NOVEL LEARNING SERIES™

Three Weeks with My Brother

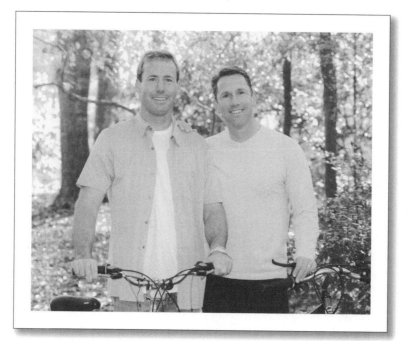

For Teacher Resources,
visit NovelLearningSeries.com.

Also by Nicholas Sparks

NICHOLAS SPARKS
AND
MICAH SPARKS

NOVEL LEARNING SERIES™

Three Weeks with My Brother

GRAND CENTRAL
PUBLISHING

NEW YORK   BOSTON

Three Weeks with My Brother was originally published by
Hachette Book Group in 2004.

Grand Central Publishing
Hachette Book Group
237 Park Avenue
New York, NY 10017
www.HachetteBookGroup.com

Printed in the United States of America

RRD-C

First Student Guide Edition: April 2012
10 9 8 7 6 5 4 3 2 1

Grand Central Publishing is a division of Hachette Book Group, Inc.
The Grand Central Publishing name and logo is a trademark of
Hachette Book Group, Inc.

Novel Learning Series is a trademark of Willow Holdings, Inc.

The Hachette Speakers Bureau provides a wide range of authors for speaking
events. To find out more, go to www.hachettespeakersbureau.com or call
(866) 376-6591.

The publisher is not responsible for websites (or their content)
that are not owned by the publisher.

The Library of Congress Control Number for the hardcover edition of
Three Weeks with My Brother is:
2003117048

ISBN 978-1-4555-1561-5 (student guide)

For our family, with love

Contents

Contents

Contents

NOVEL LEARNING SERIES™

Three Weeks with My Brother

Introduction to the Novel Learning Series™

The purpose of the Novel Learning Series™ is threefold:

1. to provide you with an opportunity to read and analyze a memoir independently,
2. to provide study questions and writing prompts that are aligned with the Common Core State Standards for English Language Arts, and
3. to prepare you for rigorous high-stakes tests, such as the SAT and ACT, by providing multiple-choice questions that are similar in both form and content to the questions on those tests.

The first part of this book contains the memoir *Three Weeks with My Brother*, which is divided into sixteen sections for the purpose of this guide: the prologue and chapter 1; chapters 2 and 3; chapter 4; chapter 5; chapter 6; chapter 7; chapter 8;

chapter 9; chapter 10; chapter 11; chapter 12; chapter 13; chapter 14; chapter 15; chapter 16; and chapter 17 and the epilogue. After each of these sixteen sections of the memoir, there is a series of multiple-choice questions. You should read the chapters of the memoir first and then answer the questions. The information following each question explains *how* to answer the preceding question. If you are confident in your answer, use this information to confirm your thought process. If you are unsure of how to answer the question, the explanation can guide your decision-making process.

The final part of this guide contains critical reading questions related to a given passage, short answer assignments, and essay assignments. A rubric—a list of various essay elements and descriptions used to gauge quality in essay responses—is also provided. The rubric and the guide to understanding the rubric are designed to walk you through the writing process as you organize your thoughts and craft your response.

At this time, please turn the page, read the prologue and chapter 1, and answer the questions that follow.

A friend is always loyal, and a brother is born
to help in the time of need.

Proverbs 17:17

Prologue

This book came about because of a brochure I received in the mail in the spring of 2002.

It was a typical day in the Sparks household. I'd spent a good part of the morning and early afternoon working on my novel *Nights in Rodanthe*, but it hadn't gone well and I was struggling to put the day behind me. I hadn't written as much as I'd intended nor did I have any idea what I would write the following day, so I wasn't in the best of moods when I finally turned off the computer and called it quits for the afternoon.

It isn't easy living with an author. I know this because my wife has informed me of this fact, and she did so again that day. To be honest, it's not the most pleasant thing to hear, and while it would be easy to get defensive, I've come to understand that arguing with her about it has never solved anything. So instead of denying it, I've learned to take her hands, look her in the eyes, and respond with those three magic words that every woman wants to hear:

"You're right, sweetheart."

Some people believe that because I've been relatively successful as an author, writing must come effortlessly to me. Many people imagine that I "jot down ideas as they come to me" for a few hours each day, then spend the rest of my time relaxing by the pool with my wife while we discuss our next exotic vacation.

In reality, our lives aren't much different from that of your average middle-class family. We don't have a staff of servants or travel extensively, and while we do have a pool in the backyard surrounded by pool chairs, I can't remember a time that the chairs have ever been used, simply because neither my wife nor I have much time during the day to sit around doing nothing. For me, the reason is my work. For my wife, the reason is family. Or more specifically, kids.

We have five children, you see. Not a big number if we were pioneers, but these days it's enough to raise a few eyebrows. Last year, when my wife and I were on a trip, we happened to strike up a conversation with another young couple. One topic led to another, and finally the subject of kids came up. That couple had two kids and mentioned their names; my wife rattled off the names of ours.

For a moment, the conversation ground to a halt while the other woman tried to figure out whether she'd heard us correctly.

"You have five kids?" the woman finally asked.

"Yes."

She laid a sympathetic hand on my wife's shoulder.

"Are you insane?"

Our sons are twelve, ten, and four; our twin daughters are coming up on three, and while there's a lot that I don't know about the world, I *do* know that kids have a funny way of helping you keep things in perspective. The older ones know that I write novels for a living, though I sometimes doubt that either of them understands what it means to create a work of fiction.

For instance, when my ten-year-old was asked during a class presentation what his father did for a living, he puffed his chest out and proudly declared, "My daddy plays on the computer all day!" My oldest son, on the other hand, often tells me—with utter solemnity—that, "Writing is easy. It's just the typing that's hard."

I work out of the house as many authors do, but that's where the resemblance ends. My office isn't some upstairs, out-of-the-way sanctuary; instead, the door opens directly onto the living room. While I've read that some authors must have a quiet house in order to concentrate, I'm fortunate that I've never needed silence to work. It's a good thing, I suppose, or I never would have ever written at all. Our house, you have to understand, is a whirlwind of activity literally from the moment my wife and I get out of bed until the moment we collapse back into it at the end of the day. Spending the day at our home is enough to exhaust just about anyone. First off, our kids have energy. Lots and lots of energy. *Ridiculous* amounts of energy. Multiplied by five, it's enough energy to power the city of Cleveland. And the kids somehow magically feed off each other's energy, each consuming and mirroring the other's. Then our three dogs feed off it, and then the *house itself* seems to feed on it. A typical day includes: at least one sick child, toys strewn from one end of the living room to the other that magically reappear the moment after they've been put away, dogs barking, kids laughing, the phone ringing off the hook, FedEx and UPS deliveries coming and going, kids whining, lost homework, appliances breaking, school projects due tomorrow that our children somehow forget to tell us about until the last minute, baseball practice, gymnastics practice, football practice, Tae Kwon Do practice, repairmen coming and going, doors slamming, kids running down the hallway, kids throwing things, kids teasing each other, kids asking for snacks, kids crying because they fell, kids cuddling up on your lap, or kids crying because they need you RIGHT THIS MINUTE! When my in-laws leave after visiting for a week, they can't get to the airport soon enough. There are deep bags under their eyes and they carry the dazed, shell-shocked expression of veterans who just survived the landing on Omaha Beach. Instead of saying good-bye, my father-in-law shakes his head and whispers, "Good luck. You're going to need it."

My wife accepts all of this activity in the house as normal. She's patient and seldom gets flustered. My wife seems to actually *enjoy* it most of the time. My wife, I might add, is a saint.

Either that, or maybe she *is* insane.

In our house, it's my job to handle the mail. It has to be done, after all, and in the course of our marriage, this is one of those little responsibilities that has fallen in my lap.

The day that I received the brochure in the mail was a day like any other. Lexie, who was six months old, had a cold and refused to let my wife put her down; Miles had painted the dog's tail with fluorescent paint and was proudly showing it off; Ryan needed to study for a test but forgot the textbook at school and had decided to "solve" the problem by seeing how much toilet paper could be flushed down the toilet; Landon was coloring on the walls—again—and I can't remember what Savannah was doing, but no doubt it was something distressing, since at six months old she was already learning from her siblings. Add to that the television blaring, dinner cooking, dogs barking, a ringing phone, and the chaotic roar seemed to be reaching a fever pitch. I suspected that even my saintly wife might be nearing the end of her rope. Pushing away from the computer, I took a deep breath and stood from my desk. Marching into the living room, I took one look around at the world gone crazy, and—with instincts only men seem to possess—I knew exactly what to do. I cleared my throat, felt everyone's attention momentarily swing to me, and calmly announced:

"I'm going to see if the mail's come in yet."

A minute later, I was out the front door.

Because our house is set a ways back from the road, it usually takes five minutes to walk out to the mailbox and back. The moment I closed the door behind me, the mayhem ceased to exist. I walked slowly, savoring the silence.

Once back in the house, I noticed that my wife was trying to clean the cookie crumb drool from her shirt while holding both babies simultaneously. Landon was standing at her feet, tugging at her jeans, trying to get her attention. At the same time, she was helping the older boys with their homework. My heart surged with pride at her ability to multitask so efficiently and I held up the stack of mail so she could see it.

"I got the mail," I offered.

She glanced up. "I don't know what I'd do without you," she answered. "You're such a big help around here."

I nodded. "Just doing my job," I said. "No reason to thank me."

Like everyone else, I get my share of junk mail and I separated the important mail from the nonimportant. I paid the bills, skimmed through articles in a couple of magazines, and was getting ready to toss everything else into the circular file cabinet when I noticed a brochure I'd initially put in the trash pile. It had come from the alumni office at the University of Notre Dame, and advertised a "Journey to the Lands of

Sky Worshipers." The tour was called "Heaven and Earth," and would travel around the world over a three-week period in January and February 2003.

Interesting, I thought, and I began to peruse it. The tour—by private jet, no less—would journey to the Mayan ruins in Guatemala, the Incan ruins in Peru, the stone giants of Easter Island, and the Polynesian Cook Islands. There would also be stops at Ayers Rock in Australia; Angkor Wat and the Killing Fields and Holocaust Museum in Phnom Penh, Cambodia; the Taj Mahal and the Amber Fort of Jaipur in India; the rock cathedrals of Lalibela, Ethiopia; the Hypogeum and other ancient temples in Malta; and finally—weather permitting—a chance to see the northern lights in Tromsø, Norway, a town located three hundred miles north of the Arctic Circle.

As a child, I'd always been fascinated with ancient cultures and faraway lands, and, more often than not, as I read the description of each proposed stop, I found myself thinking, "I've always wanted to see that." It was an opportunity to take the trip of a lifetime to places that had lingered in my imagination since boyhood. When I finished looking through the brochure, I sighed, thinking, *Maybe one day . . .*

Right now, I just didn't have the time. Three weeks away from the kids? From my wife? From my work?

Impossible. It was ridiculous, so I might as well forget about it. I shoved the brochure to the bottom of the pile.

The thing is, I *couldn't* forget about the trip.

You see, I'm a realist, and I figured that Cat (short for Cathy) and I would get the chance to travel sometime in the future. But while I knew that someday it might be possible to convince my wife to travel with me to see the Taj Mahal or Angkor Wat, there wasn't a chance we'd ever make it to Easter Island or Ethiopia or the jungles of Guatemala. Because they were so far out of the way and there were so many other things to see and places to go in the world, traveling to remote areas would always fall into the category of *Maybe one day*...and I was fairly certain that *one day* would never come.

But here was the chance to do it all in one fell swoop, and ten minutes later—once the cacophony in the living room had died down as mysteriously as it had arisen—I was standing in the kitchen with my wife, the brochure open on the counter. I pointed out the highlights like a kid describing summer camp, and my wife, who has long since grown used to my flights of fancy, simply listened as I rambled on. When I finished, she nodded.

"Mmm..." she said.

"Is that a good mmm, or a bad mmm?"

"Neither. I'm just wondering why you're showing me this. It's not like we can go."

"I know," I said. "I just thought you might like to see it."

My wife, who knows me better than anyone, knew there was more to it than that.

"Mmm," she said.

Two days later, my wife and I were walking through the neighborhood. Our oldest sons were ahead of us, the other three kids were in strollers, when I brought the subject up again.

"I was thinking about that trip," I said, oh-so-casually.

"What trip?"

"The one that goes around the world. The one in the brochure that I showed you."

"Why?"

"Well..." I took a deep breath. "Would you like to go?"

11

She took a few steps before answering. "Of course I'd like to go," she said. "It looks amazing, but it's impossible. I can't leave the kids for three weeks. What if something happened? There's not a chance that we could get back in an emergency. How many flights even go to a place like Easter Island? Lexie and Savannah are still babies, and they need me. All of them need me..." she trailed off. "Maybe other mothers could go, but not me."

I nodded. I already knew what her answer would be.

"Would you mind if I went?"

She looked over at me. I already traveled extensively for my work, doing book tours two to three months a year, and my trips were always hard on the family. Though I wasn't always willing to dive headfirst into the chaos, I'm not *completely* worthless around the house. Cat has a schedule that frequently gets her out of the house—she has occasional breakfasts with friends, volunteers regularly at school, exercises at the gym, plays bunco with a group of ladies, and runs errands—and we both know she *needs* to get out of the house to keep from going crazy. In those moments I end up being solo dad. But when I'm gone, it becomes difficult, if not impossible, for her to do anything outside the house. This is not good for my wife's state of mind.

In addition, our kids like having *both* of us around. When I'm gone, if you can imagine it, the chaos in the house multiplies, as if filling the void of my absence. Suffice it to say, my wife gets tired of my traveling. She understands it's part of my job, but it doesn't mean that she likes it.

Thus, my question was a fraught one.

"Is it really that important to you?" she finally asked.

"No," I said honestly. "If you don't want me to go, I won't. But I'd like to."

"And you'd go alone?"

I shook my head. "Actually, I was thinking about going with Micah," I said, referring to my brother.

We walked in silence for a few moments before she caught my eye. "I think," she said, "that would be a wonderful idea."

After Cat and I returned from our walk—and still in a state of partial disbelief—I went to my office to call my brother in California.

I could hear the phone ringing, the sound more distant than that on a landline. Micah never answered his home phone; if I wanted to talk to him, I had to dial his cellular.

"Hey Nicky," he chirped. "What's going on?"

My brother has caller ID, and still tends to call me by my childhood name. I was, in fact, called Nicky until the fifth grade.

"I have something I think you'll be interested in."

"Do tell."

"I got this brochure in the mail and . . . anyway, to make a long story short, I was wondering if you want to go with me on a trip around the world. In January."

"What kind of trip?"

I spent the next few minutes describing the highlights, flipping through the brochure as I spoke. When I finished, he was quiet on the other end.

"Really?" he asked. "And Cat's going to let you go?"

"She said she would." I hesitated. "Look, I know it's a big decision, so I don't need an answer now. We've got plenty of time until we have to confirm. I just wanted to get you thinking about it. I mean, I'm sure you'll have to clear it with Christine. Three weeks is a long time."

Christine is my brother's wife; in the background, I could hear the faint cries of their newborn baby girl, Peyton.

"I'm sure she'll think it's okay. But I'll check and call you back."

"Do you want me to send the brochure?"

"Of course," he said. "I should probably know where we're going, right?"

"I'll FedEx it today," I said. "And Micah?"

"Yeah?"

"This is going to be the trip of our lives."

"I'm sure it will be, little brother." I could almost see Micah grinning on the other end. "It will be."

We said our good-byes, and after hanging up the phone I found myself eyeing the family photographs that line the shelves of my office. For the most part, the pictures are of the kids: I saw my children as infants and as toddlers; there was a Christmas photograph of all five of them, taken only a couple of months earlier. Beside that stood a photograph of Cathy, and on impulse I reached for the frame, thinking of the sacrifice she'd just made.

No, she wasn't thrilled with the idea of me leaving for three weeks. Nor was she thrilled that I wouldn't be around to help with our five children; instead, she'd shoulder the load while I traveled the world.

Why then, had she said yes?

As I've said, my wife understands me better than anyone, and knew my urgent desire to go had less to do with the trip itself than spending time with my brother.

This, then, is a story about brotherhood.

It's the story of Micah and me, and the story of our family. It's a story of tragedy and joy, hope and support. It's the story of how he and I have matured and changed and taken different paths in life, but somehow grown even closer. It is, in other words, the story of two journeys; one journey that took my brother and me to exotic places around the world, and another, a lifetime in the making, that has led us to become the best of friends.

Chapter 1

Many stories begin with a simple lesson learned, and our family's story is no exception. For brevity's sake, I'll summarize.

In the beginning, we children were conceived. And the lesson learned—at least according to my Catholic mother—goes like this:

"Always remember," she told me, "that no matter what the church tells you, the rhythm method *doesn't* work."

I looked up at her, twelve years old at the time. "You mean to say that we were all *accidents*?"

"Yep. Each and every one of you."

"But good accidents, right?"

She smiled. "The very best kind."

Still, after hearing this story, I wasn't sure quite what to think. On one hand, it was obvious that my mom didn't regret having us. On the other hand, it wasn't good for my ego to think of myself as an accident, or to wonder whether my sudden appearance in the world came about because of one too many glasses of champagne. Still, it did serve to clear things up for me, for I'd always wondered why our parents hadn't waited before having children. They certainly weren't ready for us, but then, I'm not exactly sure they'd been ready for marriage either.

Both my parents were born in 1942, and with World War II in its early stages, both my grandfathers served in the military. My paternal grandfather was a career officer; my dad, Patrick Michael Sparks, spent his childhood moving from one military base to the next, and growing up largely in the care of his mother. He was the oldest of five siblings, highly intelligent, and attended boarding school in England before his acceptance at Creighton University in Omaha, Nebraska. It was there that he met my mom, Jill Emma Marie Thoene.

Like my dad, my mom was the oldest child in her family. She had three younger brothers and sisters, and was mostly raised in Nebraska where she developed a lifelong love of horses. Her father was an entrepreneur who ran a number of different businesses in the course of his life. When my mom was a teenager, he owned a movie theater in Lyons, a tiny town of a few hundred people nestled just off the highway in the midst of farmland. According to my mom, the theater was part of the reason she'd attended boarding school as well. Supposedly, she'd been sent away because she'd been caught kissing a boy, though when I asked about it, my grandmother adamantly denied it. "Your mother always was a storyteller," my grandmother informed me. "She used to make up the darnedest things, just to get a reaction from you kids."

"So why did you ship her off to boarding school?"

"Because of all the murders," my grandmother said. "Lots of young girls were getting killed in Lyons back then."

I see.

Anyway, after boarding school, my mother headed off to Creighton University just like my dad, and I suppose it was the similarities between my parents' lives that first sparked their interest in each other. Whatever the reason, they began dating as sophomores, and gradually fell in love. They courted for a little more than a year, and were both twenty-one when they married on August 31, 1963, prior to the beginning of their senior year in college.

A few months later, the rhythm method failed and my mom learned the first of her three lessons. Micah was born on December 1, 1964. By spring, she was pregnant again, and I followed on December 31, 1965. By the following spring, she was pregnant with my sister, Dana, and decided that from that point on, she would take birth control matters into her own hands.

After graduation, my dad chose to pursue a master's degree in business at the University of Minnesota and the family moved near Watertown in the autumn of 1966. My sister, Dana, was born, like me, on December 31, and my mother stayed home to raise us while my father went to school during the day and tended bar at night.

Because my parents couldn't afford much in the way of rent, we lived miles from town in an old farmhouse that my mother swore was haunted. Years later, she told me that she used to see and hear things late at night—crying, laughing, and whispered conversations—but as soon as she would get up to check on us, the noises would fade away.

A likelier explanation was that she was hallucinating. Not because she was crazy—my mom was probably the most stable person I've ever known—but because she must have spent those first few years in a foggy world of utter exhaustion. And I don't mean the kind of exhaustion easily remedied by a couple of days of sleeping in late. I mean the kind of unending physical, mental, and emotional exhaustion that makes a person look like they've been swirled around in circles by their earlobes for hours before being plunked down at the kitchen table in front of you. Her life must have been absolute *hell*. Beginning at age twenty-five, with three babies in *cloth* diapers—with the exception of those times when her mother came to visit—she was completely isolated for the next two years. There was no family nearby to lend support, we were poor as dirt, and we lived in the middle of nowhere. Nor could my mom so much as venture into the nearest town, for my father took the car with him to both school and work. Throw in a couple of Minnesota winters where snow literally reached the roof, subtract my always busy dad from the equation, throw in the unending whining and crying of babies and toddlers, and even then I'm not sure it's possible to imagine how miserable she must have been. Nor was my father much help—at that point in his life, he simply couldn't. I've often wondered why he didn't get a regular job, but he didn't, and it was all he could do to work and study and attend his classes. He would leave first thing in the morning and return long after everyone else had gone to bed. So with the exception of three little kids, my mother had absolutely no one to talk to. She must have gone days or even weeks without having a single adult conversation.

Because he was the oldest, my mom saddled Micah with responsibilities far beyond his years—certainly with more responsibility than I'd ever trust *my* kids with. My mom was notorious for drumming old-fashioned, Midwestern values into our heads and my brother's command soon became, "It's your job to take care of your brother and sister, no matter what." Even at three, he did. He helped feed me and my sister, bathed us, entertained us, watched us as we toddled around the yard. There are pictures in our family albums of Micah rocking my sister to sleep while feeding her a bottle, despite the fact that he wasn't all that much bigger than she was. I've come to understand that it was good for him, because a person has to *learn*

a sense of responsibility. It doesn't magically appear one day, simply because you suddenly need it. But I think that because Micah was frequently treated as an adult, he actually believed he *was* an adult, and that certain rights were owed him. I suppose that's what led to an almost adult sense of stubborn entitlement long before he started school.

My earliest memory, in fact, is about my brother. I was two and a half—Micah a year older—on a late-summer weekend, and the grass was about a foot high. My dad was getting ready to mow the lawn and had pulled the lawn mower out from the shed. Now Micah loved the lawn mower, and I vaguely remember my brother pleading with my father to let him mow the lawn, despite the fact that he wasn't even strong enough to push it. My dad said no, of course, but my brother—all thirty pounds of him—couldn't see the logic of the situation. Nor, he told me later, was he going to put up with such nonsense.

In his own words, "I decided to run away."

Now, I know what you're thinking. *He's three and a half years old—how far could he go?* My oldest son, Miles, used to threaten to run away at that age, too, and my wife and I responded thus: "Go ahead. Just make sure you don't go any farther than the corner." Miles, being the gentle and fearful child that he was, would indeed go no farther than the corner, where my wife and I would watch him from the kitchen window.

Not my brother. No, his thinking went like this: "I'm going to run *far away*, and since I'm always supposed to take care of my brother and sister, then I guess I have to take them with me."

So he did. He loaded my eighteen-month-old sister in the wagon, took my hand, and sneaking behind the hedges so my parents couldn't see us, began leading us to town. Town, by the way, was two miles away, and the only way to get there was to cross a busy two-lane highway.

We nearly made it, too. I remember marching through fields with weeds nearly as tall as I was, watching butterflies explode into the summer sky. We kept going for what seemed like forever before finally reaching the highway. There we stood on the shoulder of the road—three children under four, mind you, and one in *diapers*—buffeted by powerful gusts of wind as eighteen-wheelers and cars rushed past us at sixty miles an hour, no more than a couple of feet away. I remember my brother telling me, "You have to run fast when I tell you," and the sounds of honking horns and screeching tires after he screamed "Run!" while I toddled across the road, trying to keep up with him.

After that, things are a little sketchy. I remember getting tired and hungry, and finally crawling into the wagon with my sister, while my brother dragged us along like Balto, the lead husky, pushing through Alaskan snow. But I also remember being proud of him. This was *fun*, this was an *adventure*. And despite everything, I felt safe. Micah would take care of me, and my command from my mother had always been, "Do what your brother tells you."

Even then, I did as I was told. Unlike my brother, I would grow up doing what I was told.

Sometime later, I remember heading over a bridge and up a hill; once we reached the top, we could see the town in the valley below. Years later, I understood that we must have been gone for *hours*—little legs can only cover two miles so fast—and I vaguely remember my brother promising us some ice cream to eat. Just then, we heard shouting, and as I looked over my shoulder, I saw my mother, frantically rushing up the road behind us. She was screaming at us to STOP! while wildly waving a flyswatter over her head.

That's what she used to punish us, by the way. The flyswatter. My brother hated the flyswatter.

Micah was unquestionably the most frequent recipient of the flyswatter punishment. My mom liked it because even though it *stung*, it didn't really *hurt*, and it made a loud noise when connecting with the diaper or through pants. The sound was what really got to you—it's like the popping of a balloon—and to this day, I still feel a strange sort of retributive glee when I swat insects in my home.

It wasn't long after the first time Micah ran away that he did it again. For whatever reason, he got in trouble, and this time it was my dad who went for the flyswatter. By then, Micah had grown tired of this particular punishment, so when he saw my father reaching for it, he said firmly, "You're not going to swat me with it."

My dad turned, flyswatter in hand, and that's when Micah took off. Sitting in the living room, I watched as my four-year-old brother raced from the kitchen, flew by me, and headed up the stairs with my dad close behind. I heard the thumping upstairs as my brother performed various, unknown acrobatics in the bedroom, and a moment later, he was zipping back down the stairs, past me again, through the kitchen and blasting through the back door, moving faster than I'd ever seen him move.

My dad, huffing and puffing—he was a lifelong smoker—rumbled down the stairs, and followed him. I didn't see either of them again for hours. After it was dark, when I was already in bed, I looked up to see my mom leading Micah into our room. My mom tucked him in bed and kissed him on the cheek. Despite the darkness, I could see he was filthy; smeared with dirt, he looked like he'd spent the past few hours underground. As soon as she left, I asked Micah what happened.

"I told him he wasn't going to swat me," he said.

"Did he?"

"No. He couldn't catch me. Then he couldn't find me."

I smiled, thinking, *I knew you'd make it.*

Questions and Explanations for the Prologue and Chapter 1

The questions in this book serve multiple purposes. Not only are they designed to check your comprehension and understanding of *Three Weeks with My Brother*, but they also encourage you to think critically about the text. It's important not only to know what happens in the memoir, but also to be able to analyze the text and make connections outside of it. In addition, the questions check your knowledge of essential literary terms and your knowledge of standard grammar and usage rules, as well as your vocabulary. The formats of the questions mirror those found in important standardized tests, such as the ACT and SAT.

You should do your best to answer each question. If you are having difficulty, a detailed explanation to guide your reasoning process is provided after each question. It is designed to teach you *how* to answer the question rather than just providing you with the correct answer. Reading the explanation will be beneficial even if you are certain of your response; use it to verify that you have the correct response.

The ten questions on the prologue and chapter 1 focus on grammar and usage, vocabulary, comprehension, style, and characterization. Some of the questions combine two or more of these areas, requiring you to synthesize your knowledge, make inferences, and interpret the text. The questions are designed to determine both your current level of understanding of the memoir and your ability to answer higher-level questions.

The following sentence tests your ability to recognize grammar and usage errors. The sentence contains either a single error or no error at all. If the sentence contains an error, select the one underlined part that must be changed to make the sentence correct. If there is no error, select choice D.

1. Even though his brother, Micah, was becoming more
                             A

   and more enthusiastic about their upcoming trip Nicho-
                         B   **C**

   las's enthusiasm remained tepid. No error
                                         D

In order to answer this question correctly, you must be able to understand what is being tested. Choice A checks to see if you know how to punctuate an appositive. Choice B tests the use of the homophone *their*, and choice C checks the appropriate punctuation of an introductory adverb clause.

An *appositive*, choice A, is a word or group of words that follows a noun or pronoun and identifies or explains it. An example of this might be, "A new syndicated column by Nicholas Sparks, *popular novelist and screenwriter*, will appear in

27

the *Times-Gazette, a local paper.*" Information about Nicholas Sparks and the *Times-Gazette* is added.

An appositive is set off by commas when the information is not necessary to understanding the meaning of the sentence. Nicholas Sparks has only one brother, so the meaning of the sentence is clear without the name *Micah* in it.

Choice B tests your knowledge of the homophones *their*, *there*, and *they're*. *Their* is a possessive pronoun, showing joint ownership—for example, "The house belongs to Nicholas and Cat; it is *their* house." *There* is an adverb of place, as in, "Put it *there*." *They're* is a contraction for "they are"—for example, "*They're* going to the Arctic Circle."

Choice C checks your knowledge of the correct punctuation to use after an introductory adverb clause.

The following two questions test your vocabulary. Choose the word or set of words that, when inserted in the sentence, best fits the meaning of the sentence as a whole.

2. Nicholas wanted to be certain that Christine would not _____ at the brothers' desire to take the trip around the world together.

   A. glance
   B. balk
   C. marvel
   D. pare

This question tests both your comprehension and your vocabulary. The approval of the brothers' wives, Cat and Christine, is essential to their ability to take the trip. *Glance*, choice A, means to look at quickly. *Balk*, choice B, means to hinder or thwart. *Marvel*, choice C, means to wonder. *Pare*, choice D, means to trim off excess.

3. Because of the typical _____ in the Sparks household, taking a five-minute walk to get the daily mail provided a brief relief from the _____ of five young children at play.

   A. mayhem...cacophony

   B. chaos...harmony

   C. order...dissonance

   D. confusion...euphony

This question also tests both your comprehension and your vocabulary. In order to determine the correct answer, remember that both words need to make sense in the sentence and to be accurate.

The first thing you need to determine is what a typical day in the Sparks household, with five young children behaving as children do, looks like and sounds like. Clearly the synonyms *mayhem* (a state of rowdy disorder), *chaos* (a state of confusion), and *confusion* (disorder and upheaval) are closer to the reality than *order*, so choice C can be eliminated.

Now you may either recognize the definitions of the second words, *cacophony* (a harsh mixture of sounds), *harmony* (a pleasing arrangement of sounds), *euphony* (pleasant sounds), and select the best choice. Or you may realize that two of the words are very close in meaning to one another and probably eliminate each other from logical consideration.

Question 4 asks you to analyze how an author's choices contribute to overall structure and meaning.

4. Stylistically the single-sentence first paragraph of the memoir produces the following effects EXCEPT:

   A. The single sentence connects the brochure, the trip, and the memoir—on the surface, something seemingly quite simple yet actually is quite complex.

   B. It builds suspense.

   C. The reader experiences an effect of reading something out of the blue, in a manner similar to the way Nicholas Sparks first read the brochure.

   D. It reveals the primary focus of the memoir.

Three out of the four choices are effects of the single-sentence opening paragraph and can be eliminated. Choice A states that the opening sentence appears to be simple but is actually complex in the same manner that the trip and memoir initially seem to be simple—a travelogue—but is actually something much more than that. If this seems to be true, then eliminate choice A.

Choice B claims that the sentence builds suspense. If readers want to keep reading (did you stop after the first paragraph?), eliminate choice B.

Most introductory paragraphs are longer than a single sentence; thus, this single-sentence paragraph is not typical. In a sense, it hits the reader out of the blue, just as the brochure arrives unexpectedly in Nicholas's mailbox. Eliminate choice C.

Choice D indicates that the trip is the primary focus of the memoir. Yet, having read the entire prologue and first chapter, very little of the trip is discussed so far. Thus, the trip is only a part of the memoir.

Question 5 checks your comprehension.

5. Although both Nicholas and Micah Sparks are listed as the coauthors of *Three Weeks with My Brother*, whose narrative voice do readers experience?

   A. an omniscient third-person narrator's

   B. both brothers' in alternating chapters

   C. Micah's

   D. Nicholas's

Narrative voice refers to the person who is telling the story—the narrator. Third-person narrators use the pronouns *he, she,* and *they* as they refer to characters in the story, and the narrator is not a character him- or herself. Because you have read the pronoun *I* multiple times, eliminate choice A.

Do the prologue and chapter 1 have different narrators? If so and each brother has a turn telling the story, select choice B.

Although both brothers speak in the memoir, as indicated by the dialogue, only one of them is telling the story. If the *I* telling the story is Micah, select choice C, and if it's Nicholas, select choice D.

Question 6 asks you to make an inference based on textual evidence.

6. The tone of the memoir, as established in the prologue and chapter 1, is best described as:

   A. austere and stuffy

   B. precise and muted

   C. informal and conversational

   D. bitter and humorous

Remember, both words need to be correct in order for the choice to be correct. In choice A, *austere* means solemn and serious, and *stuffy* means dull or tedious. In choice B, *precise* means definitely stated, and *muted* means giving serious topics a softened intensity. In choice C, *informal* means casual and familiar, and *conversational* means having the characteristics of spoken words. In choice D, *bitter* refers to an intense hostility, and *humorous* means light and amusing.

Question 7 asks you to make an inference based on textual evidence.

7. What is the primary purpose of the prologue?

   A. to provide exposition

   B. to build suspense

   C. to establish the main themes

   D. to list the various settings of the trip

In the question, the word *primary* means main. Thus, although all of these choices may exist in the prologue, the most important one is the primary purpose. Also, realize that if one of the choices encompasses another (or all others), then that will probably be a better answer, for it is a more complete and thorough choice.

The *exposition*, choice A, is the background information, which answers all the questions that a reporter asks—who, what, where, when, why, and how? The exposition usually occurs at the beginning of the narrative, providing information about characters and the situations they are in, as well as introducing the conflict and important thematic topics. Choice B, *suspense*, is the situation where more questions are raised than are answered. The goal of building suspense is to entice the reader to keep on reading. Choice C mentions the thematic topics of the memoir, which we may or may not realize at this early stage, depending on how closely we have been reading and paying attention. Choice D refers to a simple listing of the sites that the brothers will visit on the trip.

Question 8 asks you to analyze the impact onomatopoeia has on a passage.

8. When describing the time the siblings ran away, Sparks describes "the sounds of the honking horns and screeching tires after he screamed 'Run!' while I toddled across the road, trying to keep up with him." The use of onomatopoeia achieves which primary effect?

   A. It enables readers to get a sense of what it might be like to pass through traffic.

   B. It creates a euphonious sound that captures the highway traffic.

C. It contrasts the view that the adult Nicholas has describing a childhood event.

D. It demonstrates Nicholas's appreciation of very subtle details.

Onomatopoeia is a word that suggests the very sound it describes. The two examples of onomatopoeia in the passage are "honking" and "screeching." Ask yourself, what effect do these words have on the scene? Picture the scene in your mind and hear the sounds. Now determine how hearing these sounds affects your appreciation of the scene.

If you think the words help you experience the scene, select choice A. If you think the words are creating a pleasant sound, select choice B. If you think that this is an adult perspective more than a child's memory, select choice C. And if you think the sounds were faint and difficult to perceive, select choice D.

Question 9 asks you to make an inference based on textual evidence.

9. The use of humor in the prologue and chapter 1 results in each of the following EXCEPT:

    A. the creation of a desired tone

    B. an unreliable narrator

    C. the ability for readers to relate to the narrator

    D. a sense of authenticity to the narrative voice

The word *except* reveals that three of the four choices will be eliminated because they are effects of the humor. If the Sparks brothers are purposely using humor to establish a desired narrative tone or attitude, then eliminate choice A. If the narrator cannot be trusted because of his use of humor, eliminate choice B. If the humor provides an opportunity for the reader to relate the stories that the brothers are sharing to his or her own experiences, eliminate choice C. And if the details and examples, as well as the narrative voice that is developed through the use of humor, give the prose a genuine feel, eliminate choice D.

Question 10 asks you to determine the meaning of words as they are used in the text.

10. Nicholas states that "a person has to *learn* a sense of responsibility." This statement is important to the development of each of the following EXCEPT:

   A. character

   B. plot

   C. style

   D. theme

The word *except* reveals that three of the four choices will be eliminated because they are developed through the statement "a person has to *learn* a sense of responsibility."

Choice A, *character*, refers to the individuals in the story. Because the word *person* is in the sentence, it's a safe decision to eliminate choice A.

The *plot*, choice B, refers to the selection and arrangement of all the incidents in the memoir. If the details and examples of what and how responsibility is learned are evident in the text, eliminate this option.

Style, choice C, is the way the text is written. Basically style isn't focused on *what* is said, but rather on *how* it is said. If the sentence is talking about stylistic choices, then eliminate choice C.

Theme, choice D, refers to a central idea. If this sentence is a debatable claim that can be supported with details and examples, eliminate choice D.

Chapter 2

A couple of days after I sent Micah the information about the trip, the phone rang. I was at my desk in the office, struggling through another difficult day of writing, and when I picked up the receiver Micah began rattling on almost immediately.

"This trip is...amazing," he said. "Have you seen where we're going to be going? We're going to Easter Island and Cambodia! We're going to see the Taj Mahal! We're going to the Australian outback!"

"I know," I said, "doesn't it sound great?"

"It's more than great. It's awesome! Did you see that we're going on a dogsled ride in Norway?"

"Yeah, I know..."

"We'll ride elephants in India!"

"I know..."

"We're going to Africa! Africa, for God's sake!"

"I know..."

"This is going to be great!"

"So Christine said you could go?"

"I told you I'm going."

"I know. But is Christine okay with it?"

"She's not exactly thrilled, but she okayed it. I mean . . . Africa! India! Cambodia! With my brother? What's she going to say?"

She could have said no, I thought. They had two kids—Peyton was only a couple of months old, Alli was nine—and Micah was planning to leave for a month shortly after Peyton's first birthday. But I was certain that Christine, like Cathy, understood that Micah needed to see me as much as I needed to see him, albeit for different reasons. As siblings, we'd come to depend on each other in times of crisis, a dependence that had grown only stronger as we aged. We'd supported each other through personal and emotional struggles, we'd lived each other's ups and downs. We'd learned a lot about ourselves by learning about each other, and while siblings by nature often are close, with Micah and me, it went a step further. The sound of his voice never failed to remind me of the childhood we'd shared, and his laughter inevitably resurrected distant memories, long-lost images unfurling without warning, like flags on a breezy day.

"Nick? Hello? You still there?"

"Yeah, I'm here. Just thinking."

"About what? The trip?"

"No," I said. "I was thinking about the adventures we had when we were little kids."

"In Minnesota?"

"No," I said. "In Los Angeles."

"What made you think of that?"

"I'm not exactly sure," I admitted. "Sometimes it just happens."

In 1969, we moved from the cold winters of Minnesota to Inglewood, California. My dad had been accepted into the doctoral program at the University of Southern California, and we moved to what some might consider the projects. Smack dab in the center of Los Angeles, the community where we lived still smoldered with the angry memories of the Watts riots in 1965. We were one of only a few white families in the run-down apartment complex we called home, and our immediate neighbors included prostitutes, drug dealers, and gang members.

It was a tiny place—two bedrooms, living room, and a kitchen— but I'm sure my mom viewed it as a vast improvement over her life in Minnesota. Even though she still didn't have the support of family, for the first time in two years she had neighbors to talk to, even if they were different from the folks she grew up with in Nebraska. It was also possible for her to walk to the store to buy groceries, or at least walk outside and see signs of human life.

It's common for children to think of their parents reverentially, and as a child, I was no different. With dark brown eyes, dark hair, and milky skin, my mom seemed beautiful to me. Despite the harshness of our early life, I never remember her taking her frustrations out on us. She was one of those women who were born to be a mother, and she loved us unconditionally; in many ways, we were her *life*. She smiled more than anyone I've ever known. Hers weren't those fake smiles, the kind that seem forced and give you the creeps. Hers were genuine smiles that made you want to run into her arms, which were always held open for us.

My dad, on the other hand, was still somewhat of a mystery to me. With sandy, reddish hair, he had freckles and was prone to sunburns. Among all of us, only he had an appreciation for music. He played the harmonica and the guitar, and he whistled compulsively when he was stressed, which he always seemed to be. Not that anyone could blame him. In Los Angeles, he settled into the same grueling routine that he had in Minnesota: classes, studying, and working evenings as a janitor and bartender in order to provide us with the basic necessities of life. Even then, he had to rely on both his and my mom's parents to help make ends meet.

When he was around the house, he was often preoccupied to the point of appearing absentminded. My most consistent memory of my father is of him sitting at the table, head bowed over a book. A true intellectual, he wasn't the kind of dad who liked to play catch or ride bikes or go hiking, but since we'd never experienced anything different, it didn't bother us. Instead, his purpose—to us kids, anyway—was to be provider and disciplinarian. If we got out of hand—which we did with startling frequency—my mother would threaten us by saying she was going to inform our dad when he got home. I have no idea why the very notion terrified us so, since my dad was not abusive, but I suppose it's because we didn't really know him.

Our years in Minnesota had driven us together as siblings. For years, Micah, Dana, and I had been one another's only friends, and in Los Angeles that continued. We shared the same bedroom, played with the same toys, and were almost always in one another's company. On Saturday mornings, we huddled around the television to watch cartoons, and we could spend hours playing with action figures from the now defunct Johnny West cowboy series. Like G.I. Joe action figures, there were cowboys (The West family—Johnny, Jane, and the kids), soldiers (General Custer and Captain Maddox), an outlaw (Sam Cobra), and Indians (Geronimo, Chief Cherokee, and Fighting Eagle), as well as paraphernalia that included forts, cowboy wagons, horses, and herds of cattle. Over the years, we must have collected every item of the set three or four times over. We played with the figures, conjuring up one adventure after the next, until they literally fell apart.

Because my sister was the youngest, she tended to stay inside with my mom while my brother and I gradually began to discover the outside world. My parents seemed to believe—rather naively, I now think—that we'd be safe together no matter how dangerous the streets were, and allowed us to freely explore the neighborhood on our own before I reached the age of five. Our only requirement was to be home in time for dinner. Neither my mother nor father ever bothered setting limits on how far we could travel, as long as we upheld our end of the bargain, and we took this freedom to extremes. Wherever my brother went, I'd tag along behind him with a rapidly growing sense of hero worship. We'd spend our afternoons exploring run-down apartments, or visit with our adult female neighbors as they stood along the boulevard soliciting customers. We could endlessly watch teenagers doing car repairs in the parking lot, and sometimes sat on the steps with various gangs as they drank beer and made out with their girlfriends. It was great fun—there was always something to see and do—and even when occasional gunshots sounded in the distance, I don't remember Micah or I ever being overly frightened by them.

For whatever reason, we *were* safe there. I suppose it's because everyone, even gang members, knew that not only weren't we a threat, we were probably poorer than they were. We were desperately poor. As kids, we were raised on powdered milk, potatoes, and oatmeal—I didn't know milk came in *liquid* form until I headed off to school. We never went out to eat, visited museums, went to a ball game or even a movie. The car my dad had purchased to get to work and the university had cost less than a hundred dollars. Once we started school, we'd get one pair of shoes and one pair of pants a year; if they ripped, my mother would iron on patches and keep ironing more on until our jeans looked as if they'd been originally designed with knee pads. Our few toys—primarily Tinkertoys, Lincoln Logs, and the aforementioned Johnny West figures—had all been Christmas or birthday gifts; we gave up asking for anything we saw when we went to the store with my mom.

It's only now that I realize that we were probably living well below the poverty line. We certainly didn't know it at the time, nor, to be honest, did we care. And my mom wouldn't have put up with our complaints, even if we did. My mom was a big believer in toughness. She hated whining, she hated moping, she hated excuses, and she was intent on eradicating these traits in her children. If we ever said something along the lines of, "But I want it," her response was always the same. She'd shrug and reply evenly, "Tough toenails, tiger. What you want and what you get are usually two entirely different things."

Her views on "toughness" would make most contemporary parents shudder. When Micah started school, for instance, school busing was being used to force greater integration of the inner-city schools. As a result, the school down the street wasn't open to him; instead, he had to walk nearly a mile to the bus stop—along busy avenues, through rough neighborhoods, with a shortcut through a junkyard. On the first day of kindergarten, she walked with him to the bus stop; the day after that, he walked by himself. Within a week, he told my mom that some older girls, seventh grade or thereabouts, but *huge* to a kindergartener, had cornered him in the junkyard and taken his milk money. Then they threatened him; they said that if he didn't bring them a nickel every day, they were going to hurt him.

"They said they're going to beat me up bad," Micah cried.

There are a number of ways a parent could handle such a situation. My mom could have started walking him to school regularly, for instance, or walked with him one day, confronted the girls, and threatened to call the police if another incident occurred. Perhaps my mom could have found out who their parents were and talked to them, or found someone to carpool with. Maybe she could have even talked to someone at the school.

Not my mom. Instead, after Micah told his story, she rose from the table and left the room for a few minutes. When she returned, she was carrying an old Roy Rogers lunchbox; rusty and dented, it had been her younger brother's years before. "We'll put your lunch in this tomorrow, instead of a brown bag," she said, "and if they try to take your money, just wind up and hit 'em with it. Like this..."

43

Cocking her arm like a lion tamer, she began swinging the lunchbox in wide arcs, demonstrating while my brother sat at the table watching.

The next day, my six-year-old brother marched off to school with his hand-me-down lunchbox. And just as they'd threatened, the girls surrounded him when he wouldn't give them his nickel. When the first one charged, he did exactly as my mom had told him.

In our bedroom that night, Micah related to me what happened.

"I swung with everything I had," he said.

"Weren't you scared?"

With his lips pressed together, he nodded. "But I kept swinging and hitting them until they ran away crying."

The girls, I might add, never bothered him again.

In 1971, we moved again, this time to Playa del Rey—another section of Los Angeles. For obvious reasons (the nightly gunshots began sounding awfully close) our parents believed it was safer for us than Inglewood.

I'd started kindergarten by then, but given the year separating us and the fact that Los Angeles continued to bus my brother, Micah and I found ourselves in different schools. While the students in my class resembled students that might be found in an Iowa suburb, Micah was bused to one of the schools in the inner city, and was the only white child in his class.

Still, in the afternoons, we were together, and we spent our time as we had in Inglewood, a couple of little kids with no fear of the world. We'd leave our apartment complex and spend hours going anywhere we wanted—we'd walk a couple miles down to the marina where we'd look at the boats docked in their slips or climb up the underside of highway bridges or utility poles looking for bird eggs, or explore vacant, decaying, or burned-out homes in search of something interesting that might have been left behind. Other times, we'd head behind our apartment complex, cross a few avenues, and hop a few fences to visit the high school. In the late afternoons, it was usually empty, and we used to love the wide-open fields, which were much larger than the ones at our elementary schools. We'd race or hide, or simply walk the hallways, looking into the classrooms. One day, we spotted a raven in the trees, and were instantly captivated. We began following it as it moved from tree to tree. After that, whenever we went to the school, we'd look for the raven, and surprisingly, we'd almost always find it. After calling to it for a while, we'd head off to do something else. Yet, soon enough, we'd see the raven again, in one of the trees near where we were playing. Pretty soon, we weren't able to go anywhere near the school *without* seeing the raven. It was *always* around. The raven, we soon realized, was following us.

We began to feed it. We'd toss some bread on the ground; the raven would swoop down and eat it, then fly away. Gradually, it stayed long enough for us to approach. From there, we moved to feeding it plums, and the raven grew more comfortable with us. We got to the point where we could hold the plum outstretched on the ground and the raven wouldn't hesitate to fly close and begin to eat. It struck us that it was becoming something of a pet, and we began to refer to it that way. Borrowing the camera from mom, we were even able to take up-close pictures of it, and we proudly showed them off when the photos were developed. We named the raven Blackie. Blackie was great. Blackie was cool. Blackie, we eventually discovered, was a monster.

As interested as we were in the bird, we found out that the

bird had become far more interested in us. Particularly our hair. Because we were blond, our hair gleamed in the sunlight, and ravens, we came to discover, love shiny things. Ravens also build nests. Put one together with the other, and you can imagine what happened next.

We were at the school one afternoon when Blackie suddenly came swooping toward us, diving at our heads over and over, like a fighter plane attacking a ship. It was cawing at us, and we scrambled away. Blackie followed. His wingspan seemed to have grown exponentially overnight—and soon we were running and screaming for our lives as Blackie buzzed over our heads. We hid for a while near some Dumpsters, trying to figure out how to get back home, and finally ventured out again. With the coast clear, we took off running.

Keeping up with Micah was impossible, and gradually I slowed. In that instant, Blackie swooped down and landed on my head, which was quite simply the most terrifying thing ever to happen to me in my young life. I panicked, unable to breathe, unable to move a muscle. I could feel Blackie's claws digging into my head, and—as if to amplify the horror—Blackie began to peck *hard*, its head bobbing up and down like the oil pumps in Oklahoma. I screamed. Blackie pecked harder. And that's how it went. Peck, scream. Peck, scream. Peck, scream. Peck, scream. It felt as if the raven was doing his best to drill a hole into my skull in order to suck my brains out.

I vaguely remember my brother receding into the distance—he was oblivious to Blackie's return—until the first scream. Wheeling around, Micah ran back toward me, shouting at me to push the bird off. My mind, however, was blank, and I was frozen. All I could do was stand there while Blackie killed me, one peck at a time.

Micah, of course, knew what to do. Screaming and waving his hands wildly, he was able to dislodge the evil demon bird from my scalp. Then, as Blackie continued to swoop at us, Micah took off his shirt and waved it around like a flag. Finally, Blackie retreated to the safety of the trees.

On our way home, I was embarrassed by how frightened I'd been. Micah hadn't been frightened. Micah had taken on Blackie while I'd panicked. Micah fought while I froze. I came to believe that Micah, unlike me, could do anything. And as I struggled to keep up with him, I wanted more than anything to be just like him.

Chapter 3

After confirming and reserving our places on the trip around the world, Micah and I began to make the necessary preparations. Among other things, we needed to obtain a number of vaccinations, including yellow fever and Hepatitis A and B, as well as send off our passports for the visas for India, Ethiopia, and Cambodia.

As spring turned to summer, my brother and I talked about the trip frequently, but strangely, the more we talked, the more our responses to the upcoming adventure diverged. While Micah grew more excited about the places we would see, I grew anxious at the thought of leaving; when he called wanting to talk about the trip, I found myself avoiding the subject.

Call it buyer's remorse, but I gradually began to feel as if the decision to go had been a mistake. As exciting as the idea was, as much as I wanted to visit all those places, I couldn't imagine taking weeks to do it. Between work and family, time was the one thing that I hadn't had enough of in what seemed like ages. If my home life was chaotic, my career was even busier, and the thought of traveling for pleasure not only increased my anxiety, but left me feeling guilt-ridden. If I had a month to spare, shouldn't I spend the time with the kids? Or with my wife? If I barely had time to do everything now, how on earth could I even think of taking a month off to travel for fun?

Everything about the trip felt wrong. But then, if you knew where I was in 2002, you would understand why.

I like to think of life in terms of a stream, rapids, and waterfall. There are periods in everyone's life when things just seem to float along. You're in your canoe, paddling leisurely, enjoying the view. One day flows into the next, everything gets done, and somehow there's still time to relax. Then, ever so slowly, the stream starts to move faster; it's still possible to manage everything, but it takes a little more effort. Next come the rapids, and all of a sudden, everything is more challenging. Maybe there's a new project at work, maybe someone in the family gets sick, maybe you move or get laid off. Whatever the reason, you spend those periods steering the canoe, struggling to stay afloat. You wake up in the mornings feeling you're already behind, and each day becomes a frantic race against the clock in order to get everything done. And then the rapids begin to roil even faster, and you go right along with them. You "have to," you "need to," you "have no other choice." You go, go, go. And in the distance, you hear the roar of the waterfall, and you convince yourself that your only option is to paddle even harder. You've got to steer through those rapids and somehow get to safety. Otherwise, the waterfall's going to take you.

That's where I was throughout 2002: in the middle of the rapids, steering frantically, with the waterfall growing louder. Mentally. Physically. Emotionally. And I'd been there for the previous three years.

I'm not proud of this. It's not a sign of success. It's a life without any sort of balance, and in the long run the waterfall will eventually take you. I know that now. The problem was that I didn't know that then.

My wife, however, understood this. Cat is one of those rare people who find it easy to keep everything in perspective. She's not only an attentive mother, but has dozens of friends she talks to regularly. She is close to her family, and yet, as busy as she was (five children, with three under two, will keep any mom busy), she spent her days with none of the frantic urgency that I couldn't seem to escape. She, more than anyone, knew I needed an escape; she also knew that my natural inclination was to deny that I needed one and to suddenly think of an excuse not to go on the trip. Or worse, refuse to enjoy it and relax, even if I did.

Lying in bed one night, she asked me about the trip and I mumbled again that I was having second thoughts.

She rolled over and faced me.

"You'll have fun," she urged. "And you need to go. You've never done something like this."

"I know. But it's not really a good time."

"It'll never be a good time to go. You'll always be busy. It's part of your nature."

"No it isn't."

"Of course it is. In fact, you never let yourself not be busy."

"Just for the last couple of years."

Cathy shook her head. "No, sweetheart. You've been busy since I've known you. You can't not be busy."

"Really?"

"Really."

I thought about that. "For the next couple of years, I'll be really busy. But after that, it'll slow down. In a couple of years, I'm sure I'll have time for something like this."

"You said the same thing a couple of years ago."

"Did I?"

"Yes."

I paused. "I guess I was wrong then. But I'm sure I'm right this time."

Beside me, I heard my wife sigh.

Despite her words, my feelings of anxiety about the trip only grew stronger as autumn approached. My brother, like my wife, sensed my ambivalence on the phone, and began to call more frequently, doing his best to bolster my interest.

"Hey Nicky," Micah said into the receiver. "Did you get the package TCS sent us?"

TCS was the company in charge of the tour. I was at my desk in the office working on my new novel, *The Guardian*; stacked in the corner were two large boxes, still sealed, that had remained untouched for two weeks.

"Yeah, I got 'em, but I haven't opened them yet."

"Why not?"

"I haven't had the time."

"Well open them," he said. "They sent us a bunch of cool stuff. They sent us a jacket, backpack, and suitcase—and other gizmos, too. There's also an itinerary..."

"I'll get to it this weekend."

"You should open it now," he insisted. "In fact, I think you were supposed to send in one of the health forms already. And, you're supposed to make a decision about which site you want to see in Guatemala. It's either the ruins or the market downtown. You have to send that by the end of the week."

I closed my eyes, fretting that something else had just been added to my plate.

"Okay," I said. "I'll get to it tonight if I get the chance."

There was a long pause on the other end.

"What's wrong with you?" he asked.

"Nothing," I answered.

"You don't sound like you're too excited about this."

"I will be. When it's time to go, I mean. Right now, I've got so much work that I haven't had time to think about it much. I'll get more excited the closer we get. Right now, I'm swamped."

He took a deep breath. "You're making a mistake," he said.

"What do you mean?"

"Haven't you learned yet?" he asked. "The anticipation is an essential part of this whole trip. The excitement of going, the places we'll see, the people we'll meet. That's part of the joy of this whole thing."

"I know. But—"

He cut me off.

"You're not listening to me, little brother. Never forget that anticipation is an important part of life. Work's important, family's important, but without excitement, you have nothing. You're cheating yourself if you refuse to enjoy what's coming."

I closed my eyes, knowing he was right, but still lost in all that I had to do. "It's just that right now, I've got different priorities."

"That's part of your problem," he said, his voice steady. "You've always had different priorities."

Whereas suspension came to be a regular aspect of Micah's early school life, I found that I loved school. Everything about my first year was easy—my teacher was sweet, the kids were nice, and nothing we learned seemed difficult. Still, because he was a year older, Micah was nonetheless more advanced in most subjects than I. Or, so I assumed.

Our parents had us join the Cub Scouts, and one of our projects was to carve a wooden rocket, powered by a CO_2 cartridge and held in place by a wire, which we later raced against other rockets made by other Cub Scouts. Micah and I walked the couple of miles to the recreation hall alone, both of us nervous about how we would do. My rocket lost in the first round. Micah's won, however, and continued to win. In the end, Micah's rocket ended up placing second overall, and I was both proud of him and jealous at the same time. It was the first time I'd ever experienced the feeling of jealousy toward my brother, and the feeling only grew stronger when he received a red ribbon amidst applause. He could not only do everything, I realized, but do everything better than I. Meanwhile, the ribbon I received—which was given to everyone who, like me, hadn't placed, soon made me feel even worse. I was just learning letters and sounds—I could read small words, but longer words were often incomprehensible. I had no idea what the ribbon said; all I knew was that it was given to people who didn't do well.

Still, I tried my best to read the ribbon. It had two words, and the second one was "Mention." I knew that much right away, but the first word didn't seem to make much sense, so I tried to sound it out. It started with an HO, had an R in the middle, and ended with BLE . . . my lips began forming the word, when I suddenly paled.

Oh no, I thought. *It can't be . . .*

I stared at the word trying to blink it away. But it was right there, for everyone to see.

The world began to spin as it finally dawned on me. Of course, I thought, it made sense. I felt my stomach lurch and I wanted to cry. In the distance, I could see my brother proudly showing off his rocket and ribbon, standing among the people

53

who'd done Great. Meanwhile, people like me had done exactly what the ribbon said. Horrible. They'd given me a ribbon that said *Horrible Mention*.

I don't remember leaving, but I do remember walking home. Micah knew I was upset but I kept shaking my head when he asked why. Finally, when the feelings became too overwhelming, I thrust the ribbon toward him.

"See!" I cried. "I did horrible. That's what the ribbon says."

"Your ribbon doesn't say that."

"Look at it!"

He stared at the word, trying to sound it out like I had, then slowly looked up at me as if he were about to cry, too. "That's not very nice," he mumbled.

Oh...no...I was *right*. I realized I'd been holding on to a ray of hope that somehow I'd read it wrong. That I'd made a mistake. But I hadn't, and I felt the dam holding back my emotions begin to burst.

"I tried my hardest...I really tried..." I blubbered, and all at once I began to cry. My shoulders shuddered violently, and Micah put his arms around me, pulling me close.

"I know. And your rocket wasn't horrible."

"But they said it was."

"Who cares about them. I think your rocket was one of the best."

"No you don't."

"Yes I do. You did a great job with it. I'm proud of your rocket. And I'm not going back to Cub Scouts ever again. Not if they'd do something like that."

I don't know whether his words made me feel better or worse; all I knew was that I needed him.

By then I wanted to forget all about it, but Micah wouldn't let it go.

"I can't believe they said you were horrible," he kept murmuring in disbelief, and every time he said it, my shoulders slumped even more.

When we finally reached home, we found my mom cooking in the kitchen. She turned toward us.

"Hey guys! How'd you do?"

For a long moment, neither of us answered. Micah offered his ribbon, holding it low, almost as if embarrassed. "I got second place," he said.

My mom took his ribbon and held it up. "Wow! Congratulations! Second, huh?"

"I almost won," he said.

"Well, second place is great. How'd you do, Nick?"

I shrugged without answering, trying to hold back the tears.

Her face softened. "You didn't get a ribbon?"

I nodded.

"You did get a ribbon?"

I nodded again. "It doesn't matter though."

"Sure it matters. Can I see it?"

I shook my head.

"Why not, sweetie?"

"Because," I finally said, beginning to break down. "It says I did horrible!" The tears started flowing, and I squeezed my eyes tight, trying to stop them.

"It doesn't say that," my mom said.

"Oh yeah, it does," Micah said. "It says he did horrible."

I began crying even harder and my mom put her arms around me.

"Can I see it?"

Perhaps it was the security I felt in my mom's arms, but I finally summoned the will to reach into my pocket and pull out the wrinkled ribbon. My mom glanced at it for a moment before using her finger to turn my chin toward her.

"It doesn't say horrible," she said, "it says honorable. That's a good thing, sweetie. It's saying they're proud of the job you did. You did an honorable job."

At first, I wasn't sure I heard her right. And a moment later, when she sounded out the word for me, I even felt a little better. Still, part of me wished I'd never received a ribbon at all.

In 1971, a series of earthquakes convulsed Los Angeles. The first one struck in the middle of the night, and I remember waking up and feeling the bed shake violently, as if someone were attempting to toss me out of it.

Dana woke up about the same time and started screaming. I could hear the rumbling and crackling of the walls, saw toys toppling over. The ground was vibrating, looking almost like liquid, and though I didn't know what was happening, I knew it wasn't a *good* thing, and I suspected we were in danger. Micah understood this as well, and jumped out of bed to grab my sister and me. He was pulling us to the center of the room as if to huddle, when my dad came bursting through our bedroom door. He was buck naked and wild-eyed. None of us had ever seen him naked before, and the sight of him standing in the doorway was in some ways even more shocking than what was happening around us. My mom was right behind him—unlike him, she was wearing a gown. Surging into the room, they enveloped us and forced us down to the floor, piling us together. Then, they both lay on top of us in an attempt to protect us from falling debris.

The ground continued to rumble, the walls continued to sway, but there was something calming about being heaped together as a family. As scary as it was, I remember suddenly feeling that we were going to be okay—that somehow this obvious sign of parental love and concern was enough to protect us. It wasn't until I saw the damage on television that I realized how bad it had been. Throughout the city, buildings had crumbled and freeways had buckled. The Richter scale had estimated the quake at a magnitude of 7.2, making it one of the largest quakes ever measured in the area.

For my brother and me, the quake required that we inspect the damage ourselves, and we spent the next few days probing and searching like FEMA representatives. Perhaps it was our way of trying to get the fear out of our system, and it seemed to work during the daytime. At night, though, we'd lie in bed, having trouble falling asleep, and suffering from nightmares.

The aftershocks continued for days after that first big quake. In the beginning, my parents would continue to rush into our room as they had the night of the first quake. But as the aftershocks continued, their responses grew slower, until finally they stopped getting up to check on us at all. After that, the three of us would rush into *their* room.

In the midst of yet another aftershock we kids thundered into their room, launched ourselves airborne from the foot of the bed, and heard the *whumph* of air escape our parents' lungs as we landed on top of them. My dad, obviously tiring of this sort of thing awakening him in the middle of the night, heard my mom's exhortations to "Do something, Mike!" and decided to put a stop to it once and for all. Getting out of bed—naked again, but by then we'd grown used to it—he suddenly performed what resembled an Indian rain dance in the middle of the bedroom. Waving his arms, he spun in circles, chanting, *"Stop earthquake, stop, oh, yey, mighty earthquake be gone…"* and in the moment that he stopped circling and chanting, *the earth suddenly stopped shaking.*

All we could do was stare at him. We were awestruck as he crawled back into bed and shooed us from the room.

I don't suppose I need to explain the significance of such an event to young minds, and after we crawled under the covers in our own beds, my brother and I understood exactly what this meant. Coincidence? I think not.

As Micah explained solemnly, "Our dad has magic powers."

This, of course, made us see our father in a completely different light, a new and *exciting* light, and I must say that when I got back to school, I wasn't reticent in sharing this information with others in my class. They, too, were amazed.

In addition to stopping earthquakes, my father was also able to stop the rain from falling. Not all the time, mind you, but only when we were driving in the car, and only for a little while. It didn't matter how hard the rain might be coming down, but as we hurtled down the highway, my dad would glance over his shoulder and sometimes ask us if we were ready for the rain to stop. If we said yes, he'd tell us to close our eyes, remind us not to peek, and then, in the moment that he said "Stop," *the rain would stop falling.* It would be utterly quiet for about a second—the roar against the roof completely silenced—and then, just as suddenly, we'd hear the rain begin to pound again. As he explained: "It takes a lot of energy to stop the rain—I can't keep it up for long."

It wasn't until a few years later that I noticed my father only seemed to have these powers when we were approaching a highway overpass.

*   *   *

In 1972, things began to change in our family. With my sister now in kindergarten, my mother started working, so after school we found ourselves alone. We had an older neighbor who was supposed to look in on us, but she seldom did. Instead, we'd head up to her apartment, tell her that we were home, then ignore her for the rest of the afternoon. This suited her perfectly. She was more of the "contact in case of only dire emergencies, lest I miss my soap operas" kind of babysitter, and besides, we'd been on our own in the afternoons for so long by then that we didn't really need someone to watch over us.

Unsurprisingly, my brother and I suffered an exceedingly high number of injuries during our early years. Already, I'd had my head cut open by a rock thrown by a teenager (which not only involved the police, but a visit by my father to said teen, where the teen was threatened with grave bodily harm if it ever happened again), lost a couple of teeth while learning to ride a bicycle, sprained both wrists and both ankles, and nearly cut my finger off with a piece of broken glass. My brother had the same types of injuries, only, if anything, they were more frequent and serious.

Yet, with the exception of required vaccinations, we children were seldom taken to see doctors or dentists. By seldom, what I mean is "maybe once in our lives, and only then if there was a better than even chance that we might *die*." I was eighteen years old before I ever set foot in a dentist's office. I sometimes wondered how much blood I'd actually have to lose before my parents finally broke down and brought me to a clinic. They had no religious reasons for avoiding medical care, they simply believed that seeking medical attention would not only be a waste of time, but more costly than they could afford. Add in the requirement to be tough, and the only doctors my brother and I saw were on television. I remember, for instance, that after I was struck by the rock, blood literally gushed over my face. I couldn't see well, and was barely able to stagger home.

"You'll be fine tomorrow," my mother said after taking a look at it. "You've got a thick skull."

Luckily, I did indeed have a thick skull and was able to heal on my own.

It was around that time, however, that my sister developed epiglottitis, a potentially fatal inflammation of the epiglottis. Neither Micah nor I knew exactly what was wrong with my sister that morning; all we knew was that my sister was burning up with fever, pale, delirious, and had vomited through the night. My parents, who knew a real emergency when they saw one, rushed her to the hospital. Unfortunately, without health insurance, the hospital required a deposit of $200, and after dropping the family off, my dad sped off in search of someone to lend him the money.

My mom went into the hospital with my sister; she told my brother and me to wait near a tree at the edge of a parking lot. "Don't go beyond here, there, and there," she pointed, outlining an imaginary box about twelve feet square. Even at that age, we recognized the fear in her voice, and knew enough to do exactly as she said.

It was hot that day, probably close to a hundred degrees. We'd been left with neither food nor water, and to keep our minds off the heat, we spent the next few hours climbing the tree or walking just inside the lines of the imaginary box. We made a game of getting as close to the imaginary lines as we could without stepping over. At one point, I stumbled and fell over the line. I remember standing quickly, but the thought that I'd disobeyed my mom, coupled with the stress that we were under, brought me to tears. As always, in situations like these, my brother was there to comfort me, and with his arm around me, we sat for what seemed interminable hours in the shade.

"Do you think Dana will die?" I asked eventually.

"No," he said.

"What's wrong with her?"

"I don't know."

"Then how do you know she won't die?"

"Because she won't. I just know it."

I glanced at him. "Mom looked scared. Dad, too."

He nodded.

"I don't want her to die," I said.

It was the first time I'd ever contemplated such a thing, and it scared me. We didn't have much as a family, but we'd always had one another. Even though she was younger and didn't explore like my brother and me, my sister had already taken on the best aspects of my mother's personality. She had a perennially sunny disposition; she laughed and smiled, and—on those days when I wasn't tagging along with my brother—was my best friend. Like me, she loved the Johnny West set, and at night we would play together for hours.

My brother and I were a curious and sad sight in the parking lot. Strangers would see us as they got out of the car on their way to visit someone inside; hours later, when they came back out, we'd still be sitting in the same spot. A few people offered to buy us a soda or something to eat, but we'd shake our heads and say that we were fine. We'd been taught never to take anything from strangers.

Later in the afternoon, while my brother was climbing in the tree, he lost his grip and fell to the pavement. Landing on his wrist, he screamed, and as he held it before me, I saw it begin to swell and slowly turn black-and-blue. We wondered aloud whether it was broken. We wondered whether we should disobey our mom and head into the hospital to tell her about it, and whether it might even need a cast.

We didn't move, though. We couldn't. In the end, my sister would recover, and we'd learn that Micah's wrist was sprained, not broken, but at the time, we knew nothing. Instead, we sat together with fear in our hearts, just the two of us, not saying much to each other the rest of the afternoon.

Questions and Explanations for Chapters 2 and 3

The ten questions on chapters 2 and 3 focus on grammar and usage, vocabulary, comprehension, characterization, and style. Some of the questions combine two or more of these areas, requiring you to synthesize your knowledge, make inferences, and interpret the text. The questions are designed to determine both your current level of understanding of the memoir and your ability to answer higher-level questions.

The following sentence tests your ability to recognize grammar and usage errors. The sentence contains either a single error or no error at all. If the sentence contains an error, select the one underlined part that must be changed to make the sentence correct. If there is no error, select choice D.

1. The <u>Sparkses</u> were living below poverty <u>level but</u> the
      A   **B**
   children <u>were</u> unaware of this fact. <u>No error</u>
        C   **D**

Choice A tests if you know how to make a noun ending in
s plural. Choice B checks the punctuation of a compound sentence. And choice C checks your knowledge of subject and verb
agreement.

In choice A, the name *Sparks* obviously ends with the letter *s*.
The rule is very simple: First and last names that end in the letter
s form the plural by adding -*es*.

Choice B checks the use of a coordinating conjunction (*and,
but, or, for, nor, so, yet*). If both groups of words before and after
the coordinating conjunction are complete thoughts and can
stand alone as two independent clauses, then a coordinating
conjunction by itself is not the correct way to punctuate the compound sentence—for example, "I read the paper, my wife made
dinner." Both groups of words to the left and right of the comma
are complete thoughts, so they need to be joined with a semicolon
or a comma and a coordinating conjunction. Thus, the example
above should be "I read the paper, and my wife made dinner."

Choice C checks the subject and verb agreement. Which is
correct, "children were" or "children was"?

**The following two questions test your vocabulary.
Choose the word or set of words that, when inserted
into the sentence, best fits the meaning of the sentence
as a whole.**

2. Nicholas was so impressed that his father had magical
   powers that he "wasn't _____ in sharing this information with others in my class."

A. adroit

B. fervent

C. licentious

D. reticent

In addition to checking your vocabulary, this question also checks your comprehension. And the context clues in the question indicate that the correct word will have the opposite meaning of what Nicholas did, because the question states that he "wasn't _____."

Adroit, choice A, means skillful. *Fervent*, choice B, means eager. *Licentious*, choice C, means lacking restraint. And *reticent*, choice D, means reluctant or restrained.

3. The _____ attitudes demonstrated by the brothers as they prepare for their trip reveal their vastly _____ personality types.

A. contrasting . . . different

B. distinct . . . similar

C. complimentary . . . dissimilar

D. similar . . . diverse

This question also tests both your comprehension and your vocabulary. The first thing you should do is determine whether the brothers have similar or different attitudes. If they are *contrasting*, then eliminate choice D (which is the opposite). Choice C gives the homophone for *complementary*; one of the homophones means to express admiration for someone or something, and the other means that two or more things complete a whole. If the wrong homophone is given, you can eliminate choice C. Then, realize that the context clues of the sentence requires the two words to be synonyms; this should enable you to select the correct choice.

Question 4 checks your understanding of literary terms.

4. In chapter 2, Nicholas writes that "Christine, like Cathy, understood that Micah needed to see me as much as I needed to see him, albeit for different reasons." Because the reason is not revealed until later in the memoir, this snippet serves as an example of what literary device?

   A. anaphora

   B. exposition

   C. foreshadowing

   D. flashback

Anaphora, choice A, is the repetition of a word or group of words at the beginning of successive clauses or lines. An example might be, "I want you to know the word *anaphora*. I want you to recognize the effect of anaphora in a passage. I want you to attempt to use anaphora in your own writing."

Exposition, choice B, is the background information. It answers all the questions that a reporter asks—who, what, where, when, why, and how? The exposition usually occurs at the beginning of the narrative, providing information about characters and their situations, as well as introducing the conflict and important thematic topics.

Foreshadowing, choice C, is providing hints or clues to future events or things of future importance. For example, when

Benvolio suggests to Romeo that finding a new female beauty may help Romeo get over Rosaline, it foreshadows Romeo's falling in love with Juliet when he sees her later in the play.

Flashback, choice D, refers to a break in the narrative time line that interrupts the present in order to depict an earlier event.

Question 5 asks you to make an inference regarding characterization.

5. Based on the details and examples from chapters 2 and 3, the Sparks brothers would characterize their father as all of the following EXCEPT:

   A. affectionate

   B. brainy

   C. clever

   D. musical

Think of the different anecdotes that have been shared regarding their father, and eliminate the words above that apply to each specific scenario. *Affectionate*, choice A, means demonstrating devotion or love. *Brainy*, choice B, means intellectual and smart. *Clever*, choice C, means mentally bright, intelligent, or quick-witted. *Musical*, choice D, means being fond of or skilled in music.

Question 6 asks you to make an inference based on strong and thorough textual evidence.

6. What is the primary purpose of chapter 2?

A. to establish the nature of the brothers' relationship

B. to reveal the essential conflict of the memoir

C. to provide the setting

D. to state the most important thematic topics

In this question, the word *primary* means main or most important. Thus, although more than one of these choices may occur in chapter 2, one answer is more important than the others. Think of the two narrative strands—the present and the past—that occur in the chapter, and consider the action that occurs in chapter 2.

If you think that most of the chapter is spent describing and sharing stories of the brothers' relationship, select choice A. If you now know the source of tension that is going to drive the plot of the memoir, select choice B. If knowing the different places where the boys were living as they grew up seems like the most important piece of information, select choice C. And if you feel that chapter 2 introduces the central ideas of the book, select choice D.

Question 7 tests your understanding of literary terms.

7. In the story about the raven, the brothers write the following passage: "Blackie was great. Blackie was cool. Blackie, we eventually discovered, was a monster." This snippet serves as an example of what literary device?

A. anaphora

B. exposition

C. foreshadowing

D. personification

Anaphora, choice A, is the repetition of a word or group of words at the beginning of successive clauses or lines. An example might be, "I want you to know the word *anaphora*. I want you to recognize the effect of anaphora in a passage. I want you to attempt to use anaphora in your own writing."

Exposition, choice B, is the background information. It answers all the questions that a reporter asks—who, what, where, when, why, and how? The exposition usually occurs at the beginning of the narrative, providing information about characters and their situations, as well as introducing the conflict and important thematic topics.

Foreshadowing, choice C, is providing hints or clues to future events or things of future importance. For example, when Benvolio suggests to Romeo that finding a new female beauty may help Romeo get over Rosaline, it foreshadows Romeo's falling in love with Juliet when he sees her later in the play.

Personification, choice D, is giving nonhuman things a human characteristic, such as in "Opportunity knocked on the door" and "The leaves danced in the wind."

Question 8 tests your knowledge of literary terms.

8. Nicholas Sparks compares different times of life to different types of water. Sometimes life is a stream; sometimes, it is like the rapids; and other times, life is a waterfall. This extended comparison is an example of which literary term?

   A. alliteration

   B. allusion

   C. analogy

   D. antithesis

Alliteration, choice A, is the repetition of a word's initial sound—for example, "Becky bought Bill a bad bugle." An *allusion*, choice B, is an indirect reference. Some of the most common types of allusions are historical, such as making a reference to Napoleon by saying that someone met his Waterloo; biblical, such as John Coffey in *The Green Mile* being a Christ figure; mythological, a reference to a Greek or Roman myth, such as someone having the Midas touch; and literary, a reference to a character in a work of literature, such as a couple being ill-fated like Romeo and Juliet. An *analogy*, choice C, is the illustration of an idea by using something similar or more familiar—for example, "The biological mechanism of a working human heart is similar to the workings of a pump." *Antithesis*, choice D, is the contrast or the opposite of something, when two ideas are in direct opposition—for example, "Glinda, the good witch, is often viewed as the antithesis of the Wicked Witch of the West."

Question 9 asks you to make an inference regarding characterization.

9. The differences in regards to the way that the brothers prepare for the trip illustrate all of the following about Micah and Nicholas EXCEPT:

   A. their different priorities
   B. their different personalities
   C. their different attitudes
   D. their different work ethics

Comparing and contrasting characters is an important skill to have when analyzing literature. You need to be able to notice both similarities and differences in order to draw conclusions. Sometimes, things are stated explicitly; other times, you need to make an inference based on words and actions. Three of the four choices will be eliminated because they are differences that are illustrated by the brothers' preparations for the trip.

Choice A indicates that the brothers assign different values to certain things. That is, what is most important in their lives do not match up. If you perceive them to have different priorities, eliminate choice A.

Choice B refers to the visible aspects of one's character, an embodiment of his or her qualities. If the brothers seem to possess different personalities, eliminate choice B.

Choice C states that each of their feelings toward something (in this case, the trip) is different. If they feel differently about the trip, eliminate choice C.

Choice D says that the belief in the moral benefit and importance of work and its inherent ability to strengthen character differs between the two. If this is illustrated by their trip preparation, eliminate choice D.

Question 10 asks you to make an inference regarding characterization.

10. The story about Dana's hospital visit demonstrates all of the following EXCEPT:

    A. the parents' neglect of their children's well-being

    B. the financial status of the family

    C. the concern the siblings had for each other

    D. the obedience the boys showed to their mother

Three of the four choices will be eliminated because they do illustrate something significant. If you think this episode demonstrates neglectful parenting, eliminate choice A. If you think the family's lack of financial resources is evident, eliminate choice B. If the brothers show concern for their sister, eliminate choice C. And if the boys listen to their mother despite their intense desire to do otherwise, eliminate choice D.

Chapter 4

After listening to Micah's admonition about cheating myself of the excitement about our trip around the world, I hung up the phone, thinking about what he'd said. What Cathy had been saying. What my agent had been saying. What everyone, in fact, had been saying about the trip whenever I'd mentioned it. Despite the logical arguments, despite the fact that it had been my idea to go, I still couldn't summon any excitement about the trip.

It's not that I spent my days under a cloud of doom and gloom. Yes, I was busy, but to be honest, I found tremendous satisfaction in all that I was doing. My wife was right; I was busy because I liked being busy. Perhaps, I mused, the problem was that all my energies were focused in only three areas—father, husband, and writer—with little time for anything else. As long as things fit into these neat little boxes that I'd constructed for myself, I felt in control. Not only could I function, but I could thrive. But because it was all I could do to keep up in these three areas, the idea of stepping outside the boxes to do new things—travel, adventure, or spending three weeks with my brother—not only seemed impossible, but struck me as a trade-off

I would regret. And in a rare moment of clarity in an otherwise foggy year, I suddenly realized that I had begun to take this to extremes.

If I couldn't even find excitement in the idea of taking a trip around the world, what kind of person was I? I wasn't sure. All I knew was that I didn't want to stay that way forever. Somehow, I needed to find my balance again.

Of course, there are thousands of books and talk shows offering ways to straighten out your life, and experts of every variety claim to have the answers. Instinctively, though, I wanted to figure things out with the help of the one person in my life who had lived through the same things I had: my brother.

Micah had had his own struggles over the last three years, particularly about his faith. For the most part, he'd abandoned prayer, and discussing faith had become uncomfortable to him. His wife, Christine, had talked to me about her concerns a couple of times—she was devout in her Christian beliefs, as Micah himself had once been—and I slowly began to realize that somehow there was a chance we could help each other. And in that way, I began to think of the trip less as a journey around the world than a journey to rediscover who I was and how I'd developed the way I had.

When I reflected on my childhood, I usually recalled it as light without shadow, as if the dark edges never existed. Or if they did, they were something to be reveled in, like badges of honor. Dangerous events were transformed over the years into humorous anecdotes; painful moments were modified into sweet tales of innocence. In the past, when asked about my parents, I usually responded that my mom and dad were both ordinary and typical, as was my childhood. Lately, however, I've come to realize that while my comments were true in some ways, they rang false in others, and it wasn't until I had children of my own that I finally began to understand the daily pressures that must have plagued both of them. Parenthood is fraught with worry, and my parents—despite the long leash they gave us—no doubt worried about us frequently. But if raising children is difficult, I've learned that marriage is sometimes even more challenging, and in this, my parents' was no exception.

By early 1972, my parents were struggling to keep their household intact. We were children and were unaware of the details; all we knew was that my dad had begun whistling all the time, and by then, it had begun to take on ominous significance. The sound of those nameless melodies, with their pitch rising and falling, was the first of the warning signs of my father's anger that we children grew to recognize—DEFCON 1, if you will.

In DEFCON 2, mumbling would be added to the whistling and my dad would pace in circles, refusing to talk to anyone. DEFCON 3 was indicated by the actual thinning of his lips, and in DEFCON 4, his face would begin turning red. He was sometimes able to halt the eventual progression toward nuclear launch, but if he ever hit DEFCON 5—where he would curl his tongue against his bottom teeth so that his tongue *protruded* from his mouth, held in place with his top teeth, we kids knew our best option was one of two things: run or hide. We knew he'd be reaching for his belt, which had replaced the flyswatter as the instrument of punishment.

Those moments, while still rare, were growing more frequent. Looking back, I can't say that I blame him. In 1963, he was a young, recently married, starving student; nine years later, he was still a starving student, only with the added responsibility of providing for a family of five. Working had slowed his education to a glacial pace, and trying to write a dissertation with the three of us using the apartment as our playground in the evenings was enough to drive anyone nuts.

My mom, on the other hand, continued to adore us unequivocally. When we tagged along with her to the store or she brought us to church, she was quick to display her pride to anyone who happened to be nearby. She had an uncanny ability to forget how rotten we were at times, but her ability to forgive was tempered by the same toughness she'd forever been instilling in us. As wild as we got, as far afield as we roamed, there was never a doubt in either my brother's mind or mine exactly who was in charge. If mom said to be home by dinner, we were home. If she said to clean up our bedroom, we did so right away. And if we happened to make a mistake, she'd make sure that we corrected it. She also defended us like a mother bear when she felt it was merited. When a teacher slapped Micah at school, my mom stormed in that afternoon, dragging Micah and me behind her.

"If you ever slap my child again, I'll call the police and have you arrested. You will NOT touch my child."

On the way out, Micah and I strutted like roosters, thinking, *Take that, you old bat. My mom showed you who's boss . . .*

"You're the best, Mom," Micah preened. My mom whirled around and brought a finger to his face.

"Don't think for a second that I don't know why she slapped you. You probably deserved it, and if you ever talk back to her like that again, I'll show you what a real slap feels like."

"Okay, Mom."

"You know I love you, right?"

"Yes, Mom."

"You know I'll always stand up for you, right?"

"Yes, Mom."

"But I'm still disappointed in you. And you'll be grounded for this."

Micah was grounded, but the disappointment hurt worse. We hated to disappoint her.

Despite the pressures my parents were under, my dad gradually became more comfortable with us as we grew older. At times, he would let us crawl up into his lap as he watched old horror movies on television—he absolutely *loved* horror movies—and we came to treasure these moments, pining for them like the exquisite morsels they were. Naturally, we became extremely knowledgeable in the proper ways to kill vampires and were-wolves in the event that our family was ever confronted by such a being. My brother and I had carved a collection of wooden stakes out of Popsicle sticks, which we kept under the bed.

In ever rarer quiet moments, my dad used to play the guitar for us as well. His sound was fluid and assured, and one evening he surprised us by telling us that he'd once been in a band.

The thought of my father in a band was fairly heady stuff. It meant that our dad not only had magic powers, but was cool, and of the two, this was of greater importance to us. We knew after all that we were cool, and we thought our parents were, too. But now we had *proof.*

We liked to imagine our dad playing before screaming crowds—the kind we saw on television when the Beatles played. We even had long conversations about it, but our dad simply laughed when we asked him how he'd been able to fend all those girls off.

"My band wasn't quite that popular," he tried to explain, but we didn't believe him. Why should we? The facts, after all, were clear. He was in a band. He sang and played like a professional. And he used to live in England. What could be more obvious? After a while, I think we actually convinced ourselves that he not only knew Paul McCartney and John Lennon personally, but had played no small role in their success.

And he was *our* dad.

Aside from watching spooky movies, listening to him play became our favorite activity with him. Usually, we'd be goofing off in the living room when we'd hear him start tuning his guitar. This was our signal to calm down, and we'd quickly take our places at his feet.

He never rushed. He always made sure the guitar's pitch was perfect. He seldom sang right away—I think he was shy—but instead, would simply strum through a few songs, tapping his foot in time. His fingers moved amazingly fast, as if guided by unknown forces, and when he looked at us, he'd smile, occasionally waggling his eyebrows.

Eventually he would sing, and we'd listen raptly for as long as he did. And when he finally got around to playing something by the Beatles, my brother, sister, and I would glance knowingly at one another, sharing the same thought: *"See, I told you he knew them."*

Perhaps responding to the rising tension in the house—by that time, my parents had begun arguing about everything from money to my dad's emotional absence in our lives, arguments that frequently left my mom in tears—my mom began coming into our room at bedtime, where she'd lie down with each of us in succession. Though I didn't understand it at the time—back then, it simply seemed to be another way to show her love for us—I now think she used those moments to escape the stress of her marriage, if only for a short while. While in bed, she'd ask each of us about our day, and we'd whisper our answers, sharing whatever happened to be on our minds. We'd talk about God or school or friends and though she'd sometimes speak, more often than not she'd simply let us ramble on, jumping from one subject to the next. She was warm and soft, like a heated pillow, and those stolen moments felt like heaven itself.

Later, my dad would finally come to tuck us in. Most of the time, since he got home so late, we'd already be asleep, but I always woke as soon as the door creaked open and the light from the hallway spilled in.

Sometimes, I pretended that I hadn't heard him, just to see what he would do. But my dad had a routine he always followed, whether we were sleeping or not. He went from one bed to the next, pulling the covers up, before gently stroking our hair. Then, he'd stand over us for a moment, before finally leaning down to kiss us on the cheek. By the end of the day, he looked tired and his whiskers felt like rough sandpaper. He smelled like Old Spice and cigarettes, and in a quiet voice, he'd whisper, "I love you," to each of us.

Only then would my day finally feel complete. Warm and comforted, I wouldn't wake again for the rest of the night.

That year—perhaps because our parents understood how their arguments were affecting their children—we experienced the only miracle of our young lives. I woke to find my sister nudging me awake early one morning.

"Come quick," she said, "you're not going to believe what I just saw."

"What is it?"

"Come on," she urged. "Hurry. I already woke up Micah."

Rubbing my eyes, I hurried from the room, following my brother and sister. All of a sudden they stopped, and when Micah turned, I saw his eyes widen in shock. He pointed to the kitchen table.

I followed his gaze, and for a moment all I could do was blink. There, right in the middle of the table, were two plastic swords and a plastic crown. Brand-new *toys*.

"Why are there toys there?" I asked.

"What could it mean?" Dana asked.

"It's doesn't make sense," Micah added. "It's not Christmas or our birthday."

We pulled up our chairs and stared at them. Of course, we wanted to touch them, but we didn't. We couldn't. Their unexpected arrival left us stunned.

"Do you think mom or dad got them for someone else's birthday party?" I asked.

"I don't think so," Micah answered.

"Maybe they're for us," Dana volunteered.

"Don't be ridiculous. Parents don't buy things for their kids for no reason," Micah said quickly.

"Yeah, Dana," I added. "It's like a rule or something."

But there they were, before us. Taunting us. What if they were for us? No, it was impossible.

The sword was calling to me. It would be so easy to touch and my hand began to creep forward.

"Don't," Micah warned. "Mom and dad will get mad if you touch it."

"I think they're for us," Dana said again.

"No they're not," Micah said, but he couldn't take his eyes off the new toys either. Dana, too, continued to stare.

"Maybe we should go ask mom and dad," Dana said.

"I'm not going in their bedroom," Micah said. "They're sleeping. You know how mad they get if we wake them up."

"I'm not going in there either," I said, shaking my head.

"I'll go," Dana said, rising from the table. With only the slightest hesitation, she disappeared into our parents' bedroom.

"That's a brave girl," Micah said.

"I hope she doesn't get in too much trouble," I whispered.

We waited for the shouts, but strangely, none came. Dana appeared outside the door, closed it behind her, and crept back down the hall.

"Were they still sleeping?"

Dana shook her head excitedly as she approached the table. "No—mom was awake. She said the toys were for us. She said dad brought them home for us."

For a moment, all I could do was stare. I'd heard what she said, but couldn't bring myself to believe it.

"No way!"

"That's what she said."

"So we can play with them?"

"I guess so."

"Are you sure? You've got to be sure about this, Dana."

"Mom *told* me," she insisted.

Our eyes swiveled back to the table, and with trembling hands we reached for them. The sword was light in my hands. It was brand-new. And we got it for *nothing*.

Dana took the crown and gently placed it on her head. Micah took the other sword and stood from the table. He swooshed it through the air, and smiled.

"Come on!" he cried. "Let's go outside and play!"

"What do you want to play?" Dana asked.

"You be the princess, and we'll be the knights. And we'll protect you!"

"From what?" Dana asked.

"From the dragons and the bad guys. Come on, let's go find a fort!"

"Shouldn't we get dressed first? We're still in our pajamas."

"We will in a little while," Micah said, not bothering to hide his impatience. "Let's go play first! And remember, since you asked mom and dad, you can give us orders. We'll protect you!"

So that's what we did. We played for hours, protecting our sister from harm. Micah and I slew countless imaginary creatures. Dana called us Sir Micah and Sir Nicky, and we saved her life a hundred times that day. In real life, she had almost died once; in our imagination, we would never let it happen again.

On the way home, she held both our hands. "I'll always be safe with my knights," she told us. "I love you both so much."

For weeks afterward, her nicknames for us lingered—and in the same way that our parents seemed to shelter Dana from harm, both Micah and I began to feel the need to do so, too. Unlike us, she was quiet and sweet. Unlike us, she seemed content with the world around her. Dana was our princess, and we decided then and there that we would always take care of her.

As the year wore on, my parents continued to argue even more.

Usually, these fights would occur late at night, after we'd gone to bed. We'd be sleeping soundly when their raised voices would wake us. One by one, my brother, my sister, and I would sit up in our beds and listen; with every shout we'd flinch and look at each other, wishing that it would stop and wanting nothing more than for them to be happy again. The fights could last for an hour or more. Over and over, Dana and I looked to Micah for answers, but this was a world beyond even his understanding.

"Why are they fighting?" Dana might ask.

"I don't know," Micah would answer.

"Who started it?" I'd chime in.

"I don't think grown-ups fight like that. I think they start at the same time."

"Why don't they just kiss each other and stop being mad?" Dana fretted.

"I don't know."

"Should we say a prayer?"

Micah would nod, and we'd pray and then we'd listen, trying to see if our prayers had been answered. Sometimes they would, sometimes they wouldn't, but either way, we'd finally force ourselves to lie down again. Staring at the ceiling, we'd watch the shadows, feeling more frightened than we'd ever felt while watching one of my dad's horror movies.

Questions and Explanations
for Chapter 4

T he ten questions on chapter 4 focus on grammar and usage, vocabulary, comprehension, style, characterization, and literary terms. Some of the questions combine two or more of these areas, requiring you to synthesize your knowledge, make inferences, and interpret the text. The questions are designed to determine both your current level of understanding of the memoir and your ability to answer higher-level questions.

> **The following sentence tests your ability to recognize grammar and usage errors. The sentence contains either a single error or no error at all. If the sentence contains an error, select the one underlined part that must be changed to make the sentence correct. If there is no error, select choice D.**

1. When they were growing up, neither Micah <u>nor</u> Nicholas
   A

   <u>had</u> any <u>allusions</u> regarding the nature of their mother's
   B   **C**

   love. <u>No error</u>
   D

Choice A checks the use of the correlative conjunction *nor*. Choice B tests verb tense. Choice C checks your knowledge about the use of a homophone.

For choice A, recognize this rule: When presenting options, you may use *either* and *or* together, or you may use *neither* and *nor* together. Just make sure that the words following each conjunction are grammatical matches. For example, "*Either* Nicholas was uninterested *or* preoccupied" is incorrect and should be written as "Nicholas was *either* uninterested *or* preoccupied." Likewise, the same is true in the example "Nicholas was *neither* uninterested *nor* preoccupied."

For choice B, determine whether the present tense *have* or past tense *had* is called for. In the context of the question, realize that "were growing up" indicates a time in the past.

Choice C checks your knowledge of the homophones *allusions* and *illusions*. An *allusion* is a reference to something—for example, "*Three Weeks with My Brother* is filled with historical *allusions*." An *illusion* is a mistaken idea—for example, "In spite of the evidence to the contrary, the ardent fan clung to her *illusion* regarding the team's athletic prowess."

The following two questions test your vocabulary. Choose the word or set of words that, when inserted in the sentence, best fits the meaning of the sentence as a whole.

2. The siblings' mother often sought a brief _____ from the strains of daily life by lying down next to her children at bedtime.

   A. rancor

   B. rebuttal

   C. remorse

   D. respite

This question tests both your vocabulary and your comprehension. *Rancor*, choice A, refers to bitterness. *Rebuttal*, choice B, is a refutation. *Remorse*, choice C, is guilt. And *respite*, choice D, is an interval of relief.

3. Micah's _____ regarding his brother's lack of excitement about their trip _____ the words of both Nicholas's wife and agent.

   A. admonition...echoed

   B. cautions...countered

   C. rebuke...contradicted

   D. endorsement...paralleled

This question also tests your vocabulary and your comprehension. The first thing you need to do is determine Micah's thoughts regarding his brother's apparent apathy: he is either for or against his brother's attitude. Either Micah has an *admonition* (choice A), a gentle reproof; *cautions* (choice B), warnings; a *rebuke* (choice C), a stern disapproval; *or* he has an *endorsement* (choice D), an approval. So either eliminate A, B, and C *or* eliminate D.

If you think Micah is concerned about Nicholas's attitude, then you must compare Micah's feelings to those of Cathy and Nicholas's agent. If Micah's attitude is contrary, then eliminate choice A and then differentiate between *cautions* and *rebuke* to select the better answer. If you think his words are similar to theirs, then select choice A.

Question 4 tests your knowledge of literary terms.

4. The following sentences are from the first paragraph of chapter 4: "What Cathy had been saying. What my agent had been saying. What everyone, in fact, had been saying about the trip whenever I'd mentioned it." These sentences use each of the following stylistic devices EXCEPT:

   A. anaphora

   B. chiasmus

   C. epistrophe

   D. amplification

Anaphora, choice A, is the repetition of a word or group of words at the beginning of successive clauses or lines. An example of this might be, "I want you to know the word *anaphora*. I want you to recognize the effect of anaphora in a passage. I want you to attempt to use anaphora in your own writing."

Chiasmus, choice B, is a rhetorical figure of speech that uses the repetition of ideas in reverse order—for example, "You forget what you want to remember, and you remember what you want to forget."

Epistrophe, choice C, is the repetition of a word or group of words at the end of successive clauses or lines. An example might be, "Don't you ever talk about *my friends*! You don't know any of *my friends*. You don't look at any of *my friends*. And you certainly wouldn't condescend to speak to any of *my friends*."

Amplification, choice D, refers to the repetition of a word or an idea, while adding information to it, in order to emphasize its importance or to illustrate a progression—for example, "What I wanted, what my team wanted, what the entire league wanted was an apology from the official."

Question 5 checks your comprehension.

5. Nicholas Sparks states that he realized "all my energies were focused in only three areas," referring to these areas as "neat little boxes." All of the following could serve as labels for these boxes EXCEPT:

   A. brother
   B. father
   C. husband
   D. writer

This is important for the development of Nicholas's character. If you aren't sure of the correct answer, reread the first page of chapter 4, looking for the dashes that Nicholas Sparks uses to draw attention to his categories.

Question 6 checks your knowledge of literary terms.

6. Nicholas writes that he had "a rare moment of clarity in an otherwise foggy year," though he hasn't yet elaborated on the nature of his foggy year. This is an example of what literary device?

   A. personification

   B. hyperbole

   C. foreshadowing

   D. irony

Personification, choice A, is giving nonhuman things human characteristics—for example, "The leaves danced in the wind." *Hyperbole*, choice B, is an exaggerated statement used to heighten effect and to emphasize a point—for example, "This learning guide has defined *hyperbole* a million times already."

Foreshadowing, choice C, is providing hints or clues to future events. For example, when Benvolio suggests to Romeo that finding a new female beauty may help Romeo get over Rosaline, it foreshadows Romeo's falling in love with Juliet when he sees her later in the play.

Understanding *irony* (choice D), the situation of appearance versus reality, is essential to understanding most literary texts. *Cosmic irony*, also known as irony of fate, is the situation where no matter what a character attempts to do, he or she cannot escape his or her fate. The most famous example of this is the Greek myth of Oedipus, who was fated to grow up and kill his father and marry his mother, no matter what he or anyone else tried to do to prevent it. *Dramatic irony* is when the reader knows something that the character does not know. An example of dramatic irony is when the audience knows that Juliet isn't dead but Romeo does not; when he arrives at the

Capulet tomb, he is devastated by her death, and you are devastated that he doesn't know the truth.

Situational irony is the incongruity between the expected outcome and what actually occurs. For example, Erik studies quite hard for a test yet fails it, but Mitch doesn't prepare at all for it and aces it. *Verbal irony* is to mean the opposite of what is stated; sarcasm is a form of verbal irony. When you ask Erik, who just failed the test, how he did and he responds, "Great," he doesn't really mean it. He is being sarcastic and is using verbal irony.

Question 7 asks you to make an inference based on strong and thorough textual evidence.

7. The sentence, "I began to think of the trip less as a journey around the world than a journey to rediscover who I was and how I'd developed the way I had" is important for each of the following reasons EXCEPT:

A. serving as a means to unite the two separate narratives

B. establishing both a literal and metaphorical understanding of the word *journey*

C. serving as an important part of character development

D. negating Micah's importance as a character in the memoir

The question indicates that three of the four choices will be eliminated. If the statement provides a connection between the present-day narrative and the growing-up narrative, eliminate choice A. If the word *journey* can be understood to refer to the trip around the world as well as Nicholas's journey through life, eliminate choice B. If the sentence enables readers to get a better understanding of Nicholas, eliminate choice C. And if the statement can be accurately interpreted to mean that Micah is not going to play a significant role in the memoir, eliminate choice D.

Question 8 asks you to analyze the author's stylistic choices.

8. When referring to childhood events, Nicholas writes, "Dangerous events were transformed over the years into humorous anecdotes; painful moments were modified into sweet tales of innocence." Stylistically all of the following are used in this sentence to gloss over potentially serious incidents EXCEPT:

   A. juxtaposition

   B. passive voice

   C. past tense

   D. a semicolon

Juxtaposition, choice A, is an act or instance of placing something close together or side by side, such as words or ideas, especially for comparison or contrast. The pairing of "dangerous events" with "humorous anecdotes" and "painful moments" with "sweet tales" are examples of juxtaposition. If these pairings minimize the seriousness of the situation, eliminate choice A.

Passive voice, choice B, is one of the two "voices" of verbs. A verb is in the passive voice when the subject of the sentence is acted on by the verb. For example, in "The ball was thrown by the pitcher," *the ball* (the subject) receives the action of the verb, *was thrown*, which is in the passive voice. The same sentence cast in the active voice would be "The pitcher threw the ball." *Passive voice* is a good choice when the doer of the action is less important than the action or for some purposeful reason is being obscured. If the passive voice construction seems to indicate that these transformations just happened and no one actively did this, eliminate choice B.

Past tense, choice C, refers to the expression of an action that occurred in the past but did not continue into the present— for example, "I worked there" and "I was working there." If the past tense seems to lessen the seriousness of the actions, eliminate choice C.

A semicolon, choice D, refers to the punctuation mark ; that is used to join two simple sentences into a compound sentence. The joining of two sentences indicates that the sentences have something in common. If the use of the semicolon connects the dangerous and painful events with humorous and sweet remembrances, eliminate choice D.

Question 9 tests your knowledge of literary terms.

9. Nicholas says his mother "defended us like a mother bear when she felt it was merited." This description makes use of which figure of speech?

   A. personification

   B. hyperbole

   C. metaphor

   D. simile

Personification, choice A, is giving nonhuman things a human characteristic, such as in "Opportunity knocked on the door." *Hyperbole*, choice B, is an exaggerated statement used to heighten effect and to emphasize a point—for example, "This learning guide has defined *hyperbole* a million times already." A *metaphor*, choice C, is a comparison made between two unlike things without using a connective word—for example, "LeBron James is an animal on the basketball court." And a *simile*, choice D, is a comparison between two unlike things using a connective word, such as *like*, *as*, or *than*—for example, "My love is like a red, red rose."

Question 10 checks your comprehension.

10. When discussing their childhood, Sparks states that he and his siblings "experienced the only miracle of our young lives." What was the miracle?

    A. surviving their father's DEFCON 5

    B. receiving gifts for no apparent reason

    C. listening to their father sing and play the guitar

    D. huddling at night, praying for their parents to stop fighting

All of the anecdotes mentioned in the memoir are obviously important, or they wouldn't be mentioned, but only one was referred to as a miracle. Think about the specifics of each anecdote, and if you are not able to determine the correct answer, reread the chapter. Hint: The miracle leads to an important activity as well as to important bits of character and thematic development.

Chapter 5

Fort Lauderdale, Florida
January 22–23

Duitng the days leading up to the trip, my wife and I began
shopping for the items I would need to take with me. TCS had
requested that we pack everything in a single suitcase, informing us that it was best to prepare for all types of weather. This
was easier said than done, considering we were going to be in
the Southern Hemisphere in the summer, where temperatures
in Australia would probably exceed a hundred degrees, and
three hundred miles above the Arctic Circle in the middle of
winter, when we finally finished in Norway.

Then there were toiletry items, most of which are easily
accessible in the United States, but less so in foreign countries such as Cambodia or Ethiopia, two countries in which the
median income was less than $500 a year. In the end, I brought
three pairs of pants, three pairs of shorts, and six shirts, in
addition to undergarments and everything else I thought I

needed. I got a pair of rugged walking shoes made of leather and Gore-Tex.

I'd also made arrangements to rent a satellite phone for use on the trip, but I'd been warned that it wasn't always dependable. Because of the exotic locations, varying topographies, and the ever-changing position of the satellite overhead, receiving calls would be mostly impossible. And though I would be able to call Cathy, the ever-changing time zones and flights would make it difficult to stay in touch on a regular basis. Everything fit into the suitcase and carry-on with room to spare, since I knew I'd be picking up souvenirs along the way.

My workload hadn't diminished at all—a novel that should already have been delivered was only half completed, and I had no idea where to take the story next. The feeling had begun to haunt me to the point that I couldn't sleep at night, but I promised Cat that I wasn't going to work on it. Nonetheless, I slipped a notebook into the suitcase, just in case I changed my mind.

During the last week, I spent as much time as I could with the kids—trying my best to forget the fact that it was only leaving me further behind in my work. Cat and I went out for a farewell dinner the night before my departure. At noon the following day, she drove me to the airport. Though the trip around the world wouldn't commence until Friday, January 24, my brother and I were flying to Fort Lauderdale two days early, and planned to meet at the airport.

"So this is it," I said, trying to summon enthusiasm for the trip. Despite my epiphany, I still wasn't looking forward to going. By then, I suppose, my ambivalence had become a habit.

"You have everything, right?" Cat asked. "Passport, phone, cash..."

"Got it all," I said.

She nodded. "Have a good time," she said.

"I'll try."

"No," she said patiently, "have a good time."

I gave her a hug. "I love you, Cat."

"I love you, too."

"Kiss the kids for me every night."

"I will."

"Try not to work too hard while I'm gone."

She laughed, about to say the same thing to me. "You owe me for this, you know. You can't believe how much you owe me."

"I know," I said. "I'm sure I'll be ignoring the credit card bills for months."

"More like years," she said. "Or even decades."

We kissed one last time. During my flight, all I could do was think about her, and how lucky I was to have married her. Visions of the trip never entered my mind at all.

A couple of hours later, I arrived in Fort Lauderdale under sunny skies, retrieved my luggage, and waited for my brother in the baggage section of the airport. I called Cat to tell her I made it, then took a seat on one of the benches, waiting for him.

A half hour later, Micah wasn't hard to spot walking through the airport. Tall and blond, he had a tendency to stand out in a crowd. As soon as he spotted me from across the baggage terminal, he thrust his arms above his head. I knew what was coming and cringed.

"NICKY, MY BROTHER! I HAVE FINALLY ARRIVED AND THE FESTIVITIES CAN BEGIN!"

His voice boomed in the terminal. Strangers gawked and turned to me in shock. I felt their eyes focusing on me.

"Obviously my brother doesn't get out much," I murmured.

A few moments later, amid a crowd that had suddenly given us plenty of room, we were hugging.

"You seem to be feeling pretty good, Micah."

"Had a couple of cocktails on the plane," he said easily. "Getting in the proper mood."

As soon as we separated, his eyes seemed to light up even more.

"Can you believe we're really going?" he asked. "In two days, our adventure begins." He put his hand on my shoulder. "You getting excited yet?"

"Of course."

"No you're not. This"—he said, motioning to himself—"is what excited looks like. You don't look excited."

"I'm excited on the inside."

He rolled his eyes. "How was your flight?"

"Good. And yours?"

"It was great. Sat next to a couple of neat people. I told them all about the trip. They couldn't believe it. Have you called Cat to tell her you made it?"

I nodded. "Yeah, we just talked a few minutes ago. Do you want to call Christine?"

"I will in a little while. I need to unwind first. Stretch my legs for a while. Gotta stay in shape, you know. I'm gonna do quite a bit of hiking over the next few weeks."

"You are?"

"Didn't I tell you?" His voice began to rise as he went on. "I'm going AROUND THE WORLD WITH MY BROTHER!"

The crowd parted even more, some of them looking frightened now.

"Hey, you hungry?" he suddenly asked.

"A little."

"Well, I'm starved. You want to get something to eat after we drop our luggage off at the hotel?"

"You got it."

The luggage carousel finally lurched to life, and I was busy scanning the assorted suitcases for his luggage when suddenly he pointed.

"There it is. The red one."

It was undoubtedly the largest suitcase I'd ever seen, absolutely massive. At least twice the size of mine, it was straining at the seams and bulging in the middle. Micah needed both hands and a couple of grunts to retrieve it. When he set it upright, so that it could be wheeled, it seemed to spread even wider.

"Okay, I'm ready," he said, satisfied. "Let's go."

"Are you sure you brought enough?"

"Got everything I need."

I stared at the suitcase. "It looks like you packed a small farm animal in there."

"One thing I've learned is that you can never bring too much stuff when you're traveling."

"I always thought the opposite was true."

He winked. "No, that's just a myth put out by the airlines. Don't believe it. And when you run out of things on the trip, don't worry—I'll be happy to share."

We found a restaurant in downtown Fort Lauderdale where we ate outside and watched people wander in and out of bars up and down the street.

We bantered back and forth until finally Micah paused. Leaning back in his chair, he squinted at me.

"You're still not into this, are you? What we're doing, I mean?"

"I'm getting there."

"Did you ever think you might be depressed?"

"I'm not depressed. Just busy."

"It runs in our family, you know. Some of our relatives are depressed."

"I'm not depressed."

"They have medication now. It might do you some good."

"I don't need medication."

"Denial is an ugly thing, Nicky."

"I'm not in denial."

"See what I mean? That's denial."

"You're a pain, you know that?"

"Yeah. That's what Christine says."

"She's a smart lady."

"That she is. But she's not here, and right now, we're talking about you. So why are you depressed, little brother? You're definitely not excited about this, and we're on the verge of leaving. Talk to me. I'll be your shrink."

"I'm not depressed," I said again. "Like I said, I'm swamped. You have no idea how busy I've been. It's just... not the right time for something like this."

"That's not true," he said, shaking his head. "You're choosing to let life control you, instead of the other way around. That's the big secret. You choose the kind of life you want to live."

"You always say that."

"Only because it's true. Using you as an example—you're busy because you're behind on all your deadlines and want to catch up, right?"

"Exactly."

"But what if you missed your deadline? It's not as if you're going to get fired, are you?"

"No, but—"

"But you think bad things will happen if you do," he finished for me. "So, in other words, you're making a choice. And if it's your choice, then accept it, but don't let it control you. In the same way, you can choose to be excited about the trip. That's entirely up to you."

I looked away, shaking my head. "It's not always that easy," I said slowly. "You don't choose everything. Sometimes life throws you curveballs."

"You don't think I know that?" he said softly. "Look, just so you know, this trip is going to be great. You just wait. After all this is over, you'll look back and be glad you came. And then you'll thank me for bringing you along."

"I invited you to come, remember?"

"Oh, yeah. You're right." He shrugged. "Well, in that case, be a good host, and stop ruining my buzz." He turned to get the waitress's attention. "This man needs a cocktail."

Despite myself, I laughed.

Maybe it was my brother's pep talk, or maybe it was the cocktail, but whatever the reason I gradually warmed to the idea of going. Whether I had time to go was now irrelevant, after all, and my brother's good mood was infectious. My brother has always had this effect on me. With his confidence and easygoing manner, he has always been a hit at parties, and he'd been the best man in six different weddings. *Six.*

The next day, we went by the reception room TCS had arranged to check in for the trip. We signed in, gave them our passports, and got our luggage tags. Each was large, pink, and numbered, so that the TCS crew could easily make sure every bag was accounted for. One of the nice things about the trip, we would later learn, is that TCS handled all the luggage. Our only responsibility would be to have the luggage outside our hotel room at the appointed time.

We spent the afternoon relaxing by the pool, and later that evening we attended an introductory cocktail party and dinner. It was our first chance to meet our fellow travelers.

There would be eighty-six of us on the trip, most of whom were considerably older than Micah or I. We began the gradual process of getting to know our traveling companions.

We mingled and chatted with a few people, and eventually made our way to the ballroom, where tables had been set up. As we ate, we were introduced to the TCS staff; quite a few would be traveling with us, to make sure everything went smoothly. We were introduced to guest lecturers and Jill Hannah, the physician who would attend to any medical issues that might arise.

Only a couple of years older than we were, she smiled easily, and would end up becoming one of our closest friends on the trip. Auspiciously, she was seated at our table.

"Any words of advice?" I asked her.

"Don't eat the vegetables or salads, no matter how nice the hotel is."

"Because of the fertilizers or soil?"

"No," she said. "Because they wash them in the local water, and you never know whether it's been purified."

"Anything else?"

"Don't use the tap when you brush your teeth either. Take these precautions, and you'll probably be fine. I'm going to say the same thing to the rest of the group later, when it's my turn to talk. But just wait—half these people won't listen, and they'll end up sick. You don't want to be sick when you travel like this. Trust me. It's no fun."

As she spoke, I could see her eyes darting from me to Micah and back to me again.

"You guys are brothers, right?"

We nodded.

"Twins?"

We get that quite a bit, actually. I shook my head.

"No."

"But you're older, right?"

"No, he is." I grimaced.

Micah leaned in, looking inordinately pleased by her comment. Micah enjoyed the fact that nearly everyone thought he was younger than I when they saw us together.

"I've always told him he should take better care of himself," he chided.

She smiled. "Are you guys married?"

"We both are," I answered.

"Why did you come together, and not with your wives?"

We explained about our children and showed her pictures of our families. Finally, she looked up at us again.

"I think it's great that you two are doing this together. Siblings aren't always as close as they should be. Were you always this close?"

I hesitated.

"Not always," I finally admitted.

In 1973, halfway through the school year, we moved to Grand Island, Nebraska. Or rather, everyone in the family except my dad moved. At the time, my mom told us that we were leaving so that my dad would be able to finish his dissertation, and we moved into a small duplex just around the corner from my mom's parents' house. While my dad did indeed finish his dissertation that year, he and my mother had in fact separated. It was years, however, before we ever learned the truth about this. My mom was not above keeping secrets from us if she thought the truth would hurt us.

Grand Island was a sleepy little town, nestled in the middle of the state, and as different from Los Angeles as a place could be. Wide yards separated the homes, and directly across the street from my grandparents was the elementary school we'd attend. Unlike the schools we'd been attending, Gates Elementary had massive grass fields, baseball diamonds, and—on the far side, just off the school property—a set of train tracks, where trains would come by regularly.

It didn't take long before my brother and I were laying pennies and nickels on the tracks, waiting for the train to crush and flatten them, but unlike Los Angeles, there wasn't much else to do in the way of exploring or getting in trouble. There weren't any vacant, burned-out buildings in which we could build forts, there were no bridges to climb, and though there were ravens, none of them ever attacked us. As she had in Los Angeles, my mom got a job—this time as an optometrist's assistant—and after school, we'd head to my grandparents'. There, my grandmother would make us chocolate malts and cinnamon toast (the most exquisite afternoon snack in the world) and we'd either play in the yard or go down to the basement, where my uncle Joe kept his collection of model airplanes. There were probably over a hundred models, including Spitfires and Japanese Zeros, and my uncle had assembled them as if they would someday hang in a museum. They were painted in exacting, excruciating detail, and though we weren't allowed to touch them, we spent hours looking at them.

Entering a new school halfway through the year is always hard, and for the first couple of weeks my brother and I spent most afternoons together, as we had in Los Angeles. We discovered the parks and rode our bikes there; more often than not, we'd see dozens of other kids playing games, some of whom were in our classes. A month later, they would all be there again, sledding down the hills.

But by that age, the differences between us were becoming apparent. Micah was taller, stronger, and more athletic than I, and seemed to fear nothing. He viewed the move as a new adventure, made friends easily, and carried himself with a confidence that I found elusive. I had always been less secure than he. And I worried constantly. I worried about getting in trouble, I worried about getting good grades, and I worried what other people thought about me. I worried about doing the right thing, and playing with the right kind of kids. Though I did indeed make new friends, it took far longer for me to adjust to my new surroundings.

As spring overtook winter, Micah seemed to have less and less need for my companionship, and when I tried to tag along with him, he began treating me as a nuisance. Instead, Micah would pal around with Kurt Grimminger, a boy in his class whose family owned a farm just outside town. He would go there almost every afternoon, and they would spend hours wrestling in the corn silo, riding tractors and horses, and harassing the pigs and cows with BB guns. At home, Micah would regale us with one exciting story after the next over dinner. I couldn't help feeling envious, for no matter what I had done during the day, nothing ever seemed to be as exciting as what he was doing.

Around that time, we had our first fight. I can't remember what we'd been arguing about, but one thing led to the next, and fists were flying. He punched me in the stomach, knocking the wind out of me, and slammed me to the ground. Soon, he was on top of me and hitting me over and over. I was helpless to defend myself, absorbing blow after blow. The next thing I remember is the sound of my mother screaming. Jerking Micah up, she swatted him before sending him to his room. He skulked off, and as I struggled to my feet, my mom reached for my arm.

"What happened?"

"He hates me!" I cried.

Even then, I didn't know whether my pain or humiliation was worse, and when my mom tried to comfort me, I shook her hand from my arm.

"Leave me alone!" Turning away, I began to run.

I didn't know where I was going, all I knew was that I didn't want to talk to anyone. I didn't want to see anyone. I didn't want to be small, I didn't want to live in Nebraska, and I didn't want anyone's pity. All I wanted was for things to be the way they used to be, and I kept going and going, as if somehow hoping to make time move in reverse.

Later, I found myself at the railroad tracks, some distance from home. I sat beneath a tree, watching for the train. The trains were always on schedule, and I knew that another train would follow an hour after the next. I told myself that I would stay until both of them went by. But when they did, I barely noticed them. Instead I sat with my face in my hands, shoulders quaking, wishing that our fight had never happened, and crying as I'd never cried before.

*   *   *

I could feel my family's eyes on me when I finally walked in the door. By then it was dark, and everyone was seated at the table, but my mom seemed to understand that I wasn't hungry, and she simply nodded when I asked if it was okay if I could go to my room. Or rather, our room. Again, the three of us were sharing a room, and in the darkness I lay down on my bed and stared at the ceiling.

While my anger had subsided, I was confused. I told myself that I wanted to be alone, that it was better for me to handle my feelings in my own way, yet I couldn't shake the desire I had for my mother to come into the room. Like most children, I believed that attention somehow equaled love, and of the three children I got less of the former, implying less of the latter. Micah, after all, had always been treated like an adult and because he was the first to experience everything from walking to talking to getting into trouble, he received the attention granted to those who occupy the head of the line. My sister on the other hand—both the youngest and the only girl—was accorded almost double privileges. She spent more time with my mom than either my brother or I, had fewer chores, seldom got in trouble, and was the only one of us who got more than one pair of shoes at a time, the reason being, "She's a girl."

More often than not, I was beginning to feel left out.

The knock didn't come for an hour, and by then, I was feeling downright sorry for myself.

"Come in," I said, and sitting up in bed, I wondered what my mom was going to say. When the door opened, however, it wasn't my mom who entered the room. Instead, it was Dana.

"Hi," she said.

"Oh, hey," I said, glancing over her shoulder. "Is mom coming?"

"I don't know. She wanted me to ask if you were hungry."

"No," I lied.

My sister came and sat on the bed. With long sandy-blond hair parted in the middle, pale skin and freckles, she looked like Jan Brady on early episodes of *The Brady Bunch*.

"Does your stomach hurt?"

"No."

"Are you still mad at Micah?"

"No. I don't even care about him anymore."

"Oh."

"I mean, he doesn't care about me, right?"

"Right."

"And neither does mom."

"She does, too. Mom loves you."

"Did she worry about me while I was gone?"

"No. She knew you were fine. But she does love you."

My shoulders slumped. "No one loves me."

"I love you."

Though my sister sounded utterly sincere, I wasn't in any mood to hear it.

"Gee, thanks."

"That's not why I came in here, though. To tell you that, I mean."

"I said I wasn't hungry."

"I didn't come to tell you that, either."

"Why did you come in then?"

She put her arm around me. "I came in to tell you that if Micah doesn't want to be your best friend anymore, I'd be happy to be your best friend."

"I don't need a friend."

"Okay."

I looked around the room before finally sighing. "Wanna play with the Johnny West set?"

She smiled. "Okay."

Over the next couple of months, while Micah spent time with his friends, my sister and I began to spend more time together. She wasn't as exciting as Micah, but while she never wanted to jump out of tall trees, she was amazingly easy to get along with. Still, I was occasionally too rough with her, and every so often she would end up crying and I'd beg her not to tell mom.

She would, though. Dana told my mom everything and even though she didn't intend for me to get into trouble, I'd often end up doing extra chores while my mom watched me with a frown.

Without my father around—and the terror implied by the ever-present DEFCON countdown—my brother began testing his limits. He stayed out later than he should have, began picking on me even more, talked back to my mom, and pretty much began acting like a teenager at the ripe old age of nine.

This couldn't have been easy for my mom. She was thirty years old, working full-time, and alone; the last thing she needed was any *additional* (as opposed to the *regular* and *allowable*) stress from the three of us. She began clamping down on Micah—who began talking back even more—but at nine, my brother was no match for my mom. She believed in both the carrot and the stick and wielded them expertly, like a samurai using a sword. She had no qualms with saying things like "I brought you into this world and I sure as hell can take you out," and then acting sweet as sugar a moment later, arms open for a hug.

Nor had she changed her views on sibling affection. For example, while my mom was pleased that my sister and I were spending more time together, she also recognized that things had changed between Micah and me. Though some parents would have considered our newfound sibling rivalry a passing phase, my mom didn't like it, nor was she willing to put up with it. She began making comments like, "You three will always have each other, so you'd better be nice now," and, "Friends come and go, but brothers and sisters always stick together." Though my brother and I listened—and perhaps even understood her words on an instinctive level—we continued to argue and fight and go our separate ways.

One night, however, my mom came into our room, just as we were getting ready for bed. Micah and I had been in another fight earlier in the day, this time because I'd accidentally knocked his bike over. My mom hadn't said anything about it over dinner, and I supposed she'd just chosen to ignore it this time. She helped us with our prayers as she always did, then as she turned the lights out, she sat beside Micah as he was crawling under the covers. I heard them whispering for what seemed like a long time and wondered what was going on. Then, surprising me, she came and sat beside me.

Leaning close, she ran her hand through my hair and smiled gently. Then she whispered: "Tell me three nice things that Dana did for you today. Anything. It can be big or little."

I was surprised by her question, but the answers came easily. "She played games with me, she let me watch my show on television, and she helped me clean up my toys."

Mom smiled. "Now tell me three nice things that Micah did for you today."

This, I had to admit, was a little harder.

"He didn't do anything nice for me today."

"Think about it. It can be anything."

"He was mean all day."

"Didn't he walk with you to school?"

"Yes."

"So there's one. Now think of two more."

"He didn't punch me too hard when I knocked over his bike."

She wasn't sure whether to take that one, but finally nodded. "There's two."

"And..."

I was stumped. There was nothing, absolutely nothing else to say. It took a long time for me to come up with something—and I have no idea what I eventually came up with. I think I resorted to making up something, but my mom accepted it and kissed me good night before moving to my sister's bed. It took my sister no more than ten seconds to answer the same questions, and then my mom crept from the room.

In the darkness, I was rolling over and closing my eyes when I heard Micah's voice.

"Nicky?"

"What?"

"I'm sorry about punching you today."

"It's okay. And I'm sorry about knocking over your bike."

For a moment, there was silence, until Dana chimed in, "Now, don't you both feel better?"

Night after night, my mom had us name three nice things our siblings had done for us, and each night we were somehow able to come up with something.

And to my surprise, my brother and I began to argue less and less.

Perhaps it was too hard to make up things; after a while, it just seemed easier not only to be kinder, but to notice when another was being kind to you.

We finished out the school year—I completed second grade, Micah third. In June, my grandfather decided to put a new roof on his house, an endeavor he decided Micah and I would help with. Our knowledge of roofing and experience with tools could be summed up in a single word—*huh?*—but we quickly knew we wouldn't let that stop us. It was, after all, something new, another adventure, and over the course of a couple of weeks, we learned the art of pounding nails until our hands and fingers blistered.

We worked during one of the nastiest heat waves of our young lives. The temperature was close to a hundred degrees, the humidity unbearable. More than once we grew dizzy, sitting up on the roof of the baking house. My grandfather had no qualms about having us work right near the edge of the roof, and we, of course, had no qualms about it either.

While I escaped unscathed, earning $7 for two weeks' worth of work, my brother was less fortunate. One afternoon, while taking a break, he decided to move the ladder, since it seemed to be in the way. What he didn't know was that a shingle cutter (a sharp, heavy, scissorslike tool) had been left on the uppermost rung. As he fumbled with the ladder, the shingle cutter was dislodged and came torpedoing down. It struck him an inch or so above his forehead. Within seconds, blood was gushing out of his head.

He screamed and my grandfather hustled over.

"That looks pretty deep," he said, his face grim. After a moment, he nodded. "I'd better get the hose."

Soon, water was pouring through the hose over my brother's head. That, by the way, was the sum total of his medical treatment that day. He wasn't taken to the doctor or the hospital. Nor did Micah get the rest of the day off. I remember watching the water turn pink as it flowed over the wound, thankful that Micah had a "thick skull" like me.

By the time school resumed in the fall, I'd finally become used to life in Nebraska. I was doing well in school—to that point, I'd never received a grade lower than an A—and had become friends with a few of the other kids in class. Afternoons were spent playing football, but as summer heat gradually began giving way to autumn chill, our life would be upended once more.

"We're moving back to California," my mom informed us over dinner one night. "We'll be leaving a couple of weeks before Christmas."

My parents had reconciled (though at the time we weren't even aware that they'd officially separated) and my dad had taken a job as a professor at California State University at Sacramento, where he would teach classes in management.

Our time in Nebraska came to an end as abruptly as it had begun.

Questions and Explanations
for Chapter 5

The ten questions on chapter 5 focus on grammar and usage, vocabulary, comprehension, literary terms, characterization, and style. Some of the questions combine two or more of these areas, requiring you to synthesize your knowledge, make inferences, and interpret the text. The questions are designed to determine both your current level of understanding of the memoir and your ability to answer higher-level questions.

The following sentence tests your ability to recognize grammar and usage errors. The sentence contains either a single error or no error at all. If the sentence contains an error, select the one underlined part that must be changed to make the sentence correct. If there is no error, select choice D.

1. Nicholas is often mistaken for <u>Micah's</u> older brother,
   A
   even though Nicholas is younger <u>than</u> <u>him.</u> <u>No error</u>
   B   C   D

Choice A checks the correct use of the apostrophe. Choice B tests your knowledge on the use of homophones. Choice C checks the use of a pronoun.

For choice A, remember that a singular noun demonstrates possession with an apostrophe and *s*—for example, "the boy's book, the girl's letter, the doctor's diagnosis."

Choice B asks you to differentiate between *than* and *then*. *Than* is used to compare and contrast—for example, *"The Last Song* is longer than *A Walk to Remember."* The word *then* is used when something follows or results from something else— for example, "Read the chapter, and then answer the questions."

Choice C checks whether a pronoun is used correctly. The decision here is between *he* and *him*. You know that *he* is used as the subject (doer of the action) and *him* is the object (receiver of the action)—for example, *"He* gave the ball to *him."* What's important to recognize in this sentence, though, is the elliptical clause. Sometimes in our speaking and writing, we do not complete the adverb clause that we use—for example, "I am older than you [are]." We often omit the word *are* in this sentence. Likewise, in the example "Nicholas is older than Dana," the sentence could easily be written as "Nicholas is older than she" (with the word *is* not written but understood). Because there is a missing (or elliptical) verb, the correct pronoun choice is the subjective one.

The following two questions test your vocabulary. Choose the word or set of words that, when inserted

in the sentence, best fits the meaning of the sentence as a whole.

2. A person who would become one of their best friends on the trip was _____ seated near the brothers at dinner during the opening banquet.

   A. auspiciously

   B. ominously

   C. censoriously

   D. robustly

This question tests both your vocabulary and your comprehension. *Auspiciously*, choice A, means favorably. *Ominously*, choice B, means threateningly. *Censoriously*, choice C, means critically. And *robustly*, choice D, means in a sturdy manner.

3. Micah began to consider Nicholas as _____, and the brothers ended up having their first fight; soon after this event, a closer relationship between Nicholas and Dana began to _____.

   A. an irritant...regress

   B. an annoyance...disintegrate

   C. a delight...foster

   D. a nuisance...develop

This question also checks both your comprehension and your vocabulary. First, recognize how Micah was viewing his brother at this time. Either Micah considers his brother a *delight* (choice C), one who provides a high degree of pleasure, *or* as something that's the opposite of a *delight*. So either select or eliminate choice C.

Because *irritant, annoyance,* and *nuisance* are similar, if you haven't eliminated these choices, you must differentiate among *regress* (to move backward, choice A), *disintegrate* (to deteriorate and get worse, choice B), and *develop* (to grow, choice D). Whichever word describes the situation of Dana and Nicholas growing closer is the correct answer.

Question 4 tests your knowledge of literary terms.

4. One of Micah's pearls of wisdom directed toward Nicholas is something like "You choose to control life instead of life controlling you." What stylistic device is this an example of?

   A. anaphora

   B. chiasmus

   C. epistrophe

   D. amplification

Anaphora, choice A, is the repetition of a word or group of words at the beginning of successive clauses or lines. An example of this might be, "I want you to know the word *anaphora.* I want you to recognize the effect of anaphora in a passage. I want you to attempt to use anaphora in your own writing."

Chiasmus, choice B, is a rhetorical figure of speech that uses the repetition of ideas in reverse order—for example, "You forget what you want to remember, and you remember what you want to forget."

Epistrophe, choice C, is the repetition of a word or group of words at the end of successive clauses or lines. An example might be, "Don't you ever talk about *my friends*! You don't know any of *my friends*. You don't look at any of *my friends*. And you certainly wouldn't condescend to speak to any of *my friends*."

Amplification, choice D, refers to the repetition of a word or an idea, while adding information to it, in order to emphasize its importance or to illustrate a progression—for example, "What I wanted, what my team wanted, what the entire league wanted was an apology from the official."

Question 5 tests your knowledge of literary terms.

5. After his first fight with his brother, Nicholas writes, "I didn't want to see anyone. I didn't want to be small, I didn't want to live in Nebraska, and I didn't want anyone's pity." What stylistic device is being used in these sentences?

   A. anaphora

   B. chiasmus

   C. epistrophe

   D. amplification

Anaphora, choice A, is the repetition of a word or group of words at the beginning of successive clauses or lines. An example of this might be, "I want you to know the word *anaphora*. I want you to recognize the effect of anaphora in a passage. I want you to attempt to use anaphora in your own writing."

Chiasmus, choice B, is a rhetorical figure of speech that uses the repetition of ideas in reverse order—for example, "You forget what you want to remember, and you remember what you want to forget."

Epistrophe, choice C, is the repetition of a word or group of words at the end of successive clauses or lines. An example might be, "Don't you ever talk about *my friends*! You don't know any of *my friends*. You don't look at any of *my friends*. And you certainly wouldn't condescend to speak to any of *my friends*."

Amplification, choice D, refers to the repetition of a word or an idea, while adding information to it, in order to emphasize its importance or to illustrate a progression—for example, "What I wanted, what my team wanted, what the entire league wanted was an apology from the official."

Question 6 tests your knowledge of literary terms.

6. Nicholas describes his sister as looking "like Jan Brady on early episodes of *The Brady Bunch*." This sentence contains an example of which literary device?

   A. allusion

   B. metaphor

   C. personification

   D. simile

An *allusion*, choice A, is an indirect reference. Some of the most common types of allusions are historical, such as making a reference to Napoleon by saying that someone met his Waterloo; biblical, such as John Coffey in *The Green Mile* being a

Christ figure; mythological, a reference to a Greek or Roman myth, such as someone having the Midas touch; and literary, a reference to a character in a work of literature, such as a couple being ill-fated like Romeo and Juliet.

A *metaphor*, choice B, is a comparison between two unlike things without using a connective word—for example, "Michael Phelps was a flying fish in the pool." *Personification*, choice C, is giving nonhuman things a human characteristic, such as in "Opportunity knocked on the door." And a *simile*, choice D, is a comparison between unlike things using a connective word, such as *like, as,* or *than*—for example, "My love is like a red, red rose."

Question 7 asks you to make an inference based on strong and thorough textual evidence.

7. The siblings' mother tells her children, "Friends come and go, but brothers and sisters always stick together." This statement is important to the development of each of the following EXCEPT:

   A. character
   B. conflict
   C. plot
   D. theme

Three out of the four choices will be eliminated because the quotation is important in those areas of development. *Character*, choice A, refers to the people in the memoir. If this quotation gives the reader a better understanding of Jill (Mrs. Sparks, the children's mother) or of any other character, eliminate choice A. *Conflict,* choice B, refers to the main problem of the story. If the quotation is developing the struggle between opposing characters or forces, eliminate choice B. *Plot,* choice C, refers to the selection and arrangement of all the incidents in the memoir. If the statement can be applied to the arrangement and interrelationship of the events in the memoir, eliminate choice C. And *theme,* choice D, refers to a central idea. If this statement could be considered a debatable claim, an opinion that can be supported with details and examples, eliminate choice D.

Questions 8–10 ask you to analyze an author's stylistic choices and make inferences.

The final paragraph of chapter 5 is the single sentence that follows. Read it carefully, and then answer questions 8 and 9. "Our time in Nebraska came to an end as abruptly as it had begun."

8. This final sentence of the chapter conveys:

   A. that the new move was an expected one

   B. that the move was unforeseen

   C. the sense of anticipation Nicholas had about moving back to California

   D. the bitterness Nicholas felt at being uprooted again

The last sentence says that the end to their time in Nebraska ended "abruptly," which means suddenly and unexpectedly. Thus, having an understanding of the word *abruptly* will help you to eliminate choice A. *Unforeseen,* choice B, means not known in advance. If that makes sense within the context of the sentence, select choice B. The tone of the final sentence is matter-of-fact, stating an actual occurrence. Although Nicholas may have *anticipation* (choice C) or experience *bitterness* (choice D), nothing in the sentence indicates either of these tone words, so these two choices can be eliminated.

9. The sentence makes use of each type of transition listed below EXCEPT:

   A. conclusion

   B. contrast

   C. sequence

   D. similarity

Realize that three of the four choices will be eliminated. Transitions are words and phrases that guide a reader from one idea to another; they provide coherence to the text by signaling relationships. A *conclusion* is a sense of closure and completeness or finality. If the sentence provides an end point for the time in Nebraska, eliminate choice A. *Contrast* shows opposition. If differences between the beginning and end are revealed, eliminate choice B. *Sequence* is the following of one thing after another. If the sentence provides a sense of chronological order between time spent in Nebraska and California, eliminate choice C. And *similarity* is likeness. If there is a resemblance between the beginning and ending, then eliminate choice D.

10. Stylistically the final sentence achieves each of the following effects EXCEPT:

A. the end of the chapter is as abrupt as the end of their time in Nebraska

B. the paragraph is as brief as their time in Nebraska

C. the sentence serves as both the end of the chapter and the end of the Nebraska anecdote

D. the sentence continues the pattern established in the prologue

Three out of the four choices will be eliminated. If the last sentence is somewhat abrupt, mirroring the end of their time in Nebraska, eliminate choice A. If a single-sentence paragraph can be considered brief, eliminate choice B. If the sentence provides closure to both the chapter and the story about their time in Nebraska, eliminate choice C. And if all the final paragraphs have been single sentences so far, eliminate choice D.

Chapter 6

Yaxhá and Tikal, Guatemala
January 24-25

On Friday morning, Micah and I touched down in Guatemala and stepped into a world completely different from the one we had just left.

After passing through customs, the tour group boarded vans and drove toward Petén, passing ramshackle houses and small villages that seemed to have been assembled with random bits and pieces of material. In some ways, it was like stepping back in time, and I tried to imagine what the Spanish conquistadores first thought when they arrived in this area. They were the first to discover the ruins of what was once a flourishing civilization, whose large cities included temples rising as high as 230 feet and silhouetted against the dense jungle foliage.

I'd been interested in the Maya since I first read about them as a child, and knew they'd attained intellectual heights unrivaled in the New World. In their Golden Age, from A.D. 300 to 900, their civilization encompassed the area including the Yucatán Peninsula, southern Mexico, Belize, Guatemala, parts of Honduras and El Salvador. The culture reached its height amid the jungles and swamps of Petén, Guatemala, where they built the cities of Yaxhá and Tikal.

The civilization was a study in contrasts; a sometimes brutal culture that engaged in human sacrifice, the Maya were simultaneously employing the concept of zero a thousand years before the Europeans, and were able to calculate into the hundreds of millions. Their knowledge of mathematics allowed them to chart the stars, accurately predict lunar eclipses, and develop a 365-day calendar, yet legend has it that they never used the wheel.

We arrived at the Maya Biosphere—the vast national park in Petén that was home to the ruins—where we had lunch in an open-air hut along the lake. We continued to acquaint ourselves with our companions, most of whom had traveled far more extensively than either Micah or I. An hour later we were back on the road again for our stop at Yaxhá.

Yaxhá is both the name of a lagoon and the site of a city built more than 1,500 years ago amid the jungle along its banks. Yaxhá was once the third-largest city in the Mayan empire, and approximately twenty miles from Tikal, the largest and most important ceremonial city. When we arrived, however, we saw nothing but trees and dirt pathways winding among the hills. In the background, we could hear howler monkeys, but the foliage above us was so thick it was impossible to see them.

Our guide began talking about the city and Mayan culture while pointing in various directions. I could see nothing. As he continued, I glanced at Micah, who shrugged. When the guide asked if there were any questions, I spoke up.

"When do we actually get there?" I asked. "To Yaxhá, I mean?"

"We're here, now," he answered.

"But where are the buildings?" I asked.

He motioned to the hillsides surrounding us. "Everywhere you look," he answered. "Those are not hills you see. Beneath each and every mound is a building or temple."

The trees in this part of the jungle, we learned, shed leaves three times a year. Over time, as the leaves decay, they form compost, which eventually turns to dirt. The dirt allows for initial vegetation, then eventually trees. The trees grow, mature, die and new ones grow in their place. The jungle had swallowed the buildings, one by one.

This news didn't surprise us. The city had been abandoned a thousand years ago—three thousand layers of densely packed leaves and growth—and the jungle had grown unchecked. It made sense that we would see no signs of the city.

But we were wrong. In fact, sections of Yaxhá had been completely restored less than *eighty years* earlier by archaeologists, in much the same way Tikal has been restored now. The jungle had been cut back, and dozens of buildings and temples had been completely excavated. Yet because the rains were beginning to slowly destroy the newly uncovered temples—and because lack of funds failed to keep the destruction in check—the government had no choice but to allow the jungle to encroach once more on Yaxhá, in favor of Tikal.

Micah began looking around, his expression as wondrous as that of a child.

"Can you believe that all this growth took place in only eighty years?" Micah asked me. "Our grandparents were living then."

"I can't believe it."

"I wonder what it would look like after eight hundred years."

"Probably about the same, don't you think?" I speculated. "Except that the hills might be a little bigger."

"I guess so." He squinted, trying to peer through the density of the jungle. "How on earth could someone even have discovered this place? I mean, when I see a mound of dirt, I don't automatically think there's a pyramid beneath it."

I put my arm around him. "That's why you're not an archaeologist," I said.

Our guide began leading us along a path, continuing to describe various aspects of the city. Micah and I trailed behind our group, our heads swiveling from side to side. Micah suddenly rubbed his hands together; it was something he always did when excited.

"Nick," he said, "can you believe we're here? In a buried Mayan city in the jungles of Guatemala? Six hours ago, we were in Fort Lauderdale eating bagels and cream cheese!"

"It doesn't seem real, does it?"

"No," he said. "And I'll tell you something." He motioned around him. "I never believed I could get so excited about seeing a pile of dirt."

A few minutes later, we entered what was once a plaza;

before us was one of the only temples that had been fully excavated, and for the first time the reality of what we would see on
the trip took hold. Shaped like a black and gray trapezoid, the
temple towered a hundred feet in the air. Our guide informed
us that it had been abandoned in roughly A.D. 900, some six
hundred years before Columbus arrived. It meant that the time
between the usage of the temple and Columbus's arrival, and
Columbus's arrival and the current day, were roughly the same,
and the very thought amazed me. In the ebb and flow of history, the rise and fall of civilizations, my own daily concerns
suddenly seemed minuscule in comparison.

My brother, too, was examining the temple before us with
great interest, though his thoughts were slightly different from
mine.

"Look how high it is! I've got to *climb* that thing!"

So, with our guide's permission, we did. Running up the far
side of the temple was a rickety set of rotting boards, spaced
irregularly and laced together with frayed rope. My brother and
I were the first to reach the top, and for the first few minutes we
had the place to ourselves.

The sky was overcast with black clouds hovering at the distant horizon. Beyond us, we could see the lagoon and the utter
density of the jungle spreading thirty miles in every direction.
It was impossible to see through the canopy of trees, but we saw
the tops of three or four pyramids poking through, as if trying
to reach the heavens. And with the exception of the sound of
our breathing—slightly labored from the climb—it was utterly,
completely silent. The sides of the pyramid seemed to plunge
straight down, and standing near the edge gave me a sense of
vertigo. Yet neither Micah nor I could wipe the smiles off our

faces. We had begun the trip of our lives a few hours earlier; now we were standing on what seemed to be the top of the world, in a place we'd always dreamed of seeing.

"Take my picture," Micah suddenly said. "Christine's going to love this."

"If she were here, do you think she would have come up?"

"No way. She hates heights. She would have been one of those people way down there," he said, pointing to where we'd been standing. "How about Cathy?"

"She doesn't like heights either, but she'd be up here. She wouldn't get too close to the edge, though."

I took his picture and he took mine. We took another, then still more. And we continued to gaze in wonder, even as I retrieved the satellite phone from my backpack.

"I've got to call Cat," I said, feeling the need to share this with her. I dialed the number and I heard the phone begin to ring. This amazed me. I was making a phone call from the middle of nowhere. When she answered, the first words out of my mouth were, "I'm standing on top of a Mayan temple in the jungle!" and I heard Cathy whoop with the same excitement I was feeling.

"Is it great?" she asked.

I stared around me in wonder. "It's incredible," I said. "The only way it could be any better was if you were here beside me."

"Aw," she said. "I miss you, too."

Later, when I hung up, Micah asked for the phone to call Christine. Unfortunately, she was out, and, disappointed, he hung up after leaving a message on the answering machine.

A minute later, our moment of solitude ended with the arrival of the rest of the crowd.

*   *   *

That night at the hotel, there was a cocktail party followed by dinner. Dinner was a buffet, and despite the warnings about eating salads and vegetables, we saw many people eating them anyway. And just as the doctor predicted, more than a dozen would become ill within days; some would remain sick throughout the rest of the trip.

We dined that night with Bob and Kate Devlin, who split their time between Connecticut and New York City, and with whom we formed an immediate connection. They had two sons approximately our age and they said we reminded them of their kids. For us, the connection seemed just as personal.

"Doesn't Kate remind you of mom?" Micah asked, as we were heading back to our room.

"Yeah, she does," I answered, amazed that he'd been thinking exactly the same thing as I.

Lost in thought, we didn't say much else the rest of the night.

Because it was the hub of Mayan life, Tikal has been declared a World Heritage site by UNESCO. Discovery, excavation, and repairs have been ongoing for decades, and despite the number of visitors, it takes a small army to keep the jungle at bay.

At one time, the area surrounding Tikal was home to a hundred thousand people, all of whom depended on the city for protection and trade. By the end of the tenth century, however, the civilization began to disintegrate. A number of theories abound as to the reason—overpopulation, wars, an overthrow of the ruling class, drought, famine, dwindling nutrient capacity of the soil, or simple discontent of the people that led them to find opportunities with other invading tribes. But within a few generations, the city had been completely abandoned and the people dispersed back into the countryside. The rise and sudden fall of the Maya is still considered one of the world's great mysteries, and I was thinking about it as we made our way to the ancient city.

The ruins of Tikal include some three thousand structures, including palaces, temples, platforms, ball courts, plazas, and terraces, built over a period of six hundred years. Thus, some sections are significantly older than others, and it's possible to observe the changing architecture of the Maya, which enables archaeologists to accurately date other Mayan sites throughout Central America and Mexico.

It was the sacrificial stones, however, that intrigued my brother. These were the stones upon which people had been killed as offerings to the gods. Our Maya guide was proudly discussing the historical and cultural reasons for the stones when Micah leaned over and whispered, "Have someone get a picture of me lying on the stone, while you pretend to stab me. Wouldn't that be cool?"

Actually, I found the thought a little morbid, but I reluctantly agreed. I handed over the camera and we got ourselves into position. Just as the picture was about to be taken, the guide came rushing over, waving his arms to stop us.

"No, no!" he was shouting, his face reddening. "You can't lie on the stones and take pictures! They have great religious significance!"

"I know," Micah countered, "that's why I want the picture."

"It's not allowed!"

"Just one picture."

"No!"

"Aw," he said, winking. "Just one. We won't tell anyone."

Though I laughed, the guide glowered. He was Maya, as were most Guatemalans who lived in the area, and I'm sure he thought we were insulting him or his culture. When he didn't crack a smile, Micah reluctantly got up from the stone. As we began trailing after the group, I shook my head.

"Where do you come up with these ideas?" I asked in disbelief.

Micah laughed. "He didn't like that much, did he?"

I shook my head. "He looked pretty mad, and so did the people running the tour. You're insulting their culture. You're going to get us in trouble."

"Ah, they'll get over it. They won't even remember it."

They did, of course. An hour later, one of the people who worked for TCS sidled up to us as we were walking. She was maybe a dozen years older than we were and had worked on numerous tours. She was well versed in the art of sizing people up quickly.

"You two are going to cause trouble on this trip, aren't you?" she observed.

We walked along what was once the main boulevard entering Tikal, touring the ruins of a palace while howler monkeys screeched their warnings overhead. From there, we moved on to the main plaza.

Two pyramids lie at either end of Tikal's main plaza. They are among the most photographed of all Mayan pyramids, and while one of the pyramids is off-limits to climbers, we were allowed to scale the second one.

At the top, the view was breathtaking. Micah finally reached Christine, and when he was finished with the call, we sat on the edge of the pyramid, our feet dangling beneath us. The ground was hundreds of feet below, and we could see other members of the tour, clustered in small groups throughout the ancient plaza. Since only a few wanted to make the climb, we had the place to ourselves.

"So how's Christine?" I asked.

"She's all right. Says she misses me."

"How's life on the home front so far?"

He smiled. "She's going a little crazy. Unlike Cat, she isn't used to me being gone. She kept talking about how busy she was—she hasn't stopped since I went to the airport. She said it's been four days of hell, and that she's going to call Cathy for moral support."

I smiled. "Tell her to call while the older kids are in school. Otherwise, Cat won't have a chance to talk to her. Once all five are home, the house goes crazy. Especially between five and nine. We call those the witching hours. That's when the little ones get tired, the older ones groan about having to do their homework, she starts cooking dinner—and still somehow manages to run the kids from one practice to the next. After that comes bath time, and if you've ever tried to get five kids tubbing and showering at once, you know it's not exactly relaxing. She's got such a good attitude about it. She's a great wife, but she's a genius as a mother."

Micah put his arm around me. "We married well, didn't we?"

"Yeah, we did," I admitted. "I think that's what we learned from mom. What to look for when we got married, I mean. We both married smart women with big hearts, who adore their children unequivocally. That's what mom taught us."

"Are you saying I essentially married my mother?"

"We both did."

He cocked an eyebrow. "What did we learn from dad?"

"Anger management?" I cracked. "You know, the tongue thing?"

He laughed. "Yeah, that was something, wasn't it? Man, he looked pretty scary when he did that. It still gives me nightmares." He glanced at me. "Did I tell you I did that to Alli once? Just to see how she'd react?"

"And?"

"She ran away screaming and wouldn't come out of her room."

I laughed. "No, what I think we got from dad was our love of learning," I said after a moment.

"I think so, too. Growing up, I thought mom was smart. Very smart. But dad . . . he was in his own league."

"They were quite a pair, weren't they?"

"Yeah," he said. "And they balanced each other out. Who knows how we would have turned out had they not gotten back together after our stint in Grand Island?"

On December 1, 1974, our family was reunited in Fair Oaks, California, a suburb just northeast of Sacramento. Within minutes of our arrival, my dad turned on the television to watch *Kolchak: The Night Stalker*, a campy, though utterly watchable, horror series that was far and away my dad's favorite. Soon, the three of us were seated beside my dad on the couch, eating popcorn and watching something scary on TV, almost believing that we'd never been away from him at all.

Our house—another rental, of course—had four bedrooms, an almost unfathomable luxury in our young minds, yet I couldn't help but notice that my father had claimed one of the bedrooms as his office. With the master bedroom obviously taken, that left two bedrooms for the three of us kids, and my mom quickly announced that my sister would be the one to have her own room, the reason being, "She's a girl."

Because it was so late in the first term, our parents held us out of school until after the new year, when the new term started. My parents also bought a dog, a Doberman pinscher named Brandy, and as we always did in new places, my brother and I set out to explore, this time with our dog in tow. Our street dead-ended a few houses up, bordering on what seemed like wilderness, and our first instinct was to "learn the terrain." Nowadays, Fair Oaks is almost completely developed, but back then, there were wide-open fields and hills, an abandoned house, and climbing trees—everything young boys need to have fun. Even better, we weren't the only kids our age on the street. Almost all of our neighbors had led a nomadic lifestyle, similar to ours, so it wasn't as if we were the only new kids on the block. In the afternoons, they would play on the street outside, and gradually my brother and I got to know them. And, as had happened in Nebraska, my brother soon began leaving me behind, preferring the company of his newfound friends.

Despite the fact that my parents had reunited, they continued to lead largely separate lives. My mom, who had taken another job as an optometrist's assistant, would rise with us and get us off to school while my father slept; after she got off work, she'd come home to an empty house two or three evenings a week, since my father sometimes had to teach at night. On those evenings he didn't have to teach, my dad would either grade papers and exams, or read, hoping to keep abreast in his chosen field of study. Like all professors, he was also pressed to publish, and he could frequently be heard typing in his office. Occasionally, my mom and dad would bump into each other in the kitchen, but in general they seemed to spend little time together.

While it would be easy to surmise that they didn't enjoy each other's company—neither one seemed to go out of the way to visit with the other, after all—they had a comfortable relationship. They joked and laughed at the kitchen table over dinner; I sometimes even caught my dad nuzzling the back of my mom's neck when they didn't realize I was watching. While they weren't overtly affectionate most of the time, they weren't needy, possessive, or jealous either. I never heard either of them say something negative about the other, and I seldom heard them argue anymore. They'd put the past behind them more successfully than most, and seemed to be exactly what the other one needed.

To that point, they'd lived a life of sacrifice, and I think that united them as well. Neither, after all, was living the life of their dreams. My dad wanted a life with less pressure and fewer financial worries; while he didn't desire great wealth, he was frequently discouraged by the daily struggle of keeping the family afloat. Nor could he envision any change in the future, and that weighed on him as well. My mom was no different. Once I found her crying in the bedroom, and the discovery terrified me. It was so unlike her that I began to tear up as well, and my mom pulled me close.

"I was just thinking how nice it would be to live in the country with horses like I did when I was little," she said. "Maybe with a little house, where we could go riding on the weekends…it would just be so wonderful. I wish we would have been able to give that kind of life to you kids."

Dreams are always crushing when they don't come true. But it's the simple dreams that are often the most painful because they seem so personal, so reasonable, so *attainable*. You're always close enough to touch, but never quite close enough to hold, and it's enough to break your heart.

As for Micah and me, our lives over the next four years fell into a relatively distinct pattern. My brother continued to spread his wings and found new friends easily. My sister made good friends as well, and one of them quickly became like a sister to her. I, on the other hand, had less luck in maintaining friendships, not because there was anything wrong with me per se (at least I like to think so) but rather because of simple bad luck.

My best friend in third grade was Tim; in the fourth grade, he transferred to the parochial school and our paths seldom crossed again. My best friend in fourth grade was Andy; in the fifth grade, he transferred to the parochial school as well, and I didn't see him again either. In fifth grade, my best friend was Warren; in the sixth grade, he moved to Australia. In sixth grade, my best friend was Kevin; when we went off to middle school the following year, we never had a single class together.

My brother, on the other hand, was much more fortunate, and the friendships he made grew only stronger over the years. None of the kids ever moved away, none ever transferred to a different school. Like Micah, his friends tended to be adventurous, and afternoons and weekends were spent either in the fields near our house, or at the American River a few miles away.

Meanwhile, I began to find more and more pleasure in the solitary act of reading. Because we couldn't afford to buy books and the town library was extremely small with relatively few titles, there wasn't much to choose from except for the set of *Encyclopaedia Britannica* at home. With no other options, I began with the first volume, and over the next two years I read through the entire set of twenty-six volumes, one miscellaneous entry at a time. When I finished, I read them all again. Then, I read the Bible from cover to cover.

This isn't to say I read all the time, or even most of the time. Because we were latchkey kids (again), the outside world was always beckoning, and there were even times that Micah's group of friends would get together with my friends, when it almost felt like old times.

We used to enjoy playing with the BB guns our parents got us for Christmas one year. While I suppose this is common for boys our age, what wasn't common was what we did with them. Essentially, my brother and I—along with whoever else was stupid enough to join us—quickly learned that it was less exciting to shoot at targets than at each other, and the game we developed was simple. Someone shouted "Go," we'd all scramble through the woods or into the abandoned house, then hunt each other down. There were no teams—it was every man for himself—and there was no real end to the game either. You simply kept hiding and hunting and shooting each other until dinnertime, when everyone had to go home. There were only two rules: no shooting in the face, and you could only pump the BB gun twice (which limited the velocity somewhat); but even those were more "guidelines" than strictly enforced rules. Consequently, everyone cheated. There was a perverse joy in shooting at someone, hearing them scream, and watching them dance in circles holding the wound, trying to get rid of the sting. Of course, what goes around comes around, and I spent years with welts all over my body. On more occasions than I can remember, each of us had to push out a BB that had embedded itself into our skin.

Micah, though, always seemed to suffer injuries worse than any of us. Part of it was because he was always pushing, always trying to do more. Once when he was playing with his BB gun in a garbage-strewn abandoned house, he thought it would be fun to kick out the rest of a window that had long since been broken. I suppose he was imitating what he saw people do on television, but no one told him that on TV they use special glass that doesn't shatter. Anyway, after kicking out the window and shooting someone circling the house, he knew it was time to find the next hiding place, and started to leave.

The next thing he knew, he heard a squishing noise coming from his shoe. Figuring that he must have stepped in a puddle of some unknown liquid, he kept going, trying to ignore it.

As he put it, "But I realized the squishing only seemed to be growing louder. When I looked down at my shoe, I noticed that my sock was turning pink, and my shoe was soaked. Obviously, I told myself, I'd stepped in some wine left behind by some teenagers. So there I was, step, squish, step, squish. And I could feel my foot getting slimier, and then I suddenly realized that I must have cut myself on the glass. So I sat down and took off my shoe. My sock and shoe were soaked in blood, and all of a sudden, the blood spurts from a cut over my ankle like water from a drinking fountain. It spurted high with every heartbeat. Looking back, I must have cut—or at least nicked—an artery, because it was really spurting."

He yelled for his friend, who came running. Using the bloody sock, they put a tourniquet on the ankle, and with his friend's help my brother hobbled home and called for my mom.

Because it was a weekend, she happened to be at home and she examined his ankle as it spurted blood all over the kitchen linoleum.

"Looks pretty bad," she said succinctly. And as always, she knew exactly what to do.

She stuck a Band-Aid on it.

Then she told Micah to put his hand over the Band-Aid, and told him he might want to rest it for a while before he went outside to play again.

* * *

As wild as we were, my mom always made it a point to bring us to church every Sunday, and that continued in California. My brother and I were often bored and would poke each other. The challenge, however, was that the other wasn't allowed to flinch, and the poker couldn't appear to be moving, so that our mother wouldn't catch us.

Dana didn't like this particular game very much, and while my mother didn't know what was going on, my sister certainly did. She took church very seriously—because our mom did, I suppose, and she wanted to be just like her—and in between her prayers, she would frown at us, trying to get us to stop.

Dana loved to pray. She prayed in the morning, she prayed at night. She asked God to bless everyone she knew, one at a time. She prayed for relatives and friends and strangers, dogs and cats and animals at the zoo. She prayed to become kinder and more patient, despite the fact that she didn't need help in either department. She seemed completely at ease with the world, and had a way of making others comfortable around her. In her own gentle way, my sister had quietly become the rock that my brother and I began to cling to whenever misfortune befell us.

But as much as Dana loved church and praying, it was her fault that we never arrived at Mass on time. Usually we rolled in about ten minutes late, and always after the rest of the congregation was seated. I didn't mind coming late (as I said, I was frequently bored), but I didn't like the way everyone would turn to watch us as we tried to find a seat. And in moments like those, I wished my sister would be a little more like my brother and me, at least in one respect.

Dana, despite her other wonderful qualities, was not a fast

mover. When she woke up in the morning, she never got out of bed right away. Instead, she would sit cross-legged on the mattress and simply stare into space, looking dreamy and disoriented. She would stay in that position for twenty minutes—"Waking up" as she described it—and would only then begin getting ready to go. And even then, everything was slow. She ate slowly, she dressed slowly, she brushed her hair slowly. Where our mom could tell Micah and me to get ready and we'd be dressed within minutes, my sister took her time. My brother and I had to walk to school, but more often than not, my mom would have to drive my sister in, so that she wouldn't be late. It made us crazy at times, but she never let our complaints bother her.

"People are just different," Dana used to observe serenely, whenever we'd tease her about it. And my mom never let my sister's lateness bother her. As she explained it to us, "She just needs a little more time to get ready."

"Why?" Micah or I would ask.

"Because she's a girl."

Oh.

Still, Dana had the occasional wild impulse. On our one and only cross-country vacation in the summer of 1976, the family loaded into our Volkswagen van—the only car we had from 1974 to 1982—and spent a few weeks traveling around the west. We visited the Painted Desert and Taos, New Mexico, before finally arriving at the Grand Canyon. It was, of course, one of the greatest sights in the world, but as children we didn't much appreciate it. Instead, on my sister's suggestion, we decided it would be much more fun to slip behind the viewing ropes and approach the unstable, cordoned-off edge of the canyon while our parents were buying us lunch. There, we discovered a small ledge, maybe three feet down.

"Let's go down there," my sister suggested.

Micah and I looked at each other, glanced at the ledge, and shrugged. "Okay," we replied. I mean, why not? How dangerous could it be? It didn't look *too* unstable.

Anyway, we climbed down and sat on the ledge for a few minutes, three little kids with their legs dangling free. Far beneath us, we could see the Colorado River snaking through the canyon and hawks circling below. The differing strata of rock resembled a soft-hued, vertical rainbow. After a while, however, we got bored.

"Hey," my sister said, "I have an idea. Let's pretend we slipped off the edge of the canyon and scare people."

Micah and I looked at each other again, impressed. This would normally have been one of our ideas. "Okay," we answered in unison.

Now, squatting on the ledge, we raised ourselves slowly and

poked our heads and arms over the top of the canyon. No one noticed us at first. Beyond the ropes about thirty feet away, we could see a group of people taking pictures and staring off in different directions, marveling at the natural beauty. When my sister nodded, we suddenly began screaming for help at the top of our lungs.

Heads immediately whipped in our direction, and people saw what seemed to be three little children clawing for their lives in an attempt to hold on. An older woman swooned, another grabbed at her heart, another clutched at her husband's arms. No one seemed to know what to do. They continued staring at us with wide, fearful eyes, frozen by shock and horror.

Finally, one man broke free from the spell he was under, and was stepping over the rope when we saw my mom come rushing toward us.

You can probably guess what happened next.

"Stay there while I take a picture, kids!" my mom yelled.

As fun as it was, sadly we couldn't stay at the Grand Canyon. A few minutes later, our family was told that we had to leave.

"Now," as the ranger on duty so kindly put it.

Six months later, my brother and I had our BB guns confiscated by the sheriff. Not because of the BB gun wars, but because my brother went a little too far. Basically, what happened was this: There was no one to play war with one afternoon, so my brother recruited a couple of first-graders for a different kind of game. He told them to bend over and hold the cuffs of their pant legs out, so he could shoot through the material.

"Don't move, or I might accidentally shoot your leg," Micah explained patiently. "I just want to practice my aim."

Anyway, as I said, the sheriff came and took away his gun.

A week later, they came again and took my gun, too. My brother had used it to shoot holes in a couple of neighbors' windows.

And just like that, our days playing war were over.

Questions and Explanations
for Chapter 6

The ten questions on chapter 6 focus on grammar and usage, vocabulary, comprehension, characterization, literary terms, and style. Some of the questions combine two or more of these areas, requiring you to synthesize your knowledge, make inferences, and interpret the text. The questions are designed to determine both your current level of understanding of the memoir and your ability to answer higher-level questions.

The following sentence tests your ability to recognize grammar and usage errors. The sentence contains either a single error or no error at all. If the sentence contains an error, select the one underlined part that must be changed to make the sentence correct. If there is no error, select choice D.

1. When the <u>Sparkses</u> moved to a new house in Fair Oaks,
      A
   <u>California,</u> everyone in the family was unable to get <u>their</u>
      B   **C**
   own room. <u>No error</u>
              D

Choice A checks your knowledge of how to make nouns plural. Choice B checks comma usage. And choice C tests pronoun and antecedent agreement.

In choice A, the name *Sparks* obviously ends in the letter *s*. The rule is very simple: First and last names that end in the letter *s* form the plural by adding *-es*.

In choice B, recognize that both a city and state are listed. Commas are used to separate items in addresses—for example, "Address me at 1659 Dorchester Drive, Brunswick, Ohio, after the first of July."

In choice C, recognize that *their* is a plural possessive pronoun showing joint ownership—for example, "This is their house," which indicates that more than one person has possession of the house. Also recognize that the antecedent *everyone* is singular. You can realize this in the sentence "Everyone is having a good time" because the verb *is* demonstrates a single entity (he is, she is, Rich is, and so on). Although when speaking we often consider *everyone* to be plural, in formal writing, *everyone* requires a singular verb and a singular possessive pronoun—for example, "Everyone completed his or her homework."

The following two questions test your vocabulary. Choose the word or set of words that, when inserted in the sentence, best fits the meaning of the sentence as a whole.

2. The tour guide was _____ about not taking pictures on the sacred stones, no matter how much Micah pleaded and argued.

   A. adamant

   B. adept

   C. adjure

   D. adumbrate

This question tests both your comprehension and your vocabulary. It also tests your understanding of parts of speech. Based on the sentence, you know that the missing word must be an adjective. Thus, if the possible answer is a verb, then you know to eliminate that choice as a possible correct answer. In order to select the best word, you not only need to know the definitions of the words, but you also need to insert the words into the sentence to make sure the resulting sentence makes sense.

Adamant, choice A, means utterly unyielding, despite pleas to the contrary. *Adept*, choice B, means quite skilled. *Adjure*, choice C, means to appeal to. And *adumbrate*, choice D, means to foreshadow somewhat, or give clues about future events.

3. The brothers' father made some _____ choices regarding what he _____ his children to do, such as watching *Kolchak: The Night Stalker*.

   A. mainstream...allowed

   B. typical...flouted

   C. unconventional...berated

   D. unorthodox...permitted

This question tests both your comprehension and your vocabulary. The easiest way to answer this question is to figure out the second blank first. Recall the mention of the television show. Were the Sparks kids permitted to watch it? If so, eliminate choice B and choice C. Or substitute the words into the second half of the sentence. *Flout* means to disregard with contempt, and *berate* means to scold harshly, so these choices don't make sense. Now, differentiate between *mainstream*, which means widely accepted, and *unorthodox*, meaning not customary. Did most parents in the early 1970s permit their children to stay up and watch horror shows on television with them?

Question 4 asks you to make an inference using strong and thorough textual evidence.

4. Why does the memoir, when discussing the Maya, include such details as the culture of human sacrifice along with the concept of zero?

   A. to demonstrate the contrasts within the Mayan civilization itself

   B. to demonstrate how barbaric the civilization really was

   C. to illustrate how advanced the civilization really was

   D. to illustrate the differences between then and now

In order to answer this question, recognize that the two examples provided represent vastly different aspects of Mayan civilization. Thus, although three of these choices are partially correct, the best answer incorporates them. Which is the broadest choice—the choice that integrates the other three—and therefore the best answer?

Question 5 asks you to make an inference using strong and thorough textual evidence.

5. While standing in the plaza of an excavated Mayan temple, Nicholas contemplates something the tour guide says and concludes that "In the ebb and flow of history, the rise and fall of civilizations, my own daily concerns suddenly seemed minuscule in comparison." This reflection is important for the development of each of the following EXCEPT:

   A. character
   B. external conflict
   C. plot
   D. theme

Three out of the four choices can be eliminated because the quotation is important to those areas of development. *Character* refers to the people in the memoir. If this quotation gives the reader a better understanding of Nicholas, eliminate choice A. *External conflict* refers to a problem between two characters or a character and nature. If the quotation is developing the struggle between opposing forces, eliminate choice B. *Plot* refers to the selection and arrangement of all the incidents in the memoir. If the statement can be applied to the arrangement and interrelationships of the events in the memoir, eliminate choice C. And *theme* refers to a central idea.

If this statement could be considered a debatable claim, an opinion that can be supported with details and examples, eliminate choice D.

Question 6 checks your comprehension.

6. Why were the travelers warned not to eat the salad and vegetables?

    A. They were exotic in nature.

    B. These foods were not washed.

    C. The fertilizers and soil were not compatible with American digestive systems.

    D. Local water was used to wash them.

This question requires you to make connections between chapters, for at many points, information mentioned, discussed, or revealed in a particular chapter plays an important part in a later one. If you don't remember the answer to this question, you need to reread chapter 5. Although the travelers get sick in chapter 6, the reason is revealed in the previous chapter.

Question 7 tests your knowledge of literary terms.

7. One time when Micah was playing with his BB gun, he "heard a squishing noise coming from his shoe." What literary device is being used to describe the situation?

    A. hyperbole

    B. metaphor

    C. onomatopoeia

    D. personification

Again, knowledge of literary terms is essential to answering this question. *Hyperbole*, choice A, is an overexaggeration used to make a point—for example, "Everyone who reads this learning guide will know what *hyperbole* is because hyperbole will be explained a bazillion times."

A *metaphor*, choice B, is a comparison between two unlike things without using a connective word—for example, "LeBron James is an animal on the basketball court."

Onomatopoeia, choice C, is a word that suggests the very sound it describes, like *buzz*, *sizzle*, and *boom*.

Personification, choice D, is giving nonhuman things a human characteristic, such as in "Opportunity knocked on the door."

Question 8 asks you to make an inference using strong and thorough textual evidence.

8. Based on the details in chapter 6, the brothers would most likely agree that:

   A. the only important things they learned were from their mother

   B. only their father led by example

   C. they learned important things from each of their parents

   D. their father did his best to provide for them but offered little else

This question requires you to draw a conclusion regarding information the brothers share. In this chapter they mention what they learned both explicitly and implicitly from their parents. If you do not remember what they learned from their parents, reread the chapter. If the brothers do not value what they learned from their father, select choice A. If their mother did not lead by example, select choice B. If both of their parents taught the brothers important things, select choice C. And if the only thing their father was able to offer them was doing his best, select choice D.

Question 9 checks your comprehension.

9. Because "she's a girl" becomes a standard reason to explain or excuse Dana's actions or other actions directed toward her. Which examples relied on this rationale as an explanation?

   A. Dana's receiving of her own room

   B. Dana's needing more time than the boys to get ready for church

   C. Dana's receiving a BB gun

   D. Dana's ability to make new friends quickly

In order to answer this question correctly, you need to first realize that there may be more than one correct answer. Then, remember each of the anecdotes mentioned. One of them didn't occur, so eliminate that choice. The other three did get mentioned in the chapter. If you don't remember if because "she's a girl" was used with the specific incident, skim through the chapter again to find the anecdote and reread it.

Question 10 checks your comprehension and asks you to analyze an author's stylistic choices.

10. *Three Weeks with My Brother* is a memoir with two narrative threads. Micah's desire for his picture on the Mayan tomb with Nicholas pretending to stab him echoes whose desire to photograph the siblings pretending to have slipped off the edge of the Grand Canyon?

   A. Micah's

   B. their mother's

   C. their father's

   D. Dana's

In order to answer this question correctly, first remember the incident. Eliminate the person whose idea it was to stage the event, and then think about what happens after other tourists see the "accident." If you still can't remember, reread the last two pages of chapter 6.

Chapter 7

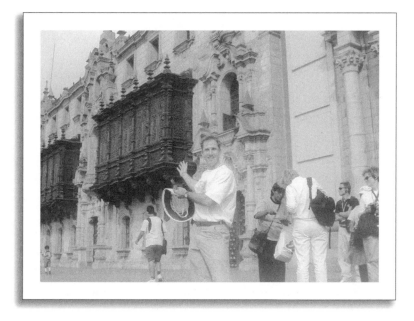

When it was time to bid farewell to Guatemala, we boarded our plane and headed to our next stop, Lima, Peru, a city of eight million and home to nearly a third of Peru's population. Once the capital of a Spanish empire encompassing Ecuador, Colombia, Bolivia, Chile, Argentina, and Peru, Lima was one of the world's wealthiest and most luxurious cities in the sixteenth, seventeenth, and eighteenth centuries. Exploitation, mismanagement, and poor planning eventually weakened the Spanish empire, however, leading to Simón Bolívar's eventual rout of the Spanish forces in 1824. A succession of governments over the next 175 years finally led to democratic elections in 1980, and I was anxious to see how the country was faring.

Lima was sweltering when we landed. It was summer in South America, far warmer than it had been in Guatemala. As we boarded buses, TCS handed out bottles of water and introduced the local tour guides, who would speak to us about the culture and history of the places we visited. We were also given a radio and earpiece, which we tuned to the same frequency as our guide. Thus, even up to a hundred feet away, we could always hear what was going on.

The central plaza was crowded when we arrived. It was one of the few open areas in the center of the city, colonial in design, and crisscrossed with curving sidewalks lined with freshly planted flowers. Kids played games in the grass and played in the fountains, trying to keep cool in the summer heat. Others did their best to sell us souvenirs, and crowded around our group the moment we stepped off the bus.

We took photographs of both the Presidential Palace and the cathedral where Francisco Pizarro was buried. Pizarro, I knew, was one in a long line of historical figures whose reputation largely depends on perspective; while known in Spain as an explorer, he had also captured Atahualpa, the leader of the Incas. When he demanded and received as ransom a roomful of gold for his release, he promptly executed the king anyway before enslaving the natives. I couldn't help but wonder what the descendants of the Incas thought about his church-sanctioned burial place.

From there, we made our way to Casa Aliaga, which was located just off the main plaza. Literally, "Aliaga's House," it was one of the most striking examples of early Spanish architecture in the city, yet from the outside it blended into the other structures on the block. Unless you knew it was there, a person could walk by without noticing it.

Beyond the doors, however, was a home that boggled the mind.

Casa Aliaga has been owned by the Aliaga family for over four hundred years, and is still occupied by the Aliagas today. Designed in typical hacienda fashion, rooms surround an open courtyard, complete with a hundred-foot-tall fig tree stretching to the sky. It is also home to one of the finest art collections in South America. Because the house is so large and expensive to maintain, the Aliagas open the house to tourists, and Micah and I wandered through with wide eyes. Everything, with the exception of the plaster walls—the banisters, door frames, crown moldings, and railings—had been intricately carved, and paintings covered every available wall space. The furniture, mostly from the seventeenth and eighteenth centuries, was so ornate that it was impossible for us to bring our cameras into focus.

As we were walking through the house, Micah finally turned to me.

"Can you believe this place?"

"No. That tree...well, everything really...it's incredible."

"I'll bet you're getting some good ideas for the next time you remodel, huh?"

I laughed. "I have to admit that it would be nice to have paintings of famous ancestors."

"You mean if we had any."

"Exactly. While the Aliaga family was building this place,

our ancestors were probably putting shoes on horses and working the farm."

He nodded and looked around. Our group had dispersed throughout various rooms in the house.

"Be honest though—would you want to live here?"

I shook my head. "No," I said. "It's...unbelievable, but it's not really my style. And the upkeep must keep the owners awake at night."

"I know what you mean. I mean, can you imagine how long it takes to dust this place? Christine would *die*."

The TCS crew began herding us together, counting heads, and making sure everyone was accounted for. After leaving Casa Aliaga, we climbed back on the bus for the ride to the hotel.

This would become our routine over the next few weeks. While a tour like ours has advantages, the schedule is carefully predetermined, and in many places there's little time to linger or explore on your own.

It was the night of the Super Bowl. The Tampa Bay Buccaneers were playing the Oakland Raiders, and a number of people in the tour wanted to watch it, including Micah. Because he lived in Sacramento, the Raiders were his favorite team and he'd even been to a few of the games that year. We weren't even sure the game would be broadcast in Peru, and there was a veritable whoop on the bus when TCS confirmed that it would be. The game would be on via satellite in the bar, and would stay tuned there throughout the game; apparently, this required quite a bit of finagling by the crew of TCS; few people in Peru care about the Super Bowl, and a soccer game—which *was* important to Peruvians—wouldn't be shown.

Wanting a good seat, Micah and I were among the first to arrive and we began ordering traditional pregame goodies. Others gradually joined us. Half the crowd favored Tampa Bay, the other half favored Oakland, and by the time it was ready for the game to begin, the hotel bar looked like a bar in any city in the United States. There wasn't a local anywhere near the place.

There was no pregame show; instead, roughly five minutes before the start of the game, the television flickered once or twice, and we found ourselves watching the teams lining up for the kickoff.

"See, everything we're doing is new," Micah said. "Be honest, who do you know who's ever watched the Super Bowl in Lima?"

"No one," I admitted.

"Having fun yet?"

"Having a blast," I answered.

"You thinking about work?"

"Nope. Just thinking about the game."

He waved a french fry at me. "Good. There's hope for you yet."

"Turn it up!" someone yelled from behind us. "We can't hear in the back!"

The bartender used the remote, and the volume began to rise. With it, the familiar sounds started to register. We heard the roar of the crowd, the names of the players as they were announced in the stadium, then the coin toss. Only then did the announcers begin their commentary.

Everyone leaned forward.

"What the hell are they saying?" someone shouted.

"I don't know," another answered. "I think they're announcing it in...*Spanish*."

Of course, it made perfect sense once you thought about it.

"Spanish?"

"It's the official language of Peru," Micah offered. "And Spain."

No one thought it was funny.

"I thought it was coming in on satellite," someone grumbled. "From the States. Maybe it's in English on another channel."

The bartender surfed around; this was it. Spanish or nothing.

I leaned toward Micah. "Now you really have a story to tell," I said. "Not only did you see your favorite team play in the Super Bowl in Lima, Peru, but you can tell them you heard it in *Spanish*."

"Now you're getting in the spirit. That's exactly what I was going to say."

We settled in to watch the game. The Raiders weren't playing well and quickly fell behind. Micah's cheers gradually grew more infrequent, and by halftime, he was shaking his head.

"You gotta have faith," I urged.

"I think I'm losing it."

"I've heard that," I said pointedly, recalling my previous conversations I'd had with his wife, Christine. "So, are you still avoiding church?"

He smiled, but didn't look at me. Faith and religion was a subject we often discussed, even through our early years. Since Micah had married, however, the subject had been coming up more regularly. Christine wasn't Catholic, and instead of going to Mass, they attended a nondenominational Christian service. Unlike the Mass I preferred, which is highly traditional, with only slight variation from week to week, Micah preferred a service with less structure and more time for personal reflection. Or, more accurately, those were his original reasons when he explained the change to me. But lately, even those differences hadn't seemed to matter.

"Let me guess. Christine told you to ask me about this on the trip, didn't she?"

I said nothing. Micah shifted in his seat.

"No, I go sometimes. But only because Christine wants me to. She thinks it's important for me to go because of the kids."

"And?"

"And what?"

"Are you getting anything out of it?"

"Not really."

"Are you praying at all?"

"I haven't prayed in three years."

A life without prayer is something I couldn't imagine. In no small way, I'd been depending on prayer for as long as he'd been avoiding it.

"Don't you feel like you're missing something?"

"I don't pray because it doesn't work," he said curtly. "Prayer doesn't fix anything. Bad things happen anyway."

"Don't you think it helps you handle those bad times, though?"

He didn't answer, and by his silence I knew he didn't want to talk about it. Not yet, anyway.

In the end, the game was a blowout. Tampa Bay had the game in hand, and Micah and I left the bar to work out in the hotel gym during the second half. We jogged and lifted weights; afterward, we went back to our room and collapsed on the bed.

"Sorry your team lost," I said.

"No big deal," he said. "I'm not like you used to be. Remember? Back when you were a kid? You used to cry whenever the Vikings lost."

The Minnesota Vikings had been my favorite team growing up; I'd picked them because it was where Dana was born.

"I remember. It broke my heart when they lost the Super Bowl."

"Which one? They lost a bunch of them."

"Thanks for reminding me."

"No problem." He paused. "You do know you were nuts when it came to the Vikings, don't you?"

"I know. I tended to go overboard in a lot of things."

"You still do."

"We all have our problems. Even you."

"That's untrue. I'm perfectly happy. Haven't you noticed? It was I who—through the sheer force of my buoyant personality—lifted you from the depths of despair only a couple of days ago."

I rolled my eyes. "That's just because we're on the trip. You have to remember—doing something like this has always been more your style than mine. You grew up loving adventure. You used to search it out. I just tagged along, trying to keep you from getting into too much trouble."

He grinned. "I did get into trouble a lot, didn't I?"

"Quite a bit, actually. Especially when it came to weapons."

A look of fond reminiscence crossed his face. "You know, I just don't understand why that happened. I wasn't a bad kid. I was just trying to have a good time."

I smiled, thinking, *good times indeed.*

My parents, being the wise and wonderful folks they were, finally realized Micah and I weren't exactly responsible when it came to BB guns, despite the good times we had had with them.

No matter how much we begged, they refused to buy us new ones. Nor would they consider giving us rifles, when we offered that by way of compromise. Instead, they bought us bows and arrows.

We had fun with those bows. Our aim wasn't too good, but what we lacked in accuracy, we made up for with velocity. We could send those arrows humming, practically burying them into trees. My brother took to it a bit more easily than I did, and eventually got to the point where he could actually hit a fairly large target from thirty feet away at least 5 percent of the time, as opposed to my 3 percent of the time.

"Hey, let's put an apple on your head and I'll try to shoot it off," he finally suggested.

"I have a better idea," I said, "let's put the apple on your head."

"Mmm. Maybe it's not such a good idea."

One day, when we were out with our bows and arrows in the woods, one of the arrows went astray, heading toward a group of workers that were framing a house. (In the years since we'd moved there, construction on new homes had begun in earnest.) Now, the arrow hadn't landed too close to the workers, but it wasn't too far away either, and one of the carpenters got pretty mad at us, even when we tried to explain that it was an accident. "Don't even *think* about shooting arrows around here," he growled, and even worse, he refused to give us the arrow back, no matter how much we pleaded. Since we had only three arrows to begin with, losing one was a big deal.

My brother and I skulked off, heading back up the hill toward our street again, seething. By the time we reached the top of the hill, my brother decided that he wasn't about to follow some stranger's orders, especially since he'd kept the arrow.

As he put it: "He can't tell *me* what to do."

My brother loaded an arrow and tightened the bow, then leaned back with the intention of shooting the arrow straight up into the sky in a statement of defiance, a sort of "take that!" He launched the arrow and it zoomed skyward, higher and higher, until it was just a speck in the sky.

Of course, he hadn't taken note of the light breeze that afternoon. Nor did my brother actually shoot straight up, though—as God is my witness—that was his intention. Instead, the arrow had just enough angle to sort of veer in the direction of the house (and workers) at the bottom of the hill, and the wind took over from there. I watched the arrow's changing trajectory, feeling my chest begin to constrict as I realized where it was heading.

"Micah—is that arrow heading where I think it is?"

"Oh, no...no...NO...NOOO...NOOOOOO!!!!!!"

My brother, turning white like me, was hopping up and down in ardent denial, as if hoping to change the obvious. We watched the arrow as it began arcing downward, toward the worker who'd confiscated the previous arrow. Had Micah aimed, had he purposely been trying, there wasn't a chance he'd ever launch an arrow two hundred yards with such accuracy.

"NOOOOO...NOOOOOO!!!!!" Micah screamed, continuing to hop up and down.

I watched the arrow descending toward doom itself, surer with every passing second that we were actually going to kill the guy. Never had I been so terrified. Time seemed to slow down; everything moved with dreadful determination. I knew we'd end up in Juvenile Hall; maybe even prison.

And then it was over.

The arrow hit the ground, less than a foot from where the man was working with a shovel, landing in a poof of dust. He jumped to the side in shock and horror.

"Oh, thank God," Micah said with a long sigh. He smiled.

"You got that right," I agreed. "That was close."

Of course, at that age—and in that particular moment—we weren't able to fathom how the worker might view this particular incident. Unlike us, he wasn't thankful at all. One minute, he's doing his job, and the next minute, he's nearly impaled by an arrow, launched by two kids at the top of the hill. No, he wasn't thankful, not even a little bit. He was ENRAGED! Even from two hundred yards, we saw him raise his eyes toward us, toss his shovel aside, and start racing for his truck.

"You think we oughta run?" I asked, turning to Micah.

But Micah was already gone, racing back toward our street, his legs moving as fast as I'd ever seen them.

I ran after him; thirty seconds later, as I was chugging across neighbors' lawns, I glanced over my shoulder and saw the truck come to a screeching halt at the edge of the woods, saw the man jump from the truck and start chasing us the rest of the way on foot.

Oh, he caught us all right, and he was even madder up close than he was far away. When my dad learned what happened, he was mad, too, and we were grounded for a couple of weeks. Even worse, later that afternoon, the sheriff came and confiscated our bows and arrows.

With the exception of the one trip to the Grand Canyon, our vacations would be spent with relatives in San Diego.

For whatever reason, the majority of both my mother's and

father's family had moved there, and consequently, we were able to visit them and enjoy the beach without having to spend much money. A good thing, I might add, for a family that didn't have any to spare.

We would always drive the ten hours it took to get there, the three of us crammed into the back of the Volkswagen van, along with Brandy (our Doberman) and assorted luggage. Though we would stop for gas twice in those ten hours, we never bought food or drinks; instead, our meals consisted of ham sandwiches, Fritos, and pink lemonade that my mom had brought from home.

Those were grand times. Our parents never required us to wear seat belts (are you really surprised by that revelation?), and we'd read, play games, or wrestle in the back as we zipped down Highway 5, heading for grandma Sparks's house. I don't mean the kind of wrestling where we'd poke each other and whine; I mean *real* wrestling complete with headlocks, punches, twisted arms and legs, and punctuated with screams and tears. Usually, my parents would ignore it for a while, but sometimes it got to the point that dad would finally look over his shoulder and scream at us to "Stop shaking the G-D-N van!" thereby initiating the inevitable DEFCON countdown, which we never seemed able to avoid. And, of course, we'd stare at our father as if he had cornstalks growing out of his ears, wondering what on earth could have possibly upset him.

"It was your fault," Micah would hiss. "You shouldn't have cried."

"But you were hurting me," I'd say.

"You need to learn to be tougher."

"You were twisting my ear! I thought you were ripping it off!"

"You're exaggerating."

"You're an idiot."

His eyes narrowed. "What'd you call me?"

"He called you an idiot," Dana would helpfully add.

Micah would glower. "I'll show you who the idiot is..."

At which point, the wrestling would begin again. I often tell people that we never actually *drove* to San Diego; for the most part, the van sort of *hopped* there.

We were also "country comes to town" when it came to visiting with our cousins. Their families tended to be better off financially than we were, and as soon as we arrived we'd go blasting through the door toward the cousins' bedroom. Beyond the door, we knew, was Nirvana itself and we'd simply stare for a moment in wonder, little tears welling in the corners of our eyes. They had more toys than we'd ever seen, and we quickly made good use of them.

"Hey what's this?" we'd ask, grabbing something. Soon we'd be wiggling pieces, trying to figure it out.

"It's the new, battery-operated construction crane," my cousin would proudly exclaim. "It can assemble entire houses from scratch—"

Snap.

The cousin would freeze in horror at the sight of the toy in two pieces.

"What happened?" we'd ask.

"You...you...broke it," he'd whimper.

"Oh, sorry about that. Hey...what's this one do?"

"It's the new electronically enhanced remote control car, complete with—"

Snap.

"Oh, sorry," we'd say again. "Hey, what's this..."

Once the toys were broken (we always wondered how so many accidents could happen in such a short time), we'd try to play with our cousins. Not that they viewed it as playing. We did nothing with them that we didn't do back home—to us, it was regular fun—but to them, it bordered on merciless torture. None of them, it seemed, had lived a childhood like ours, i.e., one without real rules. We thought it great fun, for instance, rolling the little ones up in area rugs until they were pinned and suffocated, unable to move. Then my brother and I would take turns launching ourselves from the couch onto the soft bulge where their bodies were and screaming, "Bingo!" whenever we really crunched them. Or, we might dunk them in the pool—really dunk them, for a long, long time—until they nearly passed out. Sometimes, we'd try to teach our cousins how to punch hard, demonstrating on their little arms.

"No, not like that. Cock your arm waaay back, and *really* use the knuckle. Like this . . ."

POW!

If there was one thing wrong with visiting my cousins—and it pains me to admit it, since they're family—it's that they were whiners. They cried all the time when we were around. It's a wonder how their parents ever dealt with it.

Anyway, the visit would eventually come to an end and it would be time to leave. We'd head to the van, and we'd turn around to see our cousins ghost-white and trembling as they waved good-bye to us, their little arms covered in bruises.

"See you next year!" we'd call out.

Later, on the way back to grandma's, my brother would ask, "What were they doing with their faces when we left?"

"You mean the way they were blinking, and squinching, and tilting suddenly to the side?"

"Yeah."

"I don't know. Must be a facial tic of some sort."

Micah would shake his head. "Those poor kids. They weren't like that when we got there. Must have come on suddenly."

The trips themselves were always an adventure, too. Once, when we took off for San Diego, my father had $21 in his wallet. That was it—the entire sum he'd brought for the family for an entire week's vacation. As fate would have it, the van broke down in the Tehachapi Mountains, about an hour north of Los Angeles. We were towed to the only service station nearby, where we learned that the van had an oil leak. The part would take at least a week to arrive, but the mechanic thought he could weld something together overnight that might allow us to reach our destination. Of course, it would cost money, something my dad didn't have.

My dad had a funny, almost contradictory, relationship with money. Oh, I suppose that he wanted more of it, but when push came to shove, he had no idea about how to go about earning more. At the same time, he never wanted to think about money, but, because of our family's situation, was always forced to do so. Everything had to be budgeted, and this breakdown was not in the budget. To say he was angry was an understatement; he was downright scary: He totally bypassed the DEFCON countdown and went straight to Nuclear Launch. He called his mom in San Diego, who promised to wire him the money needed for repairs, but the repairs wouldn't be completed until the following day. He spent the day pacing back and forth, whistling the tune of the dead, his tongue curled out of his mouth.

Later that afternoon, we ate the last of the ham sandwiches and Fritos and finished the lemonade, further enraging my father. Without money to buy food, or even stay in a hotel, we ended up sleeping in the back of the van with the dog that night. When we woke, there was no money for breakfast either; we wouldn't eat until we reached San Diego the following afternoon.

Still, that wasn't the worst part about our stay. Nor was it our dad's anger. When I think about that particular trip, my memories always drift back to the first day, an hour or so after we'd arrived at the garage.

As I said, my father was beyond furious at that time, and we'd learned to keep our distance in moments like those. With nothing else to do, my brother, sister, and I decided to see what the town had to offer, but quickly learned that there wasn't much. The place was more a run-down rest stop than an actual town. It was hot as blazes with only a handful of decrepit buildings lining the highway in either direction, and not a stitch of shade. There wasn't even a coffee shop or diner with a television perched in the corner that might help pass the time.

It was one of the first times we'd actually been bored. Thankfully, we soon came across a dog who seemed to enjoy our attention. We spent a few minutes petting him—he was incredibly friendly, bouncy, and happy—and we took to calling him Sparky (after us, of course). In time he scrambled to his feet and we watched him begin to trot away, tongue hanging out, looking pleased as punch. He glanced back at us, almost smiling, I still believe, and headed toward the road, where he was instantly struck by a car going sixty miles an hour.

We witnessed every detail. We heard the thump and watched the dog twist unnaturally before careening toward us, blood flying from his mouth, and skidding to a stop less than a couple of feet away. The car simply slowed; it didn't stop. The family in the car looked as horrified as we were. A moment later, after whining and whimpering and heaving a final breath, Sparky died at our feet. With my dad in such a foul mood, and my mom trying to keep him calm, all we could do was handle the latest horror the way we always had: with each other, as siblings. Just three little kids on the side of a highway, holding each other and crying, trying to understand why terrible things happened.

Questions and Explanations
for Chapter 7

The ten questions on chapter 7 focus on grammar and usage, vocabulary, comprehension, characterization, literary terms, and style. Some of the questions combine two or more of these areas, requiring you to synthesize your knowledge, make inferences, and interpret the text. The questions are designed to determine both your current level of understanding of the memoir and your ability to answer higher-level questions.

The following sentence tests your ability to recognize grammar and usage errors. The sentence contains either a single error or no error at all. If the sentence contains an error, select the one underlined part that must be changed to make the sentence correct. If there is no error, select choice D.

1. Each of the sites <u>that</u> the <u>brothers</u> visit on the tour <u>have</u>
         A   **B**   **C**
   a variety of historical and cultural significance. <u>No error</u>
                                             D

Choice A tests the use of a relative pronoun. Choice B checks the use of a plural versus the use of a possessive. And choice C checks subject and verb agreement.

Choice A is testing the choice of the relative pronoun *that*. A relative pronoun is the pronoun (*who, which, what,* or *that*) that introduces a subordinate (or dependent) clause. The entire clause acts as an adjective, modifying the noun that precedes it—for example, "A black hole is a star *that* behaves quite mysteriously."

Choice B tests whether you can differentiate between a plural noun and a possessive noun. Plural means more than one and does not require the use of an apostrophe—for example, "two sisters, three aunts, five UFOs."

Choice C checks subject and verb agreement. *Each* is a singular pronoun and thus needs a singular verb. Which is correct, "he has" or "he have"? The word *he* is also singular, so whichever verb goes with *he* should also be used with *each*.

The following two questions test your vocabulary. Choose the word or set of words that, when inserted in the sentence, best fits the meaning of the sentence as a whole.

2. When the family van broke down and there was no money to fix it or feed the family, the tension was _____ as their father bypassed his usual DEFCON countdown.

A. uncertain

B. intrepid

C. palatial

D. palpable

This question tests your vocabulary as well as your comprehension. Substitute the definition of each word in the sentence in order to determine which one makes the most sense. *Uncertain*, choice A, means doubtful. *Intrepid*, choice B, means fearless. *Palatial*, choice C, is magnificent or palacelike. *Palpable*, choice D, means plainly seen or felt.

3. The _____ scene in chapter 7, an image of three children huddled on the side of the road crying, is likely to elicit feelings of _____.

A. ultimate...pathos

B. last...bathos

C. penultimate...ethos

D. first...sympathy

This question tests your vocabulary as well as your comprehension. The first thing you need to do is determine if the scene of the siblings on the side of the road is the initial (*first*), second-to-last (*penultimate*), or final (*last, ultimate*) scene of chapter 7. Once you do that, you need to differentiate between *pathos* (pity), and *bathos* (foolish sentimentality).

Question 4 asks you to make an inference using strong and thorough textual evidence.

4. Nicholas's reflections on Pizarro demonstrate each of the following EXCEPT:

   A. his appreciation and sense of history

   B. his inquisitive nature

   C. his ability to analyze history

   D. his acceptance of official historical versions of events

This question requires you to analyze what Nicholas says regarding the famous Spanish explorer. Notice that three of the four choices will be eliminated. If Nicholas demonstrates his own historical knowledge, eliminate choice A. If Nicholas is asking questions about how Pizarro might be viewed by his descendants, eliminate choice B. If he realizes that different points of view result in different perspectives, eliminate choice C. And if he simply takes photos and appreciates the burial site of one of Spain's greatest explorers, who has a "church-sanctioned burial place," eliminate choice D.

Question 5 asks you to make an inference using strong and thorough textual evidence.

5. After "quite a bit of finagling," TCS, the company in charge of the tour, is able to get the Super Bowl shown in Peru. This was probably achieved through a combination of all of the following factors EXCEPT:

   A. the tourists had great economic power

   B. the locals, as well as the tourists, enjoyed the big game

C. the tour personnel had clout

D. TCS had an understanding of local culture and was able to manipulate events

Although Nicholas doesn't state directly what the crew members of TCS did to make this happen, think logically about the likely socioeconomic differences between the tourists and the local inhabitants, and note that three of the four choices have to be eliminated.

If the tourists were likely to spend lots of money at the bar while they watched the game, eliminate choice A. If the Peruvians would most likely enjoy the Super Bowl along with the Americans, eliminate choice B. If the TCS crew probably had a strong influence on the business's owner, eliminate choice C. And if the TCS crew probably knew the best way to pull some strings in order to get what they wanted, thus showing an appreciation of how things worked, eliminate choice D.

Question 6 asks you to analyze the development of a central idea.

6. One of the most important thematic topics in *Three Weeks with My Brother* is the notion of faith. In chapter 7, this thematic topic pertains to all of the following EXCEPT:

A. Micah's team winning the Super Bowl

B. the brothers' religious lives

C. the faith of the Incans

D. the role faith has in helping them handle difficult situations

The word *faith* can pertain to a number of things: confidence or trust in a person or thing (*faith* in another's ability), a belief that is not based on proof (having *faith* that a hypothesis will be supported), and belief in God or in the doctrines or teachings of religion (the *faith* of a particular denomination).

In chapter 7, this topic is mentioned in a variety of ways, so you are able to eliminate three out of the four choices. If Nicholas encouraged Micah to have faith in the Raiders, then eliminate choice A. If the brothers discuss their own personal faith and the current state of their religious lives, eliminate choice B. If they analyzed the religious faith of the Incans, eliminate choice C. And if they discuss how faith may help them endure bad times, eliminate choice D.

Question 7 asks you to analyze the effect onomatopoeia has on a passage.

7. During their visits to San Diego to see their cousins, the Sparks siblings often broke their cousins' toys. The word used a couple of times in the chapter is "*Snap.*" This use of onomatopoeia achieves each of the following effects EXCEPT which one?

    A. It enables readers to hear the sound of the toy breaking.

    B. It is the literal sound of the conflict between the cousins.

    C. It keeps the tone of the memoir light.

    D. It provides the anecdote with realistic details.

Onomatopoeia is a word that suggests the very sound it describes. Picture the scene in your mind, and hear the word *snap.* Now determine how hearing this sound affects your appreciation of the scene. The word *except* in the question indicates that three out of the four responses are effects of the onomatopoeia; thus, you will eliminate three of the four choices.

If the word *snap* helps you hear the toys break, eliminate choice A. If *snap* represents the conflict between the cousins, eliminate choice B. If the repetition of the word *snap* helps to create a humorous scene, keeping the story light, eliminate choice C. And if the word is a realistic sound of a toy breaking, eliminate choice D.

Question 8 asks you to make an inference based on strong and thorough textual evidence.

8. What is the primary purpose for the inclusion of the Sparky incident?

    A. to demonstrate how the siblings learn to lean on one another in tough times

    B. to illustrate their father's anger

    C. to reveal the family's lack of financial resources

    D. to express the difficulties of traveling

The word *primary* means main. Thus, although all of these things may exist in the incident, the most important one is the primary one. Also, realize that if one of the choices encompasses another (or all of the others), then that will probably be the better answer, for it is a more complete and thorough choice.

If the siblings turn to each other in a time of strife and struggle, select choice A. If the impact of their father's temper on the family's well-being is the focal point of this incident, select choice B. If the story exists to demonstrate the family's financial difficulties, select choice C. And if the incident exists to show the problems associated with traveling, select choice D.

Question 9 asks you to make an inference based on strong and thorough textual evidence.

9. The sentence "We witnessed every detail" (the first sentence of the last paragraph of chapter 7), conveys all of the following EXCEPT:

   A. that this was a shared event

   B. that the event had little impact on the siblings

   C. that the event is still vivid in their memory

   D. a sense of horror

Three out of the four choices can be eliminated. If there is a plural pronoun (*we* or *they*), then the incident is shared and choice A can be eliminated. If the words provide a sense that this was just another of many experiences that the siblings had, with no lasting effects, eliminate choice B. If the word *every* indicates that all of the details from the incident are recalled, demonstrating the significance of it, eliminate choice C. And if the word *witness* forces the reader to realize that what the siblings saw was a dog getting struck by a car traveling at least sixty miles per hour, thus creating a sense of horror, then choice D can be eliminated.

Question 10 asks you to analyze an author's stylistic choices and their impact on the text as a whole.

10. On the side of the road after having just witnessed Sparky's death, the siblings contemplate why terrible things happen. This contributes to the development of each of the following EXCEPT:

    A. character

    B. external conflict

    C. plot

    D. theme

Three out of the four choices can be eliminated because the contemplation is important in the areas of development listed. *Character* refers to the people in the memoir. If this quotation gives the reader a better understanding of Micah, Nicholas, and Dana, choice A can be eliminated. *External conflict* refers to the problem between characters or between a character and nature. If the quotation is developing the struggle between opposing forces, eliminate choice B. *Plot* refers to the selection and arrangement of all the incidents in the memoir. If the statement can be applied to the interrelationship of events in the memoir, eliminate choice C. *Theme* refers to a central idea. If this statement could be considered a debatable claim, an opinion that can be supported with details and examples, eliminate choice D.

Chapter 8

Cuzco, Machu Picchu, Peru
January 27–28

After our brief stop in Lima, we prepared to travel to Cuzco, the oldest permanent settlement in the Western Hemisphere, and the former capital of the Inca empire. With a population of 275,000, it's a city resplendent with adobe houses, red-tiled roofs, winding cobblestone streets, magnificent cathedrals, and open markets, and as we flew over the city, both Micah and I were struck by its beauty.

On the flight, we were warned about altitude sickness. Nestled in the Andes, Cuzco is situated at 11,500 feet, and we were told to move slowly as we exited the plane. Members of the TCS crew stood in various sections of the terminal, repeating their warnings over and over as our group filed past.

"Take it easy. Don't get out of breath. Go slooooow."

"You'd think we were climbing Mount Everest," Micah whispered, "not walking through an airport."

I nodded, agreeing that the whole thing was ridiculous. Maybe some of the people might be affected, but we were young and in relatively good shape. Ignoring their warnings, we walked at our normal pace and ended up having to wait quite a while for everyone else to arrive at the buses.

While we were waiting, however, a concerned look crossed Micah's face. He took a couple of deep breaths.

"You know, I think I can actually feel it," he said.

"Really?"

"A little bit. It kind of makes me feel...fuzzy."

In the end, it made us both feel *really* fuzzy, like we'd had a few too many beers. For whatever reason, we started giggling and couldn't stop. Everything struck us as outrageously funny as we rode on the bus; the clothes people were wearing, the bumpy, cobblestone roads that made our voices vibrate, and especially the name of the place we were just about to visit: Sacsayhuaman.

When pronounced correctly—Socksy Voomun—it sounded like someone with a Russian accent trying to say, "Sexy Woman." In our addled state, we couldn't drop the subject. It was all we could talk about.

"I just can't vait until vee see zee socksy voomun," Micah would say, and my oxygen-starved brain would make me double over in laughter.

"I vonder where zee socksy voomun is," he'd add. "You know I love nussing more zan a socksy voomun."

"Please...just quit, okay?" I'd plead.

"I veally, veally, veally vant to climb on a socksy voomun. You know Peru is famous for zee socksy voomum."

By then, I had tears in my eyes.

We had lunch at our hotel in Cuzco. Once a monastery, it was one of the most interesting hotels we would visit. Like Casa Aliaga, it was designed around a center courtyard, albeit on a much grander scale. Originally built in 1640, the rooms had been modified to allow oxygen to be pumped in. As Micah observed when he entered the lobby:

"Zis is even better zan a socksy voomun."

In the afternoon, after the giggles had subsided, we finally got a chance to visit the Incan fortress. It wasn't exactly what we expected. Situated on a large, open plateau just above Cuzco, it was ringed by rock walls on either side, more like an amphitheater than a defensive fort. The walls had been formed using giant blocks of granite, and the stones had been so precisely cut and stacked that, even today, it's impossible to slip a piece of paper between them.

Above us, heavy clouds lent the landscape an ominous appearance. We wandered the area with Bob and Kate Devlin, who had rapidly become good friends. As we listened to the guide talking about the intricate stone construction, they informed us they'd recently celebrated their forty-first anniversary. A little while later, while Micah and I were exploring on our own, we saw Bob and Kate standing together in the distance. For a while, we simply watched them.

"They look happy, don't they?" Micah asked.

"Yeah, they do. I think that's because they really are happy."

"Forty years is a long time. They've been married longer than I've been alive."

"So have a lot of people on this trip."

"What do you think the secret of a long-lasting marriage is?" Micah asked.

"I don't know if there's a secret. Every couple is different. What works for one might not work for another."

"I know. But if you could pick one thing, what would it be?"

I hesitated. Above me, the sky was charcoal; clouds were rolling and shifting, changing shape by the minute.

"Commitment," I finally said. "Both people have to be committed. I think if two people are committed to the marriage, if they really want to make it work, then they'll find a way to do it. No matter what happens in life. If you marry someone who isn't committed—or if you're not committed—and something goes wrong, the marriage won't make it. Marriage is hard."

"Hmm," is all Micah said.

"How about you? What do you think the secret is?"

"I have no idea. I've only been married four years. But for me and Christine, I think it's communication. When we talk about issues and really open up to each other, things are great between us. When we keep things to ourselves, grudges and resentments build up and we end up arguing."

I said nothing.

"What? You don't think communication is important?"

I shrugged. "What good is talking if neither of you are really committed? If one of you had an affair or got addicted to drugs or was abusive, simply talking about it wouldn't take the hurt away. Or fix the trust that's been lost. In the end, marriage comes down to actions. I think people talk too much about the things that bother them, instead of actually doing the little things that keep a marriage strong. You have to know what your spouse needs from you, and then you do it. And you avoid doing the things that harm the relationship. If your spouse acts the same way, your marriage can make it through anything."

He smiled. "Like you and Cat?"

"Yeah," I said quietly. "Like me and Cat."

After the fortress of Sacsayhuaman, we headed back to tour the main cathedral of Cuzco, where the wealth was enough to stagger the imagination. Larger than St. Patrick's Cathedral in New York, the cathedral was home to hundreds of frescoes and oil paintings of religious figures, while gold and silver glittered everywhere. Not only were the massive altars plated in precious metals, but entire walls as well. When one considers that the Spanish sent the vast majority of the wealth back to Spain, it was easy to understand why Pizarro had been so intent on conquering the Incas.

As fascinating as the church was, Micah seemed fixated on a particular item. With effort, he got the guide's attention.

"Um, where's the painting of Jesus eating the guinea pig?" Micah asked.

Guinea pigs, we learned, aren't regarded as pets in Peru. Instead, they're regarded as a delicacy, and are roasted for celebratory occasions. When the early Spanish missionaries were working to convert the Incas to Catholicism, they'd had to blend the religion with local culture as a way to make it more palatable to the natives. Thus when the missionaries commissioned a painting of the Last Supper, one has to wonder whether they were surprised by what the artist assumed Jesus had eaten.

We soon found ourselves staring up at the painting of Jesus

185

surrounded by his disciples. In addition to the bread and the wine, there on the platter in front of him was a roasted guinea pig.

As we were staring at it, Micah leaned over to me.

"Did you know Alli's classroom has a guinea pig for a pet?"

"She does?"

"Oh yeah. She's going to love this."

Micah surreptitiously snapped a photograph.

Museums.

Everywhere we went, we were taken to museums, so we could see the artifacts representing the history of the native peoples. In all honesty, many were quite boring. We learned, for instance, that nearly every culture in the past had—surprise!—pottery; consequently we spent a lot of time looking at jars and bowls. No matter how you sliced it, after a while this was about as exciting as looking at jars and bowls in your own kitchen cupboard. Yet our guides loved jars and bowls. It seemed like they could talk about jars and bowls for hours. They spoke with *reverence* about jars and bowls.

"And this... this is the jar they used to store water!" they'd say. "And now, over here—notice how different it is when compared to one used to store their wine! Can you see the different shape and color! It's even a different *size*! It's amazing to comprehend how advanced they were as a civilization. Different liquids, different jars! Just imagine it!"

"Wow," Micah would echo. "Just imagine it!"

"I'm trying," I'd add.

"Different liquids! Different jars!"

"It boggles the mind, doesn't it?"

Occasionally, we'd learn something truly intriguing. Bones,

for instance, usually made us pause. And weapons. And skulls. Especially the skulls. In the Cuzco museum, there was a collection of skulls behind glass. Though the placards were in Spanish, we were able to decipher a bit of the exhibit, and make out the word *surgery*.

Our guide wasn't nearly as excited about the skulls and the idea of primitive surgery as we were. He seemed to want to downplay what Micah and I were seeing, as if it somehow cast doubt on the gentility of the early Incas.

"This is not important," he urged. "Come—let me show you the jars and bowls. There are more up ahead."

"We'll catch up," we said.

It turns out the Incas engaged in brain surgery, which fascinated us. We could see the holes where they'd bored through the skulls. The holes were as big as quarters, and from the number of skulls and variations in the placement of the holes, it wasn't an uncommon practice. As we stared at them, I tried to imagine what the patient must have been going through, or what the chief said when explaining why the surgery was necessary.

"Mmm. You've been depressed, huh? Well, I'm pretty sure you have animal spirits between your ears. I think we'd better dig them out."

"Okay, Chief. As long as you know what you're doing."

"Of course I know what I'm doing. Haven't you seen our jars and bowls? We're an advanced civilization. Now hand me that jaguar bone, lean over the rock, and let me dig in."

"Okeydokey."

The next morning, we drove to the train station in Cuzco, to embark on the ride through the legendary Urubamba Valley on our way to Machu Picchu. Our guides had described the valley views as some of the most beautiful in the world, and our trip was everything it was advertised to be and more. Micah and I spent three and a half hours gawking through the windows, staring up at the towering granite cliff sides, and marveling at the river that often seemed close enough to touch. In places, it was possible to see Incan ruins that had fallen into disrepair; a wall here, a storage building there.

As we first descended through the valley, then started climbing into the Andes, the blue skies gave way to white, mist-filled clouds. The Andes became green with forest, and we disembarked at a ramshackle village perched on the banks of the by then raging Urubamba River. It was raining as we made our way down a narrow street, crowded with vendors, which also served as the town market. From there, we boarded a bus that would travel along the narrow switchback roads that ended at Machu Picchu, more than two thousand feet up.

The tale of a lost Incan city high in the Andes was regarded as little more than folklore when Hiram Bingham arrived in Peru in 1911. Wanting to prove its existence, he hired local guides and embarked on a quest to find it. The guides had been chosen because they supposedly knew its location, and after making their way through the valley, they eventually led him to a cliff whose top was shrouded in the clouds. As he and his team made their way up, they met a few natives, who remarked on the "houses just around the corner." Within minutes, Bingham soon came across the ruins of the fabled city, one that was estimated to have housed more than 2,500 people. To this day, no one is sure why the city had been built. It may have served as an outpost against invading Spanish marauders; other discoveries suggest that it may have been a place where the king rested, much like a vacation hideaway. Others have pointed to evidence that most of the occupants were women, which further complicates the theories. What is known is that the city was abandoned soon after the Spanish arrived.

Micah and I got off the bus, and at first the mist and cloud cover was thick enough to prevent us from seeing anything. Instead, as we were snaking along the edge of a cliff, the ruins materialized slowly, almost as if being casually unveiled. First, nothing was in focus; gradually images formed. Then, all at once, we could see everything, and it was enough to stun us into silence.

Part of the impact of Machu Picchu is due to sheer location; while some of the ruins are at the top of the mountain, other parts are built directly into the sides of the cliff. Terraces look like giant steps carved out of the cliff side, and just beyond them are the granite-block dwellings and temples of the ancient Incas. The roofs, originally made of wood and thatch, have long since decayed, but we could see the structures themselves. Interconnected like apartments in places, steep steps interweave among the buildings. Places to worship dotted the settlement, with open areas complete with sacrificial slabs. All around us, the lush slopes of the Andes towered in the distance. Wisps of clouds snaked through the peaks. If we'd been amazed by Tikal, we were literally rendered speechless by the architecture of Machu Picchu. It would be my favorite stop on the entire journey.

We made our way through the ruins with a guide on hand to tell us about the history and culture. Yet over and over, I felt compelled to break away from the group, simply to stand alone for a while. It was the kind of place that one should *experience*, not simply visit. Micah felt the same way. At one point, we sat quietly on the edge of one of the ruins with our feet dangling over, drinking in the spectacular view, neither of us feeling the urge to break the silence.

Over the next few hours, we continued to explore the ruins. Afterward, we were supposed to have lunch in the restaurant. Micah and I would have stayed on at the site, but the tour schedule didn't permit it, and we grudgingly made our way to join the others.

After lunch, we headed back to our hotel in Cuzco, and arrived just after dark. One of the lecturers on the tour called our room and told us to come over; when we arrived, we saw what he'd ordered from a local restaurant.

Roasted guinea pig.

"Come on," he said, "let's try it. I had one of our guides order it from a local restaurant. We'll get pictures."

Looking at it made me feel suddenly queasy. I leaned toward Micah. "It still has the head. And the claws."

Micah shrugged. "It is supposed to be a delicacy. And besides, the painting shows that it's what they served at the Last Supper."

"You're not really thinking of eating it, are you?"

"I might taste it...it's the only chance I'll get. It's not like they serve it where we live."

"Really? You're going to take a bite?"

"I think I have to. And do me a favor."

"What's that?"

"Get a picture. For Alli."

"That's mean. She's going to scream."

"No, she won't. She'll think it's funny. And I'll get a picture of you taking a bite, too."

"Me?"

"Of course. I can't let you throw away a moment like this. Like they say, When in Rome..."

I looked at the guinea pig again. "It makes me a little nause-ated to even consider it."

"That's why I'm here. To help you experience new things. To make you stretch."

"Gee, thanks."

"Hey," he said, shrugging. "What are brothers for? Now get the camera ready."

I did and snapped the picture as he took a bite. He did the same for me when I took a small bite, my stomach churning like a lava lamp on amphetamines.

"Now that wasn't so bad, was it?"

"I think I'm going to throw up," I admitted.

He laughed before putting his arm over my shoulder. "Think of it this way—it's just the latest in a long line of stupid things that we've done. And this time, it wasn't even dangerous."

During those first years in Fair Oaks, even as we began to test the limits of our courage through daredevil stunts, we continued to drift apart. Micah was spending more time with his friends, and I was spending time with mine. Occasionally, our friends would end up in the same place, but more often than not, they didn't.

Still, there were certain rites of passage that we both under-went, albeit at different times. With the fields and woods in our neighborhood disappearing as new housing developments sprang up, we both began spending more time at the nearby American River. There were bike trails and places to skimboard (sort of like water-skiing, only the board is larger and tied to a tree along the bank instead of a boat; the current keeps you upright). There was also a pedestrian bridge that spanned the river about forty-five feet above the water, and it was an accepted ritual of childhood to jump from the bridge into the chilly water below. Land wrong and the breath would be knocked clean out of you. I first jumped from the bridge when I was ten; Micah had done it a year earlier. Later, I jumped from the fence atop the bridge (intended to keep jumpers from jumping, of course), which added another ten feet to the jump. Micah had done that jump, too, well before I did. Our favorite activity, however, was riding the rope swing, and we could spend hours at it. Tied to the center of the bridge, the rope was stretched taut and with a board fastened to it. We'd jump from the bridge with the board between our legs, and clinging to the rope, feel the g-force as we swooped over the water at eighty miles an hour before swinging up toward the bridge again. It was dangerous and illegal, and frequently the sheriff arrived to confiscate our rope swing. As he did so, he'd eye me or my brother.

"Don't I know you?" he'd sometimes ask.

"I don't see how," we'd answer innocently.

Micah and I also climbed the bluffs alongside the river. They were nearly vertical and the dirt unstable; both of us slipped on more than one occasion, sometimes falling as much as thirty feet and nearly breaking our ankles and legs. Once, I nearly lost a finger bluff climbing—the cut went clear to the bone of my knuckle—but my mom told me not to worry because she knew exactly what to do. (She put a Band-Aid on it.)

But for the most part, Micah and I weren't doing these things together. If I went to the river occasionally, Micah went there almost daily. If I jumped from the bridge once, he would do it ten times and find a way to increase the danger (let's ride our bikes off it!). If I went over to a friend's house on Monday, Micah would be at a friend's each and every afternoon. Micah was simply *more* in everything, including the trouble he was beginning to get into. Though a relatively good student, he continued getting into arguments with teachers and fights with other students, and my parents were being called to the principal's office at least three times a year. I, on the other hand, spent year after year garnering perfect scores on exams and doing extra-credit assignments, all the while hearing teachers remark, "You're so much *easier* than your brother was." And I read constantly. Not only the encyclopedias and the Bible, but almanacs and atlases as well. I simply devoured them and, strangely, the information just seemed to *stick*, no matter how obscure or irrelevant. By the sixth grade, I was prodigious with trivia: If someone pointed to any country in the world, I could recite statistics, name the capital, tell you what the major exports were, or recite the average rainfall months after skimming the information. Still, it wasn't necessarily something that other kids my age found too impressive.

A group of us might be standing around at recess, for instance, when one would say to one of the others:

"Hey, how was your camping trip at Yosemite?"

"Oh, it was great. Me and my dad pitched a tent and went fishing. Man, you should have seen how many fish we caught. And we saw the sequoias, too. Man, those are the biggest trees I've ever seen."

"Did you hike around Half Dome?" another would ask.

"No, but the next time we go, my dad says we can. He says it's supposed to be awesome."

"It is. I did that last year with my dad. It was so cool."

Meanwhile, noticing me standing quietly off to the side, someone might try to include me.

"Hey, have you ever been to Yosemite, Nick?"

"No, I haven't," I'd answer. "But did you know that even

before it became a national park in 1890, the land was actually given in trust to the state of California in 1864 by the U.S. Congress, and signed into law by Abraham Lincoln? You'd think that with the Civil War in full swing, he wouldn't have had time for something like that, but he did. And in the end, the use of land trusts set the stage for Yellowstone to become the first official national park in 1872. And did you know that Yosemite Falls, which are the fifth tallest in the world at 2,450 feet, is actually made of three separate falls? Or..."

My friends' eyes would glaze over as I went on and on.

Yep, that was me. Mr. Popularity.

My sister, too, was becoming her own person. Like me, she got along with her teachers, although her grades usually hovered around a C in nearly every class. Though my parents were both college graduates and viewed education as important—my mother had received her degree in elementary education, and my father was a professor—neither seemed concerned about my sister's academic performance. They didn't push her to work harder, nor did they help her with her studies, nor did they mind if she brought home poor grades, the reason yet again being, "She's a girl."

They did, however, enroll her in horseback riding lessons, thinking a skill like that would serve her well in the long run.

The more I excelled in school, the harder I tried to do even better, if only to stand out from my siblings. Somehow, I believed that my parents would then shower me with the attention I felt was given automatically to my brother and sister. If Micah got attention because he was the oldest and my sister got attention for being the only girl, I wanted recognition for something, anything. I yearned for moments when I could be the center of attention at the dinner table, but no matter what I did, it never seemed to be enough. While I never doubted that my parents loved me, I couldn't help but think that had my mother been given Sophie's choice, I would have been the one sacrificed to save the other two. It was a terrible thing to believe—and as a parent now, I know that attention isn't the same as love—but the feeling wouldn't go away. Even worse, I began to notice those moments with ever increasing acuity. In the fall, when it was time for new school clothes, I would get a couple of new items and Micah's hand-me-downs; both Micah and Dana would receive far more than I did. And my mom, if she acknowledged my feelings at all, would simply shrug and say that "Micah's clothes *are* new for you." As I grew older, both my parents seemed oblivious to how a child like me would view their actions.

I'll never forget one Christmas when we woke up to find three bikes under the tree. Christmas was far and away the most exciting day of the year for us, because we seldom got anything we wanted the rest of the time. We would count down the days and talk endlessly about what we wanted; that particular year, bikes were on the top of the list. Bikes meant freedom, bikes meant fun, and the ones we'd owned previously had become unusable through sheer wear and tear. When we crept out to the living room, the tree lights were glowing and we stared at our gifts with wonder.

Micah's bike was new and shiny.

Dana's bike was new and shiny.

My bike was...shiny.

For a moment, I'd thought it was new as well. But...then, ever so slowly, I began to recognize it, despite the new paint job. Like a bad dream, I realized that my parents had given me *my own* bike—albeit, a repaired one. Granted, it had cost money to repair, but still, it crushed me to think I was given a gift that I already owned, while Micah and Dana got new ones.

When it came to grades, our parents used to post our report cards on the refrigerator, and I couldn't wait for my mom to get home so I could show her how well I'd done. When she saw my report card, she said that she was proud of me, but when I woke the following morning, I noticed that the report cards had been taken down and slipped into the drawer. When I asked my mom why, she said, "It hurts the other kids' feelings."

After that, the report cards were never posted at all. Perhaps, only later did I come to realize, Micah and Dana had had their own insecurities as well.

Despite these perceived childhood slights, I adored my mom. Then again, so did everyone who knew her, including all my friends and our dog, Brandy. At night, Brandy—all eighty pounds of her—would crawl up and lie in my mom's lap as she sat reading in the living room.

My mom's attitude made it hard not to like her. She was always upbeat, no matter how terrible things were, and she made light of things that most people would have found unbearable. For instance, my mom worked (as many mothers did), but she had to ride a bike to work. Whether it was pouring rain or 105 degrees, my mom would dress for work, hop on the bike, and start pedaling the four miles to the office. Her bike had a basket on the handlebars and two more behind the seat; after work, she'd ride the bike to the grocery store, load in whatever we needed, then ride home. And always—I mean *always*—she beamed when she walked in the door. No matter how hard the day had been, no matter how hot or wet she was, she made it seem as if she were the lucky one and that her life couldn't get any better.

"Hey guys! It's great to see you! I can't tell you how much I missed you today!"

197

Then, she'd visit with each of us, asking about our days. And one by one, Micah, Dana, and I would fill her in as she began cooking dinner.

She was also a giggler. My mom could laugh at anything, which naturally drew people to her. She wasn't Pollyanna, but she seemed to realize that life had both ups and downs, and it wasn't worth the energy to get upset about the downs, since not only were they inevitable, but they'd pass as well.

My mom also seemed to know *everyone's* parents, and when I'd meet someone new, this new friend would frequently mention how much *their* mom liked visiting with *my* mom. This always struck me as a mystery, because my mom had no social life. Almost all her evenings and weekends were spent at home with us, and she ate lunch alone. Nor, by the way, did my parents socialize together, or even go out on what might be considered a date. In all my years growing up, I remember my parents going out to a party together only *once*, and it was downright shocking to us when they casually mentioned that they were going out for the evening. I was thirteen at the time, and after they left, Micah, Dana, and I called a powwow to discuss the extraordinary turn of events. "They're leaving us on our own? What can they be thinking? We're just kids!" (Never mind that we were on our own *every* day...but who needs logic when you're feeling sorry for yourself?)

How, then, did people know her? It turned out that various parents of new friends were attended to by my mom at the optometrist's office, and struck up conversations with her. But it wasn't simply idle talk; my mom had a way of getting people to open up to her. People told her everything—she was the veritable Ann Landers of Fair Oaks, and occasionally, when I mentioned a new friend, she'd shake her head, and say something like, "It's fine if he comes here, but you can't go over there. I know what goes on in that house."

Yet, my mother was—and always will be—an enigma to me. While I knew she loved me, I couldn't help but wonder why she wouldn't acknowledge my successes. While we kids were the center of her life, she let us run wild in dangerous places, doing dangerous things. These inconsistencies have always puzzled me, and even now, I'm at a loss to explain them. I've long since given up trying to understand it, but if there was anything consistent in the way she raised us, it was in her refusal to allow any of us to indulge in self-pity of any kind. She achieved this through a maddening style of argument, in which the following three statements were repeated in various sequences:

A. It's your life + social commentary.
B. What you want and what you get are usually two entirely different things.
C. No one ever said that life was fair.

For example, an argument I had with her when I was eleven:

"I want to go out for the football team," I said. "There's a Pop Warner league, and all my friends are playing."

"It's your life," she answered. "But I don't want to be responsible for you hobbling around on crutches your whole life because you blew out your knee as a kid. And besides, we don't have the money for it."

"But I want to."

"What you want and what you get are usually two entirely different things."

"That's not fair. You always say that."

She shrugged. "No one ever said that life was fair."

I paused, trying another approach.

"I won't get hurt, if that's what you're worried about."

She looked me over. "Someone your size? You'd definitely get hurt. I've seen football players. You'd be nothing more than a bug on the windshield to them. You're too small."

She had a point there. I was small.

"I wish I was bigger. Like my friends are."

She put a consoling hand on my shoulder. "Oh sweetie, no one ever said life was fair."

"I know. But still . . ."

"Just remember this, okay?" she'd offer, her voice softening with maternal affection. "It'll help you later in life when you're disappointed about anything. What you want and what you get are usually two entirely different things."

"Maybe you're right. Maybe I should try another sport."

My mom would smile tenderly, as if finally conceding the argument. "Hey, do what you want. It's your life."

The older I got, the more I hated these arguments, because I lost every one of them. But still, deep down, I could never escape the feeling that my mom was probably right about most things. After all, she spoke from experience.

Questions and Explanations
for Chapter 8

The ten questions on chapter 8 focus on grammar and usage, vocabulary, comprehension, literary terms, style, and characterization. Some of the questions combine two or more of these areas, requiring you to synthesize your knowledge, make inferences, and interpret the text. The questions are designed to determine both your current level of understanding of the memoir and your ability to answer higher-level questions.

The following sentence tests your ability to recognize grammar and usage errors. The sentence contains either a single error or no error at all. If the sentence contains an error, select the one underlined part that must be changed to make the sentence correct. If there is no error, select choice D.

1. The <u>brothers'</u> developing relationship with Bob and Kate

A
   Devlin, <u>who</u> have been married for forty-one years, leads

B
   to a discussion on the keys to a successful <u>marriage,</u>

C
   both brothers have differing opinions regarding what is
   most important. <u>No error</u>

D

Choice A checks the use of the apostrophe, choice B checks the use of the relative pronoun, and choice C tests your knowledge of punctuation.

To demonstrate a plural possessive (choice A), simply add an apostrophe after the plural noun—for example, "four swimmers' towels, three monkeys' tails, two boys' jackets."

Choice B tests the selection of the relative pronoun *who*. A relative pronoun is the pronoun (*who, which, what,* or *that*) that introduces a subordinate (or dependent) clause. The entire clause acts as an adjective, modifying the noun that precedes it—for example, "My wife is an individual who pushes herself to be both a successful career woman and an amazing mother." *Who* is used to start a clause that is describing a person.

Choice C tests your knowledge of punctuation. If both groups of words before the comma and after the comma are complete thoughts and can stand alone as two independent clauses, then a comma by itself is not the correct way to punctuate the compound sentence—for example, "I read the paper, my wife made dinner." Both groups of words to the left and right of the comma are complete thoughts, so they need to be joined with a semicolon or a comma and a coordinating conjunction (*and, but, or, for, nor, so, yet*). Thus, the example should be "I read the paper, and my wife made dinner" or "I read the paper; my wife made dinner."

The following two questions test your vocabulary. Choose the word or set of words that, when inserted in the sentence, best fits the meaning of the sentence as a whole.

2. Cuzco is "a city [that is] _____ with adobe houses, red-tiled roofs, winding cobblestone streets, magnificent cathedrals, and open markets."

   A. dull

   B. humble

   C. mediocre

   D. resplendent

This question tests both your comprehension and your vocabulary. Substitute the definition of each word in the sentence in order to determine which one makes the most sense. *Dull*, choice A, means uninteresting. *Humble*, choice B, means modest. *Mediocre*, choice C, means barely adequate, and *resplendent*, choice D, means gleaming and splendid.

3. One way the Spanish missionaries made Catholicism more _____ to the natives was _____ their new religion with the local customs.

   A. pleasant...separating

   B. palatable...blending

   C. appealing...extricating

   D. unconventional...combining

This question tests your comprehension and vocabulary. The best way to determine the correct answer to this question is to answer the second blank first. The choices indicate that the new religion was either *separating* or *extricating* with the local customs, which means dividing from them, or they were *combining* or *blending* with them, which means coming together. This will immediately cut your choices in half.

Then determine what resulting effect this decision had. If it was acceptable or agreeable to the natives' minds (*palatable*), select choice B. If the decision made Catholicism more eccentric (*unconventional*), select choice D.

Question 4 tests your knowledge of literary terms.

4. When discussing the characteristics of a successful marriage, Nicholas claims that if spouses "avoid doing the things that harm the relationship," then "your marriage can make it through anything." In response to this, Micah adds, "Like you and Cat?" And although Nicholas agrees, neither brother divulges what the marriage endured. This is an example of what?

   A. foreshadowing

   B. flashback

   C. in medias res

   D. satire

Foreshadowing, choice A, is providing hints or clues to future events. For example, when Benvolio suggests to Romeo that finding a new female beauty may help Romeo get over Rosaline, it foreshadows Romeo's falling in love with Juliet when he sees her later in the play. *Flashback*, choice B, is a narrative technique that incorporates an event or series of events that occurred prior to the current time. *In medias res*, choice C, means starting in the middle of things. Each book in the Twilight series opens with a scene that actually occurs near the end of the novel and then moves back in time to tell readers how the characters got to that point. *Satire*, choice D, is a genre of writing in which the shortcomings of a society are held up to ridicule in order to not only expose them but also to offer solutions. Jonathan Swift's *A Modest Proposal* is a famous example of satire.

Question 5 tests your understanding of irony.

5. Although Nicholas and Micah are fed up with the jars and bowls, they were interested in the fact that the Incas performed brain surgery. Nicholas imagines a conversation that included these lines: "Of course I know what I'm doing. Haven't you seen our jars and bowls? We're an advanced civilization." This passage contains an example of which type of irony?

   A. cosmic irony

   B. dramatic irony

   C. situational irony

   D. verbal irony

Understanding *irony*, the situation of appearance versus reality, is essential to understanding most literary texts. *Cosmic irony*, also known as irony of fate, is a situation where no matter what a character attempts to do, he or she cannot escape his or her fate. The most famous example of this is the Greek myth of Oedipus, who was fated to grow up and kill his father and marry his mother, no matter what he or anyone else tried to do to prevent it. *Dramatic irony* is when the reader knows something that the character in the text does not know. An example of dramatic irony is when the audience knows that Juliet isn't dead but Romeo does not; when he arrives at the Capulet tomb, he is devastated by her death, and you are devastated that he doesn't know the truth.

Situational irony is the incongruity between the expected outcome and what actually occurs—for example, Erik studies quite hard for a test yet fails it, but Mitch doesn't prepare at all for it and aces it. *Verbal irony* is meaning the opposite of what is stated; sarcasm is a form of verbal irony. When you ask Erik, who just failed the test, how he did and he responds, "Great," he doesn't really mean it. He is being sarcastic; he is using verbal irony.

Question 6 tests your knowledge of literary terms.

6. When Nicholas tastes roasted guinea pig, he remembers he took a bite with "my stomach churning like a lava lamp on amphetamines." What figure of speech is used to describe how he was feeling?

   A. personification

   B. hyperbole

   C. metaphor

   D. simile

Personification, choice A, is giving nonhuman things a human characteristic, such as in "Opportunity knocked on the door." *Hyperbole*, choice B, is an exaggerated statement used to heighten effect and to emphasize a point—for example, "This learning guide has defined *hyperbole* a million times already." A *metaphor*, choice C, is a comparison made between two unlike things without using a connective word—for example, "LeBron James is an animal on the basketball court." And a *simile*, choice D, is a comparison made between two unlike things using a connective word, such as *like*, *as*, or *than*—for example, "My love is like a red, red rose."

Question 7 is asking about an author's stylistic choices.

7. After the brothers both had tasted the roasted guinea pig, Micah laughed and said, "It's just the latest in a long line of stupid things that we've done. And this time, it wasn't even dangerous." The memoir immediately transitions from the trip narrative to the story of their growing up. What types of transitions is Sparks using to move from one narrative thread to another?

    A. conclusion

    B. contrast

    C. sequence

    D. similarity

The question indicates that more than one choice will be selected. Transitions are words and phrases that guide a reader from one idea to another; they provide coherence to the text by signaling relationships. A *conclusion* is a sense of closure and completeness or finality. If the sentence provides an end point for the brothers' dinner and their time in Peru, select choice A. *Contrast* shows differences between two things. If differences between the present-day and flashback narratives exist, select choice B. *Sequence* is how one thing follows another. If the sentence provides a sense of succession from Peru to Fair Oaks, select choice C. And *similarity* is likeness. If there is a resemblance between the story in Peru and the anecdotes in California, select choice D.

Question 8 tests your knowledge of literary terms.

8. Attempting to understand his place in the family as a middle child who thought he didn't receive enough attention, Nicholas wonders about his mother being "given Sophie's choice." This is an example of what literary device?

   A. allusion

   B. metaphor

   C. personification

   D. simile

Knowing about literary devices will enable you to answer this question. An *allusion*, choice A, is an indirect reference. Some of the most common types of allusions are historical, such as a reference to Napoleon when it's mentioned that someone met his Waterloo; biblical, such as John Coffey in *The Green Mile* being a Christ figure; mythological, a reference to a Greek or Roman myth, such as someone having the Midas touch; and literary, a reference to a character in a work of literature, such as a couple being ill-fated like Romeo and Juliet. A *metaphor*, choice B, is a comparison made between two unlike things without using a connective word—for example, "Michael Phelps was a flying fish in the pool." *Personification*, choice C, is giving nonhuman things a human characteristic, such as in "Opportunity knocked on the door." And a *simile*, choice D, is a comparison made between two unlike things using a connective word, such as *like*, *as*, or *than*—for example, "My love is like a red, red rose."

Question 9 asks you to make an inference based on strong and thorough textual evidence.

9. When Nicholas is bemoaning the fact that he can't play Pop Warner league football, one of the statements that his mother makes is "What you want and what you get are usually two entirely different things." This sentence is important to the development of each of the following EXCEPT:

   A. character

   B. plot

   C. style

   D. theme

The word *except* reveals that three of the four choices will be eliminated because they are developed through the statement above.

Character, choice A, refers to the individuals in the story. If the statement enables us to get a better understanding of the brothers' mother (or any other character), eliminate choice A.

Plot, choice B, refers to the selection and arrangement of all the incidents in the memoir. If the details and examples of what someone wants and what someone gets are evident (or will probably be evident) in the text, eliminate this choice.

Style, choice C, is the way the text is written. Basically style isn't focused on *what* is said but rather *how* it is said. If the statement is talking about stylistic choices, then eliminate choice C.

Theme, choice D, refers to a central idea. If this sentence is a debatable claim that can be supported with details and examples from the text, eliminate choice D.

Question 10 tests your knowledge of literary terms.

10. Reluctantly admitting he won't be able to play football, Nicholas remarks offhandedly, "Maybe I should try another sport." He doesn't develop that idea anymore in this chapter, but another sport will eventually play an important part in his life. This is an example of what literary device?

    A. personification

    B. hyperbole

    C. foreshadowing

    D. irony

Choice A, *personification*, is giving nonhuman things human characteristics. For example, "The leaves danced in the wind." Choice B, *hyperbole*, is an exaggerated statement used to heighten effect and to emphasize a point—for example, "This learning guide has defined *hyperbole* a million times already."

Foreshadowing, choice C, is providing hints or clues to future events. For example, when Benvolio suggests to Romeo that finding a new female beauty may help Romeo get over Rosaline, it foreshadows Romeo's falling in love with Juliet when he sees her later in the play.

Understanding *irony*, the situation of appearance versus reality, is essential to understanding most literary texts. *Cosmic irony*, also known as irony of fate, is a situation where no matter what a character attempts to do, he or she cannot escape his or her fate. The most famous example of this is the Greek myth of Oedipus, who was fated to grow up and kill his father and marry his mother, no matter what he or anyone else tried to do to prevent it. *Dramatic irony* is when the reader knows something that the character in the text does not know. An example of dramatic irony is when the audience knows that Juliet isn't dead but Romeo does not; when he arrives at the Capulet tomb, he is devastated by her death, and you are devastated that he doesn't know the truth. *Situational irony* is the incongruity between the expected outcome and what actually occurs—for example, Erik studies quite hard for a test yet fails it, but Mitch doesn't prepare at all for it and aces it. *Verbal irony* is meaning the opposite of what is stated; sarcasm is a form of verbal irony. When you ask Erik, who just failed the test, how he did and he responds, "Great," he doesn't really mean it. He is being sarcastic and is using verbal irony.

Chapter 9

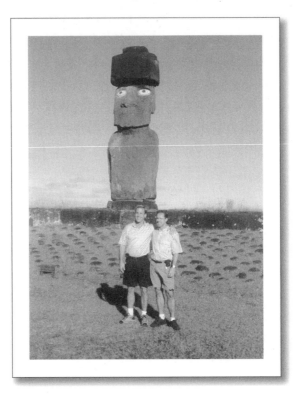

Easter Island, Chile
January 29–30

As we looked out the airplane window, Easter Island slowly
came into view, a remote and exotic sight that only underscored
how far from familiar surroundings we were.

Easter Island, like most islands in the South Pacific, was

first settled by Polynesians. But because Easter Island was so far from the rest of populated Polynesia—nearly 2,200 miles from the coast of Chile, it's the remotest inhabited island in the world—the native people developed their own unique culture, which included the carving of giant statues known as the Moai.

Of all the places listed in the original brochure, Easter Island had been the most intriguing to me. I'd read about the Moai and had longed to see and touch them ever since I was a child. Because it was so remote, I fully realized that this trip might be the only time I ever set foot on the island, and I craned my neck, looking out the window as we circled in preparation for landing.

What struck me immediately was the scarcity of trees. I suppose I'd imagined the palms and rain forests typical throughout the South Pacific, but instead the island was largely covered with grassy meadows, as if part of Kansas had been dropped into the middle of the ocean. Later, we'd find out from the archaeologists that the absence of trees partially explains the cultural history of Easter Island, but at the time I remember thinking how odd it seemed.

Another interesting thing about Easter Island is the time zone in which it is located. Because we were flying west, we would cross time zones and lose a day on our way to Australia, but it enabled us to maximize our days. If we left at ten, for instance, and flew for five hours, we might arrive only three hours after we departed, as measured by local time. But because the island is part of Chile and thus shares the Eastern Time Zone (along with New York and Miami, despite lying geographically west of California), we were told that the sun wouldn't set until 10:45 P.M.

Dinner was served outdoors, and afterward, a few of the tour members strolled over to a seaside bluff to watch the sun go down. Waves crashed violently against the rocks, the plumes rising forty to fifty feet in the air. In the west, the sky turned pink and orange, before finally changing into the brightest red I've ever seen. And then an impenetrable darkness descended.

Micah and I were sitting together, watching all of this when he finally turned to me.

"I think I know what your problem is," he said.

"What problem?"

"Why you get so stressed all the time."

"Why do you keep talking to me about this? Here I am, enjoying my first South Pacific sunset, and you want to start probing my psyche."

"Your problem," he said, ignoring me, "is that you need more friends."

"I have friends. I have a lot of friends."

"Guy friends?"

"Yeah."

"But do you do anything with them? Do you go out with them? Go fishing or boating or whatever it is you do down south?"

"Sometimes."

"Sometimes, or rarely?"

I hesitated. "Okay, so I don't do much with them. But I can't. To have the time to go out with friends, I'd have to give up time with my family. I have too many kids to do that. And besides, most of my friends have kids, too. I'm not the only one who doesn't have a lot of free time to just hang out."

"You should, though. Just hang out. Not all the time, of course, but you should try to make it more regular. Like I do. I joined an indoor soccer league and we play every Thursday.

Just a group of guys out there having fun. You should do something like that."

"We don't have an indoor soccer league. I live in a small town, remember?"

"It doesn't have to be soccer. You can do anything. The point is that you should do something. Relationships are the most important thing in life, and friends are part of that."

I smiled. "Why do I get the impression that you think the solution to all my problems is to be more like you?"

"Hey, if the shoe fits." He shrugged, and I laughed.

"So you still think you have to take care of me, huh?"

"Only when I think you need it, little brother."

"And what if I started talking to you about God, because I think you need it?"

"Go ahead," he said. "I'll listen."

Above me, the sky was filled with stars clustered together in unrecognizable constellations, and the words rose up almost unexpectedly.

"God keeps his promise, and he will not allow you to be tested beyond your power to remain firm; at the same time you are put to the test, he will give you the strength to endure it, and so provide you with a way out."

Micah glanced over at me. Despite the darkness, I could see him raise his eyebrows.

"First Corinthians," I said. "Chapter 10."

"Impressive."

I shrugged. "I just always liked that verse. It reminds me of the footprints story—you know the one where God walks with man on the beach. Scenes from the man's life flash in the sky, and during flashbacks of the most trying times of the man's life, he sees only one set of footprints. Not because God abandoned the man in times of need...but because God carried the man."

Micah was quiet for a moment. "So you don't think he abandoned us?"

"No," I said. "And I don't think he wants you to abandon him either."

The following morning, we set off to see the first of the Moai statues, which were located less than a few minutes from the hotel, just up the coast. Had we known where we'd be going, we could have seen them from our hotel room.

As we rode in the vans with the archaeologists who made their living studying them, we were informed that at one time there were roughly fourteen different tribes on the island, each with its own ruler. These rulers ordered the carving of these statues from volcanic rock—most were made to resemble said rulers—and over time, these statues grew larger and larger, as each ruler tried to impress on the people his own importance. Some of the Moai weigh up to thirty tons, and stand twelve feet high; one unfinished statue measures sixty-six feet and is estimated to weigh nearly fifty tons.

Afterward, we were told about the absence of trees.

When it was first colonized, Easter Island had resembled other islands in the Pacific, but as the population expanded, trees became the most overused of all the natural resources. They were employed in construction of dwellings and for cooking fires; mature trees were used to roll the Moai across the island. In the past when Polynesians migrated, as islands became overcrowded, people would head off in their canoes in search of new territories; because Easter Island was so isolated, there was nowhere else to go. Overcrowding and overuse of the resources led to civil wars; the wars continued through generations. Through it all, trees continued to be cut down. In the end, most had been wiped out, and the natives ended up burning anything they could in order to cook, including their homes and canoes. Shore fishing became the sole source of food, but a La Niña effect is suspected to have suddenly cooled the waters around the island. It lasted two years, killing much of the ocean reef, and the fish became much less plentiful. In the end, the natives turned to cannibalism.

Over time, a few palms eventually sprouted again, but to speed the process, mature palm trees were imported from Tahiti. These trees, however, turned out to be diseased, and they not only died, but ended up killing most of the remaining palms on the island. Now, there are only a few spots where they still remain.

The first statue we saw was fascinating. So were the second and third. By the time we viewed the fourth and fifth statues, the novelty began to wear off. Though the local archaeologists assured us that each was different, to my untrained eye they all looked pretty much the same: eye sockets, long ears, nose, and mouth, all carved from lava rock.

From there, we headed to the volcano quarry, where they'd been carved. To reach it, you had to cross the island, and the distance these statues had been transported fascinated me more than the statues themselves. As we drove, I tried to imagine how many people it had taken to move a single statue, let alone hundreds.

As we drove toward the quarry where the Moai had been

carved, lush, open pastures unfolded on either side of us. Beyond the pastures, we could see herds of wild-looking horses loping along.

Horses were a symbol of prosperity on Easter Island. They had been imported in the late 1800s, but because the island was so isolated, feed was prohibitively expensive to import. The owners allowed the horses to run free so they could forage on the island grass. Their muscles were lithe and their coats gleamed in the sunlight, inspiring Micah to take a photograph of them.

The volcano rose 1,400 feet, and everywhere along the base you could see abandoned statues. Some lay on their side, others were half buried along a trail that progressed to the far side of the island. At the quarry itself, others stood in various stages of completion. Again, there was no answer as to the reason; there was speculation about the wars, but as with so many of the places we went, nothing was certain. For all intents and purposes, it looked as if the workers had left for the day, with the full intention of returning on the next.

A winding trail leads to the peak of the volcano, and about a third of our group eventually made their way to the summit. From the top, it's possible to see the curvature of the earth, and Micah and I were the first to reach it. Under blue, cloudless skies and with temperatures in the seventies, the hike was refreshing. Surrounding the island was nothing but an endless expanse of water, and I wondered how the first Polynesians had ever survived in the open Pacific long enough to discover the island.

At the top, we took pictures before sitting near the edge of a sheer drop-off. As we relaxed, Micah pulled up the picture he'd taken of the horses. He stared at it.

"Mom would love this," Micah said. "She would have wanted to frame it."

"Yes, she would," I said. "Dana, too."

"Do you remember when we took those horseback riding lessons?"

"Actually, I don't. You and Dana did that, remember?"

"Yeah, why didn't you ride with us?"

"Because," I said, "there wasn't enough money and you two were more excited about it than I was."

He put his arm around me. "The poor middle son. Always feeling left out."

"I didn't *feel* left out. I *was* left out."

"No you weren't. Mom and dad were always proud of you. They used to tell me that I should do better in school, like you."

"That's why they took my report card down from the fridge, right?"

"They didn't do that."

"Yes they did."

"Really?"

"Really."

"I don't remember that."

"You wouldn't."

He laughed. "Isn't it funny the way memory works? We remember different things, but especially when they scarred us—you know, the kinds of events that people lie on the couch and talk to their therapists about. I remember once I asked for a stereo and headphones for Christmas. Not a big one—just one for my room, you know? I must have been about twelve or so, and I begged for that thing. I must have hounded mom for months about it, and on Christmas morning, I remember going out there and seeing it under the tree: headphones and the stereo. There was a card that said, 'to Micah.' I was so excited—it was the best gift I ever got. Then mom comes out and when I thanked her, she started saying, no, no, no. 'Just the headphones are yours. The stereo is for the family.' I was crushed. I mean, it's the only thing I wanted. And besides, what good are headphones without a stereo? It's like getting a single shoe."

"Our parents were crazy sometimes, weren't they?"

"Sometimes? Yeah. You could say that."

I sat in silence for a few moments, musing on the past. Gradually, people began leaving the summit; the tour had a schedule to maintain. "Come on," I finally said. "Let's get going. We've got to see some more statues."

When I looked at Micah, he seemed oddly contemplative. I suddenly knew he was thinking about the past as well. His eyes were focused on the horizon.

"No. Let's wait here for a couple more minutes," he said quietly. "Then we'll go."

I looked toward the horizon, following my brother's gaze. "Okay."

After descending the volcano, we journeyed to the single most photographed spot on Easter Island.

Giant statues of the Moai—about twenty or so—stand together in a straight line along the coast. Until a few years ago, all had been toppled over, some broken into pieces. The archaeologists who joined us as guides had helped not only to repair them, but position them upright once more.

These, I thought, were the statues that Jakob Roggeveen, a Dutch admiral, must have seen when he became the first European to discover the island on Easter Sunday, 1722. Legend has it that his first thought was that the island was inhabited by giants. Only when he drew nearer to shore did he realize that men of normal size were working among the statues.

The statues, however, hadn't been completely restored. Originally, we learned, all the statues on the island had eyes. Carved from wood, they were painted with pupils, but had eventually decayed, leaving nothing but the sockets and giving the statues a skeletal appearance.

"Why do you think they aren't going to put eyes in again?" Micah asked me. "They stood them upright, so it's not as if they believe the statues shouldn't be disturbed."

"I have no idea. Maybe they think it would give tourists like us the willies."

Micah stared toward the statues. "I wouldn't get the willies."

"Neither would I."

He paused. "I think they'd look better with eyes."

"Me, too."

"Maybe we should start a movement. Call it, 'Eyeballs for Statues.' "

"It has a nice ring to it. Go for it."

He continued to stare. "I really do think they'd look better, don't you?"

Standing next to Micah, I realized that there were times when we talked not because we needed to communicate anything important, but simply because we each drew comfort from the other's voice.

After taking photographs, we got back in our van and headed to Anakena, a cove fronted by a white-sand beach that was dotted with one of the few remaining groves of palm trees. For the first time, we saw a part of the island that looked tropical; an ancient Moai seemed to be standing guard at the head of the beach, watching over the bathers.

After a barbecue on the beach, Micah and I and a few others went for a swim. By then, our group had begun breaking into cliques. Some folks were adventurous and wanted to experience everything they could; others seemed to view the sights as inconveniences they had to endure between meals and cocktail parties. Some of this was age-related, some of it had to do with attitudes. Micah and I were part of the adventurous group; we always took the "fast walker" tours as opposed to the "slow walker" tours, and the chance to swim in the South Pacific wasn't something we were going to miss. Though a small thing, it would be another in a long line of "first-time-evers" we would experience together.

"They don't know what they're missing, do they?" Micah said to me, as he pointed to the people sitting on the beach.

"Maybe it's not a big deal to them. A lot of these people have traveled before."

"Maybe," he said. "Or maybe they never did it in the past, either. Some people just don't know how to have fun. They aren't even willing to try."

I glanced warily at Micah, suddenly wondering if he was talking about me.

In seventh grade, Micah went off to Barrett Junior High School, and we continued to grow apart. My sister and I, however, were growing even closer. She laughed all the time and had a quality of sweetness that almost made me feel guilty about the kind of person I was. She seldom got angry, and I sometimes overheard her talking to mom about how proud she was of us. In her eyes,

Micah and I could do no wrong, and whenever we were punished, my sister would be the one to come into our room and listen to us complain about the injustice of what our parents had done to us.

My sister always seemed to know how I felt inside; she was the only one who understood that excelling in school had more to do with an inferiority complex than any particular love of school. She would sometimes ask me to help her with her schoolwork, and used those opportunities to build my confidence. "I wish I was as smart as you," she'd say, or, "Mom and dad are so happy with how well you're doing."

Growing up, Dana was the only one of us who ever had a birthday party because, as my mom explained to us, "She's a girl." This wouldn't have been so bad—neither Micah nor I ever clamored for a party—but because my sister and I shared the same birthday, it always felt a little odd to have to watch my sister having a party, while I stood off to the side. If my mom didn't understand it, however, my sister did, and one year she came into my room early on the morning of our birthday and sat on the edge of my bed. Jostled awake, I asked her what she was doing.

She began to sing, "Happy Birthday to you..."

Afterward, I sang the song back to her, and every year after that it was our own secret ritual. We'd sing to each other, just the two of us, and we never told anyone about it. This was our secret, as it would be for years, and after singing to each other, we'd talk for a while. I'd tell her everything—my hopes and fears and struggles and successes—and Dana would do the same.

When she was twelve, I asked her, "What do you want to be when you grow up? What do you want more than anything?"

My sister looked around the room with a dreamy smile.

"I want to be married, and I want to have kids. And I want to own horses."

She got this, I knew, from my mom. More than anything in the world, my mom always wanted a horse. Growing up, she'd owned a horse named Tempo, and she often spoke of the horse and the wonderful times she used to have riding.

"That's it?" I asked.

"That's it. That's all I want out of life."

"Don't you want to be rich or famous, or do exciting things?"

"No. That's for you and Micah."

"But won't you be bored with that?"

"No," she said, with conviction. "I won't."

My sister, I knew then, wasn't the complicated bundle of nerves that I was. When she finally left the room, I remember wishing that if I couldn't be like Micah, that I could be just like her instead.

When I started at Barrett Junior High the following year, I joined Micah on the long bus ride to school, but we never sat together, or even seemed to talk. Eighth-graders occupied a completely different realm than did seventh-graders—they were the Big Men On Campus—and our paths seldom crossed in the hallways or at recess. After school and on weekends, Micah ran off to see his friends, while I stayed to compete on various athletic teams. Though a good athlete, I wasn't extraordinary, and distinguished myself neither on the football field nor when I ran track and field.

The following year, Micah started high school and we were separated again, both during and after school. By then, I'd grown used to doing my own thing.

Halfway through my eighth-grade year, in 1978, we moved to the first and only house my parents would ever own.

We handled the move ourselves. Who needs to pay a moving company when there are a couple of strong boys and a Volkswagen van on hand? So day after day, we loaded everything from the house into the back of the van and hauled it to the new home.

But Volkswagens aren't really designed for exceptionally heavy loads, and my brother and I didn't care how much we loaded into ours. We would fill the back of the van with my dad's books until there wasn't an inch to spare. It probably weighed half a ton, and the van was riding exceptionally low in the rear. Meanwhile, the nose of the vehicle actually pointed upward, like someone eyeing a distant horizon.

"We got it all loaded in, Mom."

Mom stared at the van. "It looks like it's just about to pop a wheelie."

"That's just because it's heavy in the back. It'll straighten out when we unload it."

"You think it's safe to drive?" she asked. Why she asked us, I'll never know. Neither Micah nor I even had our license.

"Of course it's safe. Why wouldn't it be?"

The good news was that the van made it to the new house. The bad news was that—even after unloading all the books—the van didn't level out. At all. We'd crushed whatever support there had been in the rear.

"Is the front still pointing toward the sky, or is it just me?" mom finally asked.

"Maybe we're looking at it crooked. Or the street's not level."

We tilted our heads, checking the van, looking up and down the road.

"I think you broke something," mom finally said.

"Nah," we said, "it'll be fine. Give it time—it'll go back to normal."

"Your dad's going to be mad."

"He won't even notice," we reassured her. "But even if he does, he won't care."

Of course my dad noticed, and the DEFCON countdown started after he got home, though we were smart enough to be long gone by then. Thankfully, by the time we got home, he had calmed down, since the van seemed to run fine, despite the crazy way it looked. And if it ran fine, that meant there was really no reason to fix it. That would be spending money we didn't have. So in the end, the van was never repaired, and for the next three years—until we traded it in for the new, improved Volkswagen van—we drove around town looking as if we were hauling baby whales to the zoo.

Our new house was small. A single-story ranch with a converted garage, it had four bedrooms, an office, a living room, and a kitchen. Two of the rooms (the office and master bedroom) had been converted from the garage. The house was twenty-five years old and in dire need of repairs. Even with the garage conversion, it was less than 1,300 square feet.

But to us, it was awesome. My brother, sister, and I each had our own room for the first time in our lives, and we all took time decorating them in our own style. My mom was tremendously proud to finally have a home she could call her own, and she spent much of the next few years fixing the place up and adding her own splashes of personality. There were sixteen walls all painted in different colors—my mom changed wall paint more often than some people change their toothbrushes—and every weekend, Micah and I had to finish our mother's "list" before we could head off to play. We spent our Saturday mornings building fences, painting walls over and over, planting bushes and trees, sanding kitchen cabinets, and executing whatever plan she happened to come up with while at work.

Because the family had little extra money to spend on such things, it was a slow process. To build the fence, for instance, my mom would buy a dozen planks of wood every week, all she could spare from her paycheck. It took her nearly five months to accumulate all the wood we needed to build the fence, but thankfully—in her opinion anyway—the labor was free. Micah and I—no doubt drawing on our roofing experience in Nebraska—were put in charge of constructing the fence, and we did. That it ended up sloping noticeably—as opposed to being straight across the top—was simply one of the outcomes my brother and I assumed our mother had foreseen before deciding to delegate the project to us.

Knowing we'd continue to do most of the work on the house, our parents began giving us tools for Christmas. It was a way of killing two birds with one stone. Not only did we get something unexpected (how could I expect to receive a hammer for Christmas if I didn't want one?), but they would save money at the same time. And it was much better than offering us weapons again. Late one Christmas morning, I sat beside Micah on the couch.

"What did you think of Christmas this year?" he asked.

"It was great," I said, "for a carpenter." I nodded toward my gifts. "What am I going to do with a *dowel* hammer? Do they want me to start building furniture next?"

Micah shook his head and sighed. "Yeah, I know what you mean. But at least you got a lot of them. I got a jigsaw. What is mom going to make me use that for? I wanted a pair of *Levi's*, for God's sake."

We sat in silence.

"Our parents are weird, aren't they?" I asked.

Micah didn't answer. When I glanced at him, I saw him staring at the jigsaw.

"What?"

He shook his head, his brow furrowed. "Nothing really. It just says on the box here that this thing can cut through hardwood, like oak."

"So."

"Isn't the hardwood in my bedroom oak?"

"I think so."

He pondered the situation. "And wouldn't you agree that our parents are a little heavy-handed?"

"Absolutely," I agreed. "They're like guards at the Gulag."

He blinked as if suddenly in the presence of a Martian. "What are you talking about, Nick?"

"Never mind."

"You're weird sometimes, too."

"I know." I'd heard this before. "But what were you saying?"

"Well, what if we use this thing to our advantage?"

"What do you mean?"

He leaned in and whispered his plan, and I had to admit he was definitely onto something. And sure enough, as soon as my parents had left for work—we were still on school break—my brother used the jigsaw to cut a hole in his closet floor that led to the crawl space beneath the house. That way, after he'd supposedly gone to bed, he could sneak out at night via his bedroom without our parents ever knowing about it.

And, of course, he did.

It was around this time that my mom decided she was tired of working full-time, and doing all the cooking and cleaning around the house. My dad was thus drafted into becoming the chef.

I remember hearing about it when I got home from school one afternoon, and I honestly believed that my dad was excited about it. He told us that he was going to make one of his favorite meals, one that he used to eat when he was a kid. He forbade us from coming into the kitchen to see what he was preparing.

"It's a surprise."

Neither Micah, Dana, nor I knew what to make of it. The only thing our dad ever cooked on his own was chicken gizzards. Not wings, not legs or breasts, but *gizzards*. My dad simply loved those things. He would fry up a plateful, and while we eventually acquired a taste for them, it was obvious that gizzards weren't on the menu that night.

Frying gizzards—frying anything—made for a pleasant aroma in the kitchen. But all *we* could smell was something burned and scorchy—like flour that caught on fire—and more than once, I heard my dad yell, "Whoops!" and race to open the back slider, so the smoke could clear the kitchen. Then, popping his head back into the living room, he'd say, "You guys are going to love this!" or, "Cooking for you guys is going to be great! I can't wait to share more of my childhood recipes. I'm really getting the hang of it now!"

Eventually, after three or four "Whoops!" he called us to the table. Mom wasn't home from work yet, and we took our seats. My dad brought the food over from the stove and set it before us.

There were two items. A plate of toast, and . . . and . . .

We looked closer, but still couldn't tell. It was in a bowl, whatever it was. Gray and brown and lumpy, sort of gravylike, with specks of black mixed in. The spoon was resting on the slowly solidifying mass.

"I might have burned it a little, but it should be fine. Eat up."
None of us moved.

"What is it, Daddy?" Dana finally asked.

"It's beans," he said. "I cooked them up using a secret recipe."

We looked at the bowl again. It sure didn't look like beans. And it didn't smell like beans, either. It smelled almost... unnatural. It reminded me of something the dog ate, partially digested, then offered up again. But okay, beans and toast and...

"What's for the main course?" I asked.

"What do you mean?"

"Like hamburger? Or chicken?"

"Don't need it. Not with this meal."

"What is this meal?" Micah asked.

"Beans on toast," he said, his voice ringing with pride. "Your mom never made this for you, did she?"

We glanced at each other, then shook our heads.

My dad reached for the bowl. "Who's going to be first?"

Neither Micah nor I moved a muscle. Dana finally cleared her throat.

"I will, Daddy."

He beamed. Placing a piece of toast on her plate, he started to scoop from the bowl. It was thick and hard, and my dad had to really work the spoon. The smell only got worse as he began to penetrate the substance. I saw my dad's nose wrinkle.

"Like I said, I might have burned it a little," he said. "But it should be fine. Enjoy."

"Are you going to eat some, Daddy?" Dana asked.

"No, you three go ahead. I'll just watch. You guys are still growing and need the energy. Micah?"

My dad dug into the bowl again, grimacing as he worked at the beans, as if he were trying to scoop frozen ice cream.

"No thanks. I'm supposed to be eating at Mark's tonight. I don't want to spoil my appetite."

"You didn't mention that before."

"I guess I forgot. But really, I should be getting ready. I was supposed to be there ten minutes ago."

He quickly rose from the table and vanished.

"Okay. How about you, Nick?"

"Yeah, okay," I said, raising my plate. I placed a piece of toast on it; the gravy-burned-bean-substance dropped like a baseball onto my plate, nearly rolling off and hitting the table.

"Just spread it out a little," my dad suggested. "It's better that way."

My sister and I began to poke at the dinner—*trying* to spread it, but getting nowhere—terrified at the thought of actually consuming it. But just when we knew we couldn't postpone it any longer, my mom walked in the door.

"Hey guys! How are you? It's great to see you—" She stopped and wrinkled her nose. "What on earth is that *stench*?"

"It's dinner," my dad said. "Come on. We're waiting for you."

She moved to the table, took one look at the food, and said, "Kids, bring those plates to the sink."

"But..." my dad said.

"No buts. I'll make spaghetti. You kids want spaghetti instead?"

We nodded eagerly, and quickly rose from the table.

"Okay. Just get the groceries from my baskets. I'll get it going in a few minutes."

For whatever reason, my dad wasn't all that upset. In fact, I think it had been his plan all along, for after that night, he was prohibited from cooking for us. And whenever my mom complained about his failure to assume more domestic responsibility, he could honestly say, "I tried. But you won't let me."

Food in general became a strange sort of obsession in our home. Because we couldn't afford the same sort of treats that other kids seemed to get—cookies, Twinkies, Ho Hos, etc.—we developed a binge mentality when the opportunity presented itself. If we were visiting someone's house for instance, we'd devour whatever we could, eating until we felt like we would burst. It was nothing for us to consume thirty or forty Oreos in a sitting. At times, we'd leave our friends in their rooms, sneak back to the friend's kitchen, raid the pantry, and eat even more.

It was the same way whenever my mom was crazy enough to buy anything sweet. Cereal, for instance. As a rule, we had only Cheerios in the house. If she happened to buy Froot Loops or Trix on a whim, we'd eat the whole box, *right away*. We simply couldn't fathom saving any for the following morning. Our thinking went, *If I don't eat it now, the other kids will, and I deserve my fair share.* We'd eat until we were sick to our stomachs. Once, after consuming five large bowls each of Froot Loops in less than half an hour, Micah and I sat beside each other on the couch, bellies bloated.

"I think there might be enough for one last bowl," Micah said.

"I know. I was just thinking about that."

"Should we leave it for Dana?"

"No. Definitely not. She ate the last bowl last time."

"That's what I was thinking. But I'm so full. I can't eat another bite."

We tried to get comfortable as we shifted around. Finally, Micah turned to me.

"Want to split it? Go half and half?"

"Okay."

My dad, too, had a sweet tooth. He always kept a stash of Oreos in the house, but knowing us, he would hide them in his office.

This led us to ransack his office in search of them. Usually, we'd find them after a few minutes, and we'd each sneak one or two, so that he wouldn't notice any were missing. We'd then go back a second and third time, always rearranging the remaining Oreos in the hope that the pack would look as if it hadn't been disturbed. By the time my dad got home from work, there'd only be a couple of broken cookies left.

Holding the mostly empty bag in front of him, he'd eye the crumbs, his eyes bulging.

"Vultures! My kids are G-D-N *vultures!*" he'd scream, and we'd hear him searching for his keys. Once he found them, he'd get in the car and drive to the store to buy another pack of Oreos. From his office, he'd give us the evil eye all night.

The next day, the search for the bag of cookies would begin again. And once we found them, we'd eat them compulsively, until only one or two broken cookies were left.

"Vultures!" we'd hear him scream. "You're all a bunch of G-D-N *VULTURES!*"

Questions and Explanations
for Chapter 9

The ten questions on chapter 9 focus on grammar and usage, vocabulary, comprehension, literary terms, and characterization. Some of the questions combine two or more of these areas, requiring you to synthesize your knowledge, make inferences, and interpret the text. The questions are designed to determine both your current level of understanding of the memoir and your ability to answer higher-level questions.

The following sentence tests your ability to recognize grammar and usage errors. The sentence contains either a single error or no error at all. If the sentence contains an error, select the one underlined part that must be changed to make the sentence correct. If there is no error, select answer choice D.

1. <u>Visiting Easter Island</u>, Nicholas and Micah <u>realize</u> that the
        A   **B**
   Moai statues are <u>very unique</u> cultural creations. <u>No error</u>
                     C   **D**

In order to answer this question, you need to be able to recognize the grammar rules being tested. Choice A checks the introductory participial phrase (a form of a verb acting as an adjective). You need to determine if the phrase "Visiting Easter Island" describes Nicholas and Micah. If it does, it is correct. Choice B checks your knowledge of subject and verb agreement. Determine which is correct, "Nicholas and Micah realize" or "Nicholas and Micah realizes." Choice C tests whether you understand that the word *unique* means one of a kind. Thus, something is either unique or it isn't; there are no degrees of uniqueness.

The following two questions test your vocabulary. Choose the word or set of words that, when inserted in the sentence, best fits the meaning of the sentence as a whole.

2. Whenever their mom brought special cereals home, the boys felt a need to devour them immediately, for they couldn't _____ not eating them right away.

   A. comprehend

   B. heed

   C. ignore

   D. undermine

This question tests both your comprehension and your vocabulary. *Comprehend*, choice A, means to fathom or understand.

Heed, choice B, means to give careful attention to. *Ignore*, choice C, means to pay little or no attention to. *Undermine*, choice D, means to attempt to subvert by stealth.

3. During their trip, the _____ between Nicholas and Micah and their ability to have serious discussions illustrate their _____.

   A. camaraderie...compatibility

   B. friendship...antagonism

   C. enmity...differences

   D. solidarity...antipathy

This question also checks your comprehension and your vocabulary. First, determine if what exists between Nicholas and Micah is positive or negative. If it's negative, *enmity* (choice C) is your only option. If you eliminate choice C, realize two things: (1) That the other three first-word choices are close in meaning, so the second word is going to be of prime importance, and (2) The first word is an illustration of the second, so both are similar in meaning. *Camaraderie*, choice A, is a spirit of familiarity and trust, and *compatibility* is the ability to coexist in harmony. *Friendship* and *antagonism* (choice B) are opposites. And *solidarity* refers to unity based on a community of shared feelings, but *antipathy* is an aversion (choice D).

Question 4 checks your comprehension.

4. According to the chapter, all of the following are reasons for the lack of trees on Easter Island EXCEPT:

A. overuse of the natural resources

B. overcrowding of people on the island

C. a La Niña effect

D. diseased imported trees

Although the lack of trees "partially explains the cultural history of Easter Island," the phenomenon is certainly as odd as Nicholas thought it was. Understanding the history of the island helps to explain this occurrence. If you are not sure of the answer, reread the first part of chapter 9, paying particular attention to the section that discusses the trees.

Question 5 asks you to identify a central idea in a text.

5. In chapter 9, Micah states that "relationships are the most important thing in life," which is an important theme of the memoir. Which of the choices listed below names a relationship that is illustrated by details and examples from the memoir to support this theme?

   A. the relationship between parents and children

   B. the relationship between siblings

   C. the relationship between spouses

   D. the relationship between individuals and their God or higher power

   E. all of the above

Being able to identify themes, or central ideas, is an important part of studying literature. Sometimes themes are explicitly stated, as in this example. It's up to a reader to recognize the details and examples that illustrate and develop that theme.

Recognize that the question indicates there will be more than one correct answer. If you can see important relationships between parents and their children in the memoir, select choice A. If the relationships between Micah, Nicholas, and Dana play an important part in the memoir, select choice B. If relationships between spouses (either the siblings' parents or their own spouses) are essential to understanding relationships and ideas in the memoir, select choice C. And if there have been important discussions regarding the role of God in personal relationships, select choice D. If all of these relationships are important in understanding the theme, select choice E.

Question 6 tests your knowledge of literary terms.

6. If Nicholas were to tell his brother, "God did not abandon you, so you should not abandon God," this sentence would be an example of what stylistic device?

    A. anaphora

    B. chiasmus

    C. epistrophe

    D. amplification

Anaphora, choice A, is the repetition of a word or group of words at the beginning of successive clauses or lines—for example, "I want you to know the word *anaphora*. I want you to recognize the effect of anaphora in a passage. I want you to attempt to use anaphora in your own writing."

Chiasmus, choice B, is a rhetorical figure of speech that uses the repetition of ideas in reverse order—for example, "You forget what you want to remember, and you remember what you want to forget."

Epistrophe, choice C, is the repetition of a word or group of words at the end of successive clauses or lines. An example might be, "Don't you ever talk about *my friends*! You don't know any of *my friends*. You don't look at any of *my friends*. And you certainly wouldn't condescend to speak to any of *my friends*."

Amplification, choice D, refers to the repetition of a word or an idea, while adding information to it, in order to emphasize its importance or to illustrate a progression—for example, "What I wanted, what my team wanted, what the entire league wanted was an apology from the official."

Question 7 checks your comprehension.

7. After his initial enthusiasm wore off, Nicholas might have compared visiting the Moai statues to what?

   A. viewing the pottery

   B. climbing the Mayan temples

   C. visiting Casa Aliaga

   D. seeing the picture of Jesus eating a roasted guinea pig

Making connections between different chapters of the memoir is extremely important to understanding and appreciating the text as a whole. In order to answer this question correctly, you must first make sure you understand how Nicholas felt after seeing the first few Moai statues. Then you must connect this feeling to something else that he has experienced on the tour; thus, you must remember how he felt during the activities that are listed in the four choices. If you can't remember, consult your notes or scan the first parts of the previous three chapters.

Questions 8 and 9 check your knowledge of literary terms.

Read the following passage, and then answer the two questions after it.

> When the brothers are discussing their parents after receiving tools for Christmas yet again, Micah called their parents "a little heavy-handed," and Nicholas said, "They're like guards at the Gulag."

8. Which figure of speech does Nicholas use to explain how he feels about his parents?

   A. hyperbole

   B. metaphor

   C. personification

   D. simile

Hyperbole, choice A, is an exaggerated statement used to heighten effect and to emphasize a point—for example, "This learning guide has defined *hyperbole* a million times already." A *metaphor*, choice B, is a comparison made between two unlike things without using a connective word—for example, "LeBron James is an animal on the basketball court." *Personification*, choice C, is giving nonhuman things human characteristics—

for example, "The leaves danced in the wind." Leaves can't really dance. And a *simile*, choice D, is a comparison made between two unlike things using a connective word, such as *like, as,* or *than*—for example, "My love is like a red, red rose."

9. In addition to using a specific figure of speech, Nicholas also uses what literary device to explain his feelings?

   A. allusion

   B. oxymoron

   C. allegory

   D. symbol

An *allusion*, choice A, is an indirect reference. Some of the most common types of allusions are historical, such as making a reference to Napoleon by saying that someone met his Waterloo; biblical, such as John Coffey in *The Green Mile* being a Christ figure; mythological, a reference to a Greek or Roman myth, such as someone having the Midas touch; and literary, a reference to a character in a work of literature, such as a couple being ill-fated like Romeo and Juliet.

Oxymoron, choice B, is a joining of two contradictory terms—for example, *jumbo shrimp, icy hot,* and *larger half.* An *allegory*, choice C, is a narrative that exists on two levels—the literal and the symbolic. *The Lord of the Flies* is often considered an allegory. On the surface, it's a novel about British boys stranded on an island, but on a deeper level, the boys as a whole represent humanity. The island stands for the world, and the fighting is essentially a war. The novel explores the notion of savagery and civilization, on the island specifically and in the world beyond the island generally.

A *symbol,* choice D, is something that has meaning in and of itself and also stands for something else. For example, the American flag is a piece of fabric with the stars and stripes on it (literally, it is a flag), but the American flag symbolizes, among other things, democracy, freedom, and the fifty states.

Question 10 tests your knowledge of literary terms.

10. When Mr. Sparks discovered that his children raided his stash of Oreos, he would give them the evil eye and scream, "Vultures!...You're all a bunch of G-D-N *VULTURES!*" Which figure of speech was he using to make his point?

    A. hyperbole

    B. metaphor

    C. onomatopoeia

    D. personification

Again, knowing about literary terms will enable you to apply your understanding to a particular passage. *Hyperbole,* choice A, is an obvious and intentional exaggeration—for example, "This learning guide has discussed hyperbole about four million times." A *metaphor,* choice B, is a comparison made between two unlike things without using a connective word—for example, "LeBron James is an animal on the basketball court." *Onomatopoeia,* choice C, is a word that suggests the very sound it describes, like *buzz, sizzle,* and *boom. Personification,* choice D, is giving nonhuman things a human characteristic, such as in "Opportunity knocked on the door."

Chapter 10

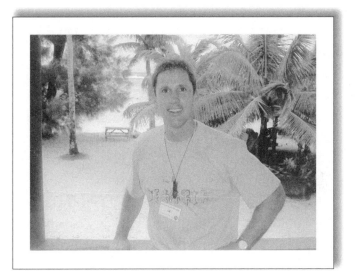

Rarotonga, Cook Islands
January 31

On our final morning on Easter Island, we rose early for breakfast and finished just as the sun was rising.

Early mornings had become typical on our trip. Usually, breakfast began at 6:30, and we'd assemble in the lobby before 8:00 to start visits to the sites. It took hours to move our group anywhere; with nearly ninety people and two hundred bags of luggage, we were more like a slow-moving caravan than a quick-strike task force. Departure time for the plane was usually around 10:00 A.M.; by that time, we'd usually been up for five hours with little to show for it.

These early mornings, late dinners, long days at the sites, and extensive travel in the previous seven days had added up; by the end of our time on Easter Island, most everyone looked tired. Yet we were only a third of the way through the trip.

The flight to Rarotonga, the main island in the cluster of South Pacific Islands known as the Cook Islands, was seven hours; we made up some of those hours on the way west, and arrived in the early afternoon. No tours were scheduled; instead, we'd be on our own for the rest of the day and would depart for Australia in the morning. We were stopping on Rarotonga to break up the fourteen-hour flight between Easter Island and Ayers Rock.

Rarotonga was steamy when we stepped off the plane, and far warmer than Easter Island had been. It was a typical island day; blue skies crowded with dense puffy clouds that portended late afternoon showers, high humidity, and a light, constant breeze. The island itself was beautiful; the main road circled the island, and the central peaks were shrouded in clouds and thick with island vegetation. Like Easter Island, it had been originally settled by Polynesians, but was probably most famous because of Captain Bligh and the mutineers of the *Bounty*, who were marooned on the islands in the late eighteenth century.

When we arrived at the hotel, the group dispersed. Some went to lunch, others retreated to nap in their rooms. Still others went to sit on the beach or by the pool; a few decided to go snorkeling. Micah and I decided to rent scooters to explore the island.

The island was roughly twenty-five miles in circumference, and, as in England, the vehicles traveled on the opposite side of the road than they did in the States. Though it took some getting used to, the roads weren't crowded, and we zipped along, stopping here and there for pictures. Palm trees stretched as far as the eye could see, and we wondered if Easter Island had once looked this way. The thought saddened us. While Easter Island had been austere and lovely in its own way, the difference between the islands was staggering.

The Cook Islands are noted for black pearls, and both Micah and I stopped to buy some for our wives. In the past week, Micah had talked to Christine twice, and I'd talked to Cat four times. None of our conversations had lasted more than a few minutes. Their lives were more hectic than usual, but their routines the same; it amazed us to think of all the places we'd been since we'd last seen them.

There is something refreshing about riding with the wind in your face, and as we circled the island my mind wandered. Part of it was that Micah and I were on our own and without a schedule. I thought about our childhood; the places we'd lived and the things we'd done. I tried to imagine what my kids were doing, and pictured the way Cathy looked as she stood in front of the mirror in the morning.

Best of all, I never thought about work as I rode, even for an instant. For the first time in years, I finally began to feel as if I were on vacation.

Micah and I grabbed some bottled water, and stopped at one of the public beaches on the far side of the island. The beaches were coral-strewn, and the waves just beyond the reef rose high before crashing against them. Micah and I were the only ones there, and from the beach we couldn't see any houses. With the exception of the faint sound of passing traffic on the road behind us, it would have been easy to believe we were the only ones on the island.

For a long time, we simply sat and watched the waves. The ocean was the color of faded turquoise, and even from our vantage point, it was possible to see through the water to the seafloor. Schools of brightly colored fish swam past us, our eyes traveling with them. Many of the South Pacific islands have their own native species; some fish found in Hawaii or Fiji can only be found there, and I wondered if I was seeing a species I would never see again.

"Now this," Micah said, "is the reason we came to Rarotonga. Beautiful beach, beautiful weather, all by ourselves. Can it get any better?"

"It's not exactly like our vacation to the Grand Canyon, is it?"

He grinned. "That was some trip, wasn't it?"

"It was great," I said.

"It was awful," he corrected. "You're just too young to remember it the way I do. By the end, we'd driven dad almost crazy. He'd drive all day, see a sight, and then we'd camp out in the Volkswagen at night because we couldn't afford hotels. And don't you remember we didn't have air-conditioning? Here we were driving through the desert in the middle of summer, sun glaring through the windows and cooking us inside. We roasted day and night, and complained all day. And we wrestled until we were slippery with sweat, screaming the whole time. Dad was pretty grouchy."

"Our dad?" I feigned disbelief. "Mr. DEFCON? You must be thinking of someone else."

He laughed. "I think we remember those moments about dad so clearly because he was such a quiet guy. I barely even knew he was around half the time, and then all of a sudden, BOOM. Our dad isn't dad—suddenly he's this super-scary guy."

"Do you remember when he brought us to the movie *Alien* on opening night because he heard it was the scariest movie ever made? Or when we watched *Salem's Lot* on television? What were we? Eleven or so?"

"Something like that."

"Would you let Alli see movies like that? I mean, in a couple of years?"

Alli, his stepdaughter, was ten years old.

"There's not a chance. Christine would kill me. She won't even let me bring scary videos into the house."

"Cathy's the same way." I sighed. "Did I ever tell you that I rented *Silver Bullet* for Miles?"

"No. What's that?"

"It's this movie about werewolves. Stephen King wrote the story it was based on, and I figured that Miles might want to watch it with me. It's what our dad used to do, right? So I let him watch it."

"And?"

"He had nightmares for months. Cathy was absolutely livid—I got glares you can't even imagine, and she still brings it up whenever I offer to bring Miles to a movie. '*He better not get nightmares,*' she warns. '*And if he does, you're the one who's going to have to sit up with him all night.*'"

Micah smiled. "Our wives and children just don't seem to have the appreciation for good horror movies that we do."

"It's a shame," I admitted. "All I wanted to do was share something with Miles that my dad shared with me growing up. Kind of like going fishing or playing catch or going to museums."

"I understand completely, little brother," he said. He put his arm around me. "You gotta give that to dad," he said. "He did teach us to appreciate the important things in life."

Once back at the hotel, we decided to go snorkeling.

While I've snorkeled in the Caribbean and Hawaii, I've never been more impressed than I was that day. Thousands of bright blue starfish, barracudas, and colorful reef fish swam in the warm, clear water, and a light current made it possible to float at the surface of the shallow water while expending little effort. Above us, clouds had filled in the sky, making it possible for us to be out without getting sunburned, and we stayed in the water, even when the rain started to fall.

Afterward, we ate on the hotel's outdoor patio. We were trying to decide what to do later in the evening; with nothing planned, it seemed like a waste to head back to our rooms. The bartender—who was also our waiter—recommended a pub crawl, and said a van would stop by the hotel around eight o'clock, if we signed up for it.

A pub crawl is essentially that: The van comes by, picks you up, and brings you from one pub to the next over the course of the evening. Whether or not a person drinks, however, is almost beside the point. Over the years, I've visited numerous countries, and I've learned that until you meet the people in a relaxed setting, doing what they normally do, you haven't actually experienced what the country is all about. Almost everyone I've ever met in situations like that is friendly; most people around the world enjoy practicing their English and hearing about America. Our country, warts and all, is a place that foreigners find both fascinating and intriguing; they love some things and hate others, but everyone has an opinion about it.

At the same time, I'm always struck by how similar people are, no matter where they live. Throughout the world, people not only want to have the chance to improve their own situation, but want their children to have more opportunities than they have. Politicians are nearly always held in low esteem; so are demagogues on both the right and the left.

Our bartender was no different, and though he was mildly disappointed that we wouldn't be traveling to New Zealand—his home country—he did add that he'd visited the United States.

"Oh yeah?" Micah said. "Where?"

"I was in Los Angeles, San Francisco, Seattle, Las Vegas, Denver, Dallas, New Orleans, Chicago, Detroit, Philadelphia, and New York. I spent a summer traveling around the country."

"Did you see the Grand Canyon?" Micah asked.

"Yes, of course," he said. "I thought it was great. Mount Rushmore, too. And the giant redwoods. Beautiful. My favorite place was Las Vegas."

"Did you win in Vegas?" I asked.

"No, I lost. I played the slots, you know? But it was fun. That's the wildest city. I love it there. Have you ever been there?"

"Of course," Micah said. "From Sacramento, it's just over an hour away by plane."

The bartender shook his head, a look of pleasure on his face. "I tell people—if you want to see America, go to Vegas. The lights, the shows, the excitement—it's America."

While we were eating, Jill Hannah, the physician, joined us. Over the past few days, she'd been busy, since so many people were developing stomach problems. Like everyone, she seemed lethargic, and when we mentioned we were going out that night, she raised her eyebrows.

"Aren't you guys tired?"

"A little," Micah answered. "But you should come, too. It'll be fun."

"Thanks, but I'm going to bed. Is anyone else going with you?"

"We'll see," Micah said. "We're going to ask around in a little while."

Not surprisingly, most everyone we asked said no, no matter how fun we tried to make it sound. We must have spoken to a couple of dozen people, but only Charles, one of the lecturers on the tour, said he'd come. We told him that we'd meet him in the lobby at eight.

"We're just going to take a short nap," Micah said, "and we'll see you then."

We headed back to our room, lay down, and fell fast asleep, neither of us waking until the following morning.

At breakfast, Charles came over to our table. "Where were you guys last night? I was waiting for you. I was all set to have a great time."

"Sorry about that," Micah said sheepishly.

"I can't believe the brothers Sparks actually got tired."

"Sometimes," Micah said, "it happens to the best of us."

As soon as Charles left, I leaned toward Micah. "I can't believe we slept through it. I guess we're getting older, huh?"

"I know what you mean. In college, it seemed like I never got tired. I could go out all night long. I was wild."

"College?" I asked. "Who are you kidding? You were wild in *high school.*"

In 1979, Micah began high school, and for the next two years my brother had a tenuous relationship with everyone in the family. He'd reached the age where he began to openly question my parents' authority, and acted out accordingly. Yet Micah, as probably could have been expected, was *more*, even when it came to being a teenager. He got drunk at the river, and my mom once found marijuana in the pocket of his jeans and grounded him for a month after threatening him with military school. At fifteen, Micah also came home with a pierced ear; my mom made him remove the earring by issuing yet another threat about military school.

She always threatened us with military school. Both of our parents had gone to boarding school and each of them had shared their horror stories, always ending with, "but at least it wasn't military school." As kids, we were terrified at the thought of these institutions, believing they'd been designed by Satan himself. But Micah was listening to our parents less and less, and he'd come to realize that he'd never actually be sent away, if only because the family couldn't afford it. Thus, his behavior got worse and worse. During his freshman year, the mood in the house was extremely tense, and my sister and I were often amazed at the way he boldly raised his voice to our mom and dad.

Image is important to most teenagers, and Micah was no exception. He was tired of being poor, and even worse, looking poor. At sixteen, he got a job as a dishwasher at an ice cream parlor, and began saving his money. He bought a used car and learned how to repair it, he bought new clothes, and began dating. He soon became serious with a girl named Juli and began spending all his free time with her. My mom didn't think it was a good idea to be so serious about a girl at such a young age, and they argued about that as well. Once, she caught the two of them napping in his room, and all hell broke loose. I don't think I'd ever seen my mother angrier about anything.

It was around that time that my mom marched into my dad's office. My dad had been all but irrelevant when it came to raising us, but my mom could go no further without his help.

"I raised them this far," she said. "Now it's your turn."

My dad simply nodded. It was, he probably thought, a lot better than cooking or cleaning.

After that, I remember evenings where I'd find Micah sitting in the office, visiting with my dad. My dad was exceptionally smart, and he read almost constantly. He taught behavioral theory and management at California State University in Sacramento, and read every conceivable book that had been written on the subjects. Seriously. There were thousands of books in his office at any given time—stacked along shelves, piled on the floor, stored in boxes—and he'd read every one. In the evenings, I could always find him sitting at his desk with his feet propped up, reading. He read amazingly fast; on average, he would finish one or two books in an evening, jotting notes as he went along. His hours were unlike anyone else's in the family. Because he taught in the afternoons, he usually stayed awake until 5:00 A.M., and then slept until noon.

Though my dad always kept his office door open, we all knew that he was most comfortable alone. He was a quiet, attentive listener; when talking to his co-workers, I was always struck by how much they seemed to adore him. My dad could listen to a person ramble on without ever feeling the need to interrupt. Nor, unless asked, would he ever offer advice. Instead, he would clarify your problem—rewording what you'd said in a way that crystallized your thoughts and allowed you to solve the problem on your own.

When talking to Micah—and later, when talking to me—his routine was always the same. He would ask what was going on regarding a specific situation, then would listen while you filled in the void. And the more Micah—or I—talked, the less he would say. Sometimes, these one-sided conversations lasted upward of an hour. We would usually leave his office thinking more clearly, and believing he was one of the smartest people we'd ever met.

In the end, my dad gave us three ironclad rules that we were bound to throughout our teenage years. They were:

A. Don't drink and drive.
B. Don't get a girl pregnant.
C. Be in by your curfew—midnight as a freshman, and increasing half an hour with every passing year in high school.

My dad, by the way, was very shrewd to offer us these particular rules when he did. We would soon be reaching the age where one or another might become an issue, but since we were following all three already, they seemed entirely reasonable at the time. Even more important, by our teenage years we'd been on our own for so long that anything more would have seemed draconian (too little, too late) and no doubt would have led to outright rebellion. These, however, seemed well thought out, and Micah agreed to abide by them.

Micah, it must be said, followed those rules, and only those rules. Everything else, it seemed, was up for grabs, and for the next couple of years he continued to press the outer limits. On more nights than I can count, I remember listening to my mom and dad fretting about him.

"He just keeps getting wilder," one would say. "What do we do?"

A long silence would follow.

"I don't know," the other one would answer.

That year brought about changes for me, too. I began competing in track and field, and though not great, I was one of the better freshmen on the team. This isn't saying much, since in the distance events, there were only a handful of us.

Still, I loved track and field, and as fate would have it, there was a genuine track and field legend who also lived in Fair Oaks. Billy Mills, an Oglala Sioux Indian raised in poverty in the Black Hills of South Dakota, had won the Olympic gold medal in the 10,000 meter run at the Tokyo games in 1964. It is still regarded as the greatest upset in Olympic track and field history. He's the only American ever to win the Olympic 10,000 meters, and proving his talent for posterity, broke the world record the following year. Years earlier, I'd read about him in one of the many almanacs I'd perused as a kid, and I'd been fascinated by his story. When I learned that he lived in Fair Oaks, I was ecstatic, and I remember running to the kitchen to tell my mother.

"Oh Billy," she said, nodding. "I know him and his wife, Pat."

My eyes widened. "You do?"

"Yeah," she said easily. "They get their glasses at our office. They're wonderful people."

All I could do was stare at her, thinking that I was standing next to someone who'd actually talked to a genuine American hero.

This was heady stuff for a kid, and after talking to my mom, I was always on the lookout for him. I'd get excited when I saw him walking into the grocery store (I'd memorized how he looked) or into a restaurant, but I couldn't summon the courage to introduce myself. When I learned that informal, neighborhood track meets were held at the local high school, I wanted to go because I suspected that he might be there as well. Sure enough, he was there, and when I saw him, I was transfixed. I'd watch him walk and think to myself, "That's how the fastest man in the world moves," and try to imitate it. Needless to say, I wanted to impress him with my talent, but to be honest, it never happened. Billy had three daughters and his youngest competed. Unlike me, however, she was *great*, and never once lost a single race.

Learning about Billy's past led me to read about other great runners. I dreamed of running like Henry Rono, Sebastian Coe, or Steve Ovett, but that's all it was—a dream. Yet I went out for the track team, and gradually I became friends with Harold Kuphaldt, a junior who was also on the team.

Like Billy, Harold was almost a legend, albeit a high school one. Harold was one of the fastest runners in the country (he would record the nation's fastest time in the two mile for juniors, and hold the American junior record for a while), and, as with Billy, I idolized him from afar. Again, there's a world of difference between the lives of freshman and upperclassmen. Yet one afternoon, toward the end of the season, the team was running as a group and I found myself running alongside Harold. We started chatting until Harold eventually grew quiet.

"I've been watching you run," Harold said to me after a few moments of companionable silence. "You can be great if you work at it. Not just good, but great. You're a natural at this."

I remember nothing about the run after that. It seemed as if I were floating, carried along by the words he'd said. There was nothing anyone could have said that would have meant more to me than what he'd told me. Not only did his words feed my fantasies, but they also touched the deeper core within myself, the one that always sought approval from my parents. *I could be great*, he'd said. *I'm a natural...*

I vowed at that moment to make his words prophetic, and instead of spending the summer goofing around as I usually did, I decided to train instead. I trained hard—harder than I'd trained during the season—and the harder I worked, the harder I wanted to work. I ran twice a day, often in temperatures exceeding a hundred degrees, and frequently ran until I vomited from exertion. Despite Harold's words, I wasn't a natural athlete, but what I lacked in talent, I made up for with desire and effort.

My brother, meanwhile, was working and earning money; in the past couple of years, he'd matured a bit and was rapidly becoming a man. And a handsome man at that. Combined with his natural confidence and charm, he quickly became irresistible to the opposite sex. The fact that he had a steady girlfriend didn't seem to matter; girls flocked to his side or admired him from afar. My brother was essentially a babe magnet.

Not so for me. I was shorter than Micah, with skinny arms and legs, and had none of the easy confidence of my brother. It didn't matter, however. Running offered me the chance to excel if I worked hard enough, and I began focusing on it to the exclusion of everything else that summer.

Well, almost everything. I was as worried about Micah as my parents were. Toward the end of the summer, after much lobbying, I convinced him to join the cross-country team with me. The team, led by Harold, was expected to be one of the best in the state, and would travel to meets in both the Bay Area and Los Angeles, where, after the meets, we would have the chance to visit amusement parks or boardwalks—places we would ordinarily never have the money or excuse to visit. "All you have to do is run fast enough to be in the top seven," I told him, "and you'll have more fun than you could ever imagine."

He finally took me up on it. Once my brother started running, he quickly made the top seven. Our team went undefeated, and for the most part, Harold did as well. Harold broke course records at nearly every meet, and ended up finishing second in the high school national championships.

While Micah didn't focus on running the way I did, with a desperate determination to excel in it, it nonetheless changed him for the better. He was part of a team, a team that counted on him, and—not surprisingly, considering the way he'd been raised—he took the responsibility seriously. Little by little, he began courting less trouble, and the more successful the team became, the more he took pride in being part of it. It didn't seem to matter to him that I was faster than he was; in fact, he was always the first to congratulate me on how I'd done.

More important to me, however, was that we were spending time together again for the first time in years. And best of all, enjoying it.

My sophomore year was transformative. Not only did I learn to love athletics and running, but it was the first time in my life that I outperformed my brother physically.

At the same time, I continued to focus on getting good grades. Unfortunately, it was becoming more and more of an obsession; not only did I want straight As, but I wanted to be the top student in every class.

I also began devouring novels. My mother, like my father, was an avid reader, and she frequented the library twice a month. There, she would check out anywhere from six to eight books, and read them all; she particularly loved the works of

James Herriot and Dick Francis. As for me, I discovered the classics—*Don Quixote, The Return of the Native, Crime and Punishment, Ulysses, Emma,* and *Great Expectations,* among others, and grew to love the works of Stephen King. Because I'd been raised on old horror movies, they struck a chord with me, and I'd read them over and over as I anxiously awaited a new title to be released.

In my sophomore year, I also had my first real girlfriend. Her name was Lisa and, like me, she ran cross-country. She was a year younger than I, and, as fate would have it, her father was Billy Mills, my boyhood hero.

We dated for the next four years, and I not only fell in love with Lisa, but with her family as well. Billy and Pat were different from my parents in that they genuinely seemed to revel in my accomplishments. More than that, Billy would talk to me about my training and the goals I wanted to reach, and had a way of making me believe they were possible.

My life was growing busier; between school, running, homework, and Lisa, I didn't have much time for anything else. Nor did I have any money, and I came to realize that this situation wasn't exactly conducive to dating. Since our parents didn't give us allowances, nor would they open their wallets if we wanted to go to the movies, I decided to follow my brother's lead. After the cross-country season ended, and on top of everything else I was doing, I got a job as a dishwasher at the same restaurant where my brother worked. In the beginning, I worked until closing two school nights a week; within a few months, I was working thirty-five hours a week, and had been moved up to busboy. Eventually, I became a waiter, and with tips was earning a tidy sum for a high school student. Every minute of every day was accounted for—I was on the go from seven in the morning until nearly midnight, seven days a week—and this schedule would remain essentially unchanged until I graduated two years later.

On our training runs, Micah and I often talked about both the past and the future; sometimes we talked about our dreams, other times we talked about money.

"Do you ever stop to think about how poor we were when we were younger?" he asked me.

"Sometimes. But to be honest, I never really knew that we were poor until a couple of years ago."

"I hated being poor," he said. "I've always hated it. I don't know what I'm going to do when I get older, but I'm not going to be poor. I want to be a millionaire by thirty-five. I don't know how, but that's what I'm going to do."

"You'll make it," I said.

"How about you?"

I smiled. "I want to be a millionaire by thirty."

Micah said nothing. Our strides moved in unison, our feet slapping the ground with almost perfect precision.

"What?" I finally asked. "You don't think I'll make it?"

"I don't know," he said. "I just think thirty-five is more realistic."

"So what are you going to do to make it?"

"Who knows. How about you?"

"I have absolutely no idea."

My brother and I ran together, worked together, and in our free time began to hang out with the same friends. Harold, Mike Lee (another member of the cross-country team), Tracy Yeates (California state champion in wrestling), Micah, and I called ourselves the Mission Gang.

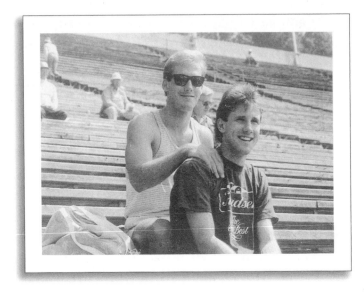

In spite of our general reputation as model student-athletes, we shared a sort of Jekyll-and-Hyde-type existence. It was with them that I got drunk for the first time in my life, and we found tremendous joy in using fireworks in ways that weren't entirely smart, or even legal. We regularly blew up various friends' mailboxes, whooping with delight when they were launched into the air with big *kabooms*. We also teepeed friends' houses with so much toilet paper that it looked like it had snowed the night before. Once, around Christmas, we came across a street where every house was decorated with twinkling lights. Over the next two hours—thinking we were *soooooo* funny—we unscrewed every lightbulb and hauled them off. We'd filled six plastic garbage bags with lights, and the houses looked as if they'd been visited by the Grinch. I really and truly can't explain why we did such things. It's juvenile and embarrassing, but I can't help but think that if we had a chance to go back in time, we'd end up doing those things again.

Due to the time we spent together, my brother and I grew close again. By then, however, our relationship had changed from what it once was. We weren't simply brothers anymore; we'd become good friends. From my sophomore year on, we never had another argument or fight about anything.

In the spring, my brother and I competed in the same events, and my training had begun to pay off. With me leading off and Harold as the anchor, we set meet record after meet record, and our distance medley team ended up running the fastest time in the country. Harold won the state championship in the two mile, and my time in the 800 was tops among sophomores nationwide.

Among my family, only Micah was there to cheer me on. My parents rarely made it to meets; in fact, in my entire career they would see me run—and break records—only once.

While some might think my parents' lack of interest as odd, it never bothered me. After all, they didn't watch Micah run, or see Dana participate on the drill team either. More important, we were doing these things for ourselves; we'd been on our own for so long by then that we didn't expect them to attend these events, and I think all three of us kids understood that our parents were so busy during the week—working, keeping up the house, tending to daily responsibilities, taking care of us, and struggling with finances—that it didn't seem fair to ask them to devote their weekends to us as well, when we all understood that other activities were more relaxing for them.

My mom, for instance, loved to work in the yard or on the house, and nothing made her happier than planting bushes or trees, or painting one of the rooms. Whenever I'd return from a meet, she'd have a smudge of dirt or paint on her cheeks; her jeans were spotted and stained like a laborer's. My dad, on the other hand, used the weekends to catch up on work in a quiet house, and enjoyed organizing—and reorganizing—the books that lined his shelves. And no doubt it was nice to have a quiet house once in a while. Whether they took advantage of that to spend some quality time together, none of us ever knew. Our parents were very private when it came to their personal relationship and told us little about their days. And none of us ever bothered to ask.

Micah trained with me the following summer, and as a senior he'd become one of the better runners in the area. At most meets, we would both finish in the top three, but Micah never became as serious about running as I did.

After graduating, he went to California State University at Sacramento and put his energies into enjoying life instead. He dated one beautiful girl after the next, skied on the weekends, took up snowboarding, and fell in love with mountain biking. He went boating and water-skiing, and spent weekends in San Francisco, Lake Tahoe, or Yosemite. He went white-water rafting, and eventually mastered it well enough to become a guide. He was a member of a yacht crew that raced on weekends. He moved into an apartment near campus and joined other students at bars and nightclubs. Every weekend, it seemed, he was doing something new, something exciting, reveling in his new-found freedom. At the same time, he kept up his grades, and worked as an intern at a commercial real estate firm.

I, on the other hand, spent my senior year as a nervous wreck. Good grades had become an *obsession*; I was on the verge of graduating valedictorian and didn't want this honor to slip from my grasp at the last moment. Furthermore, I knew that if I continued to run well, there was a chance I'd get a scholarship—a goal I'd set for myself—but I had yet to receive an offer, and wouldn't until nearly April. I continued to work thirty-five hours a week and spent whatever free time I did have with my girlfriend. The stress of keeping it all going led to horrible bouts of insomnia. I slept less than three hours a night, and felt constantly on edge.

Part of me envied the kind of life that Micah was living. I admired his ability to simply *live*, without having to *achieve*. In the hallways at school, I'd listen to friends describing their weekends at Folsom Lake, or how much fun they'd had skiing at Squaw Valley. Maybe I should try to have more fun, a voice would whisper inside me, but every time I heard it, I forced myself to push the voice away. With a shake of my head, I'd tell myself that I didn't have time, that I couldn't risk injury, that I was too close to the finish line to quit now.

But I wasn't necessarily happy. My goals had become ends in and of themselves, and there was little joy in pursuing them. Nonetheless, I somehow survived. And just as I wanted, I graduated valedictorian. A month earlier, after running one of the fastest 800-meter times in the country, I'd accepted a full athletic scholarship to the University of Notre Dame. And three months later, I would be living in South Bend, Indiana, two thousand miles from the only family I'd ever known.

Part of me didn't want to go off to college. If you live the sort of childhood I did, you're forced to bond with your family. My brother and sister, along with my parents, had been the only constants in my life, and though I'd known for years that it was inevitable, it was still a little frightening for me to leave them behind.

While I've written a lot about Micah and myself, I don't want to leave you with the impression that my sister was any less important to me. In the early years, my sister and I played together as much as Micah and I did, albeit in different ways. She was always the one I talked to about our adventures; she was the one I talked to when I was having trouble in my relationship with Lisa. In the end, I talked to my sister about everything I'd felt growing up, and my sister, more than anyone else, seemed to understand why I'd become the person I had. Even better, my sister loved me, and she alone seemed to have the ability to put things into perspective for me. My struggles had always been her struggles, and hers had always been mine. And if you ask my brother, he would say exactly the same things about her, for he had the same type of relationship with Dana that I did.

Toward the end of my senior year, I remember hearing my sister crying in her bedroom. After knocking, I went in and found her sitting on the bed, her face in her hands.

"What's wrong?" I asked, taking a seat beside her.

"Everything."

"No tell me. What happened?"

"I hate my life," she said.

"Why?"

"Because," she said, "I'm not like you or Micah."

"I don't understand."

"You guys—both of you—you have everything. You're good at everything. You have good friends, you're good in sports, you get good grades. You're popular and you both have girlfriends. Everyone knows who you guys are, and they wish they could be more like you. I'm not like you two in any way. It's like I came from different parents."

"You've always been better," I said. "You're the sweetest person I've ever met."

"So what? No one cares about that."

I took her hand.

"What's really bothering you?"

She didn't want to answer. In the silence I looked around the room; like most teenage girls, she had various magazine pictures lining the walls. On her dresser was a collection of bells and ceramic horses. A Bible sat on her end table next to a rosary, and above her bed was a crucifix. It took a long time for her to get the words out.

"Holly got asked to the junior prom."

Holly was my sister's best friend; they'd been inseparable for years.

"That's good, isn't it?"

When she didn't answer, my heart sank as I suddenly realized why she was so upset.

"But you're upset because no one asked you."

She began to cry again and I slipped my arm around her. "You'll get asked," I said soothingly. "You're a great girl. You're beautiful and kind, and anyone who doesn't ask you is too dumb to realize what they're missing."

"You don't understand," she said. "You and Micah . . . well, all the girls think you're both cute. They always tell me how lucky I am that you're my brothers. But it's hard . . . I mean, no one ever says that I'm pretty."

"You are pretty," I insisted.

"No," she said, "I'm not. I'm average. And when I look in the mirror, I know that."

She continued to cry, and refused to say anything more. When I finally left the room, I realized for the first time that my sister struggled with the same insecurities everyone had. She had simply been hiding them all along. But as I walked away, I was certain that she'd get asked; I'd meant what I said to her.

But as the days rolled on, and no boy rode up on a horse to be her knight in shining armor, I could see the pain in her disappointed, wounded expression. It killed me to think that no one seemed to realize how special she was, how much love she could offer to anyone who simply asked. I adored my sister in the same way I'd always adored my brother, and—like my parents, I suppose—I felt the need to protect her.

So one evening, about a week before the prom, I went into my sister's room. If her friends thought I was handsome, if they thought I was popular, then I wanted nothing more than for them to see how much fun we could have together. To me, it made no difference that we were brother and sister; I would be *proud* to be seen with her and wanted the entire world to know it.

"Dana," I said seriously, "would you go to the prom with me?"

"Don't be silly," she said.

"We'll have fun," I promised. "I'll take you out to a fancy dinner, I'll rent a limousine, and we'll dance the night away. I'll be the best date you've ever had."

She smiled but shook her head. "No, that's okay. I don't want to go, anyway. I'm over it now. It doesn't matter."

I hesitated, trying to see if she meant it. "Are you sure? It would mean a lot to me."

"Yeah, I'm sure. But thank you for asking."

I looked at her. "You're breaking my heart, you know."

She gave a sad little laugh. "That's funny," she said. "It's exactly the same thing Micah said."

"What do you mean?"

"He asked me to the prom, too. Yesterday."

"And you're not going with him either?"

"No."

She wrapped her arms around me and gave me a hug. Then she kissed me on the cheek. "But I want you to know that you two are the best brothers that a sister could ever have. I get so proud when I think about you two. I'm the luckiest girl in the world, and I love you both so much."

My throat constricted. "Oh, Dana," I said, "I love you, too."

Questions and Explanations
for Chapter 10

The ten questions on chapter 10 focus on grammar and usage, vocabulary, comprehension, making inferences, literary terms, and characterization. Some of the questions combine two or more of these areas, requiring you to synthesize your knowledge, make inferences, and interpret the text. The questions are designed to determine both your current level of understanding of the memoir and your ability to answer higher-level questions.

The following sentence tests your ability to recognize grammar and usage errors. The sentence contains either a single error or no error at all. If the sentence contains an error, select the one underlined part that must be changed to make the sentence correct. If there is no error, select choice D.

1. During high school, <u>Micah's</u> relationship with Nicholas
   A
   <u>evolved, </u><u>they</u> became closer and have remained close
   BC
   ever since. <u>No error</u>
   D

Choice A tests the formation of the possessive. Choice B checks your knowledge of punctuation. Choice C checks pronoun choice.

To form the possessive case of a singular noun, whether it is a common noun or a proper noun, add an apostrophe and an s—for example, "Dana's, Jill's, Michael's."

Although choice B appears to be checking the verb tense, it is actually checking your knowledge on the use of a comma. If both groups of words before the comma and after the comma are complete thoughts and can stand alone as two independent clauses, then a comma by itself is not the correct way to punctuate the compound sentence—for example, "I read the paper, my wife made dinner." Both groups of words to the left and right of the comma are complete thoughts, so they need to be joined with a semicolon or a comma and a coordinating conjunction (*and, but, or, for, nor, so, yet*). Thus, the example should be "I read the paper, and my wife made dinner" or "I read the paper; my wife made dinner."

Choice C checks the use of *they*. The word *they* is a pronoun used as the subject (doer) of a verb—for example, "*They* ran; *they* played; *they* fought."

The following two questions test your vocabulary. Choose the word or set of words that, when inserted in the sentence, best fits the meaning of the sentence as a whole.

2. During his first couple of years of high school, Micah "had a _____ relationship with everyone in the family."

   A. beatific

   B. feral

   C. robust

   D. tenuous

This question tests both your comprehension and your vocabulary. *Beatific*, choice A, means displaying calmness and joy. *Feral*, choice B, means to be suggestive of a wild beast. *Robust*, choice C, means strong. And *tenuous*, choice D, means weak.

3. Because they were not _____ and overly harsh, the rules established by Mr. Sparks were usually _____ by his sons.

   A. draconian...followed

   B. severe...dismissed

   C. munificent...embraced

   D. ignoble...adopted

This question also tests your comprehension as well as your vocabulary. Because three of the four choices for the second blank are synonyms, determine how the brothers responded to their father's rules. If they were willing to accept them, then eliminate choice B. If not, choice B must be the correct answer.

Draconian, choice A, means unusually severe. *Munificent*, choice C, means very generous. And *ignoble*, choice D, means having low moral standards. Which of these words is the opposite of what their father's rules were?

Question 4 asks you to make an inference based on strong and thorough textual evidence.

4. What is the primary purpose of chapter 10?

    A. to describe Rarotonga of the Cook Islands

    B. to connect the brothers' time in the South Pacific to their high school years

    C. to foreshadow future conflicts

    D. to demonstrate how the brothers' friendship formed and developed

The word *primary* means main. Thus, although all of these things may exist in chapter 10, the most important purpose is the primary one. The first part of the chapter does detail the brothers' time on the island. You need to ask yourself, is the description of Rarotonga the focus of the time spent there on the island and of the chapter as a whole? If it is, select choice A. Choice B discusses the transition that is used to connect the present-day narrative to the flashback narrative. If the connection between the two is the most important part of the chapter, select choice B. Foreshadowing is an important and effective literary technique. You need to decide if it is the most important aspect of this chapter; if it is, select choice C. If the most important information—and main focus of the chapter—is the formation and development of the friendship between Nicholas and Micah that still exists today, select choice D.

Question 5 asks you to make an inference based on words used in context.

5. When describing the task of moving the entire tour group, Nicholas writes, "We'd usually been up for five hours with little to show for it." From this statement you can infer which of the following?

   A. Nicholas enjoys being an early riser.
   B. Nicholas likes the leisurely pace of travel.
   C. Nicholas is frustrated with the slow-moving pace.
   D. Nicholas is a demanding traveler.

The first part of the sentence, "We'd usually been up for five hours," is the statement of fact; the key phrase to understanding the sentence is "with little to show for it" because it reveals Nicholas's attitude. Having "little to show for it" clearly doesn't sound enjoyable or like something that he enjoys, so eliminate choice A and choice B. Choice C refers to the five hours that he has been awake without much having been accomplished, so it is a possibility. Although the information in choice D may be true, it is not indicated in the direct quotation, so you must eliminate choice D.

Question 6 tests your knowledge of literary terms.

6. Although the Mission Gang had an excellent reputation, Nicholas writes that "we shared a sort of Jekyll-and-Hyde-type existence." What literary device is he using to describe his friends?

   A. alliteration
   B. allusion
   C. analogy
   D. antithesis

Alliteration, choice A, is the repetition of a word's initial sound—for example, "Becky bought Bill a bad bugle." An *allusion*, choice B, is an indirect reference. Some of the most common types of allusions are historical, such as making a reference to Napoleon by saying that someone met his Waterloo; biblical, such as John Coffey in *The Green Mile* being a Christ figure; mythological, a reference to a Greek or Roman myth, such as someone having the Midas touch; and literary, a reference to a character in a work of literature, such as a couple being ill-fated like Romeo and Juliet. An *analogy*, choice C, is the illustration of an idea using something similar or more familiar—for example, "The biological mechanism of a working human heart is similar to the workings of a pump." *Antithesis*, choice D, is the contrast or the opposite of something—for example, "Glinda, the good witch, is often viewed as the antithesis of the Wicked Witch of the West."

Question 7 tests your knowledge of literary terms.

7. When Nicholas describes what they often did with fireworks, he writes, "We regularly blew up various friends' mailboxes, whooping with delight when they were launched into the air with big *kabooms*." What figure of speech is used to describe the sound?

   A. hyperbole

   B. metaphor

   C. onomatopoeia

   D. personification

Again, knowledge of literary terms is essential to answering this question. *Hyperbole*, choice A, is an overexaggeration used to make a point—for example, "Everyone who reads this learning guide will know what *hyperbole* is because hyperbole will be explained a bazillion times."

A *metaphor*, choice B, is a comparison made between two unlike things without using a connective word—for example, "LeBron James is an animal on the basketball court."

Onomatopoeia, choice C, is a word that suggests the very sound it describes, like *buzz*, *sizzle*, and *boom*.

Personification, choice D, is giving nonhuman things a human characteristic, such as in "Opportunity knocked on the door."

Question 8 asks you to make an inference based on strong and thorough textual evidence.

8. Based on the stories told in chapter 10, what inferences can you make regarding how the brothers viewed their father?

   A. They regretted having to spend time with him.

   B. They considered him a good listener.

   C. They respected his three rules.

   D. They were disappointed that he didn't attend their sporting events.

Recognize that more than one choice may be correct. If you find details and examples from the memoir to support the inference, select it, and if you find details and examples to contradict the choice, eliminate it.

Do the brothers share any good times they spent with their father? If yes, eliminate choice A. If not, select it. Did they have long, one-sided conversations with him, where they mostly talked, and end up leaving thinking he was incredibly smart? If yes, select choice B; if not, eliminate it. Micah followed his father's three rules. Does following rules demonstrate a type of respect for the rules? If so, select choice C; if not, eliminate it. Were the brothers bothered by their father's not being at cross-country and track meets? If yes, select choice D; if no, eliminate it.

Question 9 asks you to make an inference regarding character and thematic development.

9. The anecdote regarding scary movies and Nicholas's decision to allow his own son to watch *Silver Bullet* is presented primarily to demonstrate that:

   A. their father made bad decisions

   B. parenting strategies can't always be successfully duplicated across generations

   C. Nicholas's son Miles has a low threshold for fear

   D. *Silver Bullet* is a scarier movie than *Alien*

This question asks you to think about the anecdote and its significance. If you think it demonstrates that their father made poor parenting choices, select choice A. If you think it illustrates that what worked for Nicholas when he was a boy might not work for his own children, select choice B. If you think the focus of the anecdote is on Miles and his fears, select choice C. If you think the story primarily exists to compare horror movies across the generations, select choice D.

Question 10 checks your comprehension.

10. Which one of the following topics is NOT addressed in chapter 10?

   A. Their mother's response to their viewing of horror movies as kids.

   B. The brothers' stated financial goals.

   C. Dana's personal insecurities.

   D. Nicholas's admiration for Stephen King.

Three out of the four answers are addressed in the chapter, so they may be eliminated. Skim through the chapter to find the choices that you might not remember.

Chapter 11

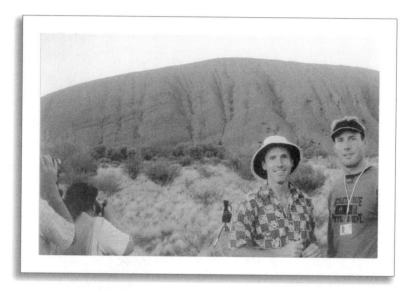

Ayers Rock, Australia
February 2–3

Unless you travel over the Pacific, it's hard to fathom how large the ocean actually is. We'd flown four hours to reach Easter Island, and another seven hours to Rarotonga. Reaching Brisbane, Australia, took another seven hours, during which we crossed over the international date line, and from there we still had another three hours until we finally reached Ayers Rock, in the Uluru–Kata Tjuta National Park, in the middle of the Australian outback.

Passing the international date line only served to make the journey longer. It's an odd feeling to realize that a day seems to have vanished from your life. Not only that, our stop in Brisbane took a couple of hours; all in all, it was over twelve hours en route, which struck me as amazing, considering that we'd already been halfway across the ocean when we started.

By the time we got to our hotel, everyone wore the look of weary travelers. In the lobby, it was possible to sign up for excursions the following day. While everyone would go to Ayers Rock in the afternoon, the morning was open. You could rent Harleys, for instance, and explore parts of the outback on your own, or take a helicopter ride over the Olgas—an outcropping of rock and canyons near Ayers Rock. There was also a walking tour through part of the Olgas as well, and a sunrise trip to Ayers Rock, which would leave the hotel before dawn.

Though my brother and I wanted to sleep, we somehow woke in time to join the sunrise expedition party. It was cool and pitch black in the desert; without lights, it was possible to see tens of thousands—if not millions—of stars. Our bus was one in a long line of buses that made their way out there that morning; we later found out that our hotel was large enough to room over three thousand guests. While this may not mean much in a city like Orlando or Chicago, in the middle of the outback, it's amazing. At any given moment, we learned, the hotel itself had a higher population than nearly every city for hundreds of miles in any direction.

Ayers Rock is the largest monolith, or single-unit stone, in the world. With a circumference of nearly five miles, it rises nearly a thousand feet in the air, and extends over three miles beneath the surface. In the predawn blackness, Ayers Rock was nothing but a darkened shadow, almost impossible to see unless you were looking directly toward it. Our disheveled group stumbled out of the bus and we made our way to the viewing area.

In time, light began glowing over the horizon, and as it slowly began to spread, our gaze was directed to the rock. Comprised of coarse-grained sandstone rich in feldspar, Ayers Rock was supposed to vary in color depending on the time of day and atmospheric conditions. Still, in the beginning anyway, it was difficult to understand why so many people found it fascinating; it had none of the fiery brilliance for which the rock had become famous. My brother and I took pictures, then more pictures, feeling disappointed. Soon, however, the sun rose high enough to brighten the eastern sky, and just when we came to the conclusion that the reputation of Ayers Rock was more hype than reality, it suddenly happened.

The sun hit the rock at such an angle that it began glowing red, like an enormous glowing coal. And for the next few minutes, all Micah and I could do was stare at it, thinking it was one of the most amazing things we'd ever seen.

Micah and I had opted for the helicopter ride instead of a walking tour through the Olgas, and by eight A.M. we were at the airport again, ready to depart.

There was, we learned, a good reason for taking the ride as early as we did. It was already hot by the time we arrived—it was summer in the desert, after all—and the canopy of the helicopter served only to intensify the heat. With five people crowded inside, everyone was sweating within moments of liftoff.

We were in the air a little more than thirty minutes, but it afforded us views impossible to see any other way. We circled Ayers Rock and flew over the Olgas; we spotted wild camels trailing through the desert. There were, we learned, tens of thousands of wild camels in Australia. They were nonindigenous—originally, they'd been imported for their survival skills to help settle the outback. A few had escaped and flourished; over time, the population had swelled. Nowadays, they were actually exported back to the Middle East.

Because of the rotating blades and the roar of the engine, conversation was impossible. But whenever I happened to glance back at Micah, I noticed that he never stopped smiling.

Once we returned from the helicopter ride, we had some free time until lunch, and we decided to go for a jog around the property.

With thousands of miles logged on our legs over the course of our lifetimes, jogging felt natural to both of us. Falling into a moderate clip, our strides quickly became synchronized.

"This is like old times," I said. "When we were back in high school."

"I was just thinking the same thing."

"How often do you jog these days?"

"Not too much," Micah answered. His breaths were even and steady. "I run when I play soccer, but if I try to do it every day, my back gets sore."

"I know what you mean. I used to run a fast twenty miles on Sundays, but these days I can't even imagine it. If I go four miles, I feel like I've really accomplished something."

"That's because we're getting older," he said. "Do you realize my twenty-year high school reunion is coming up in a few months?"

"Are you going?"

"I think so. It'll be fun to see everyone. But when I think of high school, I think about Mike, Harold, you, and Tracy. Now those were great times." For a while I listened to the sound of our feet on the compact dirt. "Do you remember when you and Harold went out on a double date that one time? When Tracy and I found you and had you roll down the car window so we could launch a bottle rocket into your car?"

I laughed. "How could I forget?" The thing had exploded at our feet, scaring the daylights out of us.

"Yeah, those are the memories that stay with me," he said. "Those guys were great, and they're the only ones I still really talk to anymore. It's hard to believe that it all happened twenty years ago."

After lunch and a shower, we headed back to Ayers Rock with the rest of our group. By then, the glare was relentless. It was over a hundred degrees, and with the sun high overhead, Ayers Rock was sandstone, its color unremarkable. Flies swarmed everywhere; you had to move continuously or they'd land on your lips or eyelashes, your arms and your back. There were *trillions* of flies. The tourists looked as if they'd taken wiggle pills.

Over the next few hours, the bus stopped in various places around Ayers Rock, which is regarded as sacred among the aborigines. We'd head out, walk around, listen to a story, then head back to the bus. We were led to some painted caves and a watering hole, where we were exposed to endless lectures about aboriginal history.

At the third or fourth stop, I turned to say something to Micah. His eyes were glassy and unfocused. At that point, we'd been listening to a story concerning one of the upper crevices on the rock. It had to do with a spirit warrior who got lost in the desert, only to fight a battle with another spirit, and somehow the images of the battle had been imprinted on the rock. This, in turn, led people to know where the watering hole was; they would search the rock for said image, thereby knowing they were close. Or something like that. The blistering heat was making me dizzy and it was difficult to keep all the characters in the legend straight.

"Have you ever noticed that the less interesting something is, the longer people want to talk about it?" Micah sighed, slapping at the buzzing flies.

"C'mon, it's interesting. It's a culture we know nothing about."

"The reason we don't know anything about it is because it's boring."

"It's not boring."

"It's a big rock in the middle of the desert."

"What about the colors?"

"We saw the colors this morning. In the daytime, it's a big rock. And I wasn't being eaten by flies or cooked in the sun while being subjected to endless stories about spirit battles."

"Doesn't it amaze you that people could actually survive out here for thousands of years?"

"It amazes me that they never left. What? You mean no aborigines ever wandered to the coast, saw the beaches and felt the cool breezes while catching fish for dinner, and said to themselves, '*Hey, maybe I should think about moving?*'"

"I think the heat's getting to you."

"Oh yeah, it's getting to me. I'm dying out here. I feel like buzzards are overhead, just waiting for me to drop my guard."

Late in the day, we headed *back* to Ayers Rock for the third time. This would be our chance to see how it changed colors at sunset.

"I'm beginning to get the impression that there's not much to do around here besides stare at Ayers Rock," Micah confided.

"It won't be so bad," I said. "I hear there's supposed to be original aborigine music tonight."

"Oh, gee," he said, throwing up his hands. "I can't wait."

As it turned out, that evening was one of the trip's most memorable. It began with a cocktail party—and yes, everyone stared at Ayers Rock when the sun started going down—but afterward we were led to a small clearing where tables had been set up, complete with white tablecloths, candle centerpieces, and beautiful floral arrangements; the setting was gorgeous and the food delicious. Among other things, on the buffet they had both kangaroo and crocodile meat, simmered in spices and cooked to perfection. The temperature cooled, and even the flies seemed to have vanished.

We ate in the desert under a slowly blackening sky; in time, the stars appeared in full. Later, the candles were blown out and an astronomer began to speak. Using a floodlight to point to various areas of the sky, she described the world above.

Not only was it dark and clear enough to make out individual stars in the vast sweep of the Milky Way, but because we were in the Southern Hemisphere, the sky was completely foreign to us. We were all spellbound. Instead of the Big Dipper and Polaris (the North Star), we saw the Southern Cross, and learned how sailors used it to navigate. Jupiter was closer to Earth than it had been in decades, and glowed bright in the sky. Saturn, too, was visible, making it the first time I'd ever seen both planets in the same sky. Even better, we found out that TCS had made arrangements for telescopes. That evening, I saw the moons of Jupiter and the rings of Saturn, and while I'd seen them in books I'd never seen them through a lens. It was a first for Micah, too.

On the way back to the hotel, he leaned his head back on the seat, the picture of contentment. "The morning was great, and the evening was the best on the trip so far."

"It's just the middle you could have done without, right?"

He smiled without opening his eyes. "You're reading my mind, little brother."

I leaned my head back and closed my eyes as well. No one on the bus was speaking; most seemed as relaxed as we were. In the silence, my mind wandered. The years had passed so quickly that I couldn't help but feel as if my life seemed surreal, almost like I were viewing it through someone else's eyes. Perhaps it was because of the evening I'd just spent, or maybe it was due to exhaustion, but in the midst of this foreign land I suddenly didn't feel like a thirty-seven-year-old author, or husband, or even a father of five. Instead, it almost seemed as if I were just starting out in the world and facing an uncertain future, similar to how I felt when I first stepped off the plane in South Bend, Indiana, in August 1984.

My first year at Notre Dame proved to be a challenge. For the first time in my life, I wasn't the smartest kid in class, and my studies were much harder than I imagined they would be. I studied an average of four hours a day and didn't do nearly as well as I'd hoped; over the next four years, the number of hours I studied would only increase.

I found it hard to be away from home. I missed my family and friends, I missed Lisa, and I didn't get along with my new roommate. Worst of all, the second week after I arrived, I strained my Achilles tendon, tried to train through the pain, and got a raging case of tendinitis. My Achilles swelled to the size of a golf ball. According to the doctors, the only thing that would allow it to heal was to stop running entirely.

By that point, running was the most important thing in my life, and the idea of not running was counter to everything I believed in. My dream was to follow in Billy Mills's footsteps; to represent the United States on the Olympic team and win the gold medal. I know now that even had I never been injured, the dream was an unattainable one. I might as well have wished to fly.

As I said, I was a good runner, but not a great one. I didn't have the natural foot speed or stamina to be world-class; indeed, I'd gotten as far as I had by training harder than most high schoolers. These realizations were only made in retrospect; at the time, the injury was devastating to me. For the first time in my life, I felt as if I were failing.

The injury raged on throughout the fall; in the winter it healed slightly before I reinjured it again. Around that time, Lisa and I broke up, high school sweethearts doomed by the distance between us. School continued to be a challenge, in part because my mind was elsewhere.

I somehow managed to scrape together a partial outdoor season, and even ended up breaking the school record as a member of one of the relay teams. It was my last meet of the year. By the time I finished the race, I could barely walk. My Achilles tendon had swollen to the size of a lemon. Any movement was excruciating; my tendon literally squeaked like a rusty hinge whenever I took a step. When I arrived back home for my summer break, I needed crutches to get off the plane.

I was miserable for the first few weeks of the summer. I had no job, no girlfriend, and because my brother had moved out, no one to hang around with. In addition, I was under doctor's orders not to run for three months, which would only put me further behind my peers.

My mom tried to come up with ways to cheer me up. At least, that's what she called it. "Paint the living room," she'd say, "it'll cheer you up." Or, "Sand the door so we can stain it a different color. It'll boost your spirits."

Had her ideas worked, I would have been the most cheerful kid on the planet. As it was, however, I simply moped around in paint-splattered clothes, working all day on various projects, and mumbling that all I wanted to do was run and wondering why God wouldn't help or listen to me. By mid-June, my mother had grown exasperated with my attitude, and, as I was lamenting my plight for the hundredth time at the kitchen table, finally shook her head.

"Your problem is that you're bored. You need to find something to do."

"I don't want to do anything but run."

"What if you can't?"

"What do you mean?"

"What if your injury never gets better? Or, even if it does, what if you can't train the way you want to anymore for fear of hurting it again? You don't want to spend your life doing nothing."

"Mom . . ."

"Hey, I'm just offering up the obvious here. I know it wouldn't be fair, but no one ever said that life was fair."

I lowered my head to the table.

"Oh no," she said firmly, "you're not going to just sit here at the table and keep acting this way. Don't just pout. Do something about it."

"Like what?"

"It's your life."

I raised my head in frustration. "Mom..."

"I don't know," she said with a shrug. Then she looked at me and said the words that would eventually change my life. "Write a book."

Until that moment, I'd never considered writing. Granted, I read all the time, but actually sitting down and coming up with a story on my own? The very notion was ridiculous. I knew nothing about the craft, I had no burning desire to see my words in print. I'd never taken a class in creative writing, had never written for the yearbook or school newspaper, nor did I suspect I had some sort of hidden talent when it came to composing prose. Yet, despite all those things, the notion was somehow appealing, and I found myself answering, "Okay."

The next morning, I sat down at my dad's typewriter, rolled in the first sheet of paper, and began to write. I chose horror as a genre and conjured up a character who caused accidental death wherever he went. Six weeks and nearly three hundred pages later, after writing six or seven hours a day, I'd finished. To this day, I can remember typing the final sentence, and I don't know that I'd ever felt a higher sense of accomplishment with anything I'd done in my life.

The only problem was the book. It was terrible and I knew it. It was atrocious in every sense of the word, but in the end, what did it matter? I didn't intend for it to be published; I'd written it to see if I could. Even then, I knew there was a big difference between starting a novel and actually finishing one. Even more surprising, I found that I'd actually enjoyed the process.

I was nineteen years old and had become an accidental author. It's funny the way things happen in life.

*   *   *

Because I was away from home eight months a year, my brother and I had little time to see each other. Micah continued to spend weekends trying new and exciting things. Meanwhile, my injury continued to plague me; I ran neither cross-country nor track, but concentrated on making a comeback.

I'd made good friends with a few other freshmen the year before, some of whom were on the track team, and they became the ones I would depend on to get me through yet another challenging year. But I'd learned something by heading off to college. My dependence on family had diminished more than it had for either my brother or sister. Dana still lived at home and was a freshman in college; though Micah was living in his own apartment, he still made it home three or four times a week. Whenever I called home, it always seemed as if he was there.

Soon after I'd left for my sophomore year, my mom mentioned that Brandy wasn't doing well. She was twelve years old—not old for some breeds, but ancient for a Doberman—and I could hear the concern in my mom's voice. My mom loved her, as we all did, and when I pressed my mom, her answers were slightly evasive.

"Well, she's lost a little weight, and her arthritis seems to be getting worse."

When I came home for fall break, I was shocked by Brandy's appearance. I hadn't seen her in two months but in those two months she'd gone from being relatively healthy to a walking skeleton. Her stomach caved in, and it was possible to count her ribs from across the room. As she slowly wandered toward me, I could see the happy recognition in her eyes. Her tail—bone thin and nearly hairless—waved a slow greeting. I crouched down and stroked her softly, feeling her shake and tremble beneath my hand. I swallowed the lump in my throat.

I spent most of the next two days with the dog, sitting beside her and patting her gently. I knew even then that she wouldn't last until Christmas; I murmured quietly to her, reminding her of all the adventures we'd had together growing up.

The day before I was to head back to Notre Dame, we woke to find that Brandy had died.

My brother and I held back our tears as we went to get our sister. Dana made no pretense of being tough, and began to sob immediately. It was the sound of her wailing that made my brother and me both begin to cry as well, and later that morning, with tears stinging our eyes, we dug a hole in the backyard and buried her. She was gone now except for memories that we would hold forever.

"She waited until you were home," Micah said earnestly. "I think she must have known you were coming back and wanted to see you one last time."

Years later, we discovered the truth of what happened to Brandy. Brandy, we learned, hadn't really died in her sleep. She'd died at the veterinarian's office earlier that morning, with my mother holding her tight as the final injection was administered. Afterward, while we were still sleeping, my mom had brought Brandy back home and placed her in the bed for us to find. She didn't want us to know that Brandy had been put down; she wanted the three of us to believe that Brandy had died peacefully in her sleep. My mom knew we would have been devastated by the idea of putting her to sleep, and thought it was important to spare our feelings.

Even though we were grown, even though she'd always stressed toughness, she didn't want Brandy's death to be harder on us than it had to be.

I had surgery on both my Achilles and my foot in April of my sophomore year. Both my Achilles and plantar fascia (a tendon that runs along the bottom of the foot) had been severely damaged by intensive training. It was touch-and-go as to whether I would ever run again. With the dream still burning, I went through rehab and began jogging in July. By mid-August, I was running without pain for the first time in years. I trained hard and was soon recording the fastest training times I'd ever run in the past; in the second hard workout of the day, for instance, I clipped through five miles in a little more than twenty-three minutes and was never out of breath.

By October, though, the pain was back and getting worse, and I had a cortisone injection at the site of the old injury. An anti-inflammatory, it numbs the area and I kept on running. When the pain came back six weeks later, I got another cortisone shot. Soon, I was getting them monthly, but I salvaged a respectable season nonetheless. By summer, I needed to receive cortisone injections weekly to continue training—I'd had nearly thirty injections since the surgery—and I had to gear myself up for one last season. Both my Achilles and plantar fascia were swollen. As I limped out to the track for a workout, I remember realizing with a sense of clear-eyed finality that I simply couldn't do it anymore.

I hung up my shoes for good, feeling sadness and—strangely—relief. With the exception of breaking a school record that still stands after nineteen years, I'd failed to reach the other goals I'd set for myself. But despite the fact that running had been the defining force in my life for the previous seven years, I knew that I'd survive without it.

I'd given it my best shot, but it wasn't meant to be. And if I had to do it all over—and fail to reach my dream again—I would. When you chase a dream, you learn about yourself. You learn your capabilities and limitations, and the value of hard work and persistence.

When I told my dad about my decision—sharing my disappointment as well as relief in knowing that I'd finally made a decision—he put his arm around my shoulder.

"Everyone has dreams," he said. "And even if yours didn't work out the way you wanted, it doesn't make me any less proud of you. Too many people never really try."

That year, my mom finally got the horse she'd always wanted. A three-year-old Arabian, she named it Chinook.

Chinook was boarded at a stable near the American River, and my mom would drop in to feed and groom the horse before and after work. She could spend hours brushing Chinook's coat, cleaning her stable, and cleaning the mud from her hooves.

Although there were riding trails along the American River, it was months before my mom could ride her. Chinook had lived most of her life in a pasture (along with a goat) and had never had so much as a saddle placed on her back, which was a big part of the reason my mom could afford to buy her. She was high-strung like many Arabians, but my mom had a natural talent when it came to calming her. Soon, Chinook allowed my mom to saddle her; when she got used to that, my mom finally crawled on. Chinook didn't seem to like it, but my mom was patient, and I remember the joy in my mom's voice one day when she called me on the phone.

"I rode Chinook for hours today!" she said. "You can't believe how wonderful it was."

"I'm happy for you, Mom," I said. My mom had lived a life of sacrifice, her own dreams always coming second to ours. I couldn't help but feel it was finally time that she got something that made her happy.

Later, she would get a second horse named Napoleon. Napoleon was good-natured and even-tempered; the kind of horse that was perfect for my father. And surprising me, my father agreed to go riding as well.

Though my dad was never comfortable in the saddle, I think it was his way of showing my mom that he was willing to work on the marriage. Years of emotional distance had strained their relationship, and Micah sometimes mentioned that he thought my mom had nearly reached the breaking point. Where once she was willing to stay married for the sake of the children, she now sometimes wondered aloud whether she would be happier without my dad. I don't know if either my mom or my dad ever seriously considered divorce; I do know, however, that my mom spoke the word with increasing frequency, both on the phone and around the house. And my dad, no doubt, had heard her speak of it as well.

Rapprochement is always difficult; when distance has grown over the years, it's sometimes impossible to overcome. Yet, horseback riding together offered my parents a way to do just that, and little by little my parents seemed to enjoy a budding sense of renewal between them.

My brother continued to live his carefree existence. After graduation from college in 1987, he and a friend went to Europe, and bicycled around Spain, France, and Italy for nearly a month.

Upon his return, he shared stories about the adventure before taking a trip to the mountains to go white-water rafting.

In August, he began working full-time as a commercial real estate broker; he continued to date energetically. He brought a different girl home every couple of weeks to meet our parents, and every date seemed crazy about him. In time, my mom called me with the news that he'd brought a particular girl over twice. For Micah, that was just about the closest thing to a steady girlfriend he'd had in years. And when he brought her by a *third* time, I think my mom knew it was serious.

At Notre Dame, I was edging toward a degree in business finance, with the hope of attending law school after graduation. In March of 1988, a few friends and I decided to drive down to Florida for our final spring break. Because one of my roommate's fathers owned a condominium on Sanibel Island, we opted to go there instead of the usual destinations like Daytona or Fort Lauderdale.

On our second night there, I noticed a woman walking with a couple of girlfriends through the parking lot of the condominium.

She was attractive—but so was practically everyone after an evening on the town—and she quickly passed from my mind. A moment later, however, when my friends and I had almost reached the lobby, we heard voices calling down to us from the external hallway on the sixth floor.

"Hey, are you guys staying here?"

When we looked up, we noticed the same three girls.

"Yes," we answered.

"Well, we're supposed to meet a couple of friends, but they're not here yet, and we *really* have to go to the bathroom. Can we use yours?"

"Sure!" we shouted. "We're on the eighth floor."

They came up and introduced themselves as seniors from the University of New Hampshire, and we let them in our room to use the bathroom. A moment later, the three of them stood in the kitchen, but my eyes were glued to the woman I had noticed earlier. Up close, she had the most beautiful eyes I'd ever seen, so unusual in color they almost looked unreal. It was all I could do not to stare.

"Hi," I finally said. "I'm Nick."

She smiled. "Hey Nick. I'm Cathy."

I would love to tell you that the initial attraction was mutual, but I'd be lying if I did. The girls stayed in our room for a half hour or so and invited us down to their friends' place. While we were there, I got their phone number from one of Cathy's friends and promised to call the next day to see if they wanted to hang out at the beach behind the condominium.

When they decided to join us the following morning, I was palpably nervous about seeing Cathy again. I hoped I'd made a good impression on her, and when I saw her and her friends coming toward us on the beach, I quickly rose to greet them.

"Hey," I said eagerly, "I'm glad you could come."

To which Cathy replied, "Oh, hey, I'm Cathy. I didn't meet you last night, did I?"

Despite the ego bruising, I wasn't about to be deterred. We ended up talking for hours. When they mentioned that they were going out to a nearby nightclub, I talked my reluctant roommates into going and immediately sought out Cathy. After dancing with her for an hour, I leaned in and said, "You know, you and I are going to get married one day."

She just laughed in disbelief and said, "I think you need another beer."

*   *   *

How could I tell so quickly that she was the one for me? It was an odd intuitive moment, but I can honestly say that *I knew*.

We had a lot in common. Like me, she was a senior who was earning a degree in business. Like me, she was Catholic and went to church every Sunday. She was also a middle child, though one of four. Like me, she had an older brother and a younger sister. Her parents, like mine, were poor before attaining middle-class status, had never been divorced, and—how's this for coincidence—shared the *same* anniversary as my parents (August 31). She was an athlete (a state champion in gymnastics). She wanted children, as did I, and she wanted to stay home to raise them, as I hoped my wife would.

But most of all, what really attracted me to her was her *manner*. She laughed a lot, and it's easy to fall for someone who can find humor in any situation. She was also intelligent, well read, and well spoken, willing to listen and confident in her beliefs. And most of all, she was warm. She treated my friends as if they'd been her friends for years, would wave and smile at both children and the elderly. She seemed genuinely interested in everyone.

I had noticed all of these things about her, and as we were dancing, it struck me that she was everything I wanted in a life-long companion.

When I got back to Notre Dame, I called my brother.

"Micah," I said, "I met the girl I'm going to marry."

"Where? When? Weren't you just on spring break?"

"Yeah. That's where I met her."

"Dude," he said, "you were on spring break. What the hell are you thinking about marriage for?"

"Just wait until you meet her."

"But it was spring break!"

"I know," I said gleefully. "Isn't it great?"

In the two months leading up to graduation, I wrote Cathy a hundred letters. She came out to visit me at Notre Dame twice, and on the day of my graduation, my parents came to visit Notre Dame for the first time. While I showed them around the place that had been my home for the previous four years, I talked mainly about Cathy and how much she'd come to mean to me in the previous two months. After graduation, while my parents flew back home, I traveled to New Hampshire to see Cat graduate. I was introduced to her parents, and ten days later I brought her to Sacramento to meet my parents.

My mom and dad greeted her with immediate hugs, and Cathy remained in the kitchen talking to my mom for an hour. That night, after Cathy had gone to bed, my mom declared, "Cathy's wonderful. She's even better than you described."

I thought my heart would burst. "I'm glad you like her, Mom," was all I said.

After graduation in May 1988, my first thought was, *what now?*

For years, I'd been a student and an athlete and had pursued those goals with an unwavering intensity. I had done as I was told, I had followed the rules. Yet, all of a sudden, both worlds were behind me, and I found myself adrift. I had no idea who I was, what I wanted to do, or where my future would lead. I'd always believed that because I'd followed the rules the world would beat a path to my doorstep. But the world didn't seem to care at all.

Despite graduating with high honors, I wasn't accepted to any of the law schools to which I'd applied, and so that door was closed even before it opened. All my friends had taken corporate jobs in New York or Chicago, but those jobs also tended to be close to the places they'd grown up. I, too, wanted to go home, and with my head filled with foggy notions of the future, I found myself on a plane back to Sacramento. My first job was waiting tables. Even with a degree, I found myself earning minimum wage.

In the meantime, I began exploring careers, trying to find an area that interested me. Though I was confused, I wasn't particularly worried, and by the time Cathy moved to Sacramento in August, I'd finally made the decision to try my hand at appraising real estate. Around the same time, Micah and I purchased two small rental houses in a run-down area of town, repaired them, and were renting them out as well. In the little spare time remaining, I wrote a second novel, titled *The Royal Murders*, an old-fashioned whodunit. I knew, however, it wasn't good enough to be published.

I began working for a local firm as an appraiser's apprentice by day while continuing to wait tables and write at night, and eventually saved enough money to buy a small diamond ring. On her birthday, October 12, 1988, I proposed to Cathy on bended knee, and she said yes.

A few days later, I asked Micah to be my best man, thinking that not only had he been by my side throughout our youth, but that he would continue to be by my side, no matter where the future took us.

Questions and Explanations
for Chapter 11

The ten questions on chapter 11 focus on grammar and usage, vocabulary, comprehension, literary terms, characterization, and style. Some of the questions combine two or more of these areas, requiring you to synthesize your knowledge, make inferences, and interpret the text. The questions are designed to determine both your current level of understanding of the memoir and your ability to answer higher-level questions.

The following sentence tests your ability to recognize grammar and usage errors. The sentence contains either a single error or no error at all. If the sentence contains an error, select the one underlined part that must be changed to make the sentence correct. If there is no error, select choice D.

1. Jill explains to Nicholas that many people have <u>less</u>
   A
   problems in <u>their</u> lives <u>than</u> he has. <u>No error</u>
   B   C   D

Choice A checks if you can differentiate between *less* and *fewer*. The word *less* is used to indicate a smaller quantity, and *fewer* is used to indicate a smaller number of individual things. Usually, a good rule of thumb is to use *less* before a singular noun and *fewer* before a plural noun. Thus, many grocery store checkouts with the signs FIFTEEN ITEMS OR LESS are incorrect.

Choice B tests your knowledge of the homophones *their*, *there*, and *they're*. *Their* is a possessive pronoun, showing joint ownership—for example, "This is their house." *There* is an adverb of place—for example, "Put it there." *There* is also an expletive, or a word used to get a sentence started—for example, "There is primarily one reason that Nicholas decides to start writing." *They're* is a contraction for the words *they are*—for example, "They're going to the beach." And if you determine that *their* is the correct homophone, make sure the noun that is showing possession is plural—for example, "Micah and Nicholas decide to try their hands at fixing up houses."

And choice C asks you to differentiate between *than* and *then*. *Than* is used to compare and contrast—for example, "*The Last Song* is a longer novel than *A Walk to Remember*." The word *then* is used when something follows or results from something else—for example, "Read the chapter, and then answer the questions."

The following two questions test your vocabulary. Choose the word or set of words that, when inserted in the sentence, best fits the meaning of the sentence as a whole.

2. "Unless you travel over the Pacific, it's hard to _____ how large the ocean actually is."

   A. abate

   B. condole

   C. declaim

   D. fathom

This question tests your comprehension as well as your vocabulary. *Abate*, choice A, means to decrease. *Condole*, choice B, means to grieve. *Declaim*, choice C, means to speak loudly. *Fathom*, choice D, means to comprehend.

3. In order to _____ its importance to development of both character and theme, Sparks wrote a single-sentence paragraph that _____ drew attention to that sentence and foreshadowed future events.

   A. divulge...often

   B. reveal...singularly

   C. minimize...surprisingly

   D. emphasize...simultaneously

This question tests your vocabulary as well as your analytical skills. Understanding the effects of a single-sentence paragraph will enable you to more easily fill in the blanks. Obviously a single-sentence paragraph is not standard; thus, it doesn't make sense to claim that this sentence has minimized importance, thus choice C can be eliminated.

Choice B can also be eliminated, because the word *singularly* refers to one thing, yet two effects are occurring, drawing attention and foreshadowing.

When deciding between choice A and choice D, compare the resulting sentences when the word substitutions are made. Although *divulge* (which means to reveal) may make sense, the more specific word in this case is *emphasize* (choice D), which means to lay stress upon. And doing two things at once, *simultaneously*, is exactly what the single-sentence paragraph is doing.

Question 4 tests your knowledge of literary terms.

4. When describing the number of flies near Ayers Rock, Nicholas writes, "There were *trillions* of flies." Although this may possibly be true, he is probably using which figure of speech for emphasis?

   A. allusion

   B. hyperbole

   C. metaphor

   D. personification

An *allusion*, choice A, is an indirect reference. Some of the most common types of allusions are historical, such as making a reference to Napoleon by saying that someone met his Waterloo; biblical, such as John Coffey in *The Green Mile* being a Christ figure; mythological, a reference to a Greek or Roman myth, such as someone having the Midas touch; and literary, a reference to a character in a work of literature, such as a couple being ill-fated like Romeo and Juliet.

Hyperbole, choice B, is an obvious and intentional exaggeration—for example, "I've been waiting here for ages."

A *metaphor*, choice C, is a comparison made between two unlike things without using a connective word—for example, "LeBron James is an animal on the basketball court."

Personification, choice D, is giving nonhuman things a human characteristic, such as in "Opportunity knocked on the door."

Question 5 asks you to make an inference regarding character development.

5. Their mother's decision to hide the truth from her children regarding Brandy's death indicates that:

   A. she didn't think they were strong enough to know the truth

   B. she didn't care enough about her children to tell them

   C. she was more concerned with her own grief than with theirs

   D. she felt she was doing the right thing to protect her children from unnecessary grief

When analyzing a character, you need to think not only about what a character does, but also about the motivation behind the action. If you think the mother believes that her children couldn't handle the truth, select choice A. If you think that the mother didn't really care for her children, select choice B. If she was more focused on her own grieving process, select choice C. And if she was continuing her role as mother as protector, doing something that she thought was truly in the best interest of her children, select choice D.

Question 6 tests your knowledge of literary terms.

6. When describing his Achilles tendon injury, Nicholas writes, "my tendon literally squeaked like a rusty hinge whenever I took a step." What is the figure of speech that he is using to help readers understand what it was like?

   A. hyperbole

   B. metaphor

   C. onomatopoeia

   D. simile

Hyperbole, choice A, is an exaggerated statement used to heighten effect and to emphasize a point—for example, "This learning guide has defined *hyperbole* a million times already." A *metaphor*, choice B, is a comparison made between two unlike things without using a connective word—for example, "LeBron James is an animal on the basketball court." *Onomatopoeia*, choice C, is a word that suggests the very sound it describes, like the noise made by the breakfast cereal Rice Krispies (*Snap, Crackle, Pop*) or the sound of a firework explosion—*kaboom.*

And a *simile*, choice D, is a comparison between two unlike things using a connective word, such as *like, as,* or *than*—for example, "My love is like a red, red rose."

Question 7 asks you to determine the meaning of words as they are used in the text.

7. When Nicholas tells his father of his decision to abandon running, his father replies, "Too many people never really try." His father's statement indicates that:

A. he is unable to provide a personal response, so he speaks in generalizations

B. he believes the attempt is as important—if not more so—than the outcome

C. he really thinks Nicholas is a quitter but is too nice to say so directly

D. he never cared for his son's athletic endeavors

In order to answer this question, you need to consider the context of the situation. Nicholas is disappointed yet relieved with his decision; he is at peace with it. Recall how his father responds, and consider what he does as well as what he says. If his father cannot and does not respond personally, select choice A. If his father echoes Nicholas's thoughts about the value of pursuing a dream and what is learned along the way, select choice B. If his father is truly disappointed in his son and is speaking indirectly, select choice C. If his father had no interest whatsoever in his son's running, select choice D.

Question 8 checks your comprehension.

8. Who first suggests to Nicholas that he should "write a book"?

   A. Micah

   B. Dana

   C. his mother

   D. his father

Nicholas Sparks wrote that these words "would eventually change my life," so clearly they are extremely important. If you don't remember who said this to him, skim through the chapter until you find the section when Nicholas returns home after his first year at Notre Dame.

Question 9 asks you to make an inference based on strong and thorough textual evidence.

9. After completing his studies at Notre Dame, Nicholas somewhat felt adrift in the world. At this time, what was the one thing in his life that he felt most confident about?

    A. his blossoming writing career

    B. his job appraising real estate

    C. working with Micah renovating houses

    D. his relationship with Cathy

Consider Nicholas's own appraisal of his second novel. If after completing it he knew for certain this was the direction his life would take, select choice A. If his newfound career seems to be pointing him in the direction that he thinks will lead him to future success and happiness, select choice B. If working with Micah provides a sense of purpose and fulfillment, select choice C. And if Cathy's moving out West to be near him results in their planning to make a life together, select choice D.

Question 10 asks you to analyze an author's style.

10. Chapter 11 closes with Nicholas asking Micah to be his best man. Nicholas explains this decision, noting that "he would continue to be by my side, no matter where

the future took us." Stylistically the closing to the chapter achieves which of the following effects?

A. Its subtle foreshadowing continues the placement of good and bad side by side.

B. It obliquely references the trip they will take together, combining both narrative threads.

C. It parallels the uncertainty that Nicholas himself was feeling at the time.

D. It states quite clearly the nature of the brothers' relationship.

E. all of the above

The question indicates that more than one answer is correct.

Even though the sentence may appear to be solely positive, if you can detect a subtle undertone that hints at tough times to come, select choice A. If Micah is literally by his brother's side during the trip around the world—a trip that at the time they had no idea they would be taking—select choice B. If Nicholas has some sense of uncertainty about his future—not that he was worried, but rather he wasn't exactly sure where he was going— then select choice C. If the sentence unequivocally states that the brothers will remain close throughout their lives, select choice D.

Chapter 12

Angkor, Cambodia
February 4–5

The temples at Angkor, Cambodia—an area encompassing nearly 120 square miles—were built from A.D. 879 to 1191 when the Khmer empire was at its zenith. More than a hundred temples have been discovered, and they were once surrounded by cities, from which the kings of the empire ruled over a domain that covered a vast portion of Southeast Asia, including Burma, Thailand, Laos, Vietnam, southern China, and Cambodia. Their rule lasted nearly five hundred years, until 1432, when the Siamese (Thai) sacked Angkor, and the capital was moved south to Phnom Penh. Angkor never regained its former stature, and eventually drifted into obscurity as the jungle continued its never-ending encroachment. In time, Angkor passed into legend—people who saw the ruins claimed they'd been built by the gods—and a few adventurous explorers from Europe circulated stories about the famous ruins among their peers. It wasn't until 1860 that the French explorer Henri Mouhot brought Angkor back to the world's attention.

The French were enchanted by the ruins and began an extensive restoration effort. Yet all that remained of Angkor were the temples themselves, which are regarded as one of mankind's greatest architectural achievements. The cities, whose buildings were constructed of wood, had long since decayed and vanished into the surrounding jungle.

The vast majority of the temples in the Angkor region are Hindu in influence; the remainder are Buddhist. At the time of their construction, both belief systems were prevalent in the empire, and as rulers came and went—Buddhists replaced by Hindus, and vice versa—temples were constructed to reflect the changing times. Still, the architecture varied only slightly; most contained a temple-mountain-like structure in the center, surrounded by square or circular walls or platforms, and enclosed within either a moat or perimeter wall.

Angkor Wat, literally "City Temple," is not only the largest temple in the Angkor complex, but the largest religious monument in existence. Constructed during the first half of the twelfth century by Suryavarman II, it's regarded as the high point of Khmer architecture. The carvings on the outer walls depict important scenes from Hindu literature, as well as events from the reign of Suryavarman II, in exacting, intricate detail. To study and fully understand the relief carvings—on walls twelve feet high and spanning over a kilometer in length—would take years. Entire books have been written on the subject of the carvings alone, and it's far beyond the scope of this volume to even attempt to comment on them.

As they say, you must see it to believe it.

The flight to Cambodia was another seven hours, and I began to grasp what a feat traveling around the world really was. In the end, we would fly 36,000 miles and spend nearly three full days in the air.

I wasn't sure what to expect when I reached Cambodia. Though I'd traveled to Hong Kong and Korea for track competitions, I wasn't prepared for the city of Phnom Penh when we landed. In a strange way, the land struck me as being both hopeful and tragic. The main thoroughfare bustled like cities around the world, but instead of cars, people drove scooters. Beyond the tenement housing were shiny new high-rises; for every man in a business suit, I saw another who'd lost a leg from the land mines that still dot the countryside. Everywhere I looked, I saw the contradiction of the country; a country struggling to put its past behind it in order to secure a more prosperous future.

Our stop in Phnom Penh was a short one. We would go to the National Museum and the Royal Palace before going straight back to the airport for our flight to Angkor.

The National Museum, I thought, was also representative of Cambodia. Outside the gates were numerous beggars, pleading with tourists for pocket change; inside were other reminders of the war that had raged for decades. Though the museum was filled with collectibles and statues of various Indian gods (Shiva, Vishnu, and Brahma), there was no glass in any of the windows. Everything inside was thus exposed to the elements; the windows had been destroyed in the war a quarter of a century earlier and there was no money to replace them. Few, if any, of the items on display were bolted down; instead, objects had simply been set on pedestals. Most of the statues were broken, and bullet holes dotted the crumbling plaster walls. The ceiling was lined with water marks, and stains ran down the walls. The floor was bare concrete.

Yet the guides spoke with pride in their voices about the museum, the culture, and the spirit of their people, and by the time we left, both my brother and I were subdued. Of all the places we'd been to up to that point, Cambodia seemed the most foreign and incomprehensible, and we both felt out of place.

We then toured the Royal Palace, which is actually a series of roughly twenty buildings and temples inside a walled compound the size of a city block. One building is the palace itself, where the king lives; another building is the Welcome Hall, a magnificent structure with high painted ceilings, long red carpet, and soaring columns, where dignitaries are brought when they want an audience with the king. In a nearby temple, still on the palace grounds, we saw the giant Silver Buddha. Unlike many of the cultural artifacts, it hadn't been destroyed in the war and it seemed to occupy a central place in the heart of Cambodians, surrounded as it was by hundreds of small offerings of flowers.

Our stop in Phnom Penh was less than three hours, though it seemed far longer. With the weight of the past bearing down on us, we set off for the jungles of Angkor, where we would arrive just after sundown.

The main road from the Angkor airport also leads to the temples, and massive hotels sprouted amid what was once jungle. The splendor of some of these establishments was dizzying (in any country in the world, they would be regarded as five-star hotels). Gleaming structures were surrounded by lavishly designed and softly lit landscaping. Towering palms and lush ferns bordered winding entry roads; flowers sprouted everywhere the eye could see. Half a dozen hotels boasted rooms that cost more than the average Cambodian earned in a year; some had health and beauty spas, and all had upscale restaurants that required jackets.

All this, while on the road out front people rode bicycles or scooters.

At our hotel, we were informed that an excursion to Angkor Wat was planned at sunrise. Most people, including Micah, opted out. It was the first and only time on the entire trip that Micah and I weren't together to see a sight. And aside from only a few moments here and there, it was the first time we hadn't been together in nearly two weeks.

On the bus ride over, I was asked by one of the members of our tour group how we were getting along.

"Fine," I said. "Micah's easy to travel with."

"Doesn't it bother you? I mean, that you're with him *all* the time?"

I thought about it, finally realizing how odd it must have

seemed. "Actually, it doesn't. We always seem to want to do the same thing—I guess we're just in sync."

"That's amazing," he said, shaking his head. "You guys get along better than most husbands and wives. If you watch closely, you can tell that some couples are already starting to get a little tired of each other."

I was anxious to see Angkor Wat. The structure itself—square with a towering temple-mountain in the center, three concentric quadrangular enclosures, and surrounding walls approximately 275 yards in length, all surrounded by a giant moat—is reached via a long causeway, and we made our way toward the outer walls. Just beyond them, our guide told us to stop. In the darkness, we could see nothing at all.

In time, the sky behind the temple began glowing red, then fanned out in vivid orange, then finally yellow. Against the changing sky, the temple was outlined by shadows, the features invisible. Yet I couldn't look away. Even from a distance and despite reading about it, the size of Angkor Wat nonetheless gave me pause. Had it been built recently, it would be considered massive. When it was built eight hundred years ago, it must have defied comprehension.

We stayed long enough to watch the sky turn from yellow to blue, and then climbed back onto the bus. As we drove, the countryside of Angkor began springing to life. The roads became crowded with scooters, zipping nimbly around the lumbering bus. There seemed to be no driving regulations; people drove on either side, wove in and out of traffic, and veered at the last second, but somehow it seemed to work.

The scooter riders were, in their own way, as impressive as

Angkor Wat. We learned that most of the scooters had been manufactured in China and cost around six hundred dollars. No bigger than a moped, they were Cambodia's version of a Chevy Suburban.

"There's four people on that scooter!" one person said, and everyone on the bus would pile toward the window to see it.

"Over here, there's five!" another would shout, and we'd all move to the windows on the other side of the bus.

"I see six!"

"No way!"

"Back there! Look!"

We did. I blinked at the sight of a scooter with six people on it; it was moving slowly, but moving nonetheless, veering like everyone else.

"You're not going to believe this," someone finally said. "Up ahead of us. Take a look."

"What?"

He pointed. "I count *seven* on that one."

And there were. A man was seated in the middle; on the scooter were what seemed to be his kids. Two little girls were seated behind the father, three more little kids were in front of him. And riding on his shoulders was his son, the youngest of the bunch, a child who looked to be about five. All were dressed in uniforms; it seemed obvious that dad was bringing the kids to school.

While we continued on toward the hotel, everyone on the bus looked unsuccessfully for a scooter carrying eight people. As if, in this remarkable environment, seven weren't enough.

Because of the heat and humidity in Cambodia, our day was divided into two segments. In the morning, we'd visit the other temples and sights—Ta Prohm, the Bayon, and the Elephant

314

Terrace. After lunch, we'd spend a few hours at the hotel. Later in the afternoon, we'd visit Angkor Wat.

Our first stop was Ta Prohm, and despite the grandiosity of Angkor Wat, it would be our favorite temple to visit. It wasn't large and lay pretty much in ruins, but the jungle growth intrigued us. Shrouded in shade, the giant roots of strangler figs and silk cotton wove around doorways and crept over walls as if the roots had been poured from the trunk. It seemed as if the jungle was in the act of devouring the temple, as it had once swallowed all the others.

The roots were unstoppable. Though the giant ones caught our attention first, closer inspection revealed the finer roots forcing their way between blocks; in time, the block would eventually be loosened. In a couple of decades, those blocks would be found on the ground with the countless others that were piled around us.

The temple, though in a terrible state of disrepair, had somehow maintained its original shape. Like all of the temples we would see, it had four concentric square walls (actually tunnels) surrounding a temple-mountain, and we gradually wove our way through the ruins toward the center. Unlike so many of the sites we'd visited, as soon as we rounded the corner, it was easy to lose sight of the others in our group.

"This is great!" Micah said.

"It's amazing, isn't it?"

"It reminds me of the Indiana Jones and the Temple of Doom ride at Disneyland."

"You're such a crass American," I complained.

"Don't you think it does? Or, it could be a movie set. Like someone had imagined what a ruined temple looked like, then built it. It looks too real to be real."

"Too real to be real?"

"Exactly," he nodded. "Like someone *planned* it."

Forty minutes later, we were back on the bus; our next stop was the Bayon. There the jungle had been cut back and we made our way through the ruins. Unlike the heat in Australia, the heat in Angkor was intensified by the humidity. Mosquitoes were prevalent, and we slathered on the bug spray.

The Bayon was unremarkable when compared to Ta Prohm. It had the same configuration as the others, though we did see our first examples of the relief carvings for which the temples are famous. In the sandstone, we could make out various images, each of which came with a story.

The stories, however, were hard to follow. Of all the languages in the countries we visited, Cambodian seemed most foreign. The linguistic sounds were so different that simple words were incomprehensible. Thus, whenever the guides spoke, even in English, we had to sift through heavy accents and long pauses as our Cambodian guides stumbled over words. It was not only hard for us to understand what they were saying, but they had an equally difficult time understanding us.

"Why do they call them relief carvings instead of just carvings?" Micah asked.

"These…uh…are…uh…*relief* carvings," our guide answered with an accommodating smile.

"But why *relief*?"

"See?" he said, pointing to the wall. "*Relief* carvings." He enunciated the word carefully. "*Relief.*"

"Ah," Micah said, knowing he wasn't getting through. "Thanks anyway."

The guide bowed. "I'm welcome."

*   *   *

The sun was directly overhead and beating down hard when we finally arrived at the Elephant Terrace. We were told the rulers used to sit atop the wall—essentially a long, thick wall with elephants carved on it—to watch performances on the plaza out front.

"What kinds of performances?" Micah asked.

"Like the...uh...uh..."

"Play?"

"No...the uh..."

"Circus?" Micah offered.

"Yes, the circus. With the swingers on the...uh..." The guide waved his hand, mimicking the word he was looking for.

"Trapeze?"

"Yes. Trapeze. And there were women...uh..." The guide moved a little, swinging his hips to the side.

"Dancers?"

"Yes, dancers. And...uh...uh..."

"Elephants?" Micah suggested.

"No, no elephants."

The three-hour break once we were back at the hotel was welcome. Both Micah and I worked out, ate, and napped before heading off to Angkor Wat. By then, we'd been told repeatedly that our two hours there wouldn't be nearly long enough to fully appreciate it.

In a way, we learned, they were right, simply because of its size and scope. And yet, unless you were well versed in the stories about the Hindu god Vishnu and had the patience to learn how those stories had been interpreted into pictures, two hours was more than enough. One of the TCS lecturers on the trip was absolutely fascinated by—and had studied intensively—the relief carvings of Angkor Wat. After making our way over the causeway to the main walls surrounding the temple, he grew giddy with excitement. As we stared and photographed portions of the carvings—and they were amazingly detailed, I have to admit—our lecturer would stop every few steps and point to the various sections of the wall, describing it in even further detail, his voice resounding with enthusiasm.

To be honest, it only confused us.

"Now this," he might say, "is where Vishnu crosses the river. Look where he's standing. See the temple in the foreground?"

We'd squint, searching for the temple and finding it, thinking, *so far, so good.* Then, unfortunately, the lecturer would go on.

"As you probably know, the temple behind him represents the cosmos as centered on Mount Meru—in other words, it's the model of the universe in microcosm! This—as with everything about Angkor Wat—is the same representation! And all these reliefs come from the Ramayana and the Mahabharata as well as the Bhagavad-Gita, which is absolutely extraordinary, if you think about it. Furthermore, as we move along, you'll also notice scenes from the life of Suryavarman II himself, who apparently decided to identify himself with Rama and Krishna, the incarnations of Vishnu, thus making himself out to be a Devaraja! You can just imagine what Jayavarman II thought about that, especially after defeating the Chams. Oh, and just up ahead, we'll see the famous relief that depicts the myth of cosmic renewal, also known as the Churning of the Sea of Milk!"

By then, Micah's eyes had acquired a familiar glassy sheen. "Milk?"

"That's what he said."

"What is that supposed to mean?" Micah went on. "And who's Rama and what on earth is a Devaraja?"

"Do you want me to ask?"

"No," he said quickly. "Maybe if no one asks, he'll eventually move on." Micah paused for a moment before shaking his head. "I mean, does he really think we know all this stuff about Shiva?"

"Vishnu. He's talking to us about the God *Vishnu.*"

"Whatever," he said. "My point is, I don't know any of this, I won't remember any of this. It's too much—I mean, the wall is ten feet high and goes all the way around the temple. It's over half a mile long. Architecturally, it's amazing, and I can see why it took decades to build it. But unless you live for this stuff, the carvings seem to run together."

"*Relief* carvings," I said. "*Relief.*"

"Whatever."

Meanwhile, our lecturer was still talking on and on, growing even more excited.

"And notice outside the four sandstone heads atop the perimeter wall! Can you see them? We think those represent the Guardians of the Four Directions, or maybe even the Bodhisattva Avalokiteshvara!"

When we reached the center of Angkor Wat and stood at the base of the temple mount, the lecturer was in full swing.

"It's interesting to compare Mahayana and Theravada Buddhism, but for historical purposes, you might keep in mind the animism that was also prevalent in the early Khmer empire—for example, the belief in Neak Ta. Perhaps you noticed the serpent god Naga near the entrance? This—"

"Excuse me?" Micah interrupted.

The lecturer paused. "Yes?"

Micah pointed to the temple-mountain. "Can we climb that thing?"

We spent the remaining hour exploring the ruins on our own. We climbed the steep, crumbling steps and wandered through the rocky corridors, posed for pictures, and surveyed Angkor Wat from the highest spots we could reach.

"I hope there's not a test on any of this," Micah said as we walked back down the causeway. "I'd flunk."

"You and me both."

He paused. "Do you realize we've been gone for two weeks?"

"It doesn't seem like it."

"It's kind of sad to think about it. I'd been dreaming about this trip for months, and we're already more than halfway through. It's going so fast."

"Dreams are funny like that," I said. "You want something so desperately, you somehow get it, then just as suddenly it's over. Like running races—all that training for a couple of minutes on the track. The secret, I've learned, is to appreciate the process."

"Are you getting philosophical on me?"

"No," I admitted. "I'm just talking to hear my head rattle."

"Good," he said. "I've had more than enough philosophy for one day."

We walked a little farther.

"Do you miss Christine?" I asked.

"Yeah," he said. "The kids, too. How about you?"

I nodded. "I've been missing them since I left."

*   *   *

Cat and I married in Manchester, New Hampshire, Cathy's hometown. In the previous six months, she'd had to make the arrangements from across the country. She'd gone home only twice; my bride-to-be, I was beginning to understand, was quite efficient when she needed to be.

We were married on July 22, 1989, in the Catholic church she'd grown up attending, and as she was led to the aisle by her father, I couldn't look away. Her eyes were luminous beneath her veil, and her hands were shaking slightly when I took them in my own. I barely remember the ceremony. The only moment that stands out in my mind was when I slipped the ring on her finger. The reception was also a blur, and we were both exhausted by the time we arrived in Hawaii for our honeymoon. The honeymoon had been a gift from Billy and Pat Mills, who had come to love Cathy as much as I did. Lisa, who'd long since found someone new in her life, jokingly began referring to me as "the ex-boyfriend that never went away."

Because the ceremony and reception had been held on the other side of the country, only a few of my friends had been able to make it. My mom, however, decided to throw a party in Sacramento in our honor. She decorated the backyard, made a cake, set out beer and food, and everyone I knew from childhood stopped by to congratulate us. The party went on for hours, and in some ways was more fun than the original reception. I had returned from honeymooning in Maui, owned two rental properties with Micah, had finished my second— albeit unpublished—novel. I was excited about a new business I was starting, and was deeply in love with my new wife. It was, I still think, one of the best evenings, and summers, I'd ever spent.

If possible, my mom was even more excited than we were. In the course of the evening, she'd mentioned that she was thinking about quitting her job in the near future. Now that we were out of college—and with my dad earning more than he ever had—there was no reason for her to keep heading into the office every day. She'd worked long enough, she said, and she wanted to spend her time enjoying the family and riding horses with my dad.

"In fact," she said, her eyes shining with excitement, "we're going riding again next weekend."

*   *   *

On the following Friday night—only six weeks after we'd been married—Cathy and I went to a barbecue at my parents' house. We were the only kids there. Micah was in Cancun—he'd be arriving back home on Saturday—and Dana was in Los Angeles with her boyfriend. It was a quiet evening. We cooked and ate dinner; afterward, we settled in the living room to watch a movie. When the hour grew late, I mentioned that Cathy and I should head on home, and kissed my mom on the cheek as she sat in her chair.

"Maybe we'll drop by tomorrow night," I said.

"Okay," she said. "We'd love to have you. Drive safe, you two."

" 'Bye, Mom," I waved.

By noon, my mom and dad were riding horses on the trails that run alongside the American River. Like most August days in the Sacramento Valley, the temperature hovered in the nineties and the dry air was still. Only a few clouds dotted the horizon, and my mom and dad shared a picnic lunch in one of the many shady areas that line the parkway. A little while later, they were riding again; because of the heat, however, the horses neither trotted nor galloped. Instead, my parents rode them at a slow walk, taking in the scenery between bits of conversation.

As the river rounded a bend, the trail narrowed and my father led Napoleon into the front, Chinook and my mom close behind. According to my dad, nothing extraordinary happened next; there were no sudden noises, no snakes, nothing to startle either horse at all. The gravel pathway was strewn with rocks, he noted; at times, there was a slight angle to it, but again, nothing that either horse should have had trouble navigating at all. Indeed, both horses—and thousands of other horses over the years—had passed over that same stretch of trail dozens of times.

Yet that day for whatever reason, Chinook stumbled.

I was in the kitchen of my apartment as the phone rang. When I answered, my father sounded breathless, on the verge of hyperventilating.

"Your mom's been in an accident..." he started. "She fell off the horse...They took her to UC Davis Medical Center..."

"Is she okay?"

"I don't know. I don't know." His voice was simultaneously panicked and robotic. "I had to bring the horses back. I haven't talked to the doctor...I've got to get down there..."

"I'm on my way."

Cathy and I drove to the hospital, terrified, and trying to convince ourselves that it wasn't serious. As soon as we rushed into the emergency room, we asked the nurse in charge what was going on.

After checking her notes and heading back to talk to someone, she rejoined us.

"Your mother's in surgery," she said. "They think she ruptured her spleen. And her arm might be broken."

I sighed with relief; I knew that though the injuries were serious, they weren't necessarily life-threatening. A moment later, Mike Marotte, an old friend from high school who was on the cross-country team with me, hurried through the door.

"What are you doing here?" I asked.

"I was running on the trail when I saw a group of people and recognized your dad. I helped him get the horses back, and came straight to the hospital from there. What's happening with your mom?"

Mike, like all my friends, loved my mom and seemed as frightened as I was.

"I don't know," I said. "They said she ruptured her spleen, but no one's come out to talk to me. You were there though? Was it serious? How was she?"

"She wasn't conscious," he said. "That's all I know. The helicopter got there just a couple of minutes after I did."

The world seemed to be whirling in slow motion.

"Is there anything you need me to do? Can I call anyone?"

"Yeah," I said. I gave him the phone numbers of relatives on both my mom's and dad's sides. "Tell them what happened, and tell them to call everyone else."

He jotted down the numbers.

"And find Micah," I said. "He's supposed to be flying in from Cancun this afternoon. He's coming into San Francisco."

"What airline?"

"I don't know."

"What time is he coming in?"

"I don't know. Do what you can . . . And find Dana, too. She's in Los Angeles with Mike Lee."

Mike nodded. "Okay," he said. "I'll take care of it."

My dad arrived a few minutes later, pale and shaking. I told him what I knew, and he burst into tears. I held him as he cried, and a moment later he was mumbling, "I'm okay, now. I'm okay," trying to stop the tears.

We took a seat, and minutes passed without a word. Ten. Twenty. I tried to look through a magazine, but couldn't concentrate on the words. Cathy sat beside me, her hand on my leg, then she moved closer to my father. He sat and rose and paced, then sat again. He rose and paced, then sat again.

By then, forty minutes had gone by, and no one knew what was going on.

*　　*　　*

Micah had just stepped off the plane when he heard his name being paged over the public-address system at San Francisco International Airport, requesting him to answer the courtesy phone.

"Please go directly to UC Davis Medical Center," the voice on the other end told him.

"What's going on?"

"That's all the message says."

Suddenly panicked, he jumped into a limousine—no cabs were available—to take him to a friend's house, where he'd left his car for the week.

He was two hours from Sacramento.

After an hour, a soft-spoken man wearing a suit came out to greet us.

"Mr. Sparks?"

We all rose, wondering if he was the doctor. He said that he wasn't.

"I work with the hospital as a counselor," he said. "I know this is hard, but please come with me."

We followed him into a small waiting room; we were the only family in the room. It seemed it had been set aside for us. It was oppressive; I felt my chest constrict, even before he said the words:

"Your wife has suffered a cerebral hemorrhage," he said to my father. His voice was gentle and ached with obvious sympathy.

Tears welled again in my father's eyes. "Is she going to be okay?" my dad whispered. His voice began growing softer; I could hear the plea contained within it. "Please...please...tell me she's going to be okay..."

"I'm so sorry," the man said, "but it doesn't look good."

The room began to spin; all I could do was stare at him.

"She's not going to die, is she?" I croaked out.

"I'm so sorry," he said again, and though he stayed with us, I don't remember him saying anything else. All I remember is suddenly reaching for Cathy and my dad. I drew them tight against me, crying as I'd never cried before.

Dana had gotten the call; she was boarding the next plane to Sacramento. I called a couple of relatives and told them what was happening; one by one, I heard them burst into tears and promise to be there as fast as they could.

Minutes crawled by, as if we were inhabiting a time warp. The three of us broke down and tried to recover again and again. An hour passed before we were able to see my mom. When we went into the room to see her, oxygen was being administered and she was receiving fluids; I could hear the heart machine beeping steadily.

For just a moment, it looked as if she were sleeping, and despite the fact that my mind knew what was happening, I nonetheless grasped at hope, praying for a miracle.

Later that evening her face began to swell. The fluids were necessary to keep her organs from being damaged in the event we would donate them, and little by little, she looked less like my mom.

Some of the relatives had arrived, and others were on the way. All had been in and out of the room but no one could stay very long. It was unbearable to be with my mom because it wasn't her—my mom had always been so full of life—but it seemed wrong to stand in the hallway. Each of us drifted back and forth, trying to figure out which alternative was less terrible.

More relatives arrived. The hallway began to crowd with friends as well. People looked to each other for support. I didn't want to believe what was happening; no one wanted to believe it. Cathy never left my side and held my hand throughout it all, but I felt myself constantly being pulled back to my mother.

When no one was in the room, I entered and closed the door behind me. All at once, my eyes welled with tears. I reached for her hand and felt the warmth I always had. I kissed the back of her hand. My voice was ragged, and though I'd already cried for most of the afternoon, I simply couldn't stop when I was with her. Despite the swelling, she looked beautiful, and I wanted—with all my heart and soul, and more than I've ever wanted any-thing—simply for her to open her eyes.

"Please, Mama," I whispered through my tears. "Please. If you're going to come out of this, you've got to do it soon, okay? You're running out of time. Please try, okay…just squeeze my hand. We all need you…"

I lowered my head to her chest, crying hard, feeling some-thing inside me begin to die as well.

Micah arrived, and as soon as I saw him I burst into tears in his arms. Dana arrived an hour after Micah did, and had to be supported as she moved down the hallway toward us. She was wailing; hers were the tears of someone not only losing a mother, but her best friend as well. In time, my brother and I led her into the room. We'd warned her about the swelling, but my sister broke down again as soon as she saw how bad it had become. My mother looked unreal, a stranger to our eyes.

"It doesn't look like mom," she whispered.

Micah held her tight. "Look at her hands, Dana," he whispered. "Just look at her hands. Those haven't changed. You can still see mom right there."

"Oh, Mama..." she cried. "Oh, Mama, please come back."

But she couldn't respond to our pleas. My mom, who had sacrificed so much in her life, who had loved her children more than any mother could, whose organs would go on to save the lives of three people, died on September 4, 1989.

She was forty-seven years old.

Questions and Explanations
for Chapter 12

The ten questions on chapter 12 focus on grammar and usage, vocabulary, comprehension, literary terms, characterization, and style. Some of the questions combine two or more of these areas, requiring you to synthesize your knowledge, make inferences, and interpret the text. The questions are designed to determine both your current level of understanding of the memoir and your ability to answer higher-level questions.

The following sentence tests your ability to recognize grammar and usage errors. The sentence contains either a single error or no error at all. If the sentence contains an error, select the one underlined part that must be changed to make the sentence correct. If there is no error, select choice D.

1. Cat and I married in Manchester, New Hampshire,
   A   B
   Cathy's hometown. No error
   C   D

Choice A tests the choice of pronoun. Choice B checks your knowledge about using commas. Choice C tests the use of the apostrophe.

For choice A, you must differentiate between *I* and *me*. When you have a subject (doer of an action), you use *I*, and when you have an object (receiver of an action), you use *me*—for example, "*I* told her to throw *me* the ball."

In choice B, recognize that both a city and state are listed. Commas are used to separate items in addresses—for example, "Address me at 1659 Dorchester Drive, Brunswick, Ohio, after the first of July."

Choice C checks the use of an apostrophe to show possession. A singular noun demonstrates possession with an apostrophe and *s*—for example, "the boy's book, the girl's letter, the doctor's diagnosis."

The following two questions test your vocabulary and comprehension. Choose the word or set of words that, when inserted in the sentence, best fits the meaning of the sentence as a whole.

2. For a variety of reasons, the sites in Cambodia were the most _____ stops on the tour.

   A. reassuring

   B. pleasurable

   C. abstemious

   D. disconcerting

This question tests your comprehension and your vocabulary. *Reassuring*, choice A, means encouraging and comforting. *Pleasurable*, choice B, means enjoyable and agreeable. *Abstemious*, choice C, means done sparingly. *Disconcerting*, choice D, means disturbing and agitating.

3. Even though their mother was an organ donor, this information provided little _____ to the siblings in their time of _____.

    A. solace...grief

    B. comfort...elation

    C. frustration...acuity

    D. provocation...angst

This question tests your comprehension and your vocabulary. First, you need to determine how the siblings were feeling at the time of their mother's death. The first words of choices A and B are synonyms, and choices C and D are near synonyms; therefore, you should be able to eliminate two of the choices immediately.

After narrowing your choices down, differentiate between *grief*, keen mental suffering following a loss, and *elation*, great joy. Or differentiate between *acuity*, sharp vision, and *angst*, a feeling of anguish.

Question 4 tests your knowledge of literary terms.

4. When describing Cambodia, Sparks writes, "the land struck me as being both hopeful and tragic." His description is an example of what?

A. foreshadowing

B. hyperbole

C. paradox

D. simile

Foreshadowing, choice A, is providing hints or clues to future events. For example, when Benvolio suggests to Romeo that finding a new female beauty may help Romeo get over Rosaline, it foreshadows Romeo's falling in love with Juliet when he sees her later in the play.

Hyperbole, choice B, is an overexaggeration used to illustrate a point. For example, if someone says, "I told you a million times what that is," you know that this person really didn't tell you a million times, just many, many times.

A *paradox*, choice C, is an apparent contradiction that upon further analysis seemingly makes sense. The famous first line of *A Tale of Two Cities*, "It was the best of times, it was the worst of times," initially doesn't make sense. But when you think about how both situations can exist simultaneously, you understand the paradox.

And a *simile*, choice D, is a comparison between two unlike things using a connective word, such as *like*, *as*, or *than*—for example, "My love is like a red, red rose."

Question 5 asks you to analyze a symbol based on textual evidence.

5. The visit to the National Museum of Cambodia and the museum itself symbolize the state of the nation in which of the following ways?

A. Numerous beggars waited outside the gates.

B. The museum contained many collectibles but no glass.

C. Many of the statues were broken.

D. The building itself was run-down.

E. all of the above

Note that the question indicates that more than one answer will be correct. A *symbol* is something that has meaning in and of itself and also stands for something else. For example, the American flag is a piece of fabric with the stars and stripes on it (literally, it is a flag), but the American flag symbolizes, among other things, democracy, freedom, and the fifty states.

If the beggars outside the gate of the museum might represent the disparity of wealth throughout the nation, select choice A. If the museum's inability to house the collection behind glass represents the lack of resources in Cambodia, select choice B. If the broken statues signify the remnants of war, which is also apparent throughout the country, select choice C. If the run-down building corresponds to the many run-down places in Cambodia, select choice D.

Question 6 asks you to make an inference based on thorough and strong textual evidence.

6. While the brothers were exploring the ruins of Angkor Wat, Micah commented upon how fast the trip was going, saying, "I'd been dreaming about this trip for months, and we're already more than halfway through." Nicholas's reply is important, as he responds with, "You want something so desperately, you somehow get it,

then just as suddenly, it's over...The secret, I've learned, is to appreciate the process." These words are important to the development of all of the following EXCEPT:

A. character

B. plot

C. style

D. theme

The word *except* reveals that three of the four choices will be eliminated because the idea in the passage is developed throughout the memoir.

Character refers to the individuals in the story. Nicholas says he learned something, so this must apply to his character development; therefore, you can eliminate choice A.

Plot, choice B, refers to the selection and arrangement of all the incidents in the memoir. If the details and examples regarding dreams and the pursuit thereof are evident in the text, eliminate this option.

Style is the way the text is written. Basically style isn't focused on *what* is said but rather *how* it is said. If the sentence seems to be about stylistic choices, then eliminate choice C.

Theme, choice D, refers to a central idea. If this sentence is a debatable claim that can be supported with details and examples, eliminate choice D.

Question 7 asks you to make an inference regarding strong and thorough textual evidence.

7. The mood of the trip during its Cambodian leg can best be described as:

A. delirious

B. disturbing

C. playful

D. whimsical

Mood is the atmosphere—the way setting and tone work together to create a feeling for the reader. In this case, Sparks uses details and examples to create a mood that enables readers to experience what those on the tour were experiencing.

Delirious, choice A, means wild with excitement and enthusiasm. *Disturbing*, choice B, means upsetting and emotionally troubling. *Playful*, choice C, means full of fun. *Whimsical*, choice D, means playfully expressive or capricious.

Question 8 tests your knowledge of literary terms.

8. While waiting to see his mother after hearing the devastating news regarding the extent of her injuries, Nicholas describes the scene as follows: "Minutes crawled by, as if we were inhabiting a time warp." What figure of speech is being used to illustrate the mood at the hospital?

   A. personification

   B. metaphor

   C. simile

   D. allusion

Knowing about figures of speech will help you to answer this question.

Personification, choice A, is giving nonhuman things a human characteristic, such as in "Opportunity knocked on the door." A *metaphor*, choice B, is a comparison made between two unlike things without using a connective word—for example, "Michael Phelps was a flying fish in the pool." A *simile*, choice C, is a comparison between two unlike things using a connective word, such as *like*, *as*, or *than*—for example, "My love is like a red, red rose." An *allusion*, choice D, is an indirect reference. Some of the most common types of allusions are historical, such as making a reference to Napoleon by saying that someone met his Waterloo; biblical, such as John Coffey in *The Green Mile* being a Christ figure; mythological, a reference to a Greek or Roman myth, such as someone having the Midas touch; and literary, a reference to a character in a work of literature, such as a couple being ill-fated like Romeo and Juliet.

Question 9 asks you to analyze how an author's choices contribute to the text's overall structure and meaning, as well as its aesthetic impact.

9. In which ways do the two narrative threads complement each other in chapter 12?

    A. The characters in both narrative threads feel out of place and inadequate.

    B. The mood of both settings—Cambodia and the hospital—are comparable.

    C. The thematic topic of loss is explored on both a personal and a global scale.

  D. The adjectives *hopeful* and *tragic* apply to both narrative threads.

  E. all of the above

Note that the question indicates that more than one answer may be correct. To *complement* is to complete; therefore, the two parts—"the two narrative threads"—work together to create one cohesive whole, which is chapter 12. If Nicholas and Micah both feel out of place in Cambodia and at the hospital, select choice A. If witnessing the poverty creates a feeling that is similar to the one the brothers experience at the hospital, select choice B. If both narratives discuss different types of loss, select choice C. And if the adjectives that Nicholas uses to describe Cambodia could also apply to the time in his life when he was just starting his married life and then experienced the death of his mother, select choice D.

Question 10 asks you to analyze an author's choices.

10. Stylistically the last paragraph of chapter 12 is a single sentence: "She was forty-seven years old." Which of the choices listed below are effects of this stylistic choice?

  A. The sentence foreshadows other impending losses and disappointments.

  B. The tone provides a sense of finality.

  C. The sudden end of the chapter mirrors the sudden ending of her life.

  D. The simple sentence emphasizes his mother's relatively young age.

The question indicates that more than one choice is correct. If something in the sentence could be providing clues to future events, select choice A. If a sense of closure is created, select choice B. If the suddenness of the sentence is as abrupt as the suddenness of the mother's death, select choice C. If the focal point of the sentence is the mother's age at the time of her death, select choice D.

Chapter 13

Phnom Penh, Cambodia
February 6

After two days in Angkor we flew back to Phnom Penh, this
time for a tour of the Holocaust Museum and a trip to the Killing Fields.

The museum is located in downtown Phnom Penh, which
had been seized by the Khmer Rouge in 1975. Pol Pot, the
leader of the Khmer Rouge, hoped to create a perfect com-
munist state, and evacuated the entire city. A million people
were forced into the countryside. With the exception of Khmer

Rouge soldiers, whose average age was twelve, Phnom Penh became largely a ghost town.

With the departure of U.S. forces from Vietnam and no other country willing to intervene, Pol Pot began his bloody reign. His first act was to invite all the educated populace back into the city, upon which he promptly executed them. Torture became a way of life and death for thousands. In time, to save the cost of bullets, most of the executions were carried out by striking the victim on the back of the head with thick bamboo poles. Over the next few years, more than a million people were killed, either through enforced hardship, or executions in what are now known as the Killing Fields.

On the flight, Micah and I anticipated our arrival with a degree of ambivalence. Though we wanted to see both the museum and the Killing Fields, our excitement was tempered by our apprehension. This, unlike so many of the sites, wasn't part of ancient history; it was modern history, home to events that people want to forget despite knowing that they never should.

From the outside, the Holocaust Museum looked unremarkable. A two-story, balconied building set off the main road, it resembled the high school it had originally been. But belying its innocuous appearance was the sinister barbed wire that still encircled it; this was the place where Pol Pot tortured his victims.

Our guide, we learned, had attended school there, and it felt disconcerting, almost surreal, when he pointed to his former classroom, before moving us to the exhibits.

They were a series of horrors: a room where they used electricity to torture victims; other rooms featured equally horrific devices. The rooms hadn't been altered since Phnom Penh had been reclaimed, and on the floors and walls, bloodstains were still visible.

So much that we saw that day seemed beyond belief; the fact that most of the Khmer Rouge were children was almost too appalling to contemplate. We were told that the Khmer Rouge soldiers dispatched their victims without remorse and with businesslike efficiency; children killing mothers and fathers and other children by striking them on the back of the head. My oldest son was roughly the same age as the soldiers, which made me sick to my stomach.

On the walls were pictures of the victims. Some pictures showed prisoners being tortured; others showed the bodies unearthed in the Killing Fields. In either corner of the main room, there were two small temples that housed the skulls of those victims who'd been discovered in the camp after the guards had fled. On the wall was a painting of a young boy in a soldier's uniform, striking and killing a victim in the Killing Fields. The artist, we learned, had lost his family there.

No one on the tour could think of anything to say. Instead, we moved from sight to sight, shaking our heads and muttering under our breath. Awful. Evil. Sad. Sickening.

More than one member of the tour had to leave; the intensity was overwhelming.

"Did you lose anyone in your family?" I finally asked the guard.

When he answered, he spoke steadily, as if he'd been asked the question a thousand times and could answer by rote. At the same time, he couldn't hide a quality of what seemed almost stunned disbelief at his own words.

"Yes, I lost almost all of them. My wife, my father, my mother. My grandparents. All my aunts and uncles."

"Did you have any siblings?"

"Yes," he said, "a younger brother."

"Is he still alive?"

"I don't know," he said. "I haven't seen him since the war. He was a member of the Khmer Rouge."

We traveled to the outskirts of Phnom Penh and turned toward the Killing Fields. On either side of the dirt road were run-down houses; halfway up the street was a garment factory, and dozens of women were clustered outside, sitting in the dirt eating lunch as we passed.

Impossible to recognize unless you knew the location, the Killing Fields appeared as a ditch-strewn field, remarkably similar to the rest of the countryside we'd passed. It was far smaller than I imagined it would be—maybe a hundred yards to each side. In the center, the only recognizable feature was a memorial temple to honor the dead.

Over the next hour, we were led from one spot to the next; this was where a hundred victims were discovered; in another spot two hundred victims were found, over here, four hundred. In another spot, we learned that the skeletons unearthed had been buried without their heads, so it was impossible to know how many had been unearthed. In this particular field, we learned that thousands had died; precise figures are impossible to know with any certainty.

Micah and I simply wandered in silence, feeling sad and sickened. Eventually, we were led to the memorial temple and went inside.

The temple, white in color, was ten feet to a side, and roughly forty feet high, making it look like a rectangular block stood on end. We didn't know what to expect, but what we found left us paralyzed. Running up the back wall to the top of the temple were glass-enclosed shelves, stacked with thousands and thousands of skulls.

On our way back to the bus, Micah summed up my own feelings in three simple words.

"This was hell."

In the strangest juxtaposition of the entire tour, one that left me feeling off balance for the rest of the day, we went from the Killing Fields straight to the Russian Market for a few hours of frivolous shopping.

Cambodia, like many Asian countries, has perfected the art of piracy, and the Russian Market was a building crowded with hundreds of vendors, selling everything from pirated DVDs to pirated clothing. DVDs cost three dollars, jeans supposedly from the Gap went for half that.

The market was crowded; it seemed that every tourist visiting the country had heard about the place and had decided to visit at the same time. Despite the fact that most of our tour group had ample financial means and could afford the real items back home, most everyone left the market with a bagful of bargains.

On our last night in Phnom Penh, there was no cocktail party, so we were encouraged to make reservations at one of the hotel restaurants, since our hotel boasted some of the best food in Cambodia. Micah and I, naturally, forgot to make them, and ended up eating at one of the casual dining spots in the hotel. It was nearly empty, and we finished our meal in half an hour.

Although initially disappointed, we ended up being pleased by our meal. As fate would have it, everything went wrong in the kitchens that night. Everyone who'd made a reservation wound up having to wait hours for their meal. Ovens broke, cooks hadn't shown up, meals came out wrong—Murphy's law was in full force. Appetizers took an hour and a half to reach the table; the main course followed two hours later. While in some circumstances that wouldn't have bothered people, we'd been on the road for thirteen days. People were tired and we had to rise early for our flight to Jaipur the following morning. On a night when everyone was looking forward to getting eight hours of sleep—as Micah and I did—most got less than five.

In our room, Micah and I were watching the Croc Hunter again. Along with CNN, *The Crocodile Hunter* was the only English-language show we'd been able to find. Every time we'd turned on the television—no matter what country we were in—Croc Hunter was always on. By Cambodia, it had become something of a long-running joke—by our reckoning, it was the most widely watched show in the world.

"Oh, isn't this snake a beauuuuuty," Steve Irwin, the ever enthusiastic Australian host, was saying. "Look at the colors. Oh, she's magnificent, isn't she? This little beauty is danger-ous—one bite can kill a dozen men!"

"The guy is nuts," Micah commented.

"He's always nuts," I said. "My kids love to watch him."

Micah was quiet for so long, I thought he'd begun to doze. When I glanced over at him, however, I saw he was staring at the ceiling.

"What are you thinking about?" I asked.

It was a long moment before he answered. "What we saw today. Earlier this morning. The museum, the Killing Fields."

"It was awful, wasn't it?"

"Yeah." He nodded. When he spoke again, his voice was subdued. "It just made me feel sad. Sad for the people here, sad about the world. Sad about everything. And empty, too. It was all so pointless. Things like this shouldn't happen." He hesitated. "It reminded me of how I felt after mom died."

I glanced over at him, not altogether surprised at his comment. Whenever either of us were sad, our conversation always returned to the topic of our family.

"Do you realize that almost everyone on this trip is older than she was when she died?" he asked. "I can't believe it's been over thirteen years. It doesn't seem like it."

"No it doesn't," I agreed.

"Do you realize that in less than ten years, *we'll* be as old as mom was when she died? Peyton would only be eleven years old then."

I said nothing. Micah drew a long breath before going on.

"And it's strange. I mean, when I think about mom, it's like she hasn't aged. In my mind, I mean. When I think about her, I always picture the way she looked the last time I saw her. I can't even imagine what she'd look like now..." He trailed off. When he spoke again, his voice was quieter. "You know what I regret?"

I looked at him, waiting.

"That I didn't get a chance to say good-bye. You and Cathy got to do that. When I left for Cancun, I was running late, and I didn't even think to call her. And the next time I saw her, she didn't look like mom anymore, and we were talking about donating her organs. It was just...unreal. And it breaks my heart to think that after sacrificing so much for us, she never got a chance to see or hold her grandkids, she never found out that you became an author, she never got to meet Christine or the kids. Mom would have been great as a grandma . . ."

He trailed off, his gaze unfocused.

"I miss her, too," I said quietly.

The months after my mom's funeral were halting steps in search of some sort of normalcy. No one in the family seemed to know how to react or what to do. Micah, Dana, and I tried to support one another as well as our dad. It seemed that every time one of us began crying, the others would fall in line. Thus we each came to the independent conclusion that no one should cry anymore. And we didn't, unless we were alone.

Our mom was gone, yet strangely, there were times when it seemed as if she wasn't. Everything in the house bore my mother's imprint; the location of the spices in the cupboard, the placement of the photographs on the shelves, the color of the walls, her nightgown draped over the chair in her bedroom. Everywhere we looked, we were reminded of her, and there were moments when I'd be standing in the kitchen when I'd suddenly begin to feel as if my mom was standing behind me. At times like those, I would pray that I wasn't imagining it. I looked for signs—movement from the corner of my eyes, perhaps, or limbs of trees swaying in the breeze. I ached for something to let me know her spirit was still with us. But there was nothing.

Yet, if the house was a constant reminder of my mom, it also began to serve notice as to how empty it had come to feel. There was no energy in the house, no vivaciousness, and the sound of laughter no longer echoed off the walls. We sometimes wondered whether we should rearrange the furniture or remove the more obvious signs of my mother's presence. Her purse, for instance. For years, she'd placed it in a basket near the front door; months after her death, no one had summoned the will to put it in the closet or even open it, to see what was left behind. We knew what we'd find; pictures of the family, letters from her mother, her lipstick and personal trinkets. Those things were so personal, so...*mom*...that we couldn't touch them for fear of somehow betraying her memory. We didn't want to forget her, and in a way those were the only things we had left. The purse, it seemed, had become our silent entreaty for her return.

That year, we didn't celebrate Christmas at the house; it was the first time in our lives we spent the holiday with other relatives. And though the company was comforting, none of us could shake the empty feeling in our hearts. Mom was gone, and Christmas at home would never be the same again.

Cat and I settled into our first year of marriage, while at the same time doing our best to take care of dad. We set aside every Thursday, and used that time to take my dad out to the movies or to dinner.

Micah and Dana decided to rent an apartment together. It was only a couple of miles from the house, and like Cat and me, they thought it would be a good way to keep an eye on him. If the death had been hard on us kids, it had been far harder on my dad. While I can't claim to understand their relationship, my mom and dad had spent twenty-seven years together, and his world was suddenly and completely altered now that she was gone.

He seemed to live by instinct alone. After the funeral, he'd begun wearing black, and only black. At first, we thought it was a phase, but as the months passed, we began to realize how lost he was without her. He'd depended on my mom as we had. Because they'd been married at such a young age, my dad had no experience in being alone, or even what it was like to be an adult without her by his side. My dad lost his best friend, his lover, his confidante, and his wife. But if that wasn't hard enough, he'd also lost the only life he'd known how to live. He had to learn to cook and how to clean the house, and had to do those things on his own. He lost a good portion of the family income, and had to learn how to budget. And he had to learn how to relate to his kids, who for the most part had been raised by his wife. We loved our dad and he loved us, but the truth was that he seemed to know as little about us as we did about him. In our own way, we each did our best to fill the void left in his life, and one by one we slowly became replacements for all that my mother had been to him.

Micah became his confidant, the only one that dad would really talk to. My dad had always admired Micah in the same way that I had, and that feeling only grew stronger after my mother died. Micah, I think, embodied many of the things my dad always wanted to be: handsome and charismatic, confident and popular. In a strange way, I think he began to seek my brother's approval. He took few actions without soliciting Micah's opinion, and listened to Micah's latest adventures with a proud twinkle in his eye. Cat became his buddy; he'd been fond of my wife since they'd first met, and whenever we'd stop by, they'd spend time together. They drank dessert wines and cooked together, they joked and laughed, and in sad times my dad turned to Cat when he needed a shoulder to cry on. And Cat responded by always saying or doing exactly what was needed. My dad also threw himself into taking care of my sister. He'd help with her bills, bought her a car, took care of her health insurance; eventually the two of them began taking care of the horses together. My dad, it seemed, was not only doing the things he thought my mom would do as a parent, but in taking care of Dana, found the strength to go on. I, too, began to play a role my mother had once had, but it was one that I would wish upon no one. With my intense schedule in high school, moving away for college, and starting a life with Cathy, I'd become the least dependent on my parents, and had been so since the age of sixteen. Maybe my dad realized this, too, for as the weeks and months wore on, I became the outlet for my dad's anger and pain.

In time, my dad began to act as if he despised me; if I asked if he needed help doing his budget, he accused me of trying to steal from him. If I cleaned up the house, he accused me of thinking he was not only helpless but a slob. If I dropped our cocker spaniel off at the house while I worked—something Cat and I had been doing since we got her—he accused me of taking advantage of him. When Cat and I visited, there were many evenings where he refused to talk to me at all; instead, he'd joke and laugh with my wife in the kitchen while I sat alone in the living room. This dynamic only grew worse over time.

I knew he didn't hate me, that he was hurting inside, struggling even more than we kids were. I knew that his anger and pain had to go somewhere, and that deep down he loved me despite the words he said and the way he'd begun to treat me. Yet even if I understood what was going on, I nonetheless sought comfort in Cathy's arms, wondering aloud what I'd done to deserve his hostility.

My brother and I did our best to continue our relationship with each other and our independent lives. Micah moved steadily forward in his real estate career; and my small business—I manufactured orthopedic wrist braces, primarily for carpal tunnel syndrome—was slowly getting off the ground. Like most young people, I thought I knew far more than I actually did about running a business, and soon accumulated credit card debts that greatly exceeded our combined annual income. Despite the fact that I had been working day and night for months, it was touch and go as to whether Cat and I could meet our obligations, and we wondered how we'd ever stay afloat. In our first year of marriage, we'd been tested in every way; Cat and I were lucky that it only served to bring us closer together.

In the hardest moments—when I wondered how I'd be able to pay the rent or put food on the table—I turned to Micah. He would treat me to pizza and beer, and we'd talk. In the end, we decided to sell the two rental houses we'd purchased earlier. The profit on both was enough for Cat and me to climb out of debt, and I gradually began to turn the corner in making my small company profitable. However, I still had to wait tables and my wife had to work as well, simply to make ends meet.

Micah, meanwhile, continued to make life seem easy. He dated, had fun on the weekends, and excelled at his job. When Cathy and I went out in the evenings with him, we would always wonder who he'd bring along this time. Most of the women barely knew him, yet they seemed as enamored of him as I was with Cathy. Yet, if he was doing well on the surface, he was struggling beneath the facade, weighed down by our dad. Dad was still having a hard time, and Micah had assumed the mantle of leadership in our family. Because dad talked to him more than to either Dana or me, Micah alone seemed to understand the depth of my father's grief. One evening in the summer of 1990, when Micah and I were out together, I couldn't help but notice that he seemed especially preoccupied.

"What's going on?" I asked.

"I'm worried about dad."

Though I was worried, too, I knew my reasons were different from his. With me, dad acted irrationally; with Micah, he seemed completely rational. Neither seemed normal.

"Why?" I asked.

"Because he's not getting over mom. It's been almost nine months, but he still cries himself to sleep at night. And he's been getting edgier, too."

I didn't know what to say.

"And then, you know he's still wearing black, but it's worse now. He got rid of his entire wardrobe and replaced it, so that everything he owns now is black. And he never leaves the house anymore, except to go to work. I know he misses mom, but we all do. And mom would want him to be happy, even without her. She'd want him to be strong."

"What do you think we should do?"

"I don't know."

"Do you want Cathy and me to try to talk to him?"

Though I knew he wouldn't listen to me, he was becoming more dependent on my wife's company.

"It won't do any good. I've tried. I've invited him over, but he never comes. And he doesn't want to go anywhere when I visit him. Does he ever go over to see you and Cat at your apartment?"

"No."

Micah shook his head. "He shouldn't close himself off from the world. That's only going to make it worse. It's only going to make him feel more alone."

"Do you tell him that?"

"All the time."

"What does he say?"

"He says he's doing fine."

As the anniversary of my mom's death approached, my dad slowly began emerging from the self-imposed shell he'd constructed around himself. Though he still wore black, Micah, Dana, and I had talked him into joining us in learning country dancing, and the evenings out seemed to revive him. Slowly but surely, he became more like his old self; even with me, he no longer seemed nearly as bitter.

Somehow, it seemed, we'd survived the first year without our mother.

Later that autumn, Cathy and I learned that she was pregnant, and like all anxious parents-to-be, we began making preparations for the baby while we awaited the moment we could first see our baby on the ultrasound.

Cathy threw herself into the pregnancy. She watched everything she ate, exercised, and learned to live with morning sickness before she went to work. Her skin began to take on the flushed glow of an expectant mother. We called our friends and family; everyone, including my dad, was thrilled with the news. In fact, dad was happier than we'd seen him in a long, long time.

When Cat was twelve weeks along, we visited the medical clinic for the ultrasound. In the room, I held Cat's hand as the technician applied the gel and ran the scope over my wife's belly.

"There it is," the technician said quickly, and both Cathy and I stared at the screen in wonder.

The image was tiny, of course, and looked nothing like a baby. A peanut, maybe, but not a baby. Still, it was our first glance, and Cathy squeezed my hand and smiled.

The nurse continued to move the scope, trying to get a better picture; within a few moments, both Cathy and I saw the technician frown.

"What is it?" Cathy asked.

"I'm not sure yet," the technician answered. She forced a smile. "Could you excuse me for a moment?" The technician got up and left the room.

We didn't know what to make of it; we had no idea whether this was normal or unexpected. A couple of minutes later, the doctor came in.

"Is anything wrong?" Cathy asked.

"Let me take a look," the doctor said. For a moment, as the technician began working the scope, we watched them both staring at the screen. The technician pointed and whispered something to the doctor. He whispered something back. Neither would answer our questions; in time, the technician rose and left the room. The doctor looked serious.

"Something's wrong, isn't it?" Cathy asked.

"I'm sorry," he said. "But we can't find a heartbeat."

Cat burst into tears; eventually, I led her from the office. Our baby had died, just as my mother had, for no apparent reason at all. A few days later, Cat had a D&C. In the wheelchair after the procedure, all she could do was wipe her tears; there was nothing I could say to ease her pain.

Later, in Micah's arms, I cried as well.

Cat and I spent the next few months worrying about the possibility of becoming parents. We didn't know how long it would take for her to get pregnant again, nor did we know whether she could carry a baby to term. We'd been told that miscarriages were common; everyone seemed to know someone who'd had one and tried to console us with the thought that everything would be fine in the long run. We knew they meant well, we knew what they were saying was true. But we also were well acquainted with the other kind of story, the kind where things didn't work out, and to Cat, the thought of never becoming a mother was unbearable. Another hard Christmas came and went, and on my birthday, when I turned twenty-five, my sister called to sing me "Happy Birthday." When she asked me what I wanted, I could think of only one thing to say.

Our prayers were answered again in late January 1991, but we kept the news to ourselves this time. We didn't want a repeat of what had happened before, but in April we learned the baby was developing normally and finally shared the good news. Cathy's belly grew over the summer, and she spent hours looking through baby-name books and reading *What to Expect When You're Expecting*.

Yet the stresses of life seemed to keep coming, one after the other, without relief. Despite working two jobs—three if you count Cat's job—we were still struggling financially, unable to get ahead. Cat had health insurance through her employer, one that covered maternity, but in early summer, while she was five months along, she was laid off. When our cocker spaniel puppy reached twenty pounds, we were evicted from our apartment and had to find a new place to live. Our one car broke down completely, and the only car we could afford as a replacement was thirteen years old and had a hundred thousand miles on the odometer. The IRS decided to audit both my business and my personal tax returns concerning the previous three years; though I would eventually be cleared completely, the stress of working two jobs while collecting the necessary documents—

they wanted receipts for *everything*—added to an already difficult summer.

Somehow I was able to squeeze in time to write a book with Billy Mills, entitled *Wokini*. Though it would end up being the first work I'd ever publish, I was under no illusions that it had to do with the quality of my writing. Rather, its merit derived from who Billy was.

In September, we rushed to the hospital when labor pains began. It was a fast labor; Cat dilated quickly, and was nearly ready to deliver by the time we reached the hospital. Cat was in back labor—the baby was facing the wrong way—and in immense pain. There was a mad scramble as the room began to be readied, but moments after the doctor arrived, the baby's heart suddenly slowed.

By the looks on the doctor's and nurse's faces, I knew it was serious. There was a chance we would lose another baby.

All at once, the world seemed to shrink; all I could think about was Cat and the baby she carried inside her. There is a panic that comes in moments like those, one that squeezes the heart with a feeling of utter helplessness. I barely remember the heated rush of activity as the doctor swung into action; I stood off to the side, praying as I'd never prayed before.

The doctor was good, and a moment later I was a father. But the baby's skin was gray, and for the longest moment, he made no sound at all. Later, we'd learn that he was anemic and that he'd bled back through the umbilical cord. But at the time, I simply wanted to hear the cry of life.

And then, after what seemed like forever, I finally did.

Within a few minutes—minutes that seem far longer when it's actually happening—the doctor assured us our son would be fine, and for the first time I relaxed enough to realize that we'd actually become parents. Cat held the baby against her. We named him Miles Andrew, and the first person I called was Micah.

"I'm a father!" I screamed into the receiver. "I have a son!"

Micah whooped on the other end. "Congratulations, Daddy! How's mama doing?"

"She's doing great—and thankfully the baby is, too. But you've got to get down here! You've got to see this little guy! He's so cute!"

He laughed again. "I'm on my way, little brother. I'm on my way."

He was the first one to reach the hospital, and after taking one look at Miles, he turned to me.

"Why, he looks just like me."

I slapped him on the back. "You should only be so lucky. You might be handsome, but you don't hold a candle to this guy!"

Despite the new life of fatherhood I was suddenly leading, my brother and I continued to make time to be together. For a short while, he helped me with my orthopedic business, but by the end of the year I eventually decided to give it up. With a new child at home, I needed something more stable, and I took a job as a pharmaceutical representative with Lederle Labs in early 1992. It was the first time in my life in which I'd officially be earning above minimum wage. I was twenty-six years old.

But if the baby—and my radically transformed life—was enough to help me keep from dwelling on mom, my dad continued to experience intense periods of ups and downs. The good mood he'd had over the summer was replaced with a funk, then replaced again with optimism. It had reached the point where we didn't know what to expect when we went to see him, and both Micah and I wondered aloud whether he was manic-depressive.

My sister, too, seemed to be having a rough time, struggling to find herself as many young adults do. Never a great student, she dropped out of college to work full-time, then proceeded to quit her job a couple of weeks later. From there, she wandered from one job to the next, working as a cocktail waitress, an aerobics instructor, a receptionist at a tanning salon. She and Micah got separate apartments again, and my dad helped her with the rent. Physically, she was changing as well. By her early twenties, she'd become something of a beauty. She was quite popular with the opposite sex all of a sudden, but like Micah, she seemed to move quickly from one relationship to the next.

"What is it with you two?" I asked Micah one night.

"What do you mean?"

"You and Dana. Can't either of you date anyone for longer than a month?"

"I dated Juli and Cindy for years."

"Half the time you say you were dating them, you were actually broken up, and you were dating other people. And then you ended it with both of them."

He smiled. "Not everyone wants to be married at twenty-three, Nick."

"I didn't plan to marry that early. It's just that I met Cathy."

"You didn't have to marry her right away."

"Yes I did. Do you know what she said to me when she decided to move to California? While I was picking her up at the airport?"

He shook his head.

"When I met her at the airport, I started telling her all this really sweet stuff—you know, how much I loved her, how glad

I was that she'd moved out here, how much I appreciated her courage. Anyway, she let me finish before she finally smiled.

" 'I love you, too, Nick. And I'm glad I came. But let's get one thing straight. As much as I love you, I'm not going to abandon my family for a relationship that might be only temporary.' So what does that mean? I asked her, and she patted my chest. 'You've got six months to propose, or I'm going back home.' "

Micah's eyes widened. "She said that?"

"Yep."

He laughed. "I love that girl. She doesn't take guff from anyone, does she?"

"Nope."

"You did the right thing, Nick. You couldn't have married anyone better."

"I know. But as I was saying earlier—what's with you?"

"It's simple, Nick," he said. "I haven't met my Cathy yet. But when I do, I'll marry her and settle down."

By 1992, three years after my mom had died, each of us had somehow found a way to move on. I had a family and a new career; Dana had a new boyfriend and was back in college. Micah continued to date and enjoy one exciting weekend after the next. Though dad was still wearing black, the ups and downs were getting less frequent, and he'd even begun to think about dating again. Our family life, as much as could be expected, was gradually regaining some semblance of normalcy.

In October, Cathy and I eventually came to the conclusion that it would be best if we moved away. While we loved California, practicalities precluded us from being able to create the kind of family life we wanted for our son. My salary, while decent, wasn't enough to enable us to live in the kind of neighborhood Cathy wanted for Miles. Nor, due to rapidly escalating housing costs, could we foresee a change in the future.

What Cat and I wanted, I suppose, was the chance to live the American dream. We dreamed of having a house we could call our own, a decent-size yard for the kids, a barbecue grill in the backyard. Just the basics, but the basics were out of reach, and after a series of long discussions with Cat, I finally talked to my boss about applying for a transfer to a territory in the southeast. My boss wasn't thrilled by my request; I'd only been with the company for eight months, had only recently completed all my training, and was doing well in my territory. He didn't want to go through the process of hiring someone new, since there was always a risk the new employee wouldn't work out. And, of course, the territory would suffer while a new employee was being trained.

That night, I called Micah.

"Micah," I said, "do you want a job selling pharmaceuticals?"

My proposal made perfect sense to me. We'd run together, waited tables together, owned houses together, and he'd been part of the small company I'd started as well. We even looked somewhat alike.

For a moment, Micah was taken aback. Though he'd done well in real estate, it was strictly commission work, and was dominated by the large brokerage houses. Because he was with a smaller firm, finding new listings required endless hustle, and he'd grown tired of the way his firm dragged out paying him what he was owed.

"What do you mean?" he finally asked.

"If I get the transfer, I'll introduce you to my boss, you can interview with him, and I bet he'll hire you."

"You think so?"

"I know so."

He thought about it overnight and called me the next morning.

"Nick," he said. "I think I want to be a pharmaceutical rep."

And lo and behold, after I received a new territory centered in New Bern, North Carolina, my brother was hired, took over my old territory in Sacramento, and I handed him the keys to my company car.

Meanwhile, Cat and I began the process of getting ready for a new life on the other side of the country.

In early November, less than a week after Micah accepted the job, I was at home and beginning the slow process of packing up our things when I got a frantic call from my father.

"You've got to get to the hospital right now," my father suddenly said. He was breathless and scattered, a reprise of that fateful call three years ago. "She's at Methodist. Do you know where that is? Bob just brought her in a couple of minutes ago."

Bob, I knew, was Dana's boyfriend, but my dad's garbled message didn't make sense.

"Who? Are you talking about Dana? Is she okay?"

"Dana... she's in the hospital..."

"Is she okay?" I repeated.

"I don't know... I've got to get down there..."

My head suddenly began spinning with a sense of déjà vu.

"Do you know what happened? Was she in an accident?"

"I don't know... I don't think so... Bob said she had a seizure of some sort... I don't know anything else... Micah's on his way... I'm heading there now."

*　　*　　*

At the hospital, Bob told us what had happened. Bob lived on a ranch in Elk Grove and worked as a local trucker delivering feed for horses and cattle. Taller and heavier than Micah or me, he wore cowboy boots and had competed in bareback rodeo riding. I'd never seem him look as frightened as he did at that moment.

"She woke up and she couldn't talk right," he said. "Her words were all mixed up, and she didn't make any sense. So I loaded her in the car, and we started for the hospital. On the way, her eyes rolled back, and she started to convulse. She was still having the seizure when we got here. They took her back, and I haven't seen her since."

Though a different hospital, it was eerily reminiscent of the one where my mother had died. So were our feelings as we paced the small corridor, waiting to hear what was going on. And so was the room where we eventually saw my sister.

Dana was tired when we saw her; she'd been given medication for the seizure, and her eyes drooped. She, like us, was frightened, and she knew no more of what had happened to her than we did. But other than exhaustion, she seemed fine. She could tap the tips of her fingers against her thumb, she could remember everything from the night before. And she remembered realizing that something was wrong when she woke up earlier that morning.

"I remember trying to talk," she said, somewhat groggily. "I can even remember hearing the words coming out, but they were the wrong words. So I'd try to repeat myself, and the same thing happened again. And the smell. I kept smelling something really bad. That's when Bob put me in the car. I don't remember anything after that, though."

Later, the doctor said she had had a grand mal seizure, though when pressed, he wouldn't speculate as to the reason until further tests came in. He did suggest that it was probably best if she rested for a while.

I was the last one to get up to leave; once the others had left the room, Dana asked me to stay.

"Nick," she said, "tell me the truth. I want to know what's going on. Why did I have a seizure?"

"There are lots of possible causes," I said. "I wouldn't worry too much."

"Like what?"

She searched my face, trusting me, wanting to know. My sister knew that I would always tell her the truth.

"Anything, really. A sudden allergy. Stress. Maybe you're epileptic, but the seizures hadn't been triggered until now. Brain tumor. Maybe you ate something bad. Dehydration. Something just made your body go haywire for a little while. Lots of people have seizures. Seizures are actually quite common."

She looked at me, zeroing in on the one cause I'd hoped she would overlook.

"Brain tumor?" she asked quietly.

I shrugged. "It can cause seizures, but believe me—it's not all that likely that you have one. I'd say it's the least likely of everything I mentioned."

She glanced toward her lap. "I don't want a brain tumor," she said.

"Don't worry," I reassured her, hoping to hide my fears. "Like I said, that's probably not the reason."

Over the next few weeks, Dana underwent a number of tests. The doctors couldn't find what was wrong with her. CAT scans were inconclusive, but since she had no more seizures, it seemed to us that the worst had passed. Still, the uncertainty weighed heavily on us; we still had no idea what had caused the seizure in the first place.

It had also come time for me to move to North Carolina.

Cat and I had talked about it numerous times since Dana had gone to the hospital; she suggested that we might consider staying, even though I'd have to find another job. Dana might need us, she said. We can put our dreams on hold for a while. At least until we know what's going on.

It was one of those choices in life without any ideal option.

"Let me talk to Micah," I finally said. "Let me see what he thinks."

That night, when I explained the guilt I felt about moving away, he put his hand on my shoulder.

"There's nothing you can do for Dana," he said. "We don't even know what's wrong yet. But you've got to think about your family. You have a baby now. You've got to do what you think is best for him."

I couldn't meet his eyes.

"I don't know..."

"I'll watch out for Dana. I'm still here, and so is dad. And you're only a flight away if we need you."

"It doesn't feel right to just leave, though."

"I don't want you to go either," he said. Then, with a smile, he added, "But remember, Nick—what you want and what you get are usually two entirely different things."

A few days before Christmas 1992, Cathy flew out with the baby to North Carolina to meet the moving van; I stayed behind to finish showing my brother around his new territory and introduce him to various doctors. Because our apartment had been emptied, I slept in my old room at my dad's house the night before my departure.

Micah came over to help me pack my remaining items in the car: I would drive it cross-country. I noticed that he was wearing a pair of shorts of mine; because we were the same size, we had borrowed each other's clothes for years.

Micah had worked a couple of summers loading trucks for Consolidated Freightways and knew how to load the items to prevent them from being damaged. With the exception of the driver's seat, the car was completely filled. We were standing just inside the door when the time came to say good-bye; I'd already said my good-byes to Dana and my dad. But it was time to go, and both Micah and I knew it.

In the house were a thousand memories; in my mind, I could hear mom's laughter from the kitchen, and see my brother and sister at the table. For the second time in my life, I was leaving my family, but this time was different. The last time I'd left, I'd been a teenager; now I had a family of my own; I knew I'd never be moving back.

"It looks like when we loaded the Volkswagen to move here, doesn't it?" I cracked.

"It's pretty full. But at least it's level this time. How long will it take you to get there?"

"Four days or so."

"Drive safe."

"I will."

We hugged. "I'm going to miss you," I said.

"I'll miss you, too."

"I love you, Micah."

He squeezed harder. "I love you, too, little brother."

When we separated, I could feel the tears coming, but tried to hold them back. We'd come to depend heavily on each other in the last three years, but I tried to diminish the significance of what was happening. I told myself that we were simply moving; it wasn't as if we wouldn't see each other again. I'd come to visit him and he'd come to see me. We'd talk on the phone.

"You're wearing my shorts," I said randomly.

"I'll give them to you tomorrow," he said without thinking. "No," he added quickly. "I won't. You'll be gone tomorrow. I can't give them to you."

At that, Micah began to cry and he leaned into me again.

"It's okay, Micah," I whispered, beginning to cry as well. "It's going to be all right."

And a few minutes later, through my own blurry tears, I saw his image in the rearview mirror grow smaller. He was standing on the lawn, forcing a smile and slowly waving good-bye.

Questions and Explanations
for Chapter 13

The ten questions on chapter 13 focus on grammar and usage, vocabulary, comprehension, literary terms, and characterization. Some of the questions combine two or more of these areas, requiring you to synthesize your knowledge, make inferences, and interpret the text. The questions are designed to determine both your current level of understanding of the memoir and your ability to answer higher-level questions.

The following sentence tests your ability to recognize grammar and usage errors. The sentence contains either a single error or no error at all. If the sentence contains an error, select the one underlined part that must be changed to make the sentence correct. If there is no error, select choice D.

1. Although the truth regarding Pol <u>Pot's</u> regime has been
   A
   known for years, only recently <u>has</u> the harmful <u>effects</u>
   B   C
   of his actions been studied in American high schools.

   <u>No error</u>
   D

Choice A checks the use of the apostrophe. Choice B checks your knowledge of subject and verb agreement. And choice C tests whether the correct homophone is used.

For choice A, remember that a singular noun demonstrates possession with an apostrophe and *s*—for example, "the boy's book, the girl's letter, the doctor's diagnosis."

For choice B, realize that the subject of the verb *has* is *effects*.

Choice C is checking whether you know the difference between the homophones *affect* and *effect*. Remember that *affect* is typically used as a verb, meaning to influence. *Effect* is typically a noun, meaning something that is produced. If someone or something is doing something, usually the correct word choice is *affect*. For example, "Research has shown that rereading a passage will affect a student's level of comprehension."

The following two questions test your vocabulary. Choose the word or set of words that, when inserted in the sentence, best fits the meaning of the sentence as a whole.

2. After their mother's death, not moving her purse became the children's "silent _____ for her return."

   A. entreaty
   B. fodder

C. modicum

D. recidivism

This question tests your comprehension and your vocabulary. *Entreaty*, choice A, is a humble prayer or petition. *Fodder*, choice B, refers to abundant raw material. *Modicum*, choice C, is a small portion. *Recidivism*, choice D, is a tendency to relapse into a previous behavior.

3. The Holocaust Museum was even _____ than Micah had _____; bloodstains were still on the floors and walls.

    A. uglier…feigned

    B. calmer…speculated

    C. pastier…envisioned

    D. more horrific…imagined

This question tests your comprehension and your vocabulary. Initially you should determine which words might fit the first blank. Clearly choices B and C should be eliminated. Then you need to differentiate between the remaining two choices' second words: *feigned*, which means faked, and *imagined*, which means to have formed a mental image.

Question 4 checks your comprehension.

4. Why are the sites called the Killing Fields?

    A. The vegetation that grows there is poisonous.

    B. The Khmer Rouge killed and buried over a million people there.

   C. Pol Pot, leader of the Khmer Rouge, was executed there.

   D. It is the location of the Holocaust Museum.

This is important historical information. If you are not sure of the answer, reread the first two pages of chapter 13.

Question 5 asks you to determine the development of a central idea in a text.

5. What is the most important thematic topic of chapter 13?

   A. killing

   B. poverty

   C. loss

   D. apathy

This question is asking you to consider both narrative threads and to make a connection between the two. *Killing,* choice A, refers to causing the death of someone or something. *Poverty,* choice B, refers to the condition of being poor. *Loss,* choice C, refers to something unable to be found or recovered. *Apathy,* choice D, refers to the lack of emotions.

Question 6 asks you to determine a central idea developed in the text.

6. The details and examples from Chapter 13 best support which of the following statements?

   A. The best way to deal with loss is to keep your emotions in check and grieve privately.

B. Because individual loss is less significant than global loss, we have no right to mourn.

C. The loss of a parent is not as great a loss as that of a child.

D. Because loss is a part of life, we must find a way to move on.

Being able to identify themes, or central ideas, is an important part of studying literature. Sometimes themes are explicitly stated; other times it's up to a reader to recognize the details and examples that illustrate and develop that topic.

Loss refers to something unable to be found or recovered. Chapter 13 obviously addresses a multitude of losses on both a personal and global scale. All four of these choices could be statements of theme for a literary text, but if the details and examples from chapter 13 don't develop the stated idea, then the statement isn't appropriate to this memoir. The best central idea will incorporate both narrative threads from chapter 13.

Because details and examples from the chapter clearly contradict the statement in choice A, eliminate this choice. Although the first half of choice B is debatable, the second half is clearly not indicated in the chapter, so eliminate choice B. Although the opinion stated in choice C is debatable, it does not pertain to the trip narrative, so eliminate choice C. Choice D is a statement that encompasses how the Sparks family will endure through its losses and how the nation of Cambodia will deal with the magnitude of its losses as well.

Question 7 checks your comprehension.

7. Nicholas Sparks experiences which of the following difficulties in chapter 13?

A. dealing with the loss of a parent

B. experiencing the loss of a child

C. deciding to move across the country

D. having a family member endure an unexpected medical condition

E. all of the above

Notice that the question indicates that more than one answer will be correct. This is an important question because it helps you understand what Nicholas is experiencing; thus, it's important for his character development. If you are not able to identify all of the difficult stresses in Nicholas's life at this time, skim through the chapter again.

Question 8 asks you to determine the meaning of a word in context.

8. After Nicholas shares Cathy's ultimatum with Micah, Micah replies, "I love that girl. She doesn't take guff from anyone, does she?" As used in this passage, *guff* most nearly means:

A. sagacity

B. imprecation

C. nonsense

D. certitude

This question tests your comprehension, your ability to make an inference, and your vocabulary. *Sagacity*, choice A, means shrewdness. *Imprecation*, choice B, is a curse. *Nonsense*, choice C, means foolish or trivial conduct. *Certitude*, choice D, means freedom from doubt.

Question 9 asks you to make an inference regarding character development.

9. Chapter 13 is one of transition for Nicholas Sparks. Which of the following best characterizes the changes he experiences?

   A. a shift in responsibilities from his father and his siblings to his wife and family

   B. a change in location that will put both literal and metaphorical distance between him and his siblings

   C. a transition from being a carefree and adventurous young man to a sensible adult

   D. a conversion from a man of faith to a man disillusioned with God

A transition is a change. If the primary focus in Nicholas's life, as indicated in chapter 13, is now his immediate family rather than his father, brother, and sister, select choice A. If the biggest change is physical—Nicholas's family moving across the country—select choice B. Although Nicholas is making a very adult decision to take care of his family, the characterization of him as a "carefree and adventurous young man" isn't accurate, so choice C must be eliminated. There is no indication that Nicholas ever lost his religious faith, so choice D can also be eliminated.

Question 10 asks you to make an inference based on strong and thorough textual evidence.

10. The final scene of chapter 13 is one of the brothers saying good-bye and Nicholas's driving away. What word best describes this scene?

A. bleak

B. bittersweet

C. elegiac

D. uplifting

Chapter 13 ends with a literal and metaphorical image of a door closing, but as one door closes, another one opens. *Bleak*, choice A, means depressing and dreary. *Bittersweet*, choice B, refers to something that is both pleasant and painful. *Elegiac*, choice C, means funeral-like. And *uplifting*, choice D, means providing hope.

Chapter 14

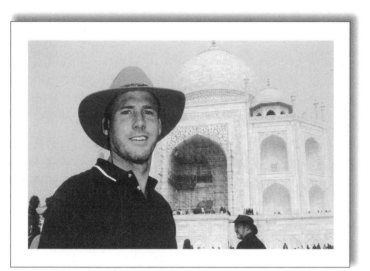

Jaipur and Agra, India
February 7–8

We landed in Jaipur, a city of two and a half million people in northern India, and the capital of the state of Rajasthan. Famous for its forts, palaces, and colorful culture, Jaipur is frequently called "The Pink City," and is the commercial center for most of the rural regions of Rajasthan.

Though we weren't sure what to expect, we quickly learned that India was a country like no other. After showing our passport in *three* different places, we boarded the bus that would take us through the city of Jaipur to the Amber Fort, which was once home to the Maharaja.

Our guide spoke perfect Indian-accented English, and as we made our way across the city of Jaipur, he informed us that Jaipur is regarded as one of India's most beautiful cities. He seemed to believe it as well. In the forty minutes it took to reach our destination, he would point out various monuments and explain what they were. His favorite words, as far as we could tell, were *Jaipur, beautiful,* and *pink.* Every description contained or ended with a variation of the following:

"Jaipur. The beautiful city. Jaipur. The pink city. Look. Can you see how beautiful it is? The landscape is beautiful, and the buildings in the old town are painted pink. Jaipur is the pink city. Jaipur is the beautiful city."

Meanwhile, Micah and I were staring out the windows with our mouths agape.

People were everywhere. The sidewalks and streets were packed, and our bus shared the roads with pedestrians, scooters, bicycles, camels, elephants, donkeys, and horse-drawn carts, all moving at different speeds and zigzagging in traffic. Cows— sacred in the Hindu culture—roamed freely throughout the city, nosing through piles of garbage along with dogs and goats.

The poverty struck us forcefully. Ragged tent sites and houses slapped together with rotting boards or whatever discarded materials could be found were home to tens of thousands of people. They lined the main thoroughfare and all the crossroads we passed. People dressed in rags were everywhere, and dozens, if not hundreds, were sleeping in the gutter. People defecated and urinated in plain view, yet no one but us seemed even to notice. The smell of diesel fuel was overwhelming.

Meanwhile, our guide continued.

"Look at the fancy houses just beyond the walls. Can you see how beautiful they are? In the old town, all the buildings are pink. Jaipur is the pink city. Jaipur is the beautiful city."

Micah leaned over to me. "Where are the fancy houses again?"

"I think he said they're behind the walls over there. See those roofs?"

"You mean behind the slums?"

"Yeah."

"And this is a beautiful city? He's got to be out of his mind."

At that point, one of the other members of our tour who was sitting behind us leaned forward.

"Actually," he said, "Jaipur is wealthy when compared to some of the other cities in India. You can't even begin to imagine what Calcutta or Bombay look like."

"It's worse than this?" Micah asked.

"By a long shot. Believe it or not, Jaipur *is* the beautiful city."

After that, all we could do was stare out the windows, wondering how on earth people survived like this.

The Amber Fort, located six miles from the city, was built atop a hill, and is surrounded by peaks and easily defended valleys that made it ideal for protection of the Maharaja.

At the base of the fort, we broke into groups of four and rode elephants up the long, winding road that led to a large courtyard that served as the entrance to the fort itself.

It took some time for our entire group to arrive at the gates—we'd needed over twenty elephants, and they moved slowly. Micah and I quickly learned that Indian vendors were even more aggressive than those in Peru. They crowded around us in groups of four to six, all of them holding trinkets, undercutting each other's prices. It didn't matter if we said no or walked away; they simply followed us, each of them almost shouting to get our attention. If we refused a second time, they closed in tighter and spoke even louder. The people in the tour first to arrive at the fort clustered in a defensive circle, backs to the crowd, trying hard to ignore the shouts. The vendors kept at it for over thirty minutes. In the end, they would follow our group right up to the door.

We toured the Amber Fort for the next hour, marveling at the blend of Hindu and Muslim architecture. There were spacious, scenic courtyards, high-quality paintings and frescoes, and individual apartments for the dozen concubines of the Maharaja. We took photographs in front of a large garden that used an ingenious system of irrigation to enable the flowers to bloom year-round, and eventually made our way to the upper levels, where we could appreciate the fort's location from a defensive standpoint.

Yet it was the Hall of Mirrors that was most impressive. It was our first exposure to the intricate marble work for which the fort had become famous, and up close the workmanship was of higher quality than anything we'd seen. Built over ten years and using two thousand workers, the Hall of Mirrors has marble walls, inlaid with tens of thousands of precious and semiprecious stones, as well as thousands of tiny mirrors. In the evening, we were told that the Maharaja would be entertained by candlelight in front of the hall, where the stones and mirrors would reflect the gentle light. While the relief carvings of Angkor Wat had been detailed, even I understood that it was far more difficult to work with marble. Every one of the tens of thousands of inlaid gems and mirrors fit perfectly.

"It's incredible," Micah whispered. "But I think it's almost too much. A little gaudy for my tastes."

"Well, that's all right. I don't think you can find anyone who even knows how to do work like this anymore. Unless you move to India, of course."

"I don't think that's going to happen."

After leaving the fort, we drove through one slum after the next, passed through a gate, and—in a way that only India can truly surprise—found ourselves in paradise.

Our hotel was once a palace owned by the Maharaja. The rooms were laid out in cabana style, and the grounds were impeccable. Lush with trees, fountains, winding paths, and flowers, there was also a full-service health spa, tennis courts, fitness center, and swimming pool. The employees were both professional and efficient; if we so much as glanced in their direction, they rushed toward us to see if there was anything they could do. Every member of the tour was escorted to his or her rooms by individuals who not only explained the features of the rooms in exceptional detail, but offered to pick up laundry and shine shoes as well, with the promise that everything would be returned within a couple of hours. It was the most luxurious hotel we would stay in on the tour, yet no matter how nice it was, neither Micah nor I could escape the reality that we knew lay just outside the door.

In the evening, we attended yet another cocktail party and had our heads wrapped in turbans for our visit to the City Palace. There, we were greeted in typically royal fashion; contingents of guards stood at attention alongside camels, white stallions, and elephants, all of which had been decorated for our arrival. We had dinner and were treated to a show with traditional Indian entertainers, but both Micah and I were tired from the day and looked forward to nothing more than getting back to our room and crashing.

In the morning, we had two choices: We could visit the museum and various shopping areas, or simply stay at the hotel.

Micah and I stayed at the hotel. Neither one of us had any desire to leave the sanctuary of our compound, and for the first time in two weeks, we did absolutely nothing at all. In the afternoon, Micah was wearing sunglasses and a bathing suit, relaxing in a lounge chair near the pool.

"Now this," Micah said, "is exactly what I needed."

"I know what you mean," I said. "I feel sort of guilty, though. It could be my last chance to see India, and we're sitting by the pool at the hotel."

"Did you really want to see another museum and go shopping?"

"No. I'm just saying that it makes me feel guilty."

"You always feel guilty. That's your problem."

"I thought my problem was that I didn't have enough friends."

"That, too."

I opened my arms wide in mock gratitude. "That's why I like you, Micah. You're always willing to offer constructive criticism."

"I'm glad to help. Besides, someone had to take over after mom died."

"She was irreplaceable."

"You know what she was?" Micah reflected. "She was like the center of the wheel in our family, and we were all the spokes. And once she was gone, we didn't have our center anymore. I think that's why the loss hit us so hard. Not only was mom gone, but we had to become a new kind of family. I think that's why you, me, and Dana started to get close again."

"What about dad?"

"I don't know," he said. "Part of it was losing mom, but I still think dad was manic-depressive. When mom was around, I think she was able to keep his mood swings under control. But after she was gone—well, dad didn't have a center either."

"Do you think he was a good dad? When we were growing up, I mean?"

"In some ways. Not so good in others. But you know, in the end, you have to give them both credit for being good parents simply because of the way their kids turned out. We're happily married, successful, ethical, and we remained close as siblings. If your kids can say the same thing later in life, won't you think you did a good job as a parent?"

"Without a doubt," I conceded.

*   *   *

In the morning, we flew to Agra, where we'd visit the Taj Mahal.

Agra held the same sights outside our bus windows as had Jaipur, with two major differences: There was far more pollution in the air, and far more roads were unpaved.

Because of the pollution, we had to change buses; to reach the Taj, we'd ride the last couple of miles in electric buses, and ended up stopping a quarter-mile from the gates.

From where we parked, it was impossible to see the Taj Mahal. What most people don't realize is that the Taj is actually part of a massive compound. Again, we waited in a long line— this one to check our bags for explosives or weapons—and we finally entered the compound. Even then, we couldn't see the monument.

Instead, we filed along a sidewalk, flanked on either side by what had essentially been apartments for guests of Shah Jahan. Up ahead and to the right was a large brick structure that served as a massive ornamental gate, and again we had to wait in line and be checked before passing through.

On the other side, however, we finally had our first glimpse of what some regard as the finest monument to love ever constructed.

The Taj Mahal was begun in 1631 by Shah Jahan, a Mughal emperor, in memory of his second wife, Mumtaz Mahal, who died after giving birth to their fourteenth child. It is, in other words, a tomb. The cenotaph honoring Mumtaz Mahal inside the Taj is inlaid with jewels and lies near that of her husband's. The Taj is one of the most symmetrical buildings ever constructed—the cenotaph of Mumtaz is directly in the center of the dome; the four corner towers are exactly the same distance from the dome; and exactly the same height.

The Taj took twenty thousand workers, one thousand elephants, and twenty-two years to build, and material was brought in from all over India and Central Asia. It is regarded as a symbol of eternal love, yet Shah Jahan spent little time there. Soon after it was completed, Shah Jahan's—and Mumtaz's—son deposed the emperor and imprisoned him in the Great Red Fort, a few miles away. While Shah Jahan could see the Taj from his prison cell, he was never allowed to set foot in the Taj Mahal again.

From where we stood, it didn't look real; set against a murky, polluted sky, the marble shone brilliantly, and the image was reflected in the long, rectangular ponds before it. Most people, when seeing pictures of the Taj Mahal (which means "Crown Palace"), believe it's constructed of white, unadorned marble; only up close does the detail of each marble block become vivid. Like the Hall of Mirrors—only on a much larger and grander scale—the Taj Mahal is adorned with precious and semiprecious stones, inlaid in the shapes of flowers and vines. After taking pictures, we made the walk to the monument itself and studied the ornamental facade.

"Now that's a lot of marble," Micah offered succinctly.

We spent a little more than an hour at the Taj Mahal, which surprisingly sufficed. The Taj, after all, is a crypt; there is not much inside other than the small room where Mumtaz and eventually Shah Jahan were buried, and most attention is directed to the detail of the marble blocks used in the construction. And it *is* amazing; yet, because the Taj had been built with such mathematical precision, the artistry seemed curiously uninspiring. If you found a design on one side, the exact same design was mechanically replicated on the opposite side. While a marvel of construction, it was strangely repetitious.

Both Micah and I were fascinated by the fact that the son had imprisoned the father and never let him set foot in the Taj Mahal—the crypt of his own mother—during the last years of Shah Jahan's life.

"You see," Micah said, with a knowing nod. "That's exactly what I was talking about. Dad was a lot better father than old Shah Jahan must have been. His kid hated him."

I nodded in agreement. And yet, as I stared up at the massive monument to Mumtaz, I found myself thinking not about my father, but about my sister.

In January 1993, less than three weeks after I moved to North Carolina, I was back in California.

Right after the new year, my sister had gone to see a new physician; he had ordered a new MRI from a different hospital. MRI scanning machines, at that time, were undergoing rapid technological change, and the newer machines were able to provide images that their predecessors were not. Dana's image, we were told, had been taken on a dated machine; a new image might provide the answers.

She lay on the bed, put earplugs in, and was rolled into the machine. The machine makes loud clanking noises—like someone banging a pan with a spoon—and within a few hours the scans were ready. And there, plain as day, was something that wasn't supposed to be there. Dana, we learned, had a brain tumor.

She was scheduled for immediate surgery at UC San Francisco, and I flew out to join Micah and my dad. In the hotel the night before, Micah and I tried to keep the mood upbeat, but my dad was extremely tense throughout the evening. It was only when Micah and I were alone that we felt comfortable enough to talk about our own fears and worries.

Our sister, our *younger* sister, had a brain tumor. As if losing our mother hadn't been hard enough, we now had to confront this.

The surgery was scheduled for early in the morning and we brought Dana to the hospital a little before seven. Because of tight schedules, however, the surgery didn't begin until nearly noon, making the day one of the longest in our lives. It wasn't until after 7:00 P.M. that the doctor came to talk to us.

He told us the surgery had gone well and that they'd removed as much of the tumor as they could. It hadn't been possible to remove it all. Parts of the tumor had spread to areas deep within her brain and other parts were intertwined with areas of the brain that performed vital functions. To have removed every speck of the tumor, the doctor informed us, would have left Dana in a vegetative state.

It took a long time for the doctor to explain Dana's condition to us in a way that we'd eventually understand. We wanted specifics—how much of the tumor is left, where is it located, what does it mean in the long run—but brain surgery, we would come to learn, is often more about judgment than rules.

"When she recovers," the doctor said, "she'll start her anti-seizure medication and begin radiation. Hopefully, that will kill whatever was left of the tumor, the parts we couldn't get to."

"What if the radiation doesn't work? What then? Do we do surgery again?"

The doctor shook his head. "Let's just hope the radiation does work. Like I said, I couldn't get to parts of the tumor without making her a lot worse."

"What are her chances? Is she going to make it?"

"It depends on the type of tumor. We're having it biopsied now. Some tumors are more susceptible to radiation than others.

Some grow quickly, and some don't. We won't know for sure until the results come in. But if the tumor's susceptible, the radiation should take care of it."

"So there's a chance she can still lead a normal life?"

The doctor shifted. "For the most part."

We waited, wondering what he meant, and the doctor finally went on. "The antiseizure medication is contraindicated in pregnancy because of possible birth defects."

The doctor paused. Micah and I glanced at each other, already knowing what was coming.

"More than likely," the doctor added, "she'll never have children."

None of us said anything for a long time.

"When can we see her?" I finally asked.

"Tomorrow. She's sleeping, and it's probably best if she rests for a while."

That night, Micah and I slept in the same hotel room. Or rather, tried to sleep. For the most part, all I could do was stare at the ceiling, thinking about a conversation Dana and I had had on our birthday long ago. *"I want to be married, and I want to have kids..."* my sister had said.

"That's it?"

"That's it. That's all I want out of life."

The memory nearly broke my heart.

My sister's head was heavily wrapped in bandages when we saw her. Mostly she slept, and when she woke, she was groggy. Her gaze was unfocused, her movements lethargic.

"Did it...go...okay?" she stammered out. Her voice was a whisper.

"It went great, sweetheart," Micah said.

"Oh...good..."

"I love you, sweetie," I said.

"Love you...both."

And then she slept again.

A week later, we had the results of the biopsy. My sister had essentially three types of cancerous cells in her brain: oligodendroglioma, astrocytoma, and glioblastoma multiforme; all are fast-growing tumors that spread in spiderlike fashion; they are only partially susceptible to radiation and chemotherapy. As we learned what we could about it, only one fact about the tumors stood out in our minds.

Though all could be deadly, one form of her tumor was essentially so. After five years the survival rate for those with glioblastoma multiforme was less than 2 percent.

My sister had just turned twenty-six.

I returned to North Carolina three days later, the morning my sister was to be released from the hospital. In addition to learning that she'd need radiation, my sister was put on the anti-seizure medication. With her head bandaged, she began the slow process of healing. The guilt I felt about not being with her left me aching for weeks, and I threw myself into work.

Yet, life eked on, bringing with it additional sources of stress. My new boss immediately began exerting pressure on me to perform; Cat and I bought our first house. In the span of three months, we'd moved, changed jobs, bought a house, began the process of remodeling, and worried incessantly about my sister.

That wasn't all. My sister's diagnosis was almost too much for my father to bear, and my relocation to North Carolina only seemed to feed the anger and guilt he felt inside. Again, I was the outlet for his rage and sense of helplessness. When I told him about our new house, for example, he responded by tersely informing me that I better not expect any help with the down payment. When he called, he spoke only to my wife; usually I stood by waiting for my chance to visit only to hear Cathy say, "Well, Nick is here. Do you want to say hi?" There would be a long pause before Cat would go on. "Oh, well, okay, then. 'Bye, Dad. Love you." Then, ever so quietly, she'd hang up the phone.

"He didn't want to talk to me?" I'd ask.

"It's not you," she'd whisper, taking me in her arms. "He's just scared."

With Dana, my dad kept up a brave front. He brought her to her appointments, and in April, when the radiation started, she moved back into the house. The radiation made her sick and caused her to lose a good deal of hair on the side of her head, but she sounded upbeat whenever I'd call. My sister, always an optimist at heart, knew she'd be okay.

"I've been praying, Nick," she told me once. "And I think it's working. It's like I can feel the tumors dying. I like to imagine them screaming in agony as they're dying."

"I'm sure they are. You're young and strong."

"Will you pray for me, too?"

"You don't have to ask, Dana. I've been praying for you every day."

"Thanks," she said.

"How's dad holding up?"

"He's been great. You can't believe how helpful he is. He cooks me soup and even bought me a television with a remote so I don't have to get up to change the channel."

"Good. I'm glad."

"So how are you doing? Anything exciting going on?"

I hesitated. There was something more, but part of me didn't want to answer. How could I tell her? At the same time, I knew my sister would find out eventually; others in the family, including Micah, already knew.

"Well, we just found out that Cat is pregnant again," I finally said. "The baby's due in September."

For a long time, my sister was silent.

"That's wonderful," she finally said. Her voice was subdued. "I'm happy for you two."

"Did you tell her?" Micah asked me a few minutes later. I'd called him immediately after hanging up with Dana.

"Yeah, I told her."

"How'd she take it?"

"About like I expected."

"It's terrible, isn't it? I mean, she'd be a great mother. She's just like mom was."

I said nothing; there was nothing really to say.

"I've been thinking about you," Micah finally added. "And the way things have been happening lately."

"What do you mean?"

"I'm talking about the highs and lows. First, you get married and you're on an incredible high. Six weeks later, mom dies, and it's impossible to get any lower. Cat gets pregnant for the first time, then has a miscarriage. You and Cat make the decision to move and you're excited about starting a new life; a month later, Dana has a seizure and we find out she has a brain tumor. Then, you learn that Cathy's pregnant again; at the same time, we find out that Dana can't have kids and she isn't likely to live more than five years. It's like you've been living on a roller coaster that's racing up and down, without hitting a level area. For you, it's been the highest of highs and the lowest of lows."

"I could say the same thing about you," I offered quietly. "And dad, too."

"I know," he said. "It kind of takes the joy out of those highs, doesn't it?"

Dana's radiation ended halfway through the summer and, remarkably, her CAT scan came back clear. The doctors were optimistic, my sister's hair began growing back slowly, and for the first time since the seizure, our worries about her were relegated to the background.

With my sister's improvement, my dad's behavior toward me changed for the better as well. He began speaking to me on the phone again; it was tentative at first, a hesitant rapprochement. He still talked to Cat at great length, however, and we learned that he'd actually begun dating again.

He'd met a woman, he said, and he liked her a lot.

Dana, too, was getting along better with Bob; after the surgery, their relationship had been rocky.

And Micah, as usual, kept humming along, escaping for long weekends and avoiding all serious relationships.

In September 1993, Ryan was born, though I wasn't at the hospital for his birth. Instead, I was out of town on business—a meeting I couldn't miss—and Cat's water broke just as the meeting was ending. I wouldn't arrive to see my son until the following day.

In November, our family reunited in Texas for Thanksgiving with my dad's younger brother Monty, and I was struck by the fact that my father seemed genuinely happy. He'd fallen in love, he said, and all three of us were pleased that he'd finally found someone whose company he enjoyed. This news, however, about our father suddenly seemed less important than what else we learned on that trip.

Dana told us that she and Bob had broken up again. This wasn't entirely unexpected; the stress of her recent illness would have been enough to test any relationship.

"Oh," I remember saying, "that's too bad. I like Bob."

"There's more though," my sister said.

"What's that?"

She smiled, offering the faintest of shrugs. "I'm pregnant," she said.

I didn't know what to say.

"Don't worry. I've stopped taking my antiseizure medicine."

There was even more. In our family, I was slowly beginning to realize, there was always something more. Not only was my sister seriously jeopardizing her health—a worry that would plague us over the next seven months—but well on her way to becoming a single mother. We soon found out that she was expecting twins.

Then, increasing our worries, right after Christmas, my dad abruptly informed my sister she had to move out of the house, despite the fact that she had nowhere else to go.

Though I never told anyone, I secretly began to wonder if my father was not only manic-depressive, but mentally ill in other ways as well.

In December, my dad learned that the woman he'd been dating—the first woman he'd dated after my mom's death—hadn't actually been divorced. Instead, she'd only been separated from her husband, and had been using my father for the little money he had. By the end of the relationship, my father was deep in debt. When he could afford nothing more, she cut off contact entirely. I don't know whether my dad kept calling the woman and she finally grew tired of his persistence, or whether it was accidental, but her husband eventually found out about the relationship. The husband was a burly police officer, and he'd physically threatened my dad in the driveway of my dad's home. My father had been terrified by the confrontation, even fearing for his life.

It was this turn of events, right around Christmas, I believe, that finally broke him emotionally.

From that point on, my dad embarked on a downward spiral that only grew worse over time. His mood and attitude were bitter, and he became not only angry, but paranoid as well. Because he couldn't go to the police—what good would it have done?—he bought guns and ammunition instead. He asked my sister to move out of the house. And then he bought a dog named Flame.

Flame, a German shepherd, had originally been trained for police duty, but because of his volatile nature, couldn't be used. Though attached to my dad, Flame made everyone else nervous. The dog growled and snapped, seemingly at random, and wasn't trustworthy. His combustible personality, combined with my father's instability, made for a dangerous mix.

During the first few months of 1994, my brother and I talked endlessly on the phone, about both our sister and our father, wondering what, if anything, we could do.

"Should I invite Dana to live out here with us?" I asked.

"She can't, Nick," Micah answered. "Her doctors are out here."

"What about dad?"

"He's adamant that she can't live at home anymore. And to

be honest, I really don't want her living there either. He's really getting strange these days. And with Flame...no, Dana can't stay there. Not if she has kids."

"Can she stay with you?"

"I've asked, but she says she doesn't want to. She says she can handle it. Her friend Olga has a small room that she says Dana can rent."

Olga lived in the old farmhouse where we boarded our horses; she'd known Dana for years.

"How's she going to handle it? She has no job, no husband, no money, she has a brain tumor..."

"I know. I try to tell her that."

"What does she say?"

"She says that she'll make do. She isn't worried at all. She's excited about having kids."

"How can she not be worried? What if she has a seizure and no one's around to help her?"

"She has faith that it'll all work out."

I hesitated. "Do you think that's enough?"

"I don't know," he answered.

Thankfully, my sister made it through her pregnancy uneventfully, and in May 1994, she delivered healthy twin boys she named Cody and Cole. Within a week of her delivery, she was back on her antiseizure medication, and she began taking care of the babies in the cramped room she called home. Micah and I sent her money, and somehow it was enough for her to survive. Dana and the twins slept on a fold-out mattress on a wooden floor for two months; by the end of the summer, however, my sister had reconciled with Bob and had decided to move in with him so the boys could live with their father. Surprising us, she hadn't told him that she'd been pregnant until right before the twins had been born.

During that time, my dad devoted most of his time to working with the dog. Despite my sister's apparent good health, his anger only grew worse. In that six-month period, he began to estrange himself from the rest of his extended family. He refused to take calls from his mother, father, or siblings; if they sent a letter, he returned it unopened. Nor would he talk to me—or Micah and Dana—about his reasons for cutting them out of his life. If we asked him what was going on, he grew furious with us—right to Nuclear Launch—and through gritted teeth would tell us that it was "none of your damn business." For whatever reason, he'd begun to blame his family for all the problems he had in his life. At the time, however, I'd been through so many ups and downs that I somehow believed my dad would get through this as well.

My father, I eventually found out, began seeing a psychiatrist around that time, which both my brother and I thought would help. But my dad, I alone seemed to recognize, had been maintaining a Jekyll-and-Hyde existence for years. He could fool people—indeed, no one at work ever mentioned that anything seemed amiss—and I think he was able to fool the psychiatrist as well. Instead of putting my father on antidepressants, which I think would have benefited him, the doctor instead prescribed Valium, which only made matters worse.

With Dana and Bob back together, the twins healthy, and dad limiting—though not cutting off—contact with us, Micah concentrated on work, excelled at his job, and continued to date.

As for me, three thousand miles from the rest of my family, life went on as usual with one small exception. Right after

Cat and I celebrated our fifth anniversary, and using my wife's grandparents as inspiration, I began writing again.

Throughout 1993 and 1994, my brother and I saw quite a bit of each other, despite the distance between us. The pharmaceutical company we worked for would hold national sales meetings to promote their new product releases. In addition, training sessions were conducted out of the home offices in New Jersey, and Micah and I would inevitably end up in the same sessions. He also visited me in North Carolina and I would make it out to California at least once a year. As always, we would talk about Dana and my dad. Because my brother was the conduit I used to follow the goings-on in the family, I needed to talk to him. Because I was the only one with whom he could speak freely, he needed to talk to me, too.

In late 1994, we were at a national sales conference and relaxing after a day of meetings when the same subjects arose.

"How's dad doing?" I asked.

"Who knows. But I think he's met someone new and he's dating again."

"Does he ever go to see the twins?"

"No, not really."

"Have you asked him why?"

"He'd rather spend the weekend with his dog."

"He didn't say that."

"Not in so many words. But that's the way he acts. It's like the dog and this new woman are the only things he cares about anymore."

"Any word on why he won't talk to his family?"

"No."

"But he's dating?"

"Yeah. Can you believe it? Half the time, I think he's getting better. But when you look at the whole picture…" He trailed off. "I hope he snaps out of it, but this time I'm not so sure. He seems so angry all the time."

"How's Dana?"

"The babies are keeping her busy. Her last CAT scan was good. There's no sign of the tumor. But man, you should see those boys. They're so cute. It almost makes me want kids."

"Almost?"

"Not now," he said quickly. "In a few years, I mean."

I laughed.

"So what do you think of all the buy-out and merger rumors we've been hearing lately?" Micah asked.

We'd heard that American Cyanamid—the parent company of Lederle Labs—was supposedly on the sales block, and thus all of the attendees at the meeting had been worried about the possibility of losing their jobs.

"Who knows. Whatever happens, happens. After everything we've been through, I'm sure we'll land on our feet."

Less than two weeks after the meeting, as 1994 was coming to a close, we learned that the company was to be bought by American Home Products. In January, the company began the slow process of restructuring; to keep my job, I had to move to Greenville, South Carolina. Micah was offered a position just south of Los Angeles. While I reluctantly took the transfer, my brother decided to give up his job.

"I can't leave," he said to me. "This is my home, and besides, I can't leave Dana and dad."

"What are you going to do?"

"I'll probably go back to real estate and see what happens. How's your novel coming?"

"It's just about done. Before editing, I mean."

"Are you going to try to get this one published?"

"I think so."

"Is it better than the first two you wrote?"

"I guess I'll find out."

"Hey, maybe you'll be out of the pharmaceutical business soon, too."

"Maybe." I sighed. "We'll see how it goes. I've given up trying to predict the future."

Questions and Explanations
for Chapter 14

The ten questions on chapter 14 focus on grammar and usage, vocabulary, comprehension, and literary terms. Some of the questions combine two or more of these areas, requiring you to synthesize your knowledge, make inferences, and interpret the text. The questions are designed to determine both your current level of understanding of the memoir and your ability to answer higher-level questions.

The following sentence tests your ability to recognize grammar and usage errors. The sentence contains either a single error or no error at all. If the sentence contains an error, select the one underlined part that must be changed to make the sentence correct. If there is no error, select choice D.

1. <u>Dana's</u> cancerous cells were <u>site specific,</u> they only
     A   B

   <u>affect</u> the brain and spinal cord. <u>No error</u>
     C   D

Choice A checks to see if the apostrophe is used correctly. To form the possessive case of a singular noun, whether it is a common noun or a proper noun, add an apostrophe and an s— for example, "Dana's, Jill's, Michael's."

Although choice B appears to be checking the subject's complement (the word that follows the verb and completes the thought), it is actually checking the use of the comma. If both groups of words before and after the comma are complete thoughts and can stand alone as two independent clauses, then a comma by itself is not the correct way to punctuate the compound sentence—for example, "I read the paper, my wife made dinner." Both groups of words to the left and right of the comma are complete thoughts, so they need to be joined with a semicolon or a comma and a coordinating conjunction (*and, but, or, for, nor, so, yet*). Thus, the example should be "I read the paper, and my wife made dinner" or "I read the paper; my wife made dinner."

Choice C checks whether you know the difference between the homophones *affect* and *effect*. Remember that *affect* is typically used as a verb, meaning to influence. *Effect* is typically a noun, meaning something that is produced. If someone or something is doing something, usually the correct word choice is *affect*—for example, "Research has shown that rereading a passage will affect a student's level of comprehension."

The following two questions test your vocabulary. Choose the word or set of words that, when inserted

in the sentence, best fits the meaning of the sentence
as a whole.

2. Following the death of his wife, Mr. Sparks became a
somewhat _____ man, often acting quite disagreeably.

   A. abstemious

   B. beneficent

   C. mellifluous

   D. cantankerous

Abstemious, choice A, means consuming in moderation.
Beneficent, choice B, is performing acts of kindness. *Mellifluous*, choice C, is having a smooth, rich flow. *Cantankerous*,
choice D, is having a stubborn disposition.

3. Using _____ such as *crashing* to indicate that he and
his brother went to sleep creates a _____ tone in the
memoir.

   A. a colloquialism...conversational

   B. a vulgarity...formal

   C. slang...heightened

   D. jargon...clichéd

First, determine how *crashing* is used in the context of the
question. If the word is a type of informal and familiar speech,
consider choice A. If it's a crude, coarse, or unrefined term,
select choice B. If it's informal usage that is derived from the
unconventional use of a standard word, consider choice C. And
if it's the technical language of a particular profession, select
choice D.

Because choices A and C have similar first words, you must differentiate between the second words in each choice. *Conversational* is characteristic of everyday speaking, and *heightened* refers to more formal language.

Question 4 asks you to determine the meaning of a word used in context.

4. The Indian guide who was leading the tour was impressed with Jaipur, referring to it as a beautiful city. In response, Sparks writes, "He seemed to believe it as well." The tone of Sparks's sentence indicates that:

   A. the brothers agree with the tour guide's assessment

   B. the brothers didn't understand the tour guide's meaning

   C. the brothers disagreed with the guide's opinion

   D. the brothers were tired of visiting so many sites

Tone is an author's or a character's attitude. You must first determine what was going through the minds of the brothers as they were looking at the city and listening to their guide. If they concur with his assessment, select choice A. If they couldn't even understand what the guide was attempting to tell them, select choice B. If the focus of the sentence is on *he* as opposed to the brothers, and they totally disagree with his assessment, then select choice C. And although the brothers may have been tired of visiting so many places, there is no indication of that in this sentence, so eliminate choice D.

Question 5 tests your knowledge of literary terms.

5. When reflecting on his mother, Micah comments, "She was like the center of the wheel in our family, and we were all the spokes." Which figures of speech are used in his description?

    A. hyperbole

    B. metaphor

    C. personification

    D. simile

Notice that the question indicates that there will be more than one correct answer. *Hyperbole,* choice A, is an exaggerated statement used to heighten effect and to emphasize a point—for example, "This learning guide has defined *hyperbole* a million times already." A *metaphor,* choice B, is a comparison made between two unlike things without using a connective word— for example, "LeBron James is an animal on the basketball court." *Personification,* choice C, is giving nonhuman things human characteristics—for example, "The leaves danced in the wind." And a *simile,* choice D, is a comparison made between two unlike things using a connective word, such as *like, as,* or *than*—for example, "She looked as fresh as the morning snow."

Question 6 asks you to make an inference based on strong textual evidence.

6. The visual images of poverty and the smell of diesel fuel result in each of the following effects EXCEPT:

    A. providing a realistic description of the city

    B. substantiating the guide's claim that Jaipur is a beautiful city

C. enabling the brothers to have a better appreciation for life in the United States

D. allowing readers to share the brothers' experience

Imagery is writing that appeals to the senses. The details and examples that an author uses to create imagery have a number of effects. If you can see the city of Jaipur more clearly based on the description, eliminate choice A. If these details support the assertion that Jaipur is a beautiful city, eliminate choice B. If the details provide a contrast to the way of life in America, enabling the brothers to better appreciate what they have at home, eliminate choice C. And if the sights and sounds enable you as a reader to gain a better understanding of what Jaipur is really like, eliminate choice D.

Question 7 tests your knowledge of literary terms.

7. Sparks writes that his father "had been maintaining a Jekyll-and-Hyde existence for years." What literary device is he using to describe his father's life?

   A. allusion

   B. hyperbole

   C. metaphor

   D. personification

An *allusion*, choice A, is an indirect reference. Some of the most common types of allusions are historical, such as making a reference to Napoleon by saying that someone met his Waterloo; biblical, such as John Coffey in *The Green Mile* being a Christ figure; mythological, a reference to a Greek or Roman myth, such as someone having the Midas touch; and literary, a reference to a character in a work of literature, such as a couple being ill-fated like Romeo and Juliet.

Hyperbole, choice B, is an obvious and intentional exaggeration—for example, "This learning guide has discussed hyperbole about four million times."

A *metaphor*, choice C, is a comparison made between two unlike things without using a connective word—for example, "LeBron James is an animal on the basketball court."

Personification, choice D, is giving nonhuman things a human characteristic, such as in "Opportunity knocked on the door."

Question 8 tests your knowledge of literary terms.

8. In a seemingly throwaway line, Sparks adds at the end of a paragraph near the end of the chapter, "and using my wife's grandparents as inspiration, I began writing again." He doesn't mention anything else about what is going to be his first published novel. This is an example of what literary device?

   A. foreshadowing

   B. flashback

   C. in medias res

   D. satire

Foreshadowing, choice A, is providing hints or clues to future events. For example, when Benvolio suggests to Romeo that finding a new female beauty may help Romeo get over Rosaline, it foreshadows Romeo's falling in love with Juliet when he sees her later in the play. *Flashback*, choice B, is a narrative technique that incorporates an event or series of events that occurred prior to the current time. *In medias res*, choice C, means starting in the middle of things. Each book in the Twilight series opens with a scene that actually occurs near the end of the novel and then moves back in time to tell readers how the characters got to that point. *Satire*, choice D, is a genre of writing in which the shortcomings of a society are held up to ridicule in order to not only expose them but also to offer solutions. Jonathan Swift's *A Modest Proposal* is a famous example of satire.

Question 9 asks you to analyze a sentence and asks you to make an inference.

9. After discussing their father, Nicholas thinks, "And yet, as I stared up at the massive monument to Mumtaz, I found myself thinking not about my father, but about my sister." What does this sentence foreshadow?

   A. their father's death

   B. the publication of Nicholas's first novel

   C. the rift in the brothers' relationship

   D. Dana's death

Foreshadowing provides hints or clues to future events. For example, when Benvolio suggests to Romeo that finding a new female beauty may help Romeo get over Rosaline, it foreshadows Romeo's falling in love with Juliet when he sees her later in the play.

In this passage, Nicholas is looking at the Taj Mahal, a monument constructed for the shah's dead wife; thus, a connection with death is a logical choice. If the focal point of the sentence seems to be Nicholas's father, select choice A. If the subject matter of Nicholas's first novel is death, select choice B. If a rift, or metaphorical death, between the brothers seems to be imminent, select choice C. And if thinking about his sister while staring at a tomb might hint at Dana's death, select choice D.

Question 10 tests your understanding of irony.

10. At the end of the growing-up narrative, Micah says to his brother, "Hey, maybe you'll be out of the pharmaceutical business soon, too." Even though at this point in time, Micah doesn't know that this will indeed be true, readers are privy to that information. This is an example of what type of irony?

   A. cosmic irony

   B. dramatic irony

   C. situational irony

   D. verbal irony

Understanding *irony*, the situation of appearance versus reality, is essential to understanding most literary texts. *Cosmic irony*, also known as irony of fate, is the situation where no matter what a character attempts to do, he or she cannot escape his or her fate. The most famous example of this is the Greek myth of Oedipus, who was fated to grow up and kill his father and marry his mother, no matter what he or anyone else tried to do to prevent it. *Dramatic irony* is when the words and actions of the characters have a different meaning for the reader than they do for the characters themselves. This is the result of the reader having more background information than the character has. For example, the audience knows that Juliet is not really dead when Romeo discovers her body in the crypt, but he does not, and so he stabs himself. *Situational irony* is the incongruity between the expected outcome and what actually occurs. For example, Macbeth's misinterpretation of the witches' prophecies is an example of situational irony, because he expects their words to mean one thing but in reality they mean something else. *Verbal irony* is meaning the opposite of what is stated; sarcasm is a form of verbal irony. For example, when Mark Antony is talking about the conspirators as he stands over the body of dead Caesar, he says, "For Brutus is an honorable man." Clearly Antony does not think Brutus is really honorable.

Chapter 15

Lalibela, Ethiopia
February 9–10

W e'd started the morning in Jaipur, had flown to Agra to see the Taj Mahal, and later that afternoon we boarded the plane once more for a flight to Addis Ababa, Ethiopia. We arrived late, landing well after dark.

Even in darkness Addis Ababa surprised us. Our impressions of Ethiopia were largely based on what we'd seen on television or read about in newspapers, and I suppose I imagined a city similar to Phnom Penh, or even Jaipur. Yet Addis was far more similar to Lima, and we were struck by its cosmopolitan atmosphere. Long, well-manicured greenbelts lined the main thoroughfare, the streets were clean, well lit, and used only by cars, and for the first time in weeks we saw elements of American culture; billboards advertised Coca-Cola and jeans from the Gap.

Our guide spoke excellent English, and when we asked him about the city, he nodded.

"Yes, Addis is a modern city. But it is not normally this clean."

"What do you mean?"

"Last week, they held a major meeting with all the nations of Africa represented. The government has been cleaning the city for weeks to make a good impression."

Still, there's only so much cleaning one could do. Addis Ababa, on the surface anyway, seemed incredibly, almost shockingly, wealthy compared to the cities we'd recently visited.

In the morning, we rode back to the airport and boarded two small propeller-driven planes for the flight to Lalibela.

Lalibela is the spiritual home of the Abyssinian (or Ethiopian) Orthodox Church, but is most famous for the monolithic cave churches carved in the thirteenth century. King Lalibela had ordered their construction, and using forty thousand slaves, eleven cave churches were carved from stone. What makes the churches unique is that they don't sit aboveground; instead, they had been carved into the earth so that the rooflines of the churches are at ground level.

The airport where we landed was located in the middle of nowhere, surrounded by peaks of the Ethiopian highlands.

Aside from the airport, there were no other buildings at all and the land was reminiscent of southern Nevada, near the Sierras. Few trees grew in the rocky soil, and low-lying scrubs stretched across the valley as far as the eye could see.

Lalibela, we learned, was roughly twenty-five miles away, and two thousand feet higher in elevation. The winding asphalt road curved through the valley and along the peaks; in the hour it took to reach our destination, we never saw another vehicle.

We did, however, see a young boy around ten years of age, eight miles from Lalibela. Walking along the road, he was hauling a monstrously overstuffed burlap bag of charcoal that he intended to deliver to the city. The bag, both taller and wider than the child, had been strapped to his back and looked many times heavier than the child himself. When he saw our bus passing, he smiled and waved a greeting before continuing his slow march to the town.

Most of the town of Lalibela was situated off the main highway, along bumpy gravel roads. Its thatched-roof adobe homes featured few glass windows, but the town boasted numerous places to eat, small, family-owned businesses, and souvenir shops. Nearly everyone we saw wore western clothing. A number of tables lined the roads, offering various T-shirts, most emblazoned with American logos. For all intents and purposes, the town of Lalibela was an Ethiopian tourist trap.

Our buses parked near the carved rock churches, and as soon as we stepped off the bus, we were besieged by teens; unlike other places we'd visited, they had no trinkets for sale. Instead, they asked for money; every child who came up to us told us that he needed money either to attend school or to buy the books he needed at the school he was currently attending.

In the end, they were forced back by Ethiopian guards swinging sticks.

Lalibela was one of the least-known sites we would visit on the trip; few knew what to expect. We weren't disappointed. The vast amount of labor needed for construction—literally carving through rock by hand—was evident as soon as we gazed upon the first church we would visit. It was far larger than we'd imagined; at least sixty feet long and forty feet wide, it was surrounded by modern scaffolding that supported a roof over the top.

"The roof is to prevent leaks," the guide informed us, "and to keep the churches from decaying."

We spent the next couple of hours wandering from one church to the next. The churches were dark inside. Few had windows, and though fluorescent lights had been strung inside, they barely permeated the blackness. The floors were slick, polished by eight hundred years of use to an almost icy smoothness. Because the churches are still in use today, throw rugs had been placed throughout. Unfortunately, they didn't cover the floor in its entirety, and we moved slowly, like blind men in foreign surroundings, to prevent us from falling.

In all, we would spend three hours in Lalibela. Toward the end of our visit, Micah and I wandered off to take pictures; because the churches were so different from everything we'd seen up to that point—carved *into* stone, rather than built *with* stone—we tried to find vantage points that could capture how unique they were.

The visits to the churches had left Micah strangely silent, and as I was snapping away, he went to sit on one of the ledges overlooking the site. I eventually walked over to join him.

"So what did you think of this place?" Micah finally asked.

"It was worth seeing, if that's what you mean."

"They're not exactly like the churches we have back home, are they?"

"I don't think the kids would appreciate having to stand the whole time during the service."

He smiled. "Are you glad you still go to Mass?"

"As opposed to what?"

"Going to another Christian church?"

I thought about it. "Yeah," I said. "I am. But Cat is Catholic, too, so we've never considered changing."

"I like the church I go to now. Or used to, anyway."

"Why?"

"I don't know. I guess I just got bored that Mass always seemed the same. And I couldn't relate the sermons to my life. I think church should make you feel close to God, but I wasn't getting that. With the new church, I did for a while."

"Do you think you'll ever feel that way again?"

"I don't know. I haven't felt...close to God lately. I'm not even sure that I believe in God anymore."

"Really?"

"Not God, per se. I think God exists, but I'm not so sure that he takes an active role in the world. I think he put everything in motion and since then he's just sitting back watching how it's going to turn out."

"Hmm," I responded. "Go on."

"It's not what they tell you in church, obviously. In church, you're supposed to pray and be thankful, but like I said before I've come to the conclusion that prayer doesn't work. And for a long time there, it wasn't easy to be thankful for much. We went through one big challenge after the next. They just didn't let up. And everyone kept telling me to be strong, that it would work out in the end."

I knew Micah wasn't looking for a response.

"And after a while, it just kind of hit me. What do I really believe? I followed the commandments, I believed in Jesus, I went to church, and I prayed all the time. And when I really needed God's help, it was like the only answer I got was, *Who cares?* I didn't want God to give me strength to endure whatever was happening, I wanted God to put an end to what was happening. And he didn't. So I quit."

I said nothing. When it comes to matters of faith, the best response is to say nothing unless you're asked directly.

"Didn't you ever feel that way?" he said.

"Yeah," I said. "All the time."

"But it didn't hit you the way it hit me?"

"No."

"Why not?"

"I don't know." I sighed. "I guess I didn't think any of the bad stuff was really God's fault in the first place. Things just happened. And if God didn't cause them, I guess I didn't expect him to change it."

He nodded, then said, "I still get sad about everything that happened. Every now and then, it just hits me. Sometimes, it takes days for me to get over it."

I put my arm around his shoulder. "That happens to me, too."

"What do you do?"

I shrugged. "Work," I offered.

He laughed. "Yeah. Your balance is totally out of whack."

"Yours, too. Work, spirituality, family, friendships, health—you can't ignore any of them or it'll get you in the end."

"Are you saying that I'm as bad as you?"

"Sure," I said. "We're brothers. We reacted to the stress in different ways, but to be honest, I think our situations are more alike than you realize. We went through the same things, didn't we?"

By early 1995, my sister had been in remission for two years and had become a mother. Her CAT scans continued to come up clear. With every passing month, our worries began to diminish. At the same time, though, all three of us became more and more concerned about our father.

His behavior outside work was growing worse. Though heavily in debt, he began spending money like crazy; he remodeled the house and bought a new SUV, and whenever he spoke to us on the phone, his only interest seemed to be in talking about Flame. Despite having a new girlfriend, his world seemed to revolve around the dog.

The estrangement from his family continued; frequently, I'd get calls from relatives wondering what was going on, yet there was nothing I could say except that I didn't understand what was happening any better than they did. He was distant and on edge whenever I called, his conversations with Cat had grown short, and Dana was busy with twins and living on the far side of town, which brought them into little contact with each other.

Even Micah was having trouble making sense of what was going on. When pressed, my dad would swear that he'd never been happier, that work was going well, that he loved his weekends with the dog and his girlfriend. Twenty minutes later, however—long after Micah had asked him how he was doing and had moved on to discussing other things—my dad would launch into DEFCON 5, suddenly turning to Micah and snarling:

"My life isn't your damn business anyway, so why don't you get the hell out of here!"

Bizarre. Hurtful. Worrisome.

Yet Cat and I were so far removed from the situation that we wouldn't learn the full story of what was going on until years later. We were caught up in yet another move, while raising two young boys. For the first couple of months, Cat had to stay in New Bern to try to sell the house, while I lived in a small apartment in Greenville. During the days, I worked at establishing a new territory; in the evenings I'd drive around looking for a house we could buy. On the weekends, I'd either head back home, or Cat would come to Greenville to view the homes that I'd found.

By the end of May, we finally moved into our new home in Greenville, and spent the first few weeks meeting our neighbors, learning the layout of the town, and making new friends. Miles had always been outgoing and friendly; he met lots of kids and frequently played with them. Ryan, not yet two, was still a toddler. He hadn't learned to talk yet and seemed much more introspective. He showed little of the curiosity that Miles had at his age and it often seemed as if his mind was elsewhere. He screamed in terror whenever we put him in the car, and seldom responded when we tried to get his attention. When we discussed it with our pediatrician, he said not to worry and assured us that Ryan would grow out of it.

"He's not even two yet," he said. "Just give him a little time."

In July, I started the process of soliciting literary agents; I sent out twenty-five query letters and the first agent to respond, Theresa Park, was willing to work with me on the novel; the next twenty-four would all end up passing on the project. By October 1995, the novel was as ready as it would ever be.

Aside from worries about my dad and the move, the year had been quiet until then. My sister had gone through yet another negative CAT scan—she was tested every three months—and my brother was doing well in real estate. My dad, if struggling in his personal life, was apparently functioning smoothly in his professional life. For a short while, it almost seemed as if things were normal; looking back, I now realize it was simply a lull before the storm broke full force.

While both my agent and I had high hopes about how the novel would be received, hopes were one thing, and reality was another. In my heart, I knew that I'd be pleased if I secured enough of an advance to pay off the credit card bills, or perhaps buy a decent car for my wife. Anything would have helped; I was living a typically middle-class lifestyle with the same budget concerns as everyone else in our neighborhood; the mortgage on my house was $125,000.

The novel, entitled *The Notebook*, was sent to publishers on a Thursday and Friday; on Monday, I listened to a message that my agent had left on my voice mail at work, one that asked me to call. It was a little before noon, and I was getting ready for a luncheon at one of the doctors' offices. I'd brought all the food, set everything up, and was waiting for the doctors to finish with their morning patients so I could tell them about the effectiveness of Lederle's antibiotics and antihypertensives.

Using the office phone, I dialed my agent, and she came straight to the point.

"You have an offer from Warner Books," she said. She sounded a little breathless on the phone.

"And?"

"Warner Books would like to offer you one million dollars for the book," she said.

I blinked, pressing the phone hard to my ear. Thinking I had heard her wrong, I asked her to repeat what she'd said. She did, and it was all I could do to sit in the chair without falling to the floor.

In one fell swoop, less than two months before my thirtieth birthday, I realized that I'd just become a millionaire.

How was I supposed to react in a situation like that? I had no idea, nor did Cathy. I can say, however, that even though I'd had my agent repeat the number not twice, but *three* times, I still believed I'd somehow been mistaken in what I'd heard. A few minutes later, however, my agent and I spoke again, and she informed me that the deal had closed.

I immediately called Cat, but she wasn't in. Nor was Micah when I tried to reach him—he happened to be out of town. Or Dana. Or my dad. None of them were home, and with the news of the sale still bubbling inside me, the doctors finally began arriving at the luncheon. Despite the earth-shaking news I'd just received, I somehow forced myself to talk to them about pharmaceuticals.

Later, when I finally reached Cat, she was flabbergasted. In excited moments, my wife's New Hampshire accent becomes pronounced.

"No suh!" she screamed. "No suh!"

"Yes suh!" I shouted in response.

Even my dad, when I told him the news, seemed genuinely

excited for me; after speaking to him, I spent much of the evening on the phone, talking to various relatives. Micah was almost the last person I talked to that day, and he was silent for a long moment after I finally told him the news.

"You're kidding," he finally said.

"It's unreal, isn't it?"

"A million dollars? For a book that *you* wrote?"

"Can you believe it?"

"Not right this moment, but give me a second." He breathed into the phone. "This is...unbelievable..." he murmured, before pausing again.

As close as we were, we weren't completely immune to sibling rivalry. Ever since we'd graduated, Micah had always been more successful in his various careers than I'd been. It had always made sense to both of us; he was the older brother, and—aside from school and track—had been more successful in everything. He was happy for me, but I also knew that part of him wished he'd been the one with the news.

Yet Micah was able to put all that aside, and his next words meant more to me than anything anyone else had said to me.

"I'm proud of you, little brother. You done good."

"Thanks, Micah."

"Now, there's just one thing left."

"What's that?"

"You have to help me figure out how to make *my* million. You made yours, so now I guess I have to do it, too."

Though the money seemed dizzying, I decided to keep my job as a pharmaceutical rep. I didn't know how well the book would do once it was released, nor did I know whether I would be able to write a second one. Cat and I viewed our windfall in much the same way we would have viewed a winning lottery ticket. Other than the purchase of a used Ford Explorer, the clearing of our credit card debt, and a new wedding ring for Cat, we spent none of the windfall. Our years in poverty had left us both extremely cautious. The money, we'd decided, would go to three areas: our mortgage, funds for the kids' college educations, and retirement.

Still, the months of November and December were thrilling. So much was new—book clubs and foreign rights sales, a film sale to New Line Cinema, even the editing process—and every day, there was something new, something exciting, to share with Cat.

Yet aside from those conversations, our lives went on as normal. Thanksgiving came and went; Christmas came and went. Dana's CAT scan was clear again—making it three years—and she called me on our birthday to sing to me. Dad, we learned, was still seeing his girlfriend, and seemed to get along well with her.

In January 1996, Miles was four and a half and Ryan two years younger when we brought Miles to the doctor to prep him for the tonsil surgery he was supposed to undergo the next day. While the doctor talked to Miles, Ryan stood quietly between my wife and me. The consultation didn't take long. When the doctor turned to engage Ryan in conversation, Ryan said nothing.

This didn't surprise either Cat or me. Ryan still hadn't learned to talk, we explained, and the doctor simply nodded. Right before we were to leave, however, the doctor asked us if he could visit with Ryan alone for a few minutes.

"Sure," we said, thinking nothing of it. We figured the doctor would give him a lollipop, or show him some of the gadgets in the office.

Strangely, however, the doctor's door remained shut for almost ten minutes. When he finally brought Ryan out of the office, we couldn't help but notice the concerned expression on his face.

"What's up?" I asked. I knew the doctor well; I'd been calling on his office for months as a pharmaceutical rep and considered him a good friend.

"I just spent some time with Ryan, going over a few things..."

He paused, drawing a long breath. He glanced down at Ryan, then back at us again.

"I think," he said slowly, "Ryan may be autistic."

I think Ryan may be autistic.

All Cat and I could do was stare at him. My stomach knotted up and all of a sudden I could barely breathe. The blood drained from Cat's cheeks, and the room closed in around us. Ryan stood by our side, his expression glazed and unfocused. We knew he couldn't talk—we'd even grown concerned enough to talk to his pediatrician—but we'd convinced ourselves that it wasn't anything serious. *He'll grow out of it,* we'd been told. *He'll be fine.*

But this?

They were, I still think, among the most frightening words a parent can hear. We both knew about autism—who hadn't seen *Rain Man*? Or read about autism in news magazines or seen shows about it on television? I stared at Ryan. Was that our son? Our *child*? Our *baby*?

No, I immediately thought, the doctor was wrong. Ryan wasn't autistic. He couldn't be. He was fine. I'm not going to believe it. I can't believe it. But...

Deep down, I knew there was something wrong with him.

Both Cat and I had known he wasn't right for months. But we had never imagined it could be this serious. It couldn't be this. Oh, please God, not this.

"What do you mean?" I stammered.

"It's a disorder..."

"I know what it is. But why?...How...?"

The doctor patiently explained what he'd seen in the office. The lack of eye contact. Lack of comprehension. Inability to talk. Intense focus on colorful items. Lack of motor skills.

We were in a daze as he went on. We already knew those things; we knew our son. We hadn't known what they meant.

"Is he going to be okay?"

"I don't know."

"What should we do?"

"He needs to be tested. There's a developmental center in town, and they can answer your questions better than I can."

At home, Cat and I found ourselves staring at Ryan as he sat quietly in the living room, feeling a tidal wave of emotions.

Denial. Guilt. Anger. Fear. Hopelessness.

We spent the rest of the afternoon looking for reasons to believe what the doctor had said, and reasons to doubt him. We talked about Ryan and what we'd noticed over the years. We went back and forth for hours, talking and worrying and crying and sitting by Ryan, trying to convince ourselves that there was nothing wrong with him at all, but somehow knowing that there was. Hoping. Praying. Pleading.

That night, when I called Micah, I could barely tell him what had happened. My hands shook when I held the receiver. My throat was tight and I couldn't get the words out without breaking down.

"Jesus," Micah said. "Are you sure?"

"No," I said. "We don't know anything for sure. We've got to bring him in for tests."

"What do you need me to do?"

I began to cry.

"Micah . . . I . . ."

"Do you want me to come out there? Help you guys through this? You want me to find out who you should talk to? I'll do whatever you need."

"No," I said. "That's okay. We don't know anything yet."

"I feel like I've got to do something."

"Just pray for Ryan, okay? Can you do that for him?"

"I'll pray for all of you," he said. "I'll start praying right now."

The only thing I remember about the next two months was a sometimes nagging, sometimes overwhelming, sense of worry about our son. At times, it was all I could think about; other times, when doing something else, I'd suddenly get the strange feeling that something was . . . *wrong* and it would take a moment before I realized I'd been subconsciously thinking about my son.

Dread. It permeated our home, seeped into the nooks and crannies of our lives.

Over the coming weeks and months, Cat shuttled Ryan to and from various doctors in search of answers. There were long waiting lists—it took six weeks to have his initial evaluation completed—and I remember sitting in the office, waiting for the words I didn't want to hear.

"Though he's thirty months of age, currently he has the developmental skills of a fourteen-month-old. There are other problems, too. Lack of eye contact, for example."

"What are you trying to say?"

"I think there's a good chance that he has autism."

"Is he going to be okay?"

"I don't know."

"Is there anything we can do?"

"I don't know."

"What can we do at home?"

"I don't know."

There were never any answers. But always, at each evaluation, they recommended another test. Again, it would take another six weeks; again, it was all we could think about until the day finally came.

At the second evaluation, in late April—after three long months of worry—we were seated before another doctor, who perused Ryan's file before finally glancing up at us.

"I'm sorry," he said, "but I think we might have been in error. We don't believe Ryan is autistic, though he may have autistic tendencies."

"What does that mean?"

"We think he might have pervasive development disorder."

"Is he going to be okay, then?"

"I don't know."

"Is there anything we can do?"

"I don't know. For the time being, however, I'd suggest getting another test. A specialized hearing test. We want to make sure he hears sounds correctly."

Another month passed. Another round of worries. Another test. Another meeting with a doctor.

"I'm sorry, but we might have been wrong. We don't think Ryan has pervasive development disorder."

"What's wrong with him?"

"Ryan," the doctor said, "is profoundly deaf."

We looked at the doctor. "Then how come he turns when the air conditioner goes on?"

"Oh, he does that?" the doctor asked. "Well, then let's give him another test."

Tests. That's all they ever recommended.

He got another hearing test, one that tests the inner ear. A month later, we talked to the doctor again.

"You were right," he said, "Ryan can hear."

"Then what's wrong with him?"

"The problem with your son is that he's severely retarded, with attention deficit disorder."

"He's not retarded," I said. "He's smart. He remembers everything."

Not knowing what else to do, they recommended yet another test.

After that, at the next meeting, they reverted to autism again, though they categorized it as mild. At the next meeting, they switched back to a diagnosis of pervasive development disorder.

No one, in other words, knew what was wrong with our son. No one could tell us what to do. No one could tell us whether he was going to be okay. No one could tell us *anything*.

My wife lived the day-to-day struggle far more intensely than I. She took Ryan from one evaluation to the next while I worked during the day; in the evenings, she handled the kids while I wrote. In the little free time I had, however, I began to read about childhood developmental disorders. I read through one book, then another, then still another. Within a couple of months, I'd read through forty books—covering the entire spectrum of possible disorders—and a couple of hundred clinical reports outlining various therapies. It was my way of trying to cope, to handle the unknown, to somehow find a way to understand my son. I was searching for something, anything, that could lead to answers.

By late August, Ryan was coming up on his third birthday. His latest evaluation showed little, if any, improvement. Now, instead of having the skills of a fourteen-month-old, he had the skills of a fifteen-month-old.

In other words, after eight months of running from doctor to doctor and after dozens of tests and evaluations, Ryan was even further behind his peers than he'd been when we'd first found out he had a problem. And he still never spoke at all.

As all-encompassing as my worries were, I continued selling pharmaceuticals by day, and by early summer had begun work on a second novel. Working in the evenings—and drawing inspiration from my dad and his struggles with grief—I started *Message in a Bottle*. The work was an escape of sorts, for only while I wrote was it possible to keep from thinking about Ryan.

Micah and I stayed in frequent touch throughout those first few months of 1996. He was the one I talked to about my fears, and he would always listen. At the same time, Micah was moving forward in his own life. In April 1996, he called to tell me that he'd decided to give up his real estate career.

"I'm thinking of buying a business instead," he said on the phone.

"What kind?"

"A manufacturing business. Garage cabinets, closet organizers, and home office systems."

"What do you know about that?"

"Nothing. But the owner says he'll train me."

"Good for you."

"There's just one thing."

"What's that?"

"Can I borrow some money? I'll be able to pay you back in a few months."

After telling me the amount, I hesitated only briefly. "Sure," I said.

"Thanks." Then, with a quieter voice, he asked: "How's Ryan doing?"

Micah, alone among my family, was the only one who never forgot to ask.

There were, however, two bright spots in the first half of 1996. Again, my sister passed her CAT scan with flying colors and seemed perfectly healthy. Other than being tired—twin two-year-old boys can do that to you—she was in good spirits, and we seldom talked about her health.

My dad, too, finally began to find his way again. As 1996 progressed, he spoke less about Flame and began talking more about the woman he was dating. He spoke about work as well—work was the one area of his life where he continued to function normally—and by the summer he'd even begun listening to my requests that he start talking to his family again.

"They miss you," I said. "They're worried about you."

"I know," he admitted. "And I'll talk to them again. I just have to be ready first."

I think that my dad's hesitation had less to do with a continuing anger than fear of how they would respond to his attempted reconciliation. In the end, he put aside whatever fears he had and called his brother. Later, I would hear from my uncle Monty that my dad did almost all of the talking, that he'd rambled a bit, but after the call, my uncle had broken down. He loved and missed my dad, and the sound of my dad's voice—even if it was less a conversation than a speech—was something he'd longed to hear. It was a step my dad had needed to make, not only for his brother, but for himself, and as the summer wore on, they began speaking more and more.

After I learned what he'd done, I told my dad that I was proud of him, and for once my dad seemed touched by my words.

"I love you, Dad," I whispered.

"Love you, too."

And a couple of weeks later, my dad called to tell me something else.

"I'm getting married," he said.

"You'll like her, Nick," Micah said on the phone.

I'd called to ask him about the woman my dad intended to marry. While I'd never met her, my brother had. "And she'll be good for dad, too."

"He seems happier."

"I think he is," Micah said. "He even went to see Dana and the twins last weekend."

"That's good," I said. I paused. "It's been a long seven years since mom died."

"Yes it has. The poor guy—I was beginning to wonder if he was ever going to be okay. Did you hear he called Uncle Monty?"

"Yeah," I said. "I'm glad. He needs his family. He always has. How's your business going?"

"It's hard. I've been working day and night, but it's paying off. Sales have been going up every month."

"Congratulations."

He paused. "There's something else, too."

"What's that?"

"I think I finally met my Cathy," he said. "But her name's Christine."

"Really? That's great!"

"Nick, you're going to love her."

"Sounds pretty serious."

"It is serious."

"Yeah, but is it marriage serious, or Micah serious?"

"Ha, ha."

My eyebrows shot up. If he wasn't willing to joke about it, I realized I already had the answer.

"Well, good for you," I said. "I can't wait to meet her."

Two days after my father told me he was engaged—and a month prior to the publication of *The Notebook*—the CBS television show *48 Hours* arrived at our house.

One of the producers, Andrew Cohen, had read an advance copy of the book in the early part of the summer, and decided to run a segment entitled "The Making of a Best Seller." In addition to filming me, they'd also been filming at Warner Books all summer; sitting in on marketing meetings, conducting interviews with Larry Kirshbaum, the CEO of Warner Books, Maureen Egen, the president, and Jamie Raab, my editor, in addition to filming a book group (composed of strangers) who would discuss the novel.

They came to the house on a Thursday; two days later, on Saturday, I was supposed to fly to Los Angeles for the Southern

California Booksellers Association dinner, which would be the first promotional event of my career. I was, as you might imagine, a basket case of nerves.

The producer and crew had arrived early in the morning and followed me throughout the day. The crew filmed me both at home and on the job, and host Erin Moriarty interviewed me throughout the day about the process of writing and whether or not the book would be a success. Though Erin and Andrew left in the early evening to catch their flight back to New York, the film crew stayed at the house to get some last-minute footage of me working on my new novel. At around 9:00 P.M., while I was staring at the screen and typing for the camera, my wife came into the office, phone in hand.

"It's Micah," she said.

"Can you tell him I'll call him back in a half hour or so?"

"He needs to talk to you now," she said. "It's important."

"What is it?"

"I don't know. But he sounds upset."

I took the phone and felt the cameras swivel toward me.

"Hey Micah. What's up?"

"It's dad," he said. He spoke in a low, dazed voice.

"What's going on?"

"I got a call from the police department near Reno. He's been in a car accident. I just called the hospital where they brought him in."

I heard him draw a long breath. I knew enough to say nothing. I could hear the cameras from *48 Hours* whirring behind me.

"He's dead, Nicky," Micah said quietly.

"Who?" I asked, already knowing the answer.

"Dad," he said. "Our daddy died an hour ago."

I was paralyzed. My eyes welled with tears at the same instant that Micah started to cry.

"Dana and I are driving up to see him now," Micah went on. "I just called her, and I'm going to pick her up on the way. I know he's gone, but we have to go see him."

"Oh...Micah..."

"I know," he said. "I gotta go..."

I hung up the phone. Throughout the conversation, Cat hadn't taken her eyes from me.

"What is it?" she asked.

I told her. My wife burst into tears and opened her arms to me. Behind us, the camera finally clicked off. Everything, I realized, had been caught on film, but the cameramen were sensitive enough to pack up and leave quietly.

I stayed up most of the night, talking and crying with Cat. My brother called me sometime in the middle of the night and said that he and Dana had reached the hospital and seen my father's body.

"I can't believe he's gone," Micah told me. He was clearly in shock. "I just talked to him last night, and now I'll never talk to him again."

"How's Dana doing?"

"Terrible. She hasn't stopped crying since we got here, but we'll be leaving in a couple of minutes. I mean...I don't know what else to do."

"I wish I was with you guys right now."

"Me, too." He paused. "When will you be coming out?"

"I don't know," I said. "As soon as I can. I'm supposed to be flying out to California for a booksellers dinner this weekend, but I'll cancel...Jesus, I still can't believe it."

"It's unreal, isn't it?"

And then we both started crying again.

In the morning, Micah called again. As we talked about dad he grew quiet.

"Nick, I've been thinking about your book tour," he finally said.

"Me, too."

"You're still going to do it, right?"

"I doubt it," I said. "How can I?"

"You've got to go," he said, growing serious.

"It seems wrong—"

"Dad was proud that you wrote the book," he said, cutting me off. "He'd be the first to insist that you've got to go. He knows how important the tour is. It's your first book. It might be the only chance you get."

"But…I don't know if I can."

"You can, Nick. And you will. I know you loved dad, and he knows you loved him. He loved you, too. But you've got your own family to consider, too. Mom and dad would want you to go."

After hanging up the phone, I thought about what he had said. He was, I thought, both right and wrong. I understood his point, but at the same time, it felt…callous. It was like trying to choose between my dreams for the future and respect for my father. If I stayed home, would I ever get another chance? And did that matter?

But if I decided to go, what then? If someone asked if I was enjoying the tour, or excited about what was happening to me, what on earth was I supposed to say?

*   *   *

There was no easy answer to that question.

I talked it over with Cat, with Dana, with Micah again, and with my relatives. I talked to my agent, publicist, and editor—all of whom said that I could cancel the tour if I felt I needed to. In the end, I reluctantly decided to go. The guilt I felt inside, however, was enormous. I couldn't shake the feeling that it was disrespectful to my dad's memory.

Andrew Cohen, the producer, called soon after. In shock, he offered sincere condolences, and I asked him not to air the footage that concerned my dad's death. We both knew the show would garner higher ratings were it to air—the current state of television bears that out—but Andrew didn't hesitate, saying he'd bury the footage. Despite my anguish over the loss of my dad, I was reminded once again of the goodness of people.

I flew to California with my stomach in knots, and somehow made it to the dinner. I remember nothing about the evening except for a feeling of disembodiment, as if I were watching what was happening through someone else's eyes. People asked about the new book and I answered on autopilot, saying all the things I was supposed to say. But as I spoke, all I could think about was my dad, how wrong this felt, and how much I longed to see my siblings.

After the dinner, I spent the following week in Sacramento with my brother and sister. Micah and I stayed at the house, which suddenly seemed to be nothing but a shell. At the same time, nothing seemed to have changed at all. There was a coffee cup on the kitchen counter, and fresh milk in the refrigerator. Mail continued to arrive; there was a stack on the table that Micah had already brought in. The grass had just been mowed. It was easy to imagine that my dad would be driving up any minute, or even that my mom was cooking in the kitchen. The memories of both of them were vivid, and as Micah and I moved from room to room, we could think of nothing to say.

I was exhausted. My mom. My sister. My dad. My son. Too many worries in too short a time. Micah had the same worn expression I did.

We made arrangements for the funeral. Relatives began flying in. Everyone was in shock, and my uncle Monty couldn't stop crying. Nor could we.

My dad was buried next to my mom, and the same people who'd gathered together seven years earlier came to the funeral. My uncle Jack spoke at my dad's grave and offered the sweetest eulogy I'd ever heard. The estrangement had wounded most of our relatives, but they loved him nonetheless. At the graveside, Cat and I held hands, as did Bob and Dana, and Micah and Christine.

This is what I thought when I was at the funeral:

My dad was a good man. A kind man. But my mom's death had wounded him, and my sister's illness had wounded him again. He spent the last seven years of his life struggling with sadness, in a world he no longer recognized. Yes, he'd been angry at times, even bitter. But he was my dad and he'd helped raise us. And I not only respected him for that, but loved him for what he did. He'd fostered independence, showed us the value of education, and taught us to be curious about the world. Even more important, he'd helped the three of us become close as siblings, which I consider to be the greatest gift of all. I could have asked for nothing more in a father. And really, who could?

Later, Micah, Dana, and I stood alone in front of the casket, our arms around one another, saying good-bye one last time. We missed him already. With the sun coming down hard, we were together and alone at exactly the same time, as orphaned siblings always are.

After the funeral, Cat and I stayed on in California for a couple of days. Miles was old enough to understand what had happened; Ryan still seemed to understand nothing at all.

Over the year, Cat and I had begun to close ranks when it came to Ryan's condition. Only she and I, we believed, fully understood how challenging the year had been, and in those early years of struggle, we divided people into two groups: good and bad. Those who were kind to Ryan, and those who ignored him.

We were under no illusions that he was like other children. He didn't laugh much, he didn't look at people when they spoke, nor did he understand what they said to him. Yet, we wanted nothing more than for Ryan to be accepted for who he was.

He was a sweet kid. A kind child. And with patience and effort, Ryan could be fun to play with. But no one, besides Cat or myself, ever made the effort. Unlike Miles, Ryan had no friends; unlike Miles, none of our neighbors' kids ever wanted to play with him. Unlike Miles, Ryan was never invited to birthday parties. Unlike Miles, no one ever tried to talk to him. And adults, sadly, were no different. More often than not, they simply ignored him, or worse, took his lack of interaction personally. "He doesn't like me," neighbors said to us. Even relatives seemed to ignore him during the course of the week—adding more stress to an already stressful week—and Cat and I would have to bite our tongues to keep from screaming, "You've got to try!"

What we really meant was, *Please, someone try. Anyone. We love him so much, and you have no idea how frightened we are for him.*

We kept this to ourselves while we divided the world into groups. We'd been handling Ryan's problems on our own, and we'd continue to do so. We didn't want people to pity Ryan, or pity us; we wanted them to love Ryan as much as we did. Even if something was wrong with him.

Two days after the funeral, Cat and I went out to pick up groceries. Micah had offered to stay with Miles and Ryan, and when we left, Micah was slogging through paperwork in my dad's office. When we got back to the house, however, Micah was no longer at the desk.

Instead, Micah was wrestling gently with Ryan in the living room, and more than that, Ryan was laughing.

Laughing.

The sound was incredible; had it come from heaven itself, it could have been no less joyous, and all Cat and I could do was stare.

"Oh hey guys," Micah said, as if nothing extraordinary was happening, "we're just having some fun."

Micah didn't have to be told how Cat and I were feeling. Micah already knew.

My book tour lasted nearly three months. Cat was on her own with the kids, continuing to haul Ryan from one doctor to the next, and the incredibly stressful year had taken its toll on our marriage.

It wasn't any single occurrence that caused the tension between Cat and myself; in large part, it had to do with the fact that our marriage had been careening from one crisis to the next almost since we walked down the aisle. Our marriage had been less a permanent state of bliss than an attempt to endure a twisted version of survival camp, and the emotions had to flow somewhere. For me, they flowed toward Cat, and for her, they flowed toward me. Our marriage was already under tremendous duress, and Ryan's problems became the breaking point.

While I worried tremendously about him, my worries were nothing compared to my wife's. I think it has something to do with motherhood. It's an almost instinctive response; she had carried Ryan in her womb, she had nursed him as a baby, and while I worked outside the home, she had been the one caring for him every minute of every day.

As the Christmas season approached, we seemed unable to enjoy each other's company as we once used to. We were also arguing more. I knew my wife not only deserved a break, but *needed* a break—she'd been on full-time duty for three months while I was on tour—and for Christmas, my gift to her was a trip to Hawaii. While she spent a week with a friend, I would stay home with the kids.

While it may strike some people as odd—if we were having trouble, why didn't I offer to go with her?—the answer is simple. Someone had to stay home to take care of Ryan. There was no family nearby to help, no neighbors willing to assist, no one, in fact, that we would trust to stay with him for a week. If my wife was to use the trip to relax, I had to stay at home. And I did.

Yet while she was gone, we got into an argument on the phone. Heated words were traded back and forth—neither of us had been treating the other well—and accusations were shouted. Finally, Cat shouted me down.

"Look," she finally ground out, "I know your year has been

hard. But do you want to know what my year has been like?" She paused to draw a ragged breath. "I wake up every morning and I think about Ryan. And I look at my beautiful child, a child that I love more than life itself, and I wonder to myself whether he'll ever have a friend. I wonder if he'll ever talk, or go to school, or play like other kids. I wonder if he'll ever have a date, or drive a car, or go to the prom. I wonder if he'll ever get married. And I spend all day driving from doctor to doctor, and no one can tell us what's wrong, and no one can tell us what to do. He'll be four years old in a little while, and I don't even know if he loves me. I think about this when I wake up, I think about this all day long, and it's the last thing I think about before I go to sleep. I wake up crying in the middle of the night because of it." Her voice was beginning to crack. "That's what my year has been like."

When my wife finished, I didn't know what to say. Yes, I was worried about our son. But—and it pains me to admit this—my worries weren't like hers. I'd split my worries—between Ryan and my dad, Dana and my book—while my wife had zeroed in on our son. He'd become her entire world.

It was the first time I realized the depths of despair that my wife was enduring, and I felt sickened by the argument I'd started.

"I'm sorry," I said quietly. "I didn't know it was like that for you."

My wife simply sniffed on the other end.

"Honey?" I whispered.

"Yeah?"

"I once made a vow to you to love you forever, and now it's time that I make another. I promise—I swear on my heart and soul—that I'm going to cure our son."

The next day, while Miles stayed at a neighbor's for the day, I went to Wal-Mart and bought a small table and chair. I bought this specific set for the simple reason that the seat had a seat belt with which I could strap my son in. Then, drawing on all the literature I'd read in the previous year, I buckled Ryan into a chair, opened a picture book, and pointed to a picture of an apple while I held a tiny piece of candy out as a reward. I said the word aloud: *Apple*. Then said it again. And again. And again.

Apple. Apple. Apple. Apple. Apple. I repeated the words, *willing* my son to talk. I don't know that my desire for anything has ever been greater; I concentrated, I focused, my entire world was centered around my son and his ability to say this one single word.

Within minutes, Ryan grew bored. Then he started to fuss and fidget. After a few more minutes, he'd begun to cry, trying to get out of the chair. After that, he started to get mad. Ferociously mad. He screamed and balled his fists, he tried to pull out his hair. He tried to claw the skin from his arms. He growled and cried out as if possessed.

And I'd take his hands, hold them against the table so he couldn't hurt himself, and say: Apple. Apple. Apple.

Over and over. He screamed and screamed and screamed. And I said it over and over. And he screamed and screamed.

After two hours, he could say *A*.

After four hours, he could say *Ap*.

And after six hours, my son—*six hours* of angry, frustrated, heartbreaking cries on Ryan's part—said in a tiny whispered voice: *Apo*.

Apple.

For a long moment, all I could do was stare at him. It had been so long, so exhausting, that I didn't believe he'd actually done it. I thought I'd heard him wrong, and I said the word again. Ryan repeated it, and when he did, I jumped up from my seat and began dancing around the room, whooping for joy. I moved toward Ryan and offered a hug; though he didn't respond to my affection, he said the word again.

It was then that I began to cry.

Simply to hear the sound of his voice, his *voice*—no screams, no grunts, no shouts—was breathtaking. It was the sound of angels, as sweet as music. But more than that, I suddenly *knew* that Ryan could *learn*. And I then understood that this had been my greatest fear all along. Cat and I had spent over a year wondering what to do for Ryan and whether he would be okay, and by saying this one, simple word, I suddenly knew that there was a possibility that he could be.

This word gave me hope; until that moment, I hadn't realized that I'd lost every bit of it.

I was under no illusions that working with Ryan would be easy or that he would improve right away. I knew the road would be long and frustrating, but he was my son.

My son who could *learn*.

I knew then that I'd walk every step of the way with him, no matter how long it took. Taking his little face in my hands, and though I knew he wouldn't understand, I whispered: "You and I are going to work through this together, okay? And I'm not going to quit, so you can't either. And you're going to be just fine."

The next day, I worked with Ryan for another six hours, and that night I called my wife in Hawaii. I apologized again for the argument we'd had, then put Miles on the phone so he could talk to his mom. When I got on the phone again, I said casually,

"By the way, Ryan has something to say to you."

I put the receiver up to Ryan's head, held out a little piece of candy, and mouthed the words I wanted him to say. The words we'd worked on all day long. And into the receiver, he said:

"I wuff you."

I love you. These were the first words Cat ever heard him say.

That night, I made the decision to quit my job selling pharmaceuticals, but I fully understood that I would continue to work a second job. In addition to writing my novels, I spent the next three years working with Ryan for three hours a day, seven days a week. And in the end, I would teach him to talk, one slow, painstaking word at a time.

It wasn't easy. Ryan didn't suddenly get better. It was a horribly frustrating process. It wasn't two steps forward, one back; it was like a half a step forward, then back almost to the beginning, then wander sideways for a while, then go further back than where you'd started in the first place, then finally tiny improvement. Months after we started, Ryan had begun to parrot words; he could say almost anything, but had no idea what words were or what they were used for. To him they were simply sounds to get a piece of candy. It would take months and months of effort to finally make him understand that the word *apple* meant something.

There were behavioral issues, too. Lack of eye contact. Poor motor skills. Food phobia. Potty training. Cat and I worked with him on all those areas as well. He was, for instance, terrified of the thought of going to the bathroom. To finally get Ryan potty-trained, I had to strip him down, have him drink glass after glass of juice, and literally sit in the bathroom with him, coaxing him to go in spite of his fears. For eight straight hours.

*　　*　　*

While the structured work with Ryan lasted three hours daily, I didn't want his entire experience with me to be one of struggle and challenge. Thus, my time with him wasn't limited to teaching and learning; I tried to spend at least an hour a day with him doing only the things he wanted to do. We would play on the jungle gym, take walks, coloring—whatever made him happy.

But at the same time I never forgot that I had another son. I remembered believing as a child that attention equaled love, and I didn't want Miles to grow up feeling as deprived as I had. I spent hours with Miles as well, doing the things he liked to do. We rode bikes and played catch, I coached his soccer teams, and he and I would eventually study Tae Kwon Do together.

Truly, my children had become my other vocation.

In May 1997, we moved back to New Bern, and began remodeling the home we live in today. It was a major construction project, one that took months, but by then, moving and remodeling—with all the associated stresses—seemed almost simple.

Cat and I continued to work with Ryan. In August, I finished my second novel, *Message in a Bottle*, and my sister called later that month to tell us that she and Bob were getting married. Soon after that, Micah and Christine got engaged as well, and would be married the following summer. Micah's business continued to grow, and he'd even begun a second business, one that manufactured entertainment centers.

Though Dana had begun getting headaches again—she'd been prone to migraines long before she'd been diagnosed—her CAT scans continued to come back negative. Nearly five years had passed since she'd first had the surgery—at which point she would technically be in remission. My sister was married in a beautiful ceremony in Hawaii. For a moment, just a moment, all seemed right in my sister's world. She had the life she'd always dreamed of; she was married, had children, and even had horses she kept at the ranch.

Then, while on her honeymoon, Dana suddenly suffered another seizure. And when she got back, the CAT scan showed something it hadn't in years.

My sister's brain tumor was growing again.

Questions and Explanations for Chapter 15

The ten questions on chapter 15 focus on grammar and usage, vocabulary, comprehension, literary terms, style, and characterization. Some of the questions combine two or more of these areas, requiring you to synthesize your knowledge, make inferences, and interpret the text. The questions are designed to determine both your current level of understanding of the memoir and your ability to answer higher-level questions.

The following sentence tests your ability to recognize grammar and usage errors. The sentence contains either a single error or no error at all. If the sentence contains an error, select the one underlined part that must be changed to make the sentence correct. If there is no error, select choice D.

1. <u>It's</u> understandable that the sad and unexpected news
    A
    regarding <u>Dana's</u> health—the CAT scan of the tumor
    B
    indicating <u>it's</u> new growth—tempered the excitement
    C
    about her new marriage. <u>No error</u>
    D

Each of these choices checks the use of the apostrophe. The contraction *it's* is a combination of the words *it is* (or *it has*). Use the substitution method to determine if the words *it is* make sense in the sentence. Choice B checks the use of an apostrophe to show possession. A singular noun demonstrates possession with an apostrophe and s—for example, "the boy's book, the girl's letter, the doctor's diagnosis." If you want the pronoun *it* to show possession, just add an s—for example, "The cat hurt its paw."

The following two questions test your vocabulary. Choose the word or set of words that, when inserted in the sentence, best fits the meaning of the sentence as a whole.

2. Nicholas Sparks resolved to work with his son Ryan three hours a day in order to _____ continued learning.

    A. censure

    B. exacerbate

    C. foster

    D. subside

This question tests your comprehension and your vocabulary. *Censure*, choice A, means to blame. *Exacerbate*, choice B, means to worsen or aggravate. *Foster*, choice C, means to encourage. *Subside*, choice D, means to settle down or grow quiet.

3. Because the scans kept coming back clean, worry about Dana _____ as concern for their father, conversely, began to _____.

    A. diminished...increase

    B. augmented...expand

    C. decreased...ebb

    D. rose...swell

This question tests your comprehension and your vocabulary. First you need to determine if the brothers' concern for Dana got larger (*augmented* or *rose*) or lessened (*diminished* or *decreased*). As soon as you have eliminated two of the choices, compare the second words. The context clues in the sentence indicate that the word used to describe their concern for their father has an opposite meaning from the word used to describe their concern for Dana. Three of the four choices are pairs of synonyms, and thus those can be eliminated.

Question 4 tests your knowledge of literary terms.

4. When the siblings were standing in front of their father's casket, Sparks writes, "We were together and alone at exactly the same time." This description is an example of what?

    A. foreshadowing

    B. hyperbole

C. paradox

D. simile

Foreshadowing, choice A, is providing hints or clues to future events. For example, when Benvolio suggests to Romeo that finding a new female beauty may help Romeo get over Rosaline, it foreshadows Romeo's falling in love with Juliet when he sees her later in the play.

Hyperbole, choice B, is an overexaggeration used to illustrate a point. For example, if someone says, "I told you a million times what that is," you know that this person really didn't tell you a million times, just many, many times.

A *paradox*, choice C, is an apparent contradiction that upon further analysis seemingly makes sense. The famous first line of *A Tale of Two Cities*, "It was the best of times, it was the worst of times," initially doesn't make sense. But when you think about how both situations can exist simultaneously, you understand the paradox.

And a *simile*, choice D, is a comparison made between two unlike things using a connective word, such as *like*, *as*, or *than*—for example, "She looked as fresh as the morning snow."

Question 5 asks you to analyze the choices an author makes.

5. The churches in Ethiopia are important for which of the following reasons?

   A. Their construction differs from every other church the brothers have visited on the tour.

   B. The churches are no longer in use.

C. They serve as a transition from Nicholas and Micah's conversation of buildings to their own attendance at church and ultimately to their attitudes regarding faith.

D. The churches are similar to the ones in Lima, Peru.

Note that the question indicates that more than one answer may be correct. If the construction of the Ethiopian churches is what makes them unique, select choice A. If the churches are no longer used for religious services, select choice B. If Sparks moves from a discussion of the churches to talking about attending church to a conversation about personal religious faith, select choice C. If these churches are similar to the ones they saw earlier in the tour, select choice D. Obviously you cannot select both choice A and choice D.

Question 6 asks you to analyze stylistic choices that an author makes.

6. When the doctor first mentioned his suspicions that Ryan may be autistic, Nicholas and Cathy are in a state of shock. The following passage describes their emotions when they returned home from the doctor's office: "Denial. Guilt. Anger. Fear. Hopelessness." The use of fragments achieves which of the following effects?

A. emphasizes their feelings

B. slows down the pace of the narrative

C. develops the characters of Nicholas and Cathy

D. enables readers to understand the varied and conflicting emotions

E. all of the above

Notice that the question indicates there will be more than one correct answer. Fragments, or incomplete sentences, are usually avoided in formal writing, but when used sparingly, they can be effective tools. If you as a reader are able to more easily relate to the feelings of Cat and Nicholas, select choice A. Shorter sentences and fragments slow down the pace of the reading. If a slower reading pace seems like an intended effect, select choice B. If you as a reader understand Nicholas's and Cat's characters better because of what they are experiencing, select choice C. And if you get a sense of the range of contradictory emotions that are running through Nicholas and Cathy, select choice D.

Question 7 checks your knowledge of literary terms.

7. When describing his son, Sparks writes, "Unlike Miles, Ryan had no friends; unlike Miles, none of our neighbors' kids ever wanted to play with him. Unlike Miles, Ryan was never invited to birthday parties. Unlike Miles, no one ever tried to talk to him." What rhetorical figure of speech is used in this passage?

   A. alliteration

   B. anaphora

   C. personification

   D. polysyndeton

Alliteration, choice A, is the repetition of a word's initial sound—for example, "Becky bought Bill a bad bugle." *Anaphora*, choice B, is the repetition of a word or group of words at the beginning of successive clauses or lines. An example of this might be, "I want you to know the word *anaphora*. I want you to recognize the effect of anaphora in a passage. I want you to attempt to use anaphora in your own writing." *Personification*, choice C, is giving nonhuman things a human characteristic, such as in "Opportunity knocked on his door." *Polysyndeton*, choice D, is the use of a number of conjunctions (*and, but, or, for, nor, so, yet*) in close succession, when one or more of them could be eliminated—for example, "lions *and* tigers *and* bears" and "neither snow *nor* rain *nor* heat *nor* gloom of night."

Question 8 asks you to analyze stylistic choices that an author makes.

8. When preparing for his father's funeral, various thoughts floated through Nicholas's mind: "My mom. My sister. My dad. My son." The use of anaphora and the syntax of the passage achieve which of the following effects?

   A. capturing the personal nature of his feelings

   B. emphasizing the extent of his loss

   C. capturing the mood of the situation

   D. mirroring his fragmented state of mind

   E. all of the above

Notice that the question indicates there will be more than one correct answer. *Anaphora* is the repetition of a word or group of words at the beginning of successive clauses or lines, and *syntax* refers to sentence structures. The word *my* is a first-person possessive pronoun. If the repeated use of the word *my* emphasizes Nicholas's feelings, select choice A. If the list

449

of family members stresses the scope of Nicholas's loss, select choice B. If the phrases characterize the mood or atmosphere that surrounds Nicholas while preparing for his father's funeral, select choice C. And if the phrases are sentence fragments and not complete sentences, which would be similar to Nicholas's state of mind, select choice D.

Question 9 checks your comprehension.

9. Nicholas Sparks credits Ryan's improvement to what?

   A. hard work, dedication, and commitment

   B. a miracle

   C. drugs and professional therapy

   D. his natural bodily development

A close reading of the chapter will enable you to identify the correct answer. This information is important for the development of character, plot, and theme. If you do not recognize the correct answer, reread the chapter.

Question 10 asks you to analyze the development of a central idea.

10. One important thematic topic addressed throughout the memoir is that bad things happen to good people. Which statement below best captures Nicholas Sparks's attitude about dealing with the highs and lows of life?

   A. It is better to have loved and lost than to have never loved at all.

B. You have no control over the bad things, but you do have control over the way you respond to them.

C. Because fate, not free will, rules the universe, it doesn't matter what choices you think you're making.

D. Praying is a waste of time because bad things still happen.

Remember that a theme is a complete sentence stating a main idea. By definition, a theme has an opinion, but it is an opinion about a topic not an opinion about a person or an event. Just because a sentence appears to be a theme does not mean it is supported by the details and examples in the text. Also, if there are two answers that seem correct and one of them incorporates the other, then the broader answer is the better choice.

Choice A is an opinion that Nicholas Sparks may or may not have, and it is a way to deal with the highs and lows in life, but can you find support for this opinion in chapter 15? Choice B recognizes and accepts that bad things are going to happen during a person's life and the only thing one can do is control the way he or she chooses to deal with these things. Choice C states that people really don't have any control over what they say or what they do. And choice D paraphrases Micah's words, not his brother's.

Chapter 16

In the previous four days—since the morning before our trip to Agra—we'd spent a total of five hours visiting both the Taj Mahal and Lalibela. Our flight time, by way of comparison, was nearly ten hours, or twice as long.

It was this slowing of the pace—and the extent of our travels to that point—that left both Micah and me feeling lethargic by the time we landed. But Malta, with its European flavor and atmosphere, energized us almost immediately.

The island was gorgeous, with white rocky cliffs plunging to the blue Mediterranean. The sky was cloudless, crisp and winter bright—it was our first stop where the temperature was cool—and after donning our jackets we boarded the buses and made our way to the various sites.

Because of the size of our group, we were split into three sections; ours would head first to the Hypogeum, an underground temple complex discovered in 1902 that was found to contain the remains of six to seven thousand bodies. The complex is a labyrinth, consisting of chambers built over three levels, and descending to a depth of nearly forty feet. Dating back to nearly 3,600 B.C., it is far older than either the Pyramids or Stonehenge. It is, in fact, the oldest known structure of any kind in the world, and had been carved from the limestone using the simplest of tools: bone, flint, and hard rocks.

Combined with the ruins in other parts of Malta that we'd visit—the Tarxien Temple, which is the oldest known freestanding statue of a deity, and the megalithic temples aboveground, which are the oldest freestanding stone buildings ever discovered—it represents one of the earliest advanced civilizations in the world. Yet no one knows who these early people were, where they came from, what happened to them, or where they went. The civilization seems to have vanished as mysteriously as it arrived.

Despite this fascinating history of the lost inhabitants, it was Malta itself that Micah seemed most interested in. As we drove along paved roads in which everyone obeyed traffic laws (by then, it seemed downright strange), I could see Micah smiling.

"You know what this reminds me of?" he asked.

"What?"

"My trip to Italy," he said. "Right after I graduated from

college, when Tracy and I went biking around. It looked just like this. Well, parts of it anyway. That trip was a blast."

"Gee, really?" I feigned surprise. "Exploring, meeting new people, having fun? That doesn't sound like your kind of thing."

He smiled, no doubt thinking back to our Mission Gang days. "Did I ever tell you what happened when we first got to Europe?"

I shook my head.

"Well, Tracy and I flew into Madrid, but because we each had free miles on different airlines, we weren't on the same flight. We were supposed to land at about the same time, but when I went to his gate to meet him, he wasn't on the plane. The thing was, Tracy had everything in his suitcase—the guidebook, directions, maps, even the tools I needed to put my mountain bike back together. And I'm in a foreign country. No one spoke English, I couldn't read any of the signs, I couldn't even figure out who to ask to find out why Tracy hadn't arrived. I didn't even know where the city was in relation to the airport."

"What did you do?"

"I finally found some guy who spoke English and he helped me. I found out that Tracy got delayed, missed his flight, and that he'd be coming in the next day. But I still had nowhere to go. I didn't even have a credit card back then. I finally found a couple of mechanics who helped me put the bike together, and after they pointed me in the direction of town, I just started pedaling. It took an hour to get downtown, and I still didn't know where to go, where I was going to sleep. I finally found a Hard Rock Cafe, and figuring I could at least find something in English, I went to get something to eat. And after that, things got a little easier."

"Why?"

He shrugged. "I asked my waitress if she wanted to go out that night. So I went out on a date."

A little while later, Micah turned back to me. He'd been busy videotaping the drive; in the end, Micah would shoot six hours of video that he'd never end up watching. On the trip, however, you would have thought he'd been filming a documentary.

"Hey Nick—have you ever heard of the Hypogeum?"

I nodded. "I've read about it."

"Isn't it just supposed to be a tomb?"

"For the most part. But it's the oldest one ever discovered. That's why it's special."

He seemed lost in thought. "You know what I want a picture of?"

"What's that?"

"A picture of me lying down in the tomb. You know, pretending I'm dead. Wouldn't that be cool?"

"I think it would be kind of disgusting."

He gave me an airy wave. "Disgusting, cool—same thing."

Alas, Micah wouldn't get a chance to have his picture taken amid the dust and microscopic remains of the humans once buried in the Hypogeum.

The Hypogeum was entirely different from any other site we'd visited to that point. For starters, it was located beneath a building entirely unremarkable on the outside. It could have been a restaurant, business, or home—like the buildings on either side of it; the only reason we knew it was a museum were the words stenciled on the glass doors.

Inside, we were met by a *very serious* guide, who explained what we could expect: The Hypogeum was essentially sealed, to prevent decay by the elements. We would walk down the steps, and should watch our heads. We would be told where remains had once been discovered. We would see a short movie about the Hypogeum first. Tours were scheduled every hour and it was imperative that we all stay together and move quickly. We should try not to interrupt, for there wasn't enough time to answer questions. We would not be allowed to take pictures. If we did, he would confiscate our cameras.

"This guy's like a prison guard," Micah whispered. "He doesn't even smile."

"Who? Mr. Cheerful?"

"I think he's sizing us up, trying to figure out who's going to follow the rules, and who isn't."

"I think he knows you're in the latter group. He keeps looking at you."

"Yeah," he said. "I noticed that. For such a happy guy, he's really pretty perceptive."

We were led into the climate-controlled, computer-enhanced, video-monitored control room and told to sit in the seats to watch the movie. There was no choice in the matter. You had to watch the movie. Our guide was taking attendance.

This, essentially, is what we learned over the next fifteen minutes: Not Much. No one knows who built it. No one knows why. No one knows what happened to the people who built it. No one knows where they came from originally. No one knows why it was designed the way it was. No one knows what the civilization was like. All they knew was that it was built long before the Pyramids.

The lights came on.

"This way, please," our guide announced. "Come, come. We will start the tour in one minute. You don't have much time, so try to stay together. Do not ask too many questions, it will only slow us down."

And with that, we were led into the Hypogeum. It's essentially a cave, and we weren't allowed to touch anything. We walked on a ramp that had been built six inches over the floor, ducked our heads, and listened to the guide talk nonstop for the next forty minutes. And this is what we learned: Not Much.

Everything he'd said seemed to have been lifted from the movie.

Nonetheless, it was a momentous feeling to wander through the oldest ruins known to mankind. And adding to the sense of gravity was our group itself. Our guide had intimidated them all. It's kind of eerie standing in a cave with twenty people—most of whom were friends by now—and not hearing so much as a whisper for an extended period of time. It was the quietest moment on the tour.

From there, we went on to the Tarxien ruins, which were located right in the middle of downtown. This time, however, instead of a building, we were led to a small vacant lot, with a few large stones scattered throughout. Machu Picchu, it was not.

"This is it?" Micah asked.

"Oh, come on. It's not that bad. At least you can shoot video now."

"There's nothing to shoot. This looks...boring. How long are we supposed to be here?"

"I think an hour."

"That's a long time, considering no one knows anything."

He was right; it was a long hour, despite the fact that we had a new guide, who actually seemed pleased to see us. Every description began with the phrase, "We think this might be one of two things..." or, "We're not exactly sure what this was used for..."

We also began to frequently hear the word *replica*.

As in: "This is a replica of the pillar, which we think might have been important because of..."

After the first few minutes, and no fewer than a dozen "replicas," Micah raised his hand.

"You keep saying the word *replica*," Micah observed.

"Yes," our guide nodded. "It's a replica."

"You mean it's not real?"

"No, the real pillar is in the museum. Most of the real pieces that have been discovered have been removed to indoor museums so they won't be further destroyed."

"And those things you just showed us?"

"They were replicas as well. But they were crafted to look exactly like the originals did." Our guide beamed. "Isn't it amazing?"

"How much of these ruins are replicas?"

Our guide motioned around her. "Almost everything you can see. But you can tell what a wonderful job they did." Our guide motioned off to the side. "For instance, we think that this wall may have been used for one of two reasons..."

Micah and I quickly lost interest. We weren't actually seeing the Tarxien ruins, we were seeing... fakes. It was like being shown a picture of the *Mona Lisa* when visiting the Louvre, instead of seeing the actual painting.

"I can't believe it's not real," Micah said, looking around. "It's like a movie set."

"Exactly," I added, "and to be honest, not even a very good one at that."

We were on our own for dinner that evening and Micah and I chose a restaurant near the hotel that served pizza and beer. As we always did when we were together, we found ourselves reminiscing about our early years.

"Do you remember Blackie?" Micah asked.

"The demon bird? How could I forget? Or Horrible Mention..."

We laughed uproariously.

"Or how about that time we loaded the van with so many books the van looked like it was being launched..."

"Or when we pretended to be falling off the edge of the Grand Canyon..."

We laughed even harder.

"Or the BB gun wars—that time I shot you in the back and we had to dig the BB out using a steak knife because it was so deep..."

"Or when Mark and I knocked over that mailbox and those guys beat the daylights out of us..."

"Or when grandpa ran the hose over my head..."

"Don't forget the infamous Band-Aid treatments..."

We told the same stories we always tell; for some reason, we never seem to get tired of hearing them. As we doubled over and slapped our knees, people at other tables stared at us, trying to figure out what was so funny.

That's the thing, though. Our stories are funny because we lived them, and we survived them. The worse the incident was when it was happening, the funnier the story had become to us over the years.

In time, Micah grew quiet. He held a warm, almost soulful look in his eyes.

"Now those were good times," he said.

I nodded. "The best."

After dinner, Micah and I ventured to the casino to try our luck. We played blackjack (Micah won, I lost), and though the casino was far smaller and quieter than those in Reno or Las Vegas, we were pleasantly surprised to learn that a band would be coming in to perform. Our dealer assured us that it was both good and very popular.

"They're local. They've been playing here for years."

"This will be fun—listening to Maltese music. I can't say that I've ever heard it before," Micah said.

"Oh," the dealer said, "lots of people will come in tonight to hear the band. It will get more crowded later. There will be dancing."

Micah smiled. "Sounds even better."

Later, we could hear the band setting up behind us; because we were concentrating on the game, we didn't turn around to watch. A few minutes later, we heard the first chords being struck. At first, we couldn't quite place it—we knew we recognized it—and just as we began to identify the song, the lead singer suddenly began belting out the lyrics from "Coward of the County."

Kenny Rogers? When we turned around, we blinked in disbelief. There, in an upscale casino in Malta, was the local band, dressed in cowboy hats. Singing American country-western songs with their boots tapping to the beat. People in the crowd were cheering and singing along. Micah and I glanced at each other, then burst out laughing.

A moment later, joining in with the chorus from the rest of the crowd, we gave each other a what-the-hell shrug and began to sing along.

Just when we thought we had the trip all figured out, something like this would happen. The world, we'd discovered, was always ready to surprise us. Never in a million years would I ever have imagined that I'd be singing a Kenny Rogers song while attempting a Maltese accent.

In the morning, we visited Hagar Qim, another replicated set of ruins. Set near a cliff, the view was more interesting than the site itself, since nothing we saw was actually real. It was, however, a good place for pictures.

From there, we traveled to see two of the main medieval cathedrals in Malta; as in Cuzco, they were amazing. With high arched ceilings, enormous gilded altars, and hundreds of paintings, the detail was overwhelming. The floors are mostly marble; each slab actually the top of a tomb in which various knights had been buried.

For lunch, we dined at a seaside café; the food was traditionally Maltese—heavy in fresh seafood and bread—and from there we traveled to the walled city of Mdina. Originally built as a fortress on high ground, miles from the main city of Valletta, the streets were paved with cobblestone and boasted a viewing area from which it was possible to see a great portion of the island.

Mdina is also home to St. Paul's Catacombs, and that was our final stop of the day. The catacombs were once the burial site of hundreds, if not thousands, of Maltese citizens, and unlike the Hypogeum, we were allowed to touch and photograph anything we wanted. Hundreds of now empty crypts had been carved into the rocky walls. The bodies had been removed and interred in cemeteries years earlier.

Micah, of course, raised his hand.

"Can I have my picture taken in one of the crypts?"

Our guide stared at Micah as if he was insane.

"You can if you want to...I guess. No one's ever asked before."

"Really? How many years have you been working here?"

"Seventeen."

Micah winked at me. "You know what that means," he whispered.

"What?"

"I might be the first guy ever to do this," he said. "After the dead guys, I mean."

He crawled in, grinning while I snapped his picture.

As we were walking along the cobblestone streets leading from Mdina back to the car, Micah surveyed our surroundings.

"I think Christine would like Malta."

"How about the other places we went?"

He glanced at me. "You couldn't drag her to India or Ethiopia. Or Easter Island, for that matter. For her, traveling to foreign countries means going to London or Paris."

I smiled. "I think Cat would have liked all the places we've gone. But since she's never been to Europe, we'll probably go there first."

"When the kids are older, you mean."

"Of course. With the kids still so young, it wouldn't be that much fun anyway."

"You know what we should do? Next summer, we should rent a big house in Italy for a month, and bring both our families out. We can make that our home base, and travel around from there."

"We'll see," I said.

"You don't think that sounds like a good idea?"

"I think it sounds like a great idea. It's just that I don't think it's all that likely. And not just because of my five kids. By then, you'll probably have another baby."

"You're probably right. But we should get some information anyway. I'd bet that most of the people on the tour have been to Italy a few times. We can find out the best place to stay."

"You really want to do this?"

"Yeah. We should live a little."

"And you don't think traveling around the world is living a little?"

He thought about it. "We should live a little *more*."

I laughed. "Would you ever have believed we actually went around the world together and seen all these places? By our age, I mean?"

Micah shook his head. "Never. But then again, if you think about it, we've lived a whole lot of life already."

After his comment, I walked in silence, remembering.

In early 1998, Micah was running two businesses, working long hours, and making plans for his wedding. Along with Bob, he also took over my father's role regarding my sister's health. He began attending all the consultations, and took notes; in the evenings, he would consult the *Physicians' Desk Reference* and peruse medical journals online, to ensure that my sister was receiving the best care possible.

Micah called me with the news as soon as he got back from the oncologist's office.

My sister's tumor, invisible only three months before, had grown to the size of a grape. While it wasn't as large as the original tumor had been—the size of an egg—it was located deeper within her brain, in an area responsible for both memory and vital motor functions. Because of that, surgery wasn't an option; there was no way to get to the tumor without causing terrible damage. My sister would be left blind and paralyzed in the best possible scenario; more likely, she would either become a vegetable or die during the operation. Nor, we learned, was radiation an option, for much the same reason. The risk was great, the possible benefits almost nonexistent. Instead my sister would be treated with chemotherapy.

After the initial consultation, my sister would be given a combination of three different drugs that had proven to be the most successful in treating the types of tumors afflicting my sister.

Yet the odds weren't good. Chemotherapy is essentially poison; the hope is that the poison kills the tumors before it kills the person. While it's effective in many types of cancer, it's far less effective in the brain. The blood-brain barrier—think of it as a wall between your brain and the rest of your body—makes reaching the high concentrations necessary to kill the tumors almost impossible to attain. They could, however, *sometimes* control the growth rate of the tumors or, if lucky, even stop the growth entirely.

"So what does that mean for Dana?" I asked Micah on the phone.

"They won't know anything until after she's on the drugs."

"But she has a chance, right?"

"Yeah, there's a chance, but . . ." Micah trailed off.

"But the odds aren't good," I finished.

"They wouldn't say. All they would tell me is that the regimen she's going on offers the best chance for her."

"What happens if the tumor stops growing, but doesn't actually die?"

"I don't know."

"Could they tell you how long the tumor might stop growing if the drug works?"

"No," he said. "To be honest, Nick, I didn't get any answers at all. Not because she doesn't have good doctors, but because they can't even begin to make an educated guess right now. I've told you all that I know. They say they'll probably know more in three months when Dana gets her next CAT scan."

"What are we supposed to do until then?"

"Wait and see what happens."

"That's what they told you?"

"In those words exactly."

After that, our life began to fall into a distinct three-month cycle, almost like a holding pattern. Dana started chemotherapy with Micah by her side. As the poison began to filter into her system, my brother held her hand.

The news about Dana made everything that much harder. Writing was a struggle the first couple of months of the year, and my book tour for *Message in a Bottle* lasted throughout March and April, again stranding Cat alone with the kids. While on the road and away from home, I worried about my sister's health, and hated the fact that I wasn't able to work with Ryan.

I continued to write when I returned; in the end, I nearly

completed a novel before throwing it out in its entirety. It simply wasn't working.

As soon as I got back, I started on Ryan's speech again, facing one struggle after the next. By then, specialists had revised the diagnosis once more—this time to CAPD, or central auditory processing disorder. Essentially, it's dyslexia of sound; for whatever reason, sounds are jumbled into something like random noise, making speech and comprehension extremely difficult. By then, neither Cat nor I cared what the experts said was wrong with Ryan; we simply continued to work with him.

After a year, he'd finally reached the point where he understood that words represented objects, and Ryan could repeat nearly everything I suggested. Questions were a massive stumbling block. He couldn't comprehend the idea behind statements beginning with what, who, when, why, or how. For weeks, I spent hours trying different ways to get through to him.

I'd point to a picture of a tree.

"Tree," I'd say.

"Tree," he'd repeat.

"Good! Great job!" I'd praise. I'd point to the tree again.

"What's this?"

"What's this?" he'd repeat.

"No, no. It's a tree."

"No, no. It's a tree," he'd repeat.

Meanwhile, the clock continued to tick. On his next birthday, he'd be five years old.

In April, while I was on tour, Dana went in for her next CAT scan, and she called me on the road with the news right after she'd received the results.

"The tumor has shrunk by half!" she said.

"That's fantastic!" I said.

"Oh, man, was I worried. I was a nervous wreck the last week and a half."

"I'll bet you were. I was, too. But this is great news."

"If it keeps working like this, it might be gone by the next time I go in."

"Did the doctors say that?"

"No, but I think it will. It's already down by half. More than half, actually."

"That's wonderful," I said again.

"I'm going to beat this thing."

"I know you will."

By May 1998, after hundreds and hundreds of hours, I finally stumbled onto something that helped Ryan understand what a question was. I began to whisper the question, and shout the answer before he could repeat the question.

"What's this?" I'd whisper, pointing to the tree. "TREE!!!!!!" I'd quickly shout.

Ryan, startled by my outburst, would say "Tree!" almost on instinct.

"That's right!" I'd cheer. "Great job! It's a *tree*."

Gradually, he learned how to respond to some questions; what and who, primarily, both major steps forward, which allowed him to finally engage in basic conversation. To learn *where* would take many more weeks. When, why, or how still eluded him completely. Nor could he ride a bike. Nor could he write with a pencil. Nor could he tie his shoes. Cat worked with him in all those areas, and she showed no less determination than I. She, like I, was determined to help Ryan get better, no matter what it took. Both of us wanted Ryan to be mainstreamed when he started school; we wanted him to attend regular classes with regular kids. We wanted Ryan to be accepted as normal.

But often it felt as if we were running out of time. In a little over a year, Ryan would be starting kindergarten. And the clock continued to tick.

At the end of May 1998, Cat and I spent a couple of weeks in California, visiting with both Micah and Dana. I served as best man in Micah's wedding, a beautiful event, attended by friends and family. A few days after he returned from his honeymoon, he took my sister in for her next appointment.

"I'm sure it's better," Dana told him on the way in, "I feel great."

But it wasn't. Instead, the tumor had grown again. Now it was the size of three grapes, with tentacles spreading out from it.

Dana's chemotherapy regimen was changed, but we all knew that the new drugs were generally not as effective as the first. Still, there was hope; in one clinical study, one patient out of twelve had been completely cured with the drugs she was now on. We still had reason to hope, the doctors assured us.

To be on the safe side, however, Micah and Dana, along with a couple of relatives, flew to MD Anderson in Houston, one of the most renowned cancer centers in the country, for a second opinion. The doctors concluded that she was receiving the highest standard of care, and that had Dana been a patient there, they would be doing nothing different.

When talking to us, Dana remained optimistic.

"I'm going to beat it," she would say.

"I know you are," both Micah and I would reassure her.

Afterward, Micah and I would say the same things to each other. Still, we spoke to each other less frequently that year than we had in the past; one or two calls a week, not the three or four calls that had once been normal. Cat and I continued working with Ryan; Micah was adjusting to married life and working hard; he'd also begun remodeling his home and was spending as much time with Dana as he could.

The phone calls were often painful. Talking to Micah reminded me of Dana, and vice versa. And even though I'd talk to Dana as frequently as I did with my brother, I could never escape the image of something terrible growing inside her, something irreversible.

That summer, drawing inspiration from my sister, I wrote *A Walk to Remember*. Jamie, the main character, embodied all the wonderful attributes of my sister, and all the worries I had for her future. It was the first time I'd ever cried while writing.

In the end, I dedicated it in memory of my parents, and to Micah and Dana.

My sister, though she knew it was about her, refused to read it.

"I don't want to know how it ends," she said.

By autumn, my sister's tumor had shrunk. Not much, but progress nonetheless. She stayed on the same drug regimen, and we bided our time until winter, when she would get another CAT scan. We continued to live from one three-month cycle to the next.

In early December, Micah and Dana, along with Bob, Christine, and the kids, flew to North Carolina to visit. While there, we all dressed in khakis and long-sleeved white shirts, and sat for a family photograph taken on the beach. It still hangs in my living room today, and no matter how long you stare at it, by their appearance, you would never know that anything was wrong with Dana or Ryan at all.

A few weeks later, my sister called me on my birthday and sang to me. By then, I couldn't help but notice that she had begun to slur words occasionally, and was beginning to have difficulty understanding some things. Still, she remained positive about her condition. But a couple of days after that, she got the results from her next CAT scan.

The second round of chemotherapy was failing. Her tumor was now the size of four grapes, and the tentacles continued to spread. She was placed on a new regimen, with new chemotherapy drugs.

"This is the last of the best," we were informed. "After this, everything we can try is pretty much experimental."

There was still hope, however. By then, hope was becoming the only thing we could cling to.

In February 1999, Micah and Dana, along with their spouses, flew to Los Angeles for the movie premiere of *Message in a Bottle.* That afternoon, before we attended the red-carpet premiere, however, we brought my sister to Cedars-Sinai Medical Center. There, we'd made arrangements for my sister to see Dr. Keith Black, one of the finest neurosurgeons in the country. We wanted to make certain that surgery wasn't an option, anywhere, by anyone, even if it entailed serious risks. While we all hoped that this latest round of chemotherapy would work, we wanted to keep every conceivable option open.

Micah, Dana, and I, along with a few relatives, were in the room when my sister's CAT scan was placed against the light. It was the first time I'd seen one of her scans, and Micah whispered that her tumor was easy to spot. Cancer shows up white on the scan, he explained.

When the light was turned on and I saw my sister's scan, my throat constricted. White seemed to be everywhere.

Still, we asked about surgery, and were told that since the tumor had crossed the midline in her brain, surgery wasn't an option. When we asked about her chemotherapy, we were told that there was a slim possibility that it could slow the growth in a case like hers.

Slow, not stop. The doctor, in his own quiet way, was telling us that it was only a matter of time.

"But they're doing everything for her that we would do here."

When we asked about experimental drugs, the doctor explained that they were experimental for a reason. Efficacy hadn't been proven. He spent a lot of time talking about quality of life; again, it was his way of telling us that my sister's chances were not good.

By then, the tumor had begun to take its toll on my sister. Though fine in ordinary conversation, she was no longer able to fully understand the details of the doctor's explanation, and she frowned at him, missing the nuances entirely.

"You're doing well," the doctor said to her. "Actually, I'm amazed at how well you're doing."

Again, we understood that he was describing her condition in relative terms; most people with a tumor like my sister's wouldn't be walking or talking at all. Toward the end of the consultation, Micah was sitting in the corner, head bowed low. As soon as the doctor left, none of us could say anything. Instead, we sat in silence for a long moment. My sister finally looked at Micah.

"What was he telling us?" Dana asked Micah.

Micah looked from Dana to me, then back to our sister again. He forced a smile.

"He says that you're taking the right medicine," Micah answered softly. "They wouldn't be doing anything different."

She nodded. "And I can't have surgery or radiation again?"

"No," he said. "They don't think it would help."

She blinked and looked from me to Micah. "But there's still more medicine they can give me, right? If the ones I'm on stop working?"

"Yeah," Micah said. "There are a couple more things they can try."

"Well...good," she said.

A couple of hours later, we were surrounded by movie stars. Dana had her picture taken with Kevin Costner and Robin Wright Penn, who were both extremely gracious to my sister. But as Dana posed for the pictures, all I could do was stare at her, wondering how much time she still had.

As if to escape the inevitability of what was happening, I began writing *The Rescue* in the spring of 1999. The story, about a boy named Kyle who couldn't talk, was deeply personal and emotional for me to write; it was inspired, of course, by Ryan, our fears for his future, and the work that Cat and I had been doing with him.

In my spare moments, I spent time with Miles and Cat, while continuing to work with Ryan. Cat had come a long way in teaching Ryan a myriad of skills, and he'd continued to improve at asking and answering questions. Still, I found myself wishing that it would be easier. I wanted nothing more than for something to suddenly click, for Ryan to start learning on his own, simply by absorbing the world around him, as other children did. But nothing ever clicked; working with him was akin to rolling boulders up a never-ending hill. It was incredibly frustrating. I wondered why I'd been given a child with so many problems; there were frequent moments when I was angry at God, angry at what had happened, angry at the lot I'd been given. With Ryan, Cat and I had been robbed of all the joys of childhood; his wonder as he discovered the world, natural affection, his ability to learn on his own. *Everything* about his childhood was a struggle without reward, and I railed at the unfairness of it all. I wanted someone else to do the work, I wanted someone to come in and magically solve the problem, I dreamed of the day that someone would invent a pill to make his problem go away. I was so tired by then; tired of it all, and I'd pray to God, begging him to make my son better. It wasn't too much to ask, was it? I just wanted what our friends had, what our neighbors had, what everyone else seemed to have. I wanted a child like other children.

And then I'd feel guilty for what I'd been thinking. Terribly guilty. It wasn't Ryan's fault. It wasn't God's or anyone's fault. And Ryan had worked so hard, harder than any young child should be expected to work, and he wasn't quitting. We'd been through fire together, and I wouldn't—couldn't—give up on him. He was my son and I loved him. And, after all, no one ever said that life was fair; what you want and what you get are usually two entirely different things. With a job to do, I'd begin work with him again.

I had no other choice. He'd be starting kindergarten in less than six months, and there was still such a long, long way to go.

*   *   *

A month later, in April 1999, we found out Cat was pregnant, and surprisingly, my sister's tumor had stabilized again. Or possibly even shrunk. Micah celebrated his first anniversary a month later, and after I called to congratulate him, he asked: "How's Ryan doing? I sure do miss that kid."

Micah always asked about Ryan. *Always.* And he *always* said something kind.

Over the summer, I continued working on *The Rescue*, working with Ryan, and spending time with Miles. Cat and I marveled at her growing belly, and I woke every morning with the renewed belief that she was the most wonderful woman in the world. We also took another trip to California; our trips out there were becoming both longer and more frequent.

In the fall, Ryan started kindergarten. We spent his first day pacing the house and worrying about him endlessly. We were terrified by the thought of what would happen to him. Though he'd improved substantially, he was still so far behind in so many areas. We worried that no one would like him, that other kids would tease him, that he wouldn't be able to handle the work. Every day, we waited for a phone call from the school, telling us that it would be best if we enrolled Ryan elsewhere. We prayed for him every single night.

Again, I had to leave town for two straight months, this time while Cat was pregnant. I toured in Europe and the U.S., promoting *A Walk to Remember*. While on the road, I worried about Cat and worried about Ryan. And halfway through the tour, I learned that my sister's tumor had reversed itself, and was growing once more. Dana was placed on experimental drugs, in experimental combinations, with no promises what-soever. And so I worried about her, too.

Almost always, interviewers would ask if I felt I'd been born under a lucky star. Or if I thought my life was blessed. I never knew what to tell them.

Throughout 1999, the phone calls between my brother and me continued regularly, and whenever we spoke I began to sense his emotional exhaustion. In addition to taking over my dad's role in shuttling Dana to and from various appointments, he'd also become my sister's confidant and cheerleader, all while trying to keep her from knowing how worried he actually was.

Like me, my brother was using work as an escape. His businesses had grown, he had nearly thirty employees, as opposed to six when he'd first started, and he pushed himself hard. He worked weekends and evenings, and by thirty-five, as once had been his goal, he'd become a millionaire as well.

Dana and I spoke on the phone, too, usually twice a week. Sometimes I'd call, but more often than not my sister would be the one to pick up the phone. She loved talking to Cat—they would talk primarily about the kids, and how tiring being a mother could be—and she followed Cat's pregnancy closely. In moments like those, it was easy to forget there was anything wrong with her.

Whether my sister was in denial or just an optimist, she downplayed her tumor. Usually, she didn't mention it at all; if she did, it was only to tell me that she was going to beat it.

"I just know it," she'd say. "I've got two kids, and they need a mother."

"I know," I'd answer. "And you're doing great—even the doctors admit that."

Sometimes, when I answered, she'd grow quiet. "You think I'll make it, too, don't you, Nick?"

"Of course I do," I'd quickly lie, fighting the lump in my throat. "You're going to be just fine."

In late December, a few days after Christmas, Micah called, sounding weary, his inflection flat.

"What's up?" I asked.

"It's Dana," he said. "We just got back from her last appointment." He paused. A moment later, into the silence, he began to cry.

"The tumor's still spreading," he said. "Her last CAT scan showed that the new drugs aren't helping at all."

I closed my eyes. Micah's voice was trembling and broken. "They put her on another regimen anyway, but they don't think it'll work. They're just doing it because they know Dana wants to try something else. They say that her attitude has been the reason she's made it as long as she has, and they don't want to break her spirit. She needs to feel like she's doing something to fight it. But..."

"She doesn't know..."

"No," he said. "When we left, she told me she was sure that this time the chemo would work."

I could feel the lump in my throat, could feel my own tears brimming. Micah continued to cry into the phone.

"Damn, Nick...she's so young...She's our baby sister..."

I began to cry as well.

"How much longer does she have?" It was all I could do to get the words out.

He took a long breath, trying to get control.

"They don't know for sure. When I cornered the doctor, though, he said that she might have six months," he whispered.

Outside, the world was darkening. The sky was filled with

stars and the moon hung white and heavy on the horizon. Leaves rustled in the winter breeze, sounding like ocean waves. It was a beautiful evening, as if all was right in the world. But it wasn't, for with Micah's call, I lost my last sliver of hope.

I didn't realize how much I'd been clinging to that improbable hope, and when I hung up with Micah, I slipped a jacket on and went outside. I walked through our yard, thinking of Dana, thinking of how strong and optimistic she'd been, thinking of her kids, thinking of the future that she would never see. And leaning against a tree, I cried into the wind.

I spent the next two days wandering aimlessly through the house. I'd start something and stop, I'd watch a show for ten minutes before realizing I didn't know or care about what was on, I'd read the same pages over and over, unable to comprehend the words on the page.

Two days later, the phone rang. Cathy was in the final month of her pregnancy, and after answering it, she brought the receiver to my office. Her eyes spilled over with tears.

"It's Dana," she said.

I took the phone, and as soon as I put it to my ear, I heard my sister begin to sing to me. It was our birthday, and I concentrated hard as I listened to her, wanting to freeze the moment in time, for I knew that it would be the last time we would ever do this for each other.

On January 11, 2000, Landon was born. With green eyes and blond hair, he looked like his mother, and I was struck by how small he was in my arms. It had been seven years since I'd held a newborn, and I never wanted to put him down.

Yet I had no other choice. I was being pulled by the feelings

I had for my other family, and three days later I flew to California to see my sister. From that point on, I'd begin flying out to California regularly. In every two-week period, I'd spend at least four days with my sister at the ranch.

Because my sister still had hope—and because hope was the only thing keeping her strong—I had to hide my reasons for coming. Though the effects of her tumor were becoming more obvious, she was still sharp enough to notice that I was suddenly visiting regularly, and she would infer the worst. I couldn't do that to her. Her spirits had kept her strong, and I didn't want to worsen the quality of life she had remaining, so in the end I found myself telling her half-truths. *I have to do some work in Los Angeles*, I'd say, *and since it's only an hour away, I'll pop up and see you*. Or, *I'm meeting friends in Las Vegas, and since I'm so close to the West Coast, I might as well drop in*.

"Great," Dana would say. "I'd love to see you."

Micah would always meet me at the airport, and we fell into a routine that didn't change. Micah and I would stop at Zelda's, a gourmet pizza parlor in downtown Sacramento, and share a pizza and beers. We'd talk for hours; about writing and his business, about our sister, and we'd share memories of our childhood. We'd laugh and shake our heads, and grow suddenly quiet as we thought about mom or dad, or what was happening to our sister. I'd sleep at Micah's the first night, and in the morning he'd drive me out to the ranch to spend the rest of my time with Dana.

On my first visit, my sister continued to pretend that nothing was wrong. She'd cook and clean, and ask if I wanted to help Cody and Cole with their homework while she napped. We'd have dinner and visit until she grew tired and finally went to bed.

But the progress of her tumor was unstoppable, and little by little there was no disguising it. On each successive visit, her naps began to grow longer and she went to bed earlier. By February, she'd begun to limp; her tumor was slowly paralyzing the left side of her body. The next time I visited, her left arm had grown weaker as well; a week after that, the left side of her face began to lose its expressive ability. Where she'd once occasionally slurred her words, the slurring now occurred with greater frequency. Abstract comprehension grew even more difficult.

My baby sister was slowly losing her battle, but even then, she somehow believed that she would make it.

"I'll be okay," she'd say. "I'm going to see Cody and Cole grow up."

Now, however, when she made comments like those, it was all I could do not to cry. I was an emotional wreck in those first couple of months of 2000. Torn between seeing Dana and spending time with my new baby, I woke each day thinking I should be somewhere else. If I was holding Landon, I'd wish I was in California holding my sister. And when I held my sister, I wished I was back in North Carolina, holding my son. I didn't know what to do, I didn't know how to balance it all, and I didn't know how long I could keep it up. I barely slept, tears would suddenly spring to my eyes in unexpected moments, and as I forced myself through the day-to-day motions of my life, I was more exhausted than I'd ever been.

When you know that someone close to you is going to die, there's a natural tendency to want to spend as much time with them as you can. As I mentioned, it was a constant struggle to maintain the balance between my current family and the family I'd grown up with. But even if I'd wanted to, there was another reason why I didn't stay in California. My visits—though everyone understood my reasons for coming—changed the dynamics of my sister's house. Guests, even family guests, always alter domestic dynamics. And remember, my sister had a new family of her own as well.

Dana had married into a wonderful situation. Bob's father lived on the ranch in a house a stone's throw away; so did Bob's stepmother and half-brother. Bob's mother and stepfather lived less than ten minutes down the highway. So did Bob's brother. All of them loved my sister, had opened their hearts to her, had accepted her into their lives. And each of them was struggling, just as Micah and I were. And maybe, I've since come to believe, their struggle was even worse than ours.

As my sister's tumor progressed and she lost energy to do everything she'd once done, various members of Bob's family moved in and out of the house, quietly filling the void. Someone would always be there, doing the dishes, washing laundry, helping with the homework. My sister, in her time of need, was never left alone.

I guess what I'm trying to say is that I visited with my sister as much as I thought I could, not how much I wanted to. I did this so that Bob's family would have the chance to spend time with my sister, without having me around. They'd earned the right, and in my heart I knew that each of them—especially Bob—also needed time to say good-bye.

I came and went, but Micah continued in the role he'd taken over from my dad. He was strong, steady, and supportive despite his fears, and in mid-March he drove with my sister to San Francisco, where she met with her oncologist. The experimental medication, as the doctors had expected, had had no effect at all. Micah sat beside my sister as the doctor explained that there was nothing left in their arsenals to try; though they could try another chemotherapy drug, there was little hope that it would do anything, other than make her sleep even more than she already was. By that point, my sister was sleeping fourteen to sixteen hours a day; if she had another round of chemo, she'd essentially sleep the rest of her life away.

At the end of the consultation, Micah said good-bye to the doctor. He held my sister's arm so she wouldn't fall, and led her outside.

They sat on the steps outside the medical complex. The day was cool, but the sky was blue and clear. On the sidewalks, people passed by, without a second glance. Cars rolled by steadily, and in the distance one or two of them honked their horns. Everywhere else, life was going on as normal, but for Micah, nothing seemed normal at all.

Like me, Micah was exhausted. Yes, he knew it would come to this. We all knew it would come to this. Yet, just as we all had at our mother's bedside, we'd never stopped wishing and praying for a miracle. There was no logical reason to expect one, but Dana was our sister and we loved her. It was the only thing we could do.

My sister said nothing. Her left eye drooped and a bit of saliva leaked from her mouth. She couldn't feel it, didn't even know it was there. Micah gently wiped her mouth.

"Hey sweetie," he said.

"Hey," my sister answered quietly. It was no longer her voice; her words sounded different now, like someone mumbling in her sleep.

Micah slipped his arm around her. "Do you understand what the doctor was saying?"

Dana looked at him, moving her head slowly. It seemed to be everything she could do to remember.

"No...more...meds?" she finally asked. The words were soft, almost too low to hear.

"Yeah, sweetie, that's right. No more medicine. You're done with all that."

My sister stared at him, trying to follow his words. Her expression saddened, half of her mouth forming a frown.

"So that's it?"

Micah's eyes immediately welled with tears. It was her way of asking Micah if she was really going to die.

"Yeah, sweetie, that's it," he whispered.

He pulled her close, kissed the top of her head, and Dana leaned into his chest.

And for the first time since she'd been diagnosed with the tumor, my little sister began to cry.

By late March, even without the chemo, my sister's sleep continued to lengthen, and on my visits I'd sit alone in the kitchen for long periods at a stretch, waiting for her to get up from her nap. In those hours, my mind would whirl with thousands of images; how she'd looked as a child, the things we'd done together, the long talks we used to have. We were running out of time and I wanted to wake her. I wanted to spend time with her, I wanted to talk to her, but I never disturbed her rest. Instead, I would go into her bedroom and lie on the bed beside her. I'd run my hand gently through her hair and whisper stories of our childhood or tell her about Landon, but my sister never stirred. Her breath was heavy and labored, like that of someone far older. In time, I would go back to the kitchen and look out the window, seeing nothing at all as I waited for her to wake, while the hours dragged on and on.

In the evenings, after dinner, we'd sit in the living room and I'd stare at Dana, concentrating on how she looked, wanting to remember her face forever. Time had dimmed the image of my mother; it was already dimming the image of my father, and I didn't want it to happen with my sister. I stared at her, noting the curve of her jaw, her gold-rimmed hazel eyes, the patch of freckles on her cheeks. I concentrated. I forced myself to see everything, to make it real forever.

Members of Bob's family would sometimes visit with me in the hours after dinner. One night toward the end of April, Bob's stepmother, Carolyn, and I were talking with Dana, when Dana finally announced she was going to bed. She'd grown steadily worse—for the most part, all she could do was mumble—but she'd smile that half-paralyzed smile of hers, and I was struck by the thought it might be the last normal conversation we'd ever have. As soon as she was behind closed doors, I broke down and cried in Carolyn's arms, sobbing uncontrollably for nearly twenty minutes.

In May, the horrible progression seemed to intensify. Dana could no longer hold a fork, so I'd feed her; a week later, she couldn't walk or talk at all. A week after that, she'd been hooked up to a catheter and could ingest only liquids; she'd have to be carried from her room.

During my last visit, in mid-May, my family came with me to say good-bye.

On our last day in town, I remember bringing Landon into her bedroom. Her eyes were the only feature that had remained immune to the ravages of the tumor, and they shone as I held the baby against her cheek. I held Dana's hand against the baby's skin; she seemed to revel in the sensation. When we were finally alone again, I knelt by the bed, taking my sister's hand in my own. I didn't want to leave her; in my heart, I knew this was the last time I'd ever speak to her.

"I love you," I finally whispered. "You're the best person I've ever known," I said, and my sister's eyes softened. With effort, she raised a finger, and pointed to me.

"You are," she mouthed.

Cody and Cole celebrated their sixth birthday the following day; my sister was carried outside and sat in a chair to watch them. That night, she slipped into a coma and never woke again. She died three days later.

Dana was thirty-three years old.

Dana was buried next to my parents, and the funeral was packed. Again, I saw the same faces in the crowd, faces that had witnessed my mom's and dad's burials. The funerals were the only time I'd seen some of these people in the last eleven years.

In the eulogy by the graveside, I told everyone how my sister and I used to sing to each other on our birthday. I told them that when I thought of my sister, I could still hear her laughter, sense her optimism, and feel her faith. I told them that my sister was the kindest person I've ever known, and that the world was a sadder place without her in it. And finally, I told them to remember my sister with a smile, like I did, for even though she was being buried near my parents, the best parts of her would always stay alive, deep within our hearts.

Micah had only been to three funerals in his life. When the service was over, we stood near the graveside, staring at the flowers covering the coffin.

Micah put his arm around me in silence. There was nothing

left to say. Nor could we cry. At that moment, neither of us had any tears remaining.

I could feel the stares of others, I could sense their despair. We were too young to have lost them all, I imagined them thinking, and they were right.

It was lonely by the grave. I should have had the rest of my family to lean on in a moment like this, but they were the reason we were here. Standing beside Micah, it dawned on me that we were the only ones left in our family. It was just the two of us now.

Brothers.

Questions and Explanations
for Chapter 16

The ten questions on chapter 16 focus on grammar and usage, vocabulary, comprehension, literary terms, characterization, and style. Some of the questions combine two or more of these areas, requiring you to synthesize your knowledge, make inferences, and interpret the text. The questions are designed to determine both your current level of understanding of the memoir and your ability to answer higher-level questions.

The following sentence tests your ability to recognize grammar and usage errors. The sentence contains either a single error or no error at all. If the sentence contains an error, select the one underlined part that must be changed to make the sentence correct. If there is no error, select choice D.

1. The reason the <u>brothers'</u> stories are funny is <u>because</u>
   _A   _B
   they lived and survived them without <u>too</u> many ill
   _C
   effects. <u>No error</u>
   _D

Choice A tests the use of the apostrophe. If a word is plural and ends in *s*, you add an apostrophe to show possession—for example, "The players' uniforms were filthy after sixty minutes of playing in the mud."

Choice B checks to see if you realize that the words *reason* and *because* should not be used together. To illustrate, "The *reason* you don't use both words is that it would create a redundancy" or "You don't use both words together, *because* that would create a redundancy." The rule of thumb is "The *reason* is never *because*."

Choice C checks your knowledge of the homophone *too*. The word *two* refers to the quantity, one more than one. The word *to* is a preposition or part of an infinitive—for example, "Go to the store" and "We have to leave early." The word *too* is an adverb meaning also or to an extent—for example, "I want to see the movie, too" and "The movie was too long."

The following two questions test your vocabulary. Choose the word or set of words that, when inserted in the sentence, best fits the meaning of the sentence as a whole.

2. Dana's death is a _____ scene in the memoir, connecting both narrative threads.

   A. paltry

   B. peripheral

C. petty

D. pivotal

This question tests your comprehension and your vocabulary. *Paltry*, choice A, means insignificant or petty. *Peripheral*, choice B, means marginal or outer. *Petty*, choice C, means trivial and unimportant. And *pivotal*, choice D, means crucial or central.

3. Although when they landed in Malta after a ten-hour flight the brothers were feeling _____, the energy and flavor on the Mediterranean island _____ them almost immediately.

    A. lethargic...revitalized

    B. tired...overwhelmed

    C. energetic...exhausted

    D. sluggish...wearied

This question tests your comprehension and your vocabulary. The first thing you need to do is to determine how the brothers felt after the long ten-hour flight. If they had an abundance of energy, select choice C; otherwise, eliminate it. Because the first word in the other choices are synonyms, you must determine the best second word. The word *although* provides a context clue that indicates that the meaning of the second word will be the opposite of the first. In choice A, *revitalized* means vigor has been restored. In choice B, *overwhelmed* means overcome completely. In choice D, *wearied* means physically or mentally exhausted.

Question 4 asks you to make an inference based on words used in context.

4. Micah seemed to be enjoying Malta because it reminded him of a trip to Italy that he had loved. Nicholas responds with feigned surprise, "Gee, really?...Exploring, meeting new people, having fun? That doesn't sound like your kind of thing." What word best describes Nicholas's tone?

   A. questioning

   B. sincere

   C. hesitant

   D. sarcastic

This question checks your ability to understand the way lines are stated. Picture this scene in your mind, and listen to the conversation between Micah and Nicholas. *Questioning*, choice A, refers to an inquiry, saying something with uncertainty. *Sincere*, choice B, means earnest and genuine. *Hesitant*, choice C, means doubtful. *Sarcastic*, choice D, refers to a biting or taunting tone; it's a form of verbal irony.

Question 5 asks you to make an inference regarding character and thematic development.

5. Dana served as inspiration for *A Walk to Remember*, and Ryan inspired *The Rescue*. These examples illustrate what adage?

   A. Success is 10 percent inspiration and 90 percent perspiration.

   B. Don't judge a book by its cover.

   C. Write about what you know.

   D. No news is good news.

An *adage* is a traditional saying, similar to a proverb. They are short sayings that many people consider to be true. In order to answer this question correctly, you need to understand what each adage means. Choice A means that every good idea requires a lot of hard work in order to be successful. Choice B means you shouldn't make judgments based on outward appearances. Choice C is advice that new writers often receive, encouraging them to draw from their own experiences. Choice D indicates that not hearing about a situation implies that there is no bad news to be heard.

Question 6 asks you to analyze the development of a central idea.

6. The juxtaposition of highs and lows—for example, touring to promote a new book while his sister has a growing brain tumor—that Sparks uses throughout the chapter illustrates what?

   A. Life is full of good and bad times.

   B. You need to find a balance between the extremes in your life.

   C. Happiness is only an illusion.

   D. You can't always get what you want.

Although choice A is true, it is more of a topic rather than a statement about the topic. Choice B is an opinion regarding how to deal with the highs and lows in life. Choice C is an opinion that really isn't supported by the details and examples in the chapter, and choice D is definitely true and is illustrated within the chapter, but it does not explain Sparks's stylistic choices or why he determined to address the highs and lows of life.

Question 7 asks you to make an inference regarding character development.

7. What is the most likely reason Nicholas often finds himself repeating his mother's words of advice?

   A. He finds comfort in them.

   B. He does it for Micah's sake.

   C. He is basically just parroting something he heard his entire life.

   D. Her words were full of applicable wisdom.

Choice A indicates that Nicholas likes repeating the words and emphasizes the act of repeating his mother's words rather than focusing on the words themselves. Choice B indicates that Nicholas gains nothing from the words themselves, but rather recognizes that saying them to Micah is beneficial for his brother. Choice C states that Nicholas merely says the words without thinking about them as a mindless response to a situation. Choice D indicates that Nicholas values the insights that his mother shared quite often and is making them a part of his own life.

Question 8 asks you to analyze an author's stylistic choices.

8. How is the pacing of chapter 16 best described?

   A. It mirrors the pace of Nicholas's life.

   B. It is slow, like the long trip and Dana's treatments.

   C. It's sometimes slow and sometimes fast, depending on the anecdote.

D. It is on an even keel, representing the balance Nicholas is yearning for in his life.

Overall, the pace of the chapter is quite quick: Nicholas's children are getting older, his wife is giving birth again, and his writing career is taking off. The pacing of the trip narrative is as energizing to you, the reader, as Malta was to Micah and Nicholas. Readers read about the last years of Dana's life in just a few pages because that mirrors how quickly the time seemed to pass for the brothers as they watched their sister die.

Question 9 asks you to analyze an image.

9. The final paragraph of chapter 16 is a single word— *Brothers*. This image achieves which of the following effects?

A. It demonstrates Nicholas and Micah's loneliness.

B. It offers a sense of unity.

C. It captures Nicholas and Micah's sense of loss.

D. The syntax mirrors Nicholas and Micah's sense of incompleteness.

E. all of the above

The final image is one of Micah and Nicholas standing next to the graves of their parents and sister. In their immediate family, there is just the two of them. And they are currently side by side. If you realize that all they feel they have left is each other—brothers—no more sister or mother or father, and this realization is somewhat lonely, select choice A and choice C. If in this time of loss, they have an understanding that there is just the two of them left and that they must cling to each other, select choice B. And if you recognize that the final paragraph is merely a sentence fragment—something incomplete and not quite whole, select choice D.

Question 10 tests your knowledge of literary terms.

10. In chapter 16, readers finally learn the reason that the Sparks brothers needed to take this trip together. This information unites both narrative threads. What is the term used to describe this decisive moment of the plot?

A. exposition

B. rising action

C. climax

D. denouement

The *exposition*, choice A, is the background information. It answers all the questions that a reporter asks—who, what, where, when, why, and how? The exposition usually occurs at the beginning of the narrative, providing information about characters and their situations as well as introducing the conflict and important thematic topics. The *rising action*, choice B, refers to the related series of incidents that move the plot toward its highest point. The *climax*, choice C, is the point of greatest tension or emotional intensity in a plot. The *denoue-ment*, choice D, is the resolution.

Chapter 17

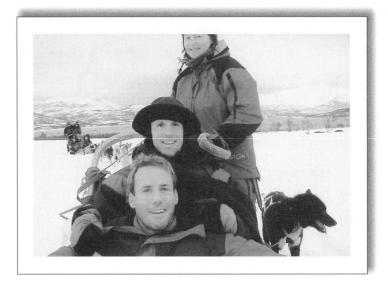

Tromsø, Norway
February 13–14

Wefe arrived in Tromsø, Norway, a picturesque coastal town located three hundred miles north of the Arctic Circle, the following afternoon. Because of the latitude, the sky was already a darkening blue, but the temperature struck me as merely chilly, not cold. Though only a thousand miles from the North Pole, the coastal waters are warmed by the Gulf Stream, making the winters far milder than other Norwegian cities farther to the south.

Boarding the bus, we wound through the town. Tromsø is set amid the mountains and a layer of snow coated the ground, making the city resemble a Christmas card. The sky was completely black by the time we arrived at our hotel. My watch showed that it wasn't quite four o'clock.

Immediately after checking in, I went to the hotel computer to e-mail Cat. I'd been e-mailing her regularly. Because of the time differences, it was often easier to reach her that way, and I typed out a letter, filling her in on what I'd been up to. Then, despite the mountains and cloud cover that would probably limit the use of the phone I'd brought, I attempted to call her, and found her at home. In the past three weeks, I'd been on the phone with her less than a dozen times, and we seldom spoke more than a few minutes. Though Cat had known it would be hard for her while I was gone, I don't think either of us knew exactly how hard it was actually going to be. I could hear the exhaustion in her voice; she sounded completely spent.

When I got back to the room, Micah was lying in bed reading when he looked up at me.

"You were gone a long time."

"Oh," I said, "I just talked to Cat."

"How's she doing? Looking forward to having you home?"

"You can say that. It's been horrible while I've been gone."

"How so?"

"She's been sick and the kids have been sick. Pretty much since the moment I left."

"Really?"

"Between the five kids and her, she's had to deal with seven colds, five flus, and three sinus infections. At any given moment over the last three weeks, there were three sick kids, all of them whining and crying. And get this—despite all that, she took them all on a ski trip. And they had to drive seven hours to get there, too."

He winced. "Seven hours? In the car with sick kids?"

"Unbelievable."

"I can't even imagine it." He was silent for a moment. "I'll bet she wasn't in the best of moods, huh?"

"Actually, she seemed to be in pretty good spirits."

"Your wife is nuts. In a good way, of course. But she's definitely nuts. I hate it when the kids whine. It's like fingernails against a chalkboard." Micah shook his head before grinning. "Gee, it's just a shame that you were traveling the world and weren't around to help her out."

"Oh, definitely a shame."

"If only you'd known, right?"

"Exactly. I probably wouldn't have gone."

He laughed. "Did you tell her to try to make sure they're all better by the time you get home?"

"I didn't want her to kill me."

He laughed again. "Christine would kill me, too. You guys are going on vacation in a couple weeks? Just the two of you, right?"

I nodded. "Yeah. We'll spend a few days relaxing at the beach."

"You know she gets to decide what to do the entire vacation."

"Oh, I know. I've already figured that out."

"I mean, every bit of it," he added for emphasis. "Instead of scuba diving, you'll be browsing through stores for hours, looking at kids' clothes. And she'll ask you whether you like the shirt with the pink bunny or the yellow duck, and you have to act as if you're giving the matter a lot of thought."

496

"I know."

"And you'll have to treat her like a queen and pretend you're enjoying yourself."

"I know."

"In fact, you're pretty much going to have to grovel."

"Believe me. I know." I shrugged. "But it's only fair."

"Ah, the trade-offs we have to make." He smiled. "Isn't marriage great?"

In the evening, we rode a gondola up the side of one of the peaks near Tromsø.

At the top, we made our way to a lodge for a mountaintop cocktail party. With windows lining two walls, we could see the lights of Tromsø twinkling in the darkness. Outside the windows there were snow flurries. It seemed hard to believe that only a few days earlier we'd been sweating in places like Ethiopia, India, and Cambodia.

It was our second-to-last night on the tour, and people were beginning to exchange phone numbers and addresses. Everyone was tired but in good spirits; it was hard to believe that our trip was nearly over.

Instead of mingling, Micah and I went to sit by the windows. We were in a reflective mood, and, watching the snow flurries, we talked about the things we'd seen, the places we'd been. We talked about the places we would visit again—both of us had Machu Picchu at the top of our list—and how much we were both looking forward to seeing our families again.

In time, Micah glanced at me.

"So how's Ryan doing these days?"

"He's doing well. On his last report card, he got two Bs and the rest As."

"And he's in third grade?"

"Yeah."

"Does he have more friends now?"

"He's in a great class," I said, "and he's been with the same group since kindergarten. The kids in his class are used to him. And they like him. It's nice. And it's funny, too—if you ask the kids how Ryan's doing, they all say that he's the smartest kid in the classroom."

"Does he play like other kids yet?"

"He's getting better. Socially, he's still a little behind, and he still has a little trouble with regular conversations. He's fine if you talk to him about his interests, but he's not too good at banter or small talk yet. I think part of it, though, is that he's shy. I don't know whether it's because of his problem, or whether he would have been shy anyway. It's one of those unanswered questions."

"You guys have come a long way with him. It's amazing how much better he is. Every time I see him, I notice how he's improving all the time."

"Thanks," I said. "I know he's come a long way, but to be honest, it's sometimes hard to remember how bad he once was. We keep focusing on the future—you know, working on his conversations, his reading comprehension, things like that. It's frustrating. You always have to figure out new ways to get through to him—it's not like you can simply give him instructions."

"He's come a long way, Nick. What you and Cathy have done is amazing. I mean it."

"Thanks," I said again.

"Did you ever find out what was wrong with him?"

I shook my head. "No. We have some ideas, but we'll never be certain. Cat thinks he just had CAPD—where he couldn't understand sound—but I'm not so sure. I mean, I've read everything about that disorder, and if Ryan did have it, it was the worst case that I ever came across. I think it might have been part of the problem, but I think there was more to it. I think he was also autistic. But, like I said, I don't think we'll ever know for sure." I took a long breath. "But we'll keep working and he'll keep getting better. In the end, I think he'll be able to lead a normal life. I think he'll go to college and get married and make mistakes like all of us. He's close now. He's not there yet, but he's close. And we're not going to give up on him. But sometimes..."

I hesitated. Micah looked at me.

"What?"

"Sometimes I wonder why we had a child like Ryan. There was so much going on already with mom, dad, and Dana. It was too much, you know. It was too hard. It's like I didn't have enough challenges, so God gave me one more." I paused. "Do you know what I always tell Miles and Ryan?"

He raised his eyebrows.

"I tell Ryan that God gave him a brother like Miles so that Ryan could learn that anything is possible and that he can be good at anything. And I tell Miles that God gave him Ryan so that Miles could learn patience and persistence and how to overcome challenges."

Micah smiled. "That's nice."

I shrugged. It was a good lesson, but part of me always wished I wouldn't have had to say it at all.

Micah put his hand on my shoulder. "I know why God gave Ryan to you and Cat."

"Yeah?"

"Yeah."

"Why? Because he wanted to test my faith?"

"No," he said quietly. "Because not all parents could have done what you two did. He gave you Ryan because he knew that you two were smart and strong enough to help him. Ryan might have been lost with someone else."

For a long moment, we sat in silence. The snow flurries danced hypnotically, and began to coat the window ledges. I thought about Ryan, and his struggles, everything he'd been through. Yes, he was better because of the work Cat and I had done. And yes, I was confident about his future. But all at once, despite those thoughts, I felt a lump in my throat, and to be honest, I wasn't sure where it came from.

Our evening at the lodge ended relatively early, and Micah and I talked a few others on the tour into visiting one of the pubs in Tromsø. There are a lot of pubs in Tromsø, by the way. When it's dark eighteen hours a day in a relatively small town, there isn't much else to do if a person wants to spend time with friends. And Norwegians, we quickly discovered, are just about the friendliest people in the world. As soon as we found a table, locals gathered around to talk to us and listened as we described the trip we'd just been on. They asked our names and our histories, and asked how we liked their town. They offered to buy us drinks, and excitedly informed us that there would be karaoke that night. Some of the Norwegians took karaoke very seriously, and gradually the bar began to fill with people who'd come in just to sing. And here I thought karaoke stopped being popular years ago. Shows me how much I know.

Now, I've never sung karaoke. I've never *wanted* to sing karaoke, mainly because I'm a terrible singer. Micah can't sing either. And neither, I eventually learned, could anyone else on our tour.

But sing we did, and gradually we warmed to the idea of performing for these Norwegians. We passed the microphone back and forth, laughing when it was someone else's turn to belt out the next set of lyrics. We did this for hours, and it was one of the best evenings (along with Ayers Rock) that we had on the tour. The bar had a large selection of music, including Kenny Rogers's "Coward of the County," which made both of us laugh. It had to be an omen, and we belted out that tune at the top of our lungs. We also sang "Greased Lightning" from the movie *Grease*, doing our best to hide our off-key singing by dancing as exuberantly as we could. We moved like John Travolta, like professionals on Broadway, like we'd been dancing our entire lives, and at the end, the crowd clapped, whistled, and cheered. Later, when we asked one of the members of our tour what they really thought about our performance, there was a short pause before she answered.

"You know those howler monkeys in Guatemala? You looked like them."

Like I said, all in all, a fabulous night.

Our late night made rising early the following morning difficult. We were tired, and spent the morning at the museum in Tromsø.

There, we were treated to long discourses on jars and bowls.

After the museum, we drove out into the countryside to go dogsledding. There were low-lying hills and trees in every direction; in the distance, the snowcapped peaks were partially hidden by clouds.

It was brisk, and we dressed in snowsuits that we could slip over our clothes. To reach the dogsleds, we had to descend a shallow hill, and were given the option of walking or riding down on an inner tube.

Most of the people walked. Micah and I rode the inner tubes. About fifty times.

We were loaded into the dogsleds in groups of three: Micah and I were joined by Jill, the physician, and as we waited we were introduced to the dogs. They were huskies, but smaller than I'd imagined they would be, maybe fifty pounds or so. And they were friendly; they seemed to enjoy being stroked and licked at our snowsuits in return.

Our driver, a middle-aged woman who'd once placed fifth in the Alaskan Iditarod, had not only trained the dogs, but owned most of the surrounding area. The business of providing dogsled rides enabled her to exercise her dogs daily. And the dogs loved to exercise.

As soon as the driver stepped on, the dogs got antsy and started barking; I suppose I expected her to yell "Mush!" but instead—and in a tone no louder than ordinary conversation—she simply said something that sounded like "Het." The dogs started pulling and the sled took off, dogs trotting ahead and looking around.

There are a few things about dogsledding you should know. First, the sled is slow, extremely bumpy, and hard on the rear end. Second, you're seated in such a way to make you feel every bit of the ride. And finally, *saying* that you went dogsledding in Norway with a team that once competed in the Iditarod is more fun than the sledding itself.

But hey, we did it. And took lots of pictures, too. And now, when I stand at a party, I can say things like,

"Yes, I remember the time I was dogsledding in the Nor-wegian Alps...training the team for the Iditarod...going

hard...with the snow swirling in my eyes...my lead dog limping but gamely carrying on...my face growing numb in the cold...and I remember thinking..."

Pause.

It's even better than the *"I remember the time I was riding the elephants on my way to ancient Amber Fort in Jaipur...the heat beating down...the elephant growing weary as we mounted the final crest...and I remember thinking..."* story.

After riding the dogsled, we joined our tour companions under a teepee; inside, they were serving reindeer stew that had been cooked over an open fire. The teepee was smoky, but it was warm and the food was enticing, especially after the morning we'd spent.

Sadly, we were informed that because of the ever-deepening cloud cover, our chance to see the aurora borealis was next to nil; in fact, we would learn that the northern lights had been rare all winter. The chance to see them had been the reason for our visit to Tromsø in the first place, and both Micah and I were disappointed.

We were, however, offered a chance to go to yet another museum, but Micah and I were museumed out by then. Instead, we spent the rest of the afternoon wandering the streets of Tromsø, talking and taking in the sights.

"Did you ever wonder why things happened the way they did?" Micah asked, apropos of nothing.

"All the time," I responded, knowing exactly what he was referring to.

"Most of my friends haven't lost anyone close to them."

"Neither have mine. And Cat hasn't either."

"Why is that?"

"Who knows. I wish I could tell you, but I can't."

Micah pushed his hands into his pockets.

"Have you ever noticed that people think of us as experts on death now? I mean, whenever a friend has someone die, he or she always calls me to talk. Does that happen to you?"

"All the time," I answered.

"What do you say?"

"It depends."

"I never know what to tell them. I mean, there's nothing you can say to make a person stop hurting. Half the time, I just feel like telling them the truth. I'd say that for three months, you're going to feel worse than you've ever felt, and you cope as best you can. And that after six months, the pain isn't so bad, but it still hurts more than you think it will. And even after years, you still find yourself thinking about the person you lost, and get sad about it. And you still miss them all the time."

"Why don't you say that?"

"Because that's not what people want to hear. They want to hear that it's going to be okay. That the pain goes away. But it doesn't. It never does. And you can't say that when the wound is fresh. It would be like pouring salt in their wound, and you can't do that to a person. So instead, I tell them what they want to hear." He paused. "What have all these losses taught you?"

"That it hurts, but you've got to go on anyway."

"That's what I learned, too. But you know, I would rather have learned it a lot later in life."

"Me, too."

"You know what else I learned?" Micah asked.

"What's that?"

"That it's a cumulative thing. Mom's and dad's deaths were hard, but it's like when you lose both of them, it's not only twice the loss. It's exponential. And then, when we lost Dana...it wasn't like we'd lost three people we loved. It's like we lost almost *everything*."

Micah shook his head before going on.

"After something like that...well, even though you try to get through it—and might seem fine on the surface—underneath you're a wreck, and you don't even know it. And sometimes, it takes a while to figure out that you're still struggling with everything that happened."

I nudged his shoulder. "You talking about me again?"

"No, not just you," he said. "Me, too. Like you said, we just reacted to the loss in different ways."

After our sister's death, Micah changed.

It was as if he'd suddenly become intimately aware of the fragility of life and how precious time really was. As a result, he made a conscious effort to simplify his life, with the goal of eliminating unnecessary stress. No longer interested in society's definition of success, he began purging his life of material things. Life, he decided, was for *living*, not for *having*, and he wanted to experience every moment that he could. At the deepest level, he'd come to understand that life could end at any moment, and it was better to be happy than busy.

He began selling things, getting rid of the clutter. Within a couple of months, he'd sold both businesses and converted his investments to cash. He sold both his boat and his jeep. He recommitted himself to his family, and when he called me, he explained his reasoning as follows.

"The more you own, the more it owns you, and I'm tired of it.

I'm tired of having to take care of everything. I'm tired of things breaking and having to fix them. It adds stress, and frankly, I'm giving myself a break."

In the end, he kept the basics: his house, his car, and his furniture. The sale of his businesses left him with more than enough money to meet his monthly obligations—for years if he had to—and for the next eight months he did nothing that might add unwanted pressure to his life.

In some ways, he reverted to the young man he'd been during his college years. He went camping and hiking, he rafted during the summer, and as soon as snow began falling in the Sierras, he snowboarded. He took a trip to Puerto Vallarta with Christine. He visited Cody and Cole at the ranch. He began exercising regularly again, and joined an indoor soccer league. He also made a point to see me as often as he could. When I had a meeting in Los Angeles, my brother flew down to spend a few days with me. When my tour brought me through Sacramento later that fall, he came with me to the promotional events. In December, six months after my sister passed away, Micah visited me in North Carolina with Christine and his stepdaughter, Alli; Bob also came, along with Cody and Cole. Our three families took a trip to New York and we stood atop the World Trade Center admiring the view, less than nine months before it would be reduced to rubble.

Three weeks after our trip to New York, my brother called me. It was my birthday, and as soon as I answered the phone, he began to sing to me, in the same way my sister always had.

I listened with my eyes closed, remembering it all.

"I guess I'll have to do this for you now," he said, when he finished. "It's a tradition, you know."

I smiled, missing my sister but thankful for my brother.

"Thanks, Micah."

"No problem, little brother."

There was one other way in which my brother changed as well.

While he still went to church, his attendance became sporadic and continued to diminish as time went on. And on those days he did go, he sat in the pew and felt nothing.

With my sister's death, my brother had lost his faith.

I, too, had suddenly become aware of the fragility of life and the preciousness of time. But as similar as Micah and I were in many ways, my reaction was exactly the opposite.

I came to believe that because life could end at any moment, I had to be prepared for any eventuality. I wanted to make sure my family was taken care of, no matter what might happen in the future. I had goals, and with the clock ticking, I had to hurry up and meet them before the unthinkable occurred. There was suddenly no time to waste. I had to hurry, I had to get things ready, I had to work. I had to *go*.

Less than two weeks after my sister's funeral, I began to work on *A Bend in the Road*, a story inspired by my brother-in-law, Bob. It was the story of a young widower with a child, and I forced myself to sit at the computer for days on end to finish it. That fall, I toured in Europe and the United States to promote *The Rescue*, and as soon as the edits on *A Bend in the Road* were completed in early 2001, I began *The Guardian*, which would eventually become my longest and most challenging book to date. Little by little, work on the novel began to consume me.

I'd become so used to stress in the last eleven years that it was as if I didn't know how to function without it, and from that point on I continually added more to my plate. In January 2001, we found out that Cat was pregnant again; a few months later we learned she was having twin girls. After three boys, it was definitely exciting, and expecting twins seemed appropriate considering the sudden increase in the pace of life.

I became the master of scheduling. Every minute was planned for during the course of a day. Time was not to be wasted, even when I didn't work, for my responsibilities didn't end there. To accomplish everything, I compartmentalized my life into little boxes: If I wasn't working, I was dad, or husband, and I focused on those areas as intensely as my work. In the same way I sought my parents' approval, I sought my family's. I couldn't be simply dad, I tried to be *super-dad*: I coached soccer teams, attended gymnastics practices, helped with homework, played catch, and spent the weekends boating, bowling, swimming, and heading to the beach. I continued working with Ryan informally—he no longer needed intense structure—and played on the carpet with Landon every night. I tried to be the best husband I could, helping around the house, and doing my best to romance my wife. Somehow, despite all that, I squeezed in time to earn a black belt in Tae Kwon Do, lift weights, and jog daily. I continued to read a hundred books a year.

I slept less than five hours a night.

It wasn't all bad news, however. In the spring of 2001, I picked up the phone to hear Micah's excited voice.

"Christine is pregnant," he said. "We just found out."

"Congratulations," I said sincerely. "When's the baby due?"

"January," he said. "Just like Landon. And the twins will be only a few months old when she's born, so they'll have fun as cousins when they get older. When are the twins due?"

"Late August. How's Christine holding up?"

"Great, so far. She wouldn't have even known that she was pregnant except for the home pregnancy test she took."

"That's wonderful," I enthused. "I'll tell you, though—it's going to change your life."

"I know. I can't wait."

"You ready for this? Being a father?"

"Of course I'm ready. I've raised Alli since she was two."

"That's when they start getting easy. Wait until there's a newborn. It's a whole different world."

"Any words of advice you want to offer? Since it's my first time, and you're the expert?"

"Yeah," I said. "Toward the end of the pregnancy, see all the movies you can."

"Why?"

"Because," I said, "you're not going to see another movie for at least a year."

"Yeah, we will. Christine loves movies."

"Trust me," I said. "Nothing can change a lifestyle more than having a baby."

"Yeah, yeah," he said. Despite myself, I smiled inwardly. He'd learn soon enough.

"And Micah?"

"Yeah?"

"Congratulations again. Everything changes, but it's a change for the better."

"Thanks, little brother." He paused. "Oh yeah, one more thing—Cat wanted me to tell you this."

"What's that?"

"Quit working so hard."

"I will when you start going to church again."

We both laughed.

"This is great," I said. "I'm happy for you and Christine."

"Me, too."

I didn't listen to my brother. Or to my wife.

By early summer 2001, one year after my sister's death, Cat was heavy with twins, and I had to take on even more responsibility, since she couldn't keep up with the toddler or the older boys. To meet those additional demands on my time, I found myself sacrificing more sleep. Throughout that summer, I averaged less than three hours a night, and though I felt like a zombie when I stumbled out of bed, I quickly poured a cup of coffee, and charged into my day.

And I went and went and went. Working. Watching the kids. Taking care of Landon. Cleaning the house. Go, go, go.

Somehow, I was pulling it off. But a pace like that isn't normal, nor is it realistic. Something had to give, and for me, it was not only sleep, but simple downtime during the day. No lazy mornings sleeping in, no poker games with friends, no time to watch sports on television. I rushed through lunch and dinner. For a while, it didn't bother me, for my schedule made it seem as if I were in control of my life. I was taking care of all that I needed to. The schedule, though, had begun to control me. Little by little, I forgot how to relax. Even worse, I began to feel as if I didn't deserve to relax. *Not until I finished* _____ (fill in the blank).

But nothing was ever finished. There was always one more page to write, one more novel to finish, one more city to add to a tour, one more interview to give. My children continued to need my attention, no matter how much time I spent with them the day before. There was always another chore around the house. I wasn't necessarily unhappy—boredom has never suited me—and the pace wasn't killing me physically. But the lack of downtime, I would eventually realize, wasn't good for me mentally or emotionally. I began waking every day with the sense that I was falling behind. Despite my best efforts, I began to feel as if I were failing. Where once I was doing all those things because I wanted to, it gradually came to feel as if I *had* to, as if I had no other choice.

I say this in retrospect. At the time, I couldn't see the forest for the trees. Back then, all I knew was that I began to wake up with a sickening sense of dread. As soon as my eyes popped open, my mind filled with all that I had to do, and how my only chance to get it done was to start right then, at that moment, and get going. My life was a long to-do list, and instead of slowing down and doing what I could, I'd roll up my sleeves, grit my teeth, and work even harder.

Again, I wasn't consciously unhappy about it. I tried to find humor in the situation. I continued to laugh. People often remarked at how optimistic I seemed or how much I smiled. Yet, slowly but surely, life was becoming a grind, and there was nothing I could do to stop it.

My brother and I continued to speak on the phone regularly that summer. Our conversations—after discussing our pregnant wives—usually went as follows:

"What's going on?" he might ask, and I'd begin telling him everything I had scheduled. When I finished, he'd say nothing for a moment.

"So when do you sleep?" he'd ask.

"When I get the chance," I answered. Strangely, I felt a sense of pride about this, as if this were an admirable quality.

"That's dumb," he said. "You gotta sleep. And you gotta take time for yourself, too. You'll go crazy if you don't. Haven't you learned the importance of balance yet? Life is all about balance, and right now, your life is seriously out of whack."

"I'll be fine."

"Well, you sound stressed."

"Just busy. I'm fine—really," I said. "So what's going on with you?"

"Just living my life. I get up whenever I want and linger over the newspaper. I work out for a while, get in the shower around noon, and then figure out what I want to do next."

"Must be nice."

"You could do it, too. Everyone chooses his own life."

"Not always," I said. "Sometimes responsibilities get in the way. Granted, I could choose to ignore them, but it wouldn't be good for my family."

"Your family will be fine. You're just making excuses. You're going to go crazy if you keep up like this."

I didn't see it that way. I knew, however, there was no use arguing with him.

"Enough about me. How are you doing?"

"The same."

"You going to church yet?"

"Not really."

"How's Christine handling it?"

"The same. She's not too happy about it."

"Don't you think you should go then? If only for her?"

"You go to church for yourself, Nick. If you go for someone else, it doesn't mean anything."

"Then go for you."

"I'm not in the mood right now. I've got nothing against it, but I'm not getting anything out of it when I do go. I feel like a hypocrite sitting there."

"You can always use the time to pray."

"I've tried praying. I prayed for Dana every day, and she still died. Praying doesn't work."

We acknowledged our standoff with a moment of silence before Micah cleared his throat.

"So how's Ryan doing?"

In early August 2001, my brother was proven correct.

Endless nights of allowing myself only three hours of sleep had left me exhausted, and something inside me finally gave way. It came out of the blue. I woke with a feeling of anxiety unlike anything I'd ever experienced. I couldn't concentrate, and all of a sudden I started crying for the first time since my sister had died. I simply couldn't stop. My wife—now approaching her thirty-fifth week of pregnancy—held me in her arms, then sat me down.

"You need a break," she said. "Go to the beach house for a couple of days. I'll be fine here."

"Yeah...okay...let me get my things..."

She put her hand on my computer. "This stays here," she said. "I want you to relax. Take long walks by the water, sleep in. Do absolutely nothing for a few days."

My first night there, I slept seventeen straight hours. When I woke, I read for a little while, then slept another nine.

My brother called me a few days later.

"Heard about your little breakdown," he said. "I told you it would catch up to you."

"You were right."

"How you doing now?"

"Better," I said. "I think I was just tired and needed sleep."

"I think you need to learn to slow down."

"Like you?"

"Hey," he said, "I'm not the one who crashed. And in fact, I think I'm ready to go back to work. I'm starting another business."

"Doing what?"

"Same thing," he said. "Making garage cabinets."

"Good for you."

"Yeah, I'm excited about it, and with Christine pregnant, it's time. Besides, I've been getting bored lately. All my friends are working. No one has time to do anything fun."

Despite myself, I laughed. "Imagine that," I said.

In the fall of 2001, despite the lessons I should have learned, I threw myself back into work with a vengeance. If anything, I grew even busier than I'd been before.

Savannah and Lexie were born on August 24; Lexie Danielle had been named for my sister. While my wife took care of the twins and recovered, I took care of the other three kids and the household, at the same time pushing myself to finish the novel. A month later, I was on the road touring the country for *A Bend in the Road*. My wife, with twins, a toddler, and two older sons, somehow managed to keep the household running smoothly.

But again, there was more. There was always more.

At birth, Lexie had a small hemangioma—a collection of excess blood vessels in the soft tissue beneath her chin. It was the size of a pencil eraser at birth; by the time I went on tour for *A Bend in the Road*, it was a bulbous, purple mass that made her chin seem small in comparison.

It ruptured while I was on tour. Cat and I were talking on the phone, when she suddenly screamed, "I've got to go! Lexie's chin is gushing blood!"

Lexie was seven weeks old when she was rolled into surgery; that night, I signed books for eight hundred people, hating myself for not being with my family.

But still, I continued to work like a demon. I finished the first draft of *The Guardian* while in Jackson, Mississippi, and as soon as I got back home, I wrote a screenplay based on the same novel. I then composed text for a Web site that had more words than my first novel. In my spare time, I began working on a television pilot based on *The Rescue* for CBS, agreeing to serve as an executive producer if the network picked it up. Then, in late December 2001, I heard from my editor.

The Guardian, I was told, would need extensive revisions— including a complete rewrite on the last half of the book—and I couldn't imagine having to start all over on the novel. Yet, with a deadline looming, I needed a novel for the coming fall. Instead of reworking the novel, I began writing *Nights in Rodanthe*, to be published that fall in its place. *The Guardian*, my publisher and I decided, would be published in spring 2003, and I would edit it when *Nights in Rodanthe* was completed. While the time pressure on *Nights in Rodanthe* was intense—it had to be completed by April—it meant I had to do something else as well; namely I would have to write a *third novel* that year, immediately after finishing *The Guardian*, to be ready for fall 2003. The preliminary title was *The Wedding*.

In other words, 2002 was shaping up to be even busier than the previous year. Not only did I have five children and a wife— all of whom needed time and attention—but I'd have to work harder and faster than I ever had, simply to get it all done. It was still doubtful, though, I'd be able to finish before the year was out.

But by then, it didn't matter. I'd been running so hard, I didn't know how to stop. Life became something to conquer, rather than live, and had I wanted to change, I couldn't have figured out how to do it. Even then, however, I think I subconsciously knew that I needed to get my life back into balance, and that only Micah could help me do that.

And, as if my prayers were finally answered, it was around this time that the brochure came in the mail.

Epilogue

On our last night in Tromsø, we had a farewell dinner. It was an early night. We would be departing first thing in the morning, and because of a two-hour layover in England, the flight home would take nearly fifteen hours.

The atmosphere on the plane varied from boisterous to quiet. People mingled in the aisles, continuing to exchange phone numbers and e-mail addresses. Micah and I said our good-byes as well; once we landed and got through customs, everyone would head off in different directions to catch their final flights back home.

Later, while Micah was napping, I gazed out the window, watching the clouds pass beneath us.

I wasn't sure how I felt. Part of me was sad that our adventure had come to an end; another part was thrilled at the thought of seeing my wife and kids. Cat and I have loved each other since the third week of March 1988, and my feelings for her have grown only stronger over the years. How could they not? We were married only six weeks when catastrophe first struck, and she was the one who held me on those first few terrible nights, when everything always seemed hardest. And she's never stopped holding me since. As hard as it's been, as heartbreaking as it's been, I know that in many ways I've been fortunate. My wife and children are proof of that. And even now, when I pray at night, I find myself thanking God for all the blessings in my life.

At heart, I suppose, I'm an optimist like my mom was. Granted, an optimist who sometimes worries too much or works too hard, but an optimist nonetheless. In those moments when I feel sad about the loss of my parents and my sister, I've found that if I look closely at my children, I see hints of my own past. In my family growing up, there were five of us; three males and two females. Among my kids, those numbers are exactly the same, and I've come to realize that as the echoes of my own family's voices gradually dim over time, they've been replaced by the excited sounds of happy childhood. As they say, the circle of life continues.

The lessons my parents taught are still with me. I keep a tighter leash when raising my kids than my parents did, but I often find myself doing or saying the same things they did. My mom, for instance, was always cheerful when coming in from work; I try to behave the same way when I finish writing for the day. My dad would listen intently when I came to him with a problem, to help me find a way to solve it on my own; I try to do the same with my own kids. At night, while I'm tucking my kids in bed, I ask them to tell me three nice things that each of their siblings did for them that day, in the hopes that it will help them grow as close as Micah, Dana, and I did. And more frequently than I ever would have imagined possible growing up, I find myself telling my children *It's your life*, or *No one ever promised that life would be fair*, and *What you want and what you get are usually two entirely different things*. And after I say these words, I turn away and try to hide my smile, wondering what my parents would think about that.

When my thoughts turn to Dana, though, it's not easy. Her death sent me into a tailspin of sorts, one that took years from which to recover. She was too young, too sweet, too much a part of me for me to accept that she's gone. Yet my sister taught me well. Alone among the family, my sister never let her illness get her down, and I've tried to learn from her example. She lived her life fully despite her fears; she laughed and smiled until the very end. My sister, you see, had always been the strongest among us all.

"What are you thinking about?" Micah asked. Waking from his nap, he stretched in his seat.

"Everything," I said. "The trip. Our family. Cat and the kids."

"Did you think about work?"

I shook my head. "Actually, I didn't."

"But you'll plunge back in as soon as you get home, right?"

"I don't think so. I think I need to spend time with the family first."

Micah nudged me. "I think you're getting better," he said. "You look better. You're not nearly as glum as when you started. You actually look...relaxed."

"I am," I said. "But how about you? Are you doing any better?"

"I don't know what you're talking about. I never had any problems to begin with."

I snorted. "Must be nice being you."

"Oh, it is. Christine is one lucky lady to have a guy like me around."

I laughed. "So what's on your agenda when you get home?"

"Oh, the usual. See the wife, see the kids." He shrugged and let out a long breath. "And I'm sure Christine will want to go to church tomorrow, so I guess I'll have to go."

I raised my eyebrows but said nothing.

"What?" he asked.

I shook my head, unable to hide the smirk. "I didn't say anything."

"Listen, I'm not going to church because of anything I learned on the trip. Or anything you told me. You're not that wise, little brother."

"Oh, I know."

"I'm serious."

"I know."

"Don't look at me like that."

"Like what?"

"With that face. It wasn't like I completely stopped going to church. I still went every now and then. I'm just going to go because I think it's good for the kids to see me there. It teaches them the right kind of lessons—that you're part of God's plan. Mom did it for us, and look how we turned out."

"Mmmm," I said, nodding, continuing to smile.

"You're smirking."

"Yeah," I said smugly. "I know."

People often ask my brother and me how we continued to function—even flourish, by most standards—in the face of so much tragedy in our lives. I can't answer that question, except to say that neither Micah nor I ever considered the alternative. We'd been raised to survive, to meet challenges, and to chase our dreams.

We made the best of our lives because we had to. Because we wanted to. We had families of our own, families that needed us, and we couldn't let them down. But in the end, both Micah and I also survived and succeeded for each other. I needed Micah's support as much as he needed mine; Micah chased his dreams because I did, and vice versa. And it wouldn't have been fair of either of us to have to worry about each other. There was too much else going on.

We didn't escape unscathed. Who could? Our sister's death hit us hard—not just her death, but all of the deaths, one after the next. Even now, any elation we feel at reaching a goal or overcoming a challenge is tempered by the knowledge that, aside from each other, our family won't be around to share in our joy. Even worse, our children will never know their grand-parents or their aunt, and that, to us, is heartbreaking.

But still, we have each other. People ask me why my brother and I are so close. The reason is simple; it's the way it should be. The loss of our family alone didn't drive us together; we were always close, even as children. We keep in touch, not because we have to, but because we want to. And we don't only love each other, but like each other as well. My brother and I haven't had an argument—or even a disagreement—since we were little kids. He is, along with my wife, my best friend in the world. And, if you asked him, he would say the same thing about me.

My parents may have been crazy, but whatever they did, it worked.

We landed in Dulles, and made our way through customs. Micah and I, like everyone else, would be going in different directions. We strolled through the terminal, weaving through weekend crowds, until we finally reached the point where our paths were forced to diverge.

We faced each other to say good-bye, and when I looked up at Micah, the first thought to go through my mind was that I might never see him again.

It's a sad thought, of course, but honest. It had happened to both of us three times before. It's what I always think when I say good-bye to my brother.

"I had a great time," I said. "Like you promised, it was the trip of a lifetime."

"It was the best," he said. He set his suitcase down and smiled. "I'll give you a call when I get back home."

"You better."

He opened his arms and I went into them. And for a long moment, my brother and I held each other in the terminal, oblivious to the crowd weaving around us.

"I love you, little brother," he whispered.

I squeezed my eyes shut.

"I love you, too, Micah."

Questions and Explanations for Chapter 17 and the Epilogue

The ten questions on chapter 17 and the epilogue focus on grammar and usage, vocabulary, comprehension, literary terms, characterization, and style. Some of the questions combine two or more of these areas, requiring you to synthesize your knowledge, make inferences, and interpret the text. The questions are designed to determine both your current level of understanding of the memoir and your ability to answer higher-level questions.

The following sentence tests your ability to recognize grammar and usage errors. The sentence contains either a single error or no error at all. If the sentence contains an error, select the one underlined part that must be changed to make the sentence correct. If there is no error, select choice D.

1. Neither of the choices <u>that</u> Nicholas <u>has</u> when facing the
   _A   _B
   difficulties of promoting his new novels <u>are ideal options</u>,
   _C
   for both touring and not touring were means of support-
   ing his family. <u>No error</u>
   _D

Choice A tests the choice of the relative pronoun *that.* A relative pronoun is the pronoun (*who, which, what,* or *that*) that introduces a subordinate (or dependent) clause. The entire clause acts as an adjective, modifying the noun that precedes it—for example, "A black hole is a star *that* behaves quite mysteriously."

Choice B checks your knowledge of subject and verb agreement. Which is correct, "Nicholas has" or "Nicholas have"?

Choice C also checks subject and verb agreement. *Neither* is a singular pronoun and it needs to be paired with a singular verb—for example, "Neither of the boys has his own motorcycle."

The following two questions test your vocabulary. Choose the word or set of words that, when inserted in the sentence, best fits the meaning of the sentence as a whole.

2. Any elation that the brothers feel "at reaching a goal or overcoming a challenge is _____ by the knowledge that, aside from each other, our family won't be around to share in our joy."

   A. acclaimed

   B. degenerated

    C. nullified

    D. tempered

This question tests your comprehension and your vocabulary. *Acclaimed*, choice A, means applauded. *Degenerated*, choice B, means to become worse. *Nullified*, choice C, means abolished. *Tempered*, choice D, means toned down or restrained.

3. Stylistically, Sparks _____ creates a single-sentence paragraph in order to _____ its importance to the development of character and theme.

    A. usually...divulge

    B. frequently...reveal

    C. surprisingly...minimize

    D. occasionally...emphasize

This question tests your vocabulary as well as your analytical skills. Understanding the effect of a single-sentence paragraph will enable you to more easily fill in the blanks. Obviously a single-sentence paragraph is not standard; thus, it doesn't make sense to claim that this is a usual or frequent technique, so choice A and choice B can be eliminated.

When deciding between choice C and choice D, compare the resulting sentences when the substitutions are made. Although *surprisingly* (which means unexpectedly) may make sense, the word *minimize* (which means to reduce or lessen the importance of) does not. Choice D states that although the occurrence only takes place now and again, it is used to stress the importance of the paragraph.

Question 4 tests your knowledge of literary terms.

4. Micah says, "I hate it when the kids whine. It's like fingernails against a chalkboard." What figure of speech is he using to explain his position?

   A. hyperbole

   B. metaphor

   C. personification

   D. simile

Hyperbole, choice A, is an exaggerated statement used to heighten effect and to emphasize a point—for example, "This learning guide has defined *hyperbole* a million times already." A *metaphor*, choice B, is a comparison made between two unlike things without using a connective word—for example, "LeBron James is an animal on the basketball court." *Personification*, choice C, is giving nonhuman things human characteristics—for example, "The leaves danced in the wind." And a *simile*, choice D, is a comparison made between two unlike things using a connective word, such as *like*, *as*, or *than*—for example, "She looked as fresh as the morning snow."

Question 5 asks you to make an inference regarding strong and thorough textual evidence.

5. Nicholas tells Ryan that God gave him a brother in order to "learn that anything is possible," and he tells Miles that God gave him a brother to "learn patience and persistence and how to overcome challenges." These ideas are significant for which of the following reasons?

A. They reflect Nicholas's attitude toward his sons.

B. The words also represent what Nicholas and Micah have in each other.

C. Universally, they represent what any brother could be for another.

D. They provide closure to both narratives in the memoir.

E. all of the above

Recognize that the question indicates that there may be more than one correct answer. If you think that Nicholas is speaking honestly about both of his sons, select choice A. If the description also aptly applies to the relationship between Nicholas and Micah, select choice B. If the ideas can be applied to the relationships of brothers outside of the memoir, select choice C. And if the words begin to provide closure to both narrative threads, select choice D.

Question 6 tests your knowledge of literary terms.

6. "The snow flurries danced hypnotically, and began to coat the window ledges." What literary device is being used to describe this scene?

A. personification

B. hyperbole

C. foreshadowing

D. irony

Personification, choice A, is giving nonhuman things human characteristics—for example, "Opportunity knocked on the door." *Hyperbole*, choice B, is an exaggerated statement used to heighten effect and to emphasize a point—for example, "This learning guide has defined *hyperbole* a million times already."

Foreshadowing, choice C, is providing hints or clues to future events. For example, when Benvolio suggests to Romeo that finding a new female beauty may help Romeo get over Rosaline, it foreshadows Romeo's falling in love with Juliet when he sees her later in the play.

Understanding *irony*, the situation of appearance versus reality, is essential to understanding most literary texts. *Cosmic irony*, also known as irony of fate, is the situation where no matter what a character attempts to do, he or she cannot escape his or her fate. The most famous example of this is the Greek myth of Oedipus, who was fated to grow up and kill his father and marry his mother, no matter what he or anyone else tried to do to prevent it. *Dramatic irony* is when the reader knows something that the character in the text does not know. For example, the audience knows that Juliet is not really dead when Romeo discovers her body in the crypt, but he does not, and so he stabs himself. *Situational irony* is the incongruity between the expected outcome and what actually occurs—for example, Erik studies quite hard for a test yet fails it, but Mitch doesn't prepare at all for it and aces it. *Verbal irony* is meaning the opposite of what is stated; sarcasm is a form of verbal irony. When you ask Erik, who just failed the test, how he did and he, knowing full well he failed it, responds, "Great," he doesn't really mean it. He is being sarcastic; he is using verbal irony.

Question 7 checks your comprehension.

7. What does Nicholas say when Micah asks him, "What have all these losses taught you?"

    A. "That it's a cumulative thing...It's exponential."

    B. "People think of us as experts on death now."

    C. "That it hurts, but you've got to go on anyway."

    D. "We just reacted to the loss in different ways."

This is an important question for character, plot, and thematic development. Although all four choices are direct quotations from the memoir, only one of these sentences is spoken by Nicholas and only one directly answers the question. If you are not sure of the answer, skim the chapter and look for the question and response immediately following it.

Question 8 asks you to make an inference regarding character development.

8. Although Micah wants to tell people who are hurting after the death of a loved one that "even after years, you still find yourself thinking about the person you lost, and get sad about it," he doesn't because "that's not what people want to hear." What can you infer about Micah as a character based on these words and actions?

    A. He is selfish.

    B. He is realistic.

    C. He is idealistic.

    D. He is stubborn.

In order to answer this question, you need to understand not only what Micah is saying but also why he is saying it, for the reasoning behind his words reveals his character. A *selfish* person, choice A, disregards the welfare of others, caring only for his own interests and comfort. A *realistic* person, choice B, is practical, seeing things as they truly are. An *idealistic* person, choice C, sees things as he or she wants them to be or thinks they should be rather than the way they really are. A *stubborn* person, choice D, is inflexible in his or her opinion.

Question 9 checks your comprehension.

9. After Dana's death, Micah changes. Which of the following are examples of the way Micah changed?

   A. He adopted a "the more you own, the more it owns you" attitude.

   B. He sold both of his businesses.

   C. He began exercising regularly and joined an indoor soccer team.

   D. He continued Dana's tradition of singing "Happy Birthday" to Nicholas.

   E. all of the above

This question is also important for character, plot, and thematic development. The changes that Micah goes through after his sister's death obviously impact himself and his immediate family, but they also affect Nicholas. Knowing that he only has his brother left and realizing that life is short, Micah makes some changes in the way he lived his life. If you are not sure of the correct answers (recognize that the question indicates there may be more than one correct answer), reread the chapter to understand how Micah responds to the third major tragedy.

Question 10 asks you to analyze an author's stylistic choices.

10. Stylistically the epilogue achieves which of the following effects?

   A. It fulfills the words of the epigraph.

   B. It provides closure to the two narratives that began in the prologue.

   C. It presents a final image that is the physical representation of a deep emotional connection.

   D. It evokes a relatable feeling of family.

   E. all of the above

This question asks you to analyze how an author's choices regarding parts of a text contribute to its overall structure and meaning. If the words of the epigraph, "A friend is always loyal, and a brother is born to help in the time of need," are realized, then select choice A. If both narrative threads are completed, select choice B. If the final image of the memoir demonstrates the closeness of the brothers, select choice C. If the main ideas of the epilogue center on the importance of family, select choice D. And if the epilogue achieves A through D, select choice E.

Post-Reading Questions and Writing Assignments

Critical Reading Questions

Answer the questions on pages 534–535 based on the information in the accompanying passage.

I work out of the house as many authors do, but that's where the resemblance ends. My office isn't some upstairs, out-of-the-way sanctuary; instead, the door opens directly onto the living room. While I've read that some authors must have a quiet house in order to concentrate, I'm fortunate that I've never needed silence to work. It's a good thing, I suppose, or I never would have ever written at all. Our house, you have to understand, is a whirlwind of activity literally from the moment my wife and I get out of bed until the moment we collapse back into it at the end of the day. Spending the day at our home is enough to exhaust just about anyone. First off, our kids have energy. Lots and lots of energy. *Ridiculous* amounts of energy. Multiplied by five, it's enough energy to power the city of Cleveland. And the kids somehow magically feed off each other's energy, each consuming and mirroring the other's. Then our three dogs feed off it, and then the *house itself* seems to feed on it. A typical day includes: at least one sick child, toys strewn from one end of the living room to the other that magically reappear the moment after they've been put away, dogs barking, kids laughing, the phone ringing off the hook, FedEx and UPS deliveries coming and going, kids whining, lost homework, appliances breaking, school projects due tomorrow that our children somehow forget to tell us about until the last minute, baseball practice, gymnastics practice, football practice, Tae Kwon Do practice, repairmen coming and going, doors slamming, kids running down the hallway, kids throwing things, kids teasing each other, kids asking for snacks, kids crying because they fell, kids cuddling up on your lap, or kids crying because they need you RIGHT THIS MINUTE! When my in-laws leave after visiting for a week, they can't get to the airport soon enough. There are deep bags under their eyes and they carry the dazed, shell-shocked expression of veterans who just survived the landing on Omaha Beach. Instead of saying good-bye, my father-in-law shakes his head and whispers, "Good luck. You're going to need it."

My wife accepts all of this activity in the house as normal. She's patient and seldom gets flustered. My wife seems to actually *enjoy* it most of the time. My wife, I might add, is a saint.

Either that, or maybe she *is* insane.

1. The passage includes a description of the author's home life primarily to:

    A. justify his father-in-law's feelings

    B. characterize his wife

    C. develop his children as characters

    D. gain sympathy from the reader

    E. illustrate his working conditions

2. The passage is primarily concerned with:

    A. advancing the plot

    B. describing a setting

    C. developing a character

    D. establishing a theme

    E. listing various daily activities

3. The narrator would most likely describe his daily life as:

    A. affectionate

    B. chaotic

    C. languid

    D. meticulous

    E. supercilious

4. The clause "the *house itself* seems to feed on it" makes use of which figure of speech?

   A. hyperbole

   B. irony

   C. metaphor

   D. personification

   E. simile

5. In the passage, the author uses each of the following rhetorical devices for emphasis EXCEPT:

   A. amplification

   B. anaphora

   C. fragments

   D. hyperbole

   E. italics

6. Which rhetorical figure of speech does the author use in the second paragraph?

   A. allusion

   B. analogy

   C. anaphora

   D. antithesis

   E. apostrophe

Answer the questions on pages 537–539 based on the information in the accompanying passage.

The following morning, we set off to see the first of the Moai statues, which were located less than a few minutes from the hotel, just up the coast. Had we known where we'd be going, we could have seen them from our hotel room.

As we rode in the vans with the archaeologists who made their living studying them, we were informed that at one time there were roughly fourteen different tribes on the island, each with its own ruler. These rulers ordered the carving of these statues from volcanic rock—most were made to resemble said rulers—and over time, these statues grew larger and larger, as each ruler tried to impress on the people his own importance. Some of the Moai weigh up to thirty tons, and stand twelve feet high; one unfinished statue measures sixty-six feet and is estimated to weigh nearly fifty tons.

Afterward, we were told about the absence of trees.

When it was first colonized, Easter Island had resembled other islands in the Pacific, but as the population expanded, trees became the most overused of all the natural resources. They were employed in construction of dwellings and for cooking fires; mature trees were used to roll the Moai across the island. In the past when Polynesians migrated, as islands became overcrowded, people would head off in their canoes in search of new territories; because Easter Island was so isolated, there was nowhere else to go. Overcrowding and overuse of the resources led to civil wars; the wars continued through generations. Through it all, trees continued to be cut down.

In the end, most had been wiped out, and the natives ended up burning anything they could in order to cook, including their homes and canoes. Shore fishing became the sole source of food, but a La Niña effect is suspected to have suddenly cooled the waters around the island. It lasted two years, killing much of the ocean reef, and the fish became less plentiful. In the end, the natives turned to cannibalism.

Over time, a few palms eventually sprouted again, but to speed the process, mature palm trees were imported from Tahiti. These trees, however, turned out to be diseased, and they not only died, but ended up killing most of the remaining palms on the island. Now, there are only a few spots where they still remain.

1. What is the primary purpose of this passage?

   A. to describe Easter Island

   B. to explain why the island has few trees

   C. to suggest why the islanders resorted to cannibalism

   D. to narrate a day on the island

   E. to analyze the Moai

2. The sentence, "Had we known where we'd be going, we could have seen them from our hotel room" (lines 3–5) suggests that:

   A. the author is excited about the close proximity of the Moai

   B. the Moai exist extensively throughout the island

   C. the Moai are the reason for the depletion of trees

  D. the tour guides never communicate with the tourists

  E. Easter Island is too commercial

3. What is the primary function of the third paragraph?

  A. to compare and contrast the past with the present

  B. to illustrate a cause and effect

  C. to describe the current condition of the island

  D. to explain a process analysis

  E. to transition between topics

4. According to the passage, which of the reasons listed below LEAST affected the loss of trees on Easter Island?

  A. La Niña

  B. overpopulation

  C. ongoing warfare

  D. diseased trees

  E. transporting the Moai

5. The use of passive voice in the final paragraph primarily achieves what stylistic effect?

  A. It illustrates the destructive nature of the diseased trees.

  B. It demonstrates the shortsightedness of the islanders.

  C. It emphasizes the effect of the action rather than the doer of the action.

  D. It illustrates the connection between form and theme.

  E. It transitions the reader from the past to the present.

6. The tone of the final paragraph is best described as:

   A. critical

   B. despairing

   C. emotional

   D. objective

   E. terse

Short Answer Questions (paragraph response)

1. What role does religion play in the Sparks brothers' lives? Compare and contrast the brothers, as well as their adult lives with their childhoods.
2. How would you categorize Nicholas and Micah's parents? Use details and examples from the memoir to support your assertion.
3. Which death has the greatest impact on Nicholas Sparks? On Micah? On the relationship between the brothers?
4. Which stop on the tour was the most significant one for Nicholas Sparks? For Micah?
5. How has Nicholas Sparks's personal life affected his professional life?

Writing Assignments (essay response)

1. Although this memoir is nonfiction, in many ways it reads like a novel. Analyze the narrative techniques Sparks uses in *Three Weeks with My Brother*. What impact do these techniques have on the text as whole?

2. One important thematic topic in *Three Weeks with My Brother* is fate versus free will. Consider the numerous events that could be considered fate throughout the memoir. Which are the most significant? Then, using specific details and examples from the text, write an essay in which you analyze what the memoir seems to support regarding fate and free will. Avoid mere plot summary.

3. Stylistically, Nicholas Sparks made an interesting choice in the structure of *Three Weeks with My Brother*. The narrative is told from two interrelated narrative threads; thus, the time line shifts within a single chapter. Using details and examples from the text, trace the development of plot, characters, and themes. Then articulate the effect this change has on the memoir as a whole.

4. Select a moment or scene from *Three Weeks with My Brother* that you find especially memorable. Write an essay in which you identify the passage, explain its relationship to the work as a whole, and analyze the reasons for its effectiveness.

5. Although Nicholas Sparks is a popular writer and *Three Weeks with My Brother* was a best seller, many aspects of the memoir suggest a more literary text. Evaluate the literary merit of the memoir. Then write an essay arguing for either the inclusion or exclusion of *Three Weeks with My Brother* in a high school curriculum.

Understanding the Rubric

It is important to understand the various sections of the rubric and to use it while you are drafting your essay. The following sections are designed to help you understand the rubric for your literary essay.

Thesis

A strong essay relies on the quality of its thesis. Thus, a strong thesis—a precise opinion about a limited topic, a debatable claim, a main idea, or a central idea—is essential for a strong, interpretative, analytical essay.

A strong thesis has the following characteristics:

- a clearly defined opinion
- one idea
- something worth saying
- specific terms

A thesis may be weak if it is a retelling of the plot: An example of a weak thesis is *"Three Weeks with My Brother* is a memoir that recounts a trip around the world that Nicholas Sparks took with his brother Micah." It is also weak if it merely mentions a topic. An example of this type of weak thesis is *"Three Weeks with My Brother* is a memoir about brothers and family."

Your thesis must not be too broad: "In *Three Weeks with My Brother*, Sparks shows in many ways the importance of family." Instead, focus your topic: *"Three Weeks with My Brother* demonstrates that family is the most important thing in life."

A strong thesis is clearly stated and focused: "In his memoir *Three Weeks with My Brother*, Sparks shares intimate details about his personal life and the tragedies that he and his brother endured in order to demonstrate that family is the most important thing in life."

Rubric for Essays

CATEGORY	OUTSTANDING	STRONG	MEETS EXPECTATIONS	EMERGING	UNACCEPTABLE
Thesis	A clearly stated, focused, and persuasive opinion	A clearly stated and focused claim	Although the opinion may be legitimate, it is too broad for the scope of the assignment	More of a topic than thesis OR thesis does not address assignment	No thesis evident OR thesis is a retelling of plot
Organization	Introduction grabs attention; variety of transitions used within and between paragraphs; topic sentences have ample support; meaningful conclusion ties essay together well	Introduction sparks some interest; some variety of transitions used within and between paragraphs; topic sentences have support; satisfying conclusion completes the argument	Evidence of an introduction, body paragraphs, and a conclusion; transitions used within and between paragraphs	Introduction and/or conclusion does not flow with rest of argument; body paragraphs lack topic sentences or support; few transitions used	Introduction and/or conclusion missing; topic sentences not evident OR topic sentences are summaries; transitions not used

Support from the Text	Every body paragraph has multiple supports from text; evidence from text persuasively supports your argument; all citations are incorporated smoothly	Every body paragraph has some support from text; evidence supports your argument; most citations are incorporated smoothly	Every body paragraph has support from text, though the evidence may be superficial; some citations stand alone	Evidence does not support topic sentences; most citations stand alone and are not incorporated smoothly into argument	Little or no textual support
Analysis	All support material is introduced and commented upon; cumulative weight of the evidence is convincing	Most support material is introduced and commented upon; analysis is clearly connected to thesis	Ideas support thesis but are obvious and basic	Analysis misrepresents evidence OR is an illogical argument OR ideas are not fully developed	Analysis not attempted OR restates evidence OR does not address the assignment
MUGS (Mechanics, Usage, Grammar, Spelling)	Varied sentences; sophisticated vocabulary; no editing errors	Some variety in sentence structure; advanced vocabulary; few editing errors	Little sentence variety; adequate vocabulary; some editing errors	Lack of sentence variety and clarity; limited vocabulary; many editing errors	Fragments and/or run-ons; errors with word choice; editing errors handicap readers

An outstanding thesis is not only clearly stated and focused but also persuasive: "*Three Weeks with My Brother* illustrates that every negative situation can be used to create good."

Organization

An essay has three distinct sections: the introduction, the body, and the conclusion. The introduction should be about 15 percent of your paper; the body should be about 75 percent; and the conclusion should comprise about 10 percent of the entire essay.

INTRODUCTION

The introduction should contain the following elements:

- motivator
- title and author
- basic plot summary/overview
- thesis

The *motivator* is the first part of your introduction. It is something that captures your reader's attention and entices him or her to keep on reading. A good introduction announces the topic and sets the tone—for example, an amusing anecdote is not appropriate for a paper about political torture. You want to entice your reader (motivate him or her) to keep reading. And you want to state—either explicitly or implicitly—your opinion. Here are some suggestions for possible motivators:

- general background
- history

- definitions
- quotation
- anecdote
- personal experience
- arresting statement
- interesting details (facts, figures, statistics)
- directly stated thesis
- a question

Here are some examples of poor beginnings:

- In this paper I intend to . . .
- Wars have always affected mankind.
- As you may know, having too little time is a problem for many of us.
- In the modern world today, . . .

Here are some examples of stronger beginnings:

- Although Dana is an important minor character in *Three Weeks with My Brother*, readers are seldom privy to her interior world; rather, we are dependent on her words and actions in order to get to know the real person.
- Nicholas Sparks's control over pacing and his ability to intertwine two narrative threads in *Three Weeks with My Brother* are essential to his success in showing the importance of brothers and sisters sticking together no matter what.
- Nicholas Sparks creates a conversational tone from the onset of *Three Weeks with My Brother* by admitting, "It isn't easy living with an author."

- Is it better to have loved and lost than to have never loved at all? For Nicholas Sparks and his brother, Micah, it is, as they share in their memoir *Three Weeks with My Brother*.

BODY

Each body paragraph should have a topic sentence—that is, a sentence that states the main idea of the paragraph. All of the topic sentences in your essay should develop and illustrate your thesis. If they do, your essay will have unity. Within the paragraph, all of your details and examples should develop and illustrate your topic sentence. If they do, then your paragraph will have unity.

In order to allow your reader to follow your train of thought, you need to use transitions—standard devices and hooks to connect ideas—that give your essay coherence. Use transitions within and between paragraphs.

CONCLUSION

Your conclusion is your last chance to make your case. Compare it to an attorney's closing argument in a trial. Rather than restating your thesis and main support for it, you should demonstrate how the cumulative weight of the evidence in your essay works together to prove your point.

Support from the Text

Support from the text can come in one of three forms: summaries, paraphrases, or direct quotations. The most effective support is a direct quotation because you are using the exact words of the original text in support of your assertions.

None of your citations should be used as a stand-alone sentence in your essay; rather, you should incorporate citations into your own sentences.

Analysis

Although having citations in your essay is important, citations alone are not enough. You must be certain that you are using the citations to develop your ideas.

You do this by following a four-part process:

1. Introduce
2. Use
3. Cite
4. Comment upon

When you make the cited material a part of your own sentence, you integrate it smoothly into your essay by introducing the quoted material before you use it. This prepares the reader of your essay for the information that is going to follow.

After introducing the source material, you use it. Make sure you use quotation marks for all passages that you cite verbatim—that is, exactly—from the memoir.

Follow the documentation style required by your teacher, which is typically MLA (Modern Language Association). Sometimes you may be asked to use the *Chicago Manual of Style* or APA (American Psychological Association) documentation guidelines, including footnotes or endnotes. Although the specific formats vary, all documentation styles exist to indicate the location of the cited material in the original text and to credit the original text properly. If in doubt, ask your teacher for documentation guidelines.

The most important aspect of using citations is your explanation of the significance of the text evidence you are citing. When you discuss the passage, quoting lines from the memoir helps develop your interpretation. Providing individual instances of textual support is a good thing, and when all of the quotations in your essay work together, they create a cohesive whole.

Another part of your analysis is addressing details and examples that may initially indicate a counterinterpretation. The best interpretations are those that address and incorporate the significant words and actions on both sides of the argument.

MUGS

MUGS refers to the editing portion of your essay. MUGS stands for "mechanics, usage, grammar, and spelling." This is the last step of the writing process, when you clean up any surface-level errors.

Mechanics are the rules regarding how you put a sentence together—using capital letters and punctuation marks. In addition, they require you to use a variety of sentence types. Sometimes a simple sentence is effective, such as "Nicholas loves Cat." Other times, a complex sentence is more effective, such as "Although Nicholas loves Cat, he still has a void in his life due to the early deaths of his mother and sister."

Usage refers to various forms of agreement—subject and verb agreement (*he is, they are*) and pronoun and antecedent agreement (*not* "Micah and me are going on a world tour" or

"Everybody has their luggage")—as well as dangling and mis-placed modifiers. A dangling modifier is using a word or group of words to modify something that isn't in the sentence—for example, "Hiking up the hill, a temple came into view." In this sentence, the temple wasn't hiking up the hill, so the phrase "hiking up the hill" is considered dangling. To correct the error, rewrite the sentence: "While Micah and Nicholas were hiking up a hill, a temple came into view." A vague pronoun reference occurs when a pronoun could possibly reference more than one word, which can create confusion—for example, "Micah tossed a stick at the pottery and broke it." Did he break the stick or the pottery?

Grammar is the overarching term that covers all the rules of language and composition. And spelling is self-evident.

Three Sample Essays and Application of the Rubric

Following are a copy of essay question 5 and three sample essays, each written at different and improving levels, based on the rubric. Sample Essay 1 is an example of a below-level essay. Sample Essay 2 takes some of the shortcomings (as identified on the rubric) from Sample Essay 1, makes some revisions based on the rubric, and thus improves the essay. Sample Essay 3 is an outstanding essay fully utilizing the essential elements of the rubric and thus improving Sample Essay 2.

Essay Question 5. Although Nicholas Sparks is a popular writer and *Three Weeks with My Brother* was a best seller, many aspects of the memoir suggest a more literary text. Evaluate the literary merit of the memoir. Then write an essay arguing for either the inclusion or exclusion of *Three Weeks with My Brother* in a high school curriculum.

Sample Essay 1 (example of a poor essay)

In *Three Weeks with My Brother*, Nicholas Sparks writes a memoir that also serves as travelogue. Readers learn alot about Nicholas Sparks and his brothers' trip around the world as well as about their lives growing up. Its a good read and an important book.

In the Prologue we find out that Nicholas gets a brochure about taking the trip. Initially he is interested but doesn't think he has the time, so he buries it in the pile of mail. But he couldn't forget about the trip. Cautiously mentioning the trip to his wife a couple of times, he eventually gets around to telling her that he was considering taking the trip with his brother, Micah. "That would be a wonderful idea" (13) Cat, short for Cathy, his wife tells him. And almost as soon as he agrees to go, Nicholas Sparks seemingly regrets his decision.

Although Micah is quite excited about the trip, Nicholas has a hard time gaining enthusiasm. Eventually he does, and then the memoir is broken down into two parts. One is the story of the trip; the other is the story of the brothers growing up. Eventually, the two story lines come together. *Three Weeks with My Brother* is a memoir about growing up as well as the trip around the world. But the more important story is the story of their lives together. It is "a story about brotherhood" (14).

This memoir about brothers is quite literally because of what is in the book. There are alot of examples of figures of speech and foreshadowing. And there is lots of character development. This is nonfiction but it reads just like a novel. And since the book takes place all over the world, there are many different settings and different locations of where the story takes place. The most important thing that makes this book literary is the fact that it explores many important themes, like brotherhood, death, faith, growing up, love, marriage, and relationships.

Because of these themes, *Three Weeks with My Brother* should be a part of the high school curriculum. Also because it's more interesting to read than other nonfiction things, like "Sinners in the Hands of an Angry God," "Civil Disobedience," and "I Have a Dream." When you are interested in what your reading, you read it more often (or at least more of it). Some parts did slow down, but overall this was a really good book.

- thesis is a retelling of plot
- evidence of introduction, body paragraphs, and a conclusion; transitions used between paragraphs
- too few citations. The two stand alone and are not incorporated smoothly into argument
- analysis restates evidence but does not completely address the prompt
- little sentence variety
- many editing errors

Sample Essay 2 (example of a competent essay)

"That would be a wonderful idea" (13) Cathy Sparks tells her husband Nicholas when he suggests that he and his brother, Micah, take a three-week trip around the world. And thus begins *Three Weeks with My Brother*, a memoir and travelogue all in one. Cat, short for Cathy, knew that Nicholas had a need to spend time with his brother. In the Prologue, readers are not privy to the information, though Nicholas does write that the book is "a story about brotherhood" (14) and about two journeys: one that took them to "places around the world" and the other that "has led us to become the best of friends" (15). *Three Weeks with My Brother* is a quality piece of literary nonfiction that should be read in an American literature class.

Even though Sparks mentions in the Prologue that the memoir is about two journeys, the initial chapters are mostly about his life growing up. These chapters serve as the exposition for both stories that are going to be told in *Three Weeks with My Brother.* Sparks paints a portrait of his parents that enables readers to get to know them and their values; they are developed through their own words and actions in the early chapters as well as throughout the rest of the text. Although the brothers grow up in poverty conditions, they neither realized it nor cared. In retrospect, Nicholas writes that "we didn't have much as a family, but we'd always had one another" (61). This idea of favoring family above all else resonates throughout the memoir and is one of the most important thematic topics.

Gradually, Sparks begins to tell the story of their trip around the world. The tour takes the brothers to many exotic locations, such as the Mayan and Incan ruins, Easter Island, India, Africa, and Norway. Through Sparks's inclusion of meticulous details, readers are able to share the trip with Nicholas and Micah. This trip narrative is both educational and enlightening, as readers learn that Cuzco, Peru, is the "oldest permanent settlement in the Western Hemisphere" (181) and that Ayers Rock is the "largest monolith, or single-unit stone, in the world" (278). This type of information is mixed in with the details of typical touristy activities—visiting museums, shopping, and sightseeing; all of these details provide background information about the different sites, as well as creating images for the reader to share in the experience.

Although the chapters begin with the name of the specific location and important information about each stop on the tour is shared, the more important narrative is the one that follows the family's life as the brothers were growing up. This is the story line that develops the three siblings—for their sister Dana is also a significant character in the memoir—and enables readers to relate to the Sparks family. From this incredible family, the brothers learn some of their most important life lessons. From their father, they learned their "love of learning" (135), and their mother taught them, among other things, that "what you want and what you get are usually two entirely different things" (43). These values and attitudes enable the brothers to gain a healthy and secure outlook on life, and they ended up living fulfilled lives based on this solid foundation.

The lessons that the Sparks brothers learned from their parents are universal and are enough to make *Three Weeks with My Brother* should be a part of the high school curriculum. In addition, many students may find this memoir more interesting to read than many classical nonfiction texts that students often encounter in American literature classes, such as Thoreau's "Civil Disobedience," and Martin Luther King, Jr.'s "I Have a Dream." I'm not advocating abandoning these, but often American literature starts at the beginning and continues chronologically, never providing students an opportunity to read something contemporary. A balance between classical and contemporary texts would be an acceptable compromise. Because *Three Weeks with My Brother* is a nonfiction text that reads like a novel, students will be able to use their analytical skills on an accessible piece of writing while simultaneously learning a number of new things. And if students were excited about reading, analyzing, and learning, that "would be a wonderful idea."

- a clearly stated and focused claim
- introduction sparks some interest
- some variety of transitions used within and between paragraphs
- topic sentences have support
- a conclusion exists
- most support material is introduced and commented upon
- analysis is clearly connected to thesis
- some variety in sentence structure
- few editing errors

Sample Essay 3 (example of an outstanding essay)

"That would be a wonderful idea" (13) Cathy Sparks tells her husband Nicholas when he suggests that he and his brother, Micah, take a three-week trip around the world. And thus begins *Three Weeks with My Brother*, a book that is both a memoir and travelogue. Cat, short for Cathy, knows that Nicholas has a desire and need to spend time with his brother, even though in the Prologue readers are not privy to the information. Later in the opening section, Nicholas writes that the book is "a story about brotherhood" (14) and about two journeys: one that took them to "places around the

Direct quotation does not stand alone

world" and the other that "has led us to become the best of friends" (15). In essence, *Three Weeks with My Brother* tells two stories, a trip narrative and a growing-up narrative. <u>Together, these two threads intertwine to create an outstanding piece of literary nonfiction that ought to become a staple in every American literature class.</u>

Introduction ends with a thesis that addresses the prompt

Three Weeks with My Brother is not a story that is told chronologically; if the entire story was told in linear fashion, the opening is in the middle of the two main narratives—the brothers are already grown and have lost their parents and sister, but they haven't taken the trip yet. <u>But a linear narration is not nearly as effective as the use of the framing technique and flashbacks that enable two stories to unfold simultaneously.</u> The trip narrative serves as a frame around the narrative of their lives together growing up. Even though Sparks mentions that the memoir is about two journeys, the initial chapters are mostly about his life growing up. These chapters serve as the exposition for both narratives. Sparks paints a portrait of his parents that enable readers to get to know them and their values; they are developed through their own words and actions in the early chapters, as well as throughout the rest of the text. Although the brothers grow up in poverty, they neither realized it nor cared. In retrospect, Nicholas writes that "we didn't have much as a family, but we'd always had one another" (61). <u>This idea of favoring family above all else resonates throughout the memoir and is one of the most important thematic topics.</u> When asking his brother about taking the trip,

Insight about structure

Explanation of support

Nicholas tells Micah, "This is going to be the trip of our lives" (14). Although his statement is explicitly about their tour around the world, it also refers to the story of their lives. And readers are about to share both narratives with the Sparks brothers.

The tour takes the brothers to many exotic locations, such as the Mayan and Incan ruins, Easter Island, India, Africa, and Norway. Through Sparks's inclusion of meticulous details, readers are able to share the trip with Nicholas and Micah. This trip narrative is both educational and enlightening, as readers learn that Cuzco, Peru, is the "oldest permanent settlement in the Western Hemisphere" (181) and that Ayers Rock is the "largest monolith, or single-unit stone, in the world" (278). This type of information is mixed in with the details of typical touristy activities—visiting museums, shopping, and sightseeing; all of these details provide background information about the different sites, as well as creating images for the reader share in the experience.

Although the chapters begin with the name of the specific location and important information about each stop on the tour is shared, the more important narrative is the one that follows the family's life as the brothers were growing up. This is the story line that develops the three siblings—for their sister Dana is also a significant character in the memoir—and enables readers to relate to the Sparks family. From this incredible family, the brothers learn some of their most important life lessons. Specifically, from their father they learned their "love of learning" (135), and their mother taught them,

Analysis of memoir

Use of direct quotations to support writer's argument

Analysis of structure

Direct quotations develop both character and theme

556

among other things, that "what you want and what you get are usually two entirely different things" (43). And through their suffering, they are able to recognize things that are both "hopeful and tragic" (310) in the world—whether it is life in Cambodia or dealing with the deaths of their immediate family members. Through it all, the brothers grow up to be "happily married, successful, ethical" (381), outstanding characteristics that anyone would value. These values and attitudes enable the brothers to gain a healthy and secure outlook on life, and they ended up living fulfilled lives based on this solid foundation. It's no wonder that the memoir ends with brothers in a close embrace unashamedly telling each other "I love you" (522), for this is a book about brothers and brotherly love.

One of the main ways the Sparks brothers learned things was by doing. From an early age, Micah helped to raise his brother and sister because "a person has to *learn* a sense of responsibility" (21–22). Their parents demonstrated this lesson through their own actions and not through their words. And Micah demonstrates that he indeed learned this lesson when years later, when preparing to embark on their world tour, he tells Nicholas, "You choose the kind of life you want to live" (100), words that instruct his brother as well as readers to take responsibility for their own actions. And Nicholas teaches his own sons this as well. This connection between words and actions is essential to the stylistic development of character, plot, and theme, for *Three Weeks with My Brother* is an outstanding text for literary analysis.

Most—if not all—of the reading and analytical goals that exist for an American literature class can be achieved through the study of this memoir. The text offers a variety of central ideas, stated explicitly, such as "Friends come and go, but brothers and sisters always stick together" (110), and some inferred through the words and actions of the Sparks siblings. Stylistically, the form of the text often creates meaning, as when a single sentence paragraph, "Our time in Nebraska came to an end as abruptly as it had begun" (114) abruptly ends a chapter in the same way that the siblings' life in Nebraska ended so quickly. Techniques such as flashbacks and foreshadowing mix with figures of speech such as similes, anaphora, and metaphors to create a rich reading experience. Because the lessons that the Sparks brothers learned from their parents are universal, *Three Weeks with My Brother* should become a part of the high school curriculum. In addition to these themes, many students may find this memoir more interesting to read than many classical nonfiction texts that students often encounter in American literature classes, such as Thoreau's "Civil Disobedience," and Martin Luther King, Jr.'s "I Have a Dream." I'm not advocating abandoning these, but often American literature starts at the beginning and continues chronologically, never providing students an opportunity to read something contemporary. A balance between classical and contemporary texts would be an acceptable compromise. Because *Three Weeks with My Brother* is a nonfiction text that reads like a

Details and examples support writer's assertion }

novel, students will be able to use their analytical skills on an accessible piece of writing while simultaneously learning a number of new things. <u>And if students were excited about reading, analyzing, and learning, that</u> "would be a wonderful idea."

Return to moti-
vator brings
essay full circle.

About the Author

With over 77 million copies of his books sold, Nicholas Sparks is one of the world's most beloved storytellers. His novels include ten #1 *New York Times* bestsellers, and all his books, including *Three Weeks with My Brother*, the memoir he wrote with his brother, Micah, have been *New York Times* and international bestsellers and were translated into more than forty languages. Seven of Nicholas Sparks's novels—*The Lucky One, The Last Song, Dear John, Nights in Rodanthe, Message in a Bottle, A Walk to Remember*, and *The Notebook*—were also adapted into major motion pictures. The author lives in North Carolina with his wife and family. You can visit him at www.nicholassparks.com.

Available Books in the Novel Learning Series™

Novel Learning Series:
The Notebook by Nicholas
Sparks
ISBN: 978-1-4555-1559-2

Novel Learning Series:
A Walk to Remember by
Nicholas Sparks
ISBN: 978-1-4555-0856-3

Novel Learning Series:
Three Weeks with My Brother:
A Memoir by Nicholas and Micah
Sparks
ISBN: 978-1-4555-1561-5

Novel Learning Series:
The Last Song by Nicholas
Sparks
ISBN: 978-1-4555-1560-8

For more information
www.novellearningseries.com